China Since 1919 – Revolution and Reform

Has China's modernization over the last 100 years depended on turning to the West? What new problems has growing prosperity created for China? This sourcebook tells the momentous history of China since 1919 mainly from the viewpoints of participants. Over 150 extracts from political statements, telegrams, speeches, memoirs, letters, and poems illuminate the historical development of China from the May 4th Movement onwards.

The collection begins with the cultural renaissance of the early twentieth century, the rebellion against Western and Japanese imperialism after 1919, the rise of the Nationalist and Communist movements and their conflict in mainland China until the Communist victory of 1949. After that, the focus is on the revolutionary changes under Mao Zedong's regime, and the ideological struggles after his death. Under Deng Xiaoping economic reform promoted rapid growth but also led to calls for greater political freedom, culminating in the Tiananmen protests of 1989. The final chapters illustrate the problems the regime faces today, such as the ambitions of the Tibetan minority and social issues such as unemployment and corruption. Key foreign policy issues affecting domestic policies – the Chinese role in the Korean War and, in particular, changing relations with the USA and Soviet Union – are also covered.

The collection includes classic documents as well as less accessible extracts, including a number only recently in the public domain. Anyone interested in the modern history of China will find *China Since 1919* an invaluable source of information.

Alan Lawrance taught history at colleges and universities in the USA, Canada and England. His publications include *China's Foreign Relations Since 1949* (1975), *Mao Zedong: A Bibliography* (1991), and *China Under Communism* (1998).

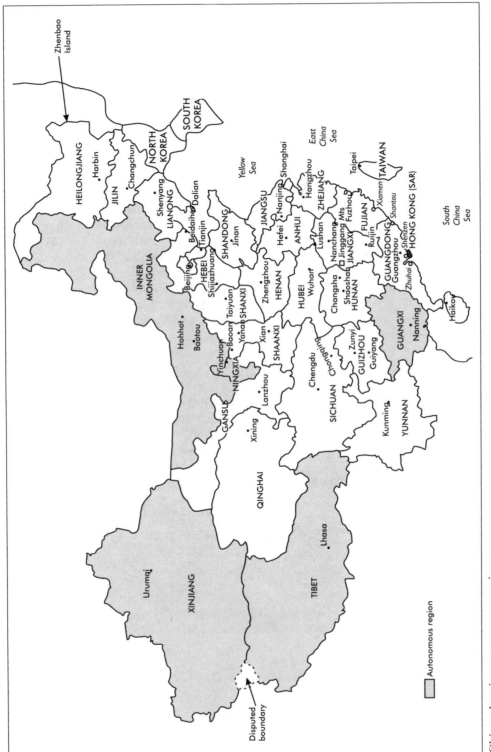

China, showing autonomous regions

Zhenbao Island

HEILONGJIANG
Harbin

JILIN
Changchun

NORTH KOREA

SOUTH KOREA

INNER MONGOLIA

Shenyang
LIANONG
Dalian
Beidaihe

Hohhot
Baotou

Beijing
HEBEI
Tianjin
Shijiazhuang

SHANDONG
Jinan

Yellow Sea

JIANGSU
Nanjing
Shanghai

Hangzhou
ZHEJIANG
Lushan

East China Sea

Taipei
TAIWAN

Taiyuan
SHANXI
Yanan

Zhengzhou
HENAN

HUBEI
Wuhan

Nanchang
Jinggang Mts
JIANGXI
Ruijin
FUJIAN
Fuzhou
Xiamen
Shantou

HONG KONG (SAR)
Shenzen
GUANGDONG
Guangzhou
Zhuhai

South China Sea

Xian
SHAANXI

Chengdu
Chongqing
SICHUAN

Changsha
Shaosha
HUNAN

Zunyi
GUIZHOU
Guiyang

GUANGXI
Nanning

Haikou

Yinchuan
NINGXIA
GANSU

Lanzhou

Kunming
YUNNAN

Xining

QINGHAI

Urumqi
XINJIANG

Lhasa

TIBET

Disputed boundary

Autonomous region

China Since 1919 – Revolution and Reform

A SOURCEBOOK

Alan Lawrance

Routledge
Taylor & Francis Group

LONDON AND NEW YORK

First published 2004
by Routledge
11 New Fetter Lane, London EC4P 4EE

Simultaneously published in the USA and Canada
by Routledge
29 West 35th Street, New York, NY 10001

Routledge is an imprint of the Taylor & Francis Group

Typeset in Baskerville and Gill Sans by Bookcraft Ltd, Stroud, Gloucestershire
Printed and bound in Great Britain by TJ International Ltd, Padstow, Cornwall

British Library Cataloguing in Publication Data
A catalogue record for this book is available from the British Library

Library of Congress Cataloging in Publication Data
China since 1919 : Revolution and reform: a sourcebook / edited by Alan Lawrance
p. cm.
Includes bibliographical references.
1. China–History–Republic, 1912–1949–Sources. 2. China–History–1949–Sources.
3. China–History–Republic, 1912–1949. 4. China–History–1949–
I. Title: revolution and reform: a sourcebook. II. Lawrance, Alan.
DS773.89.C474 2003
951.05–dc21   2003008285

ISBN 0–415–25141–9 (hbk)
ISBN 0–415–25142–7 (pbk)

Contents

Documents

THE CULTURAL RENAISSANCE

THE UNITED FRONT AND ITS BREAKDOWN

MAO–ZHU IN THE COUNTRYSIDE AND THE LONG MARCH

THE NANJING DECADE (1927–37) AND WORLD WAR TWO (1937–45)

YANAN: THE FORMATIVE YEARS, 1936–44

THE CIVIL WAR AND COMMUNIST VICTORY

THE SINO-SOVIET ALLIANCE, THE KOREAN WAR, AND THE EARLY YEARS OF THE PEOPLE'S REPUBLIC, 1949–55

THE HUNDRED FLOWERS

THE GREAT LEAP FORWARD

THE CULTURAL REVOLUTION

YEARS OF TRANSITION

MODERNIZATION IN THE 1980s

DEFINING THE CHINESE NATION: HONG KONG, TIBET, AND THE MINORITIES

CHINA ENTERS THE TWENTY-FIRST CENTURY

Acknowledgements

The publishers wish to thank the following for permission to reproduce copyright material:

1.1 Extracts from *China's Response to the West* by Ssu-yü Teng and John King Fairbank, reprinted with permission of the publisher from 'Ch'en Tu-hsiu's "Call to Youth", 1915', pp. 240–3, Cambridge, Massachusetts: Harvard University Press, © 1954, 1979 by the President and Fellows of Harvard College, © renewed 1982 by Ssu-yü Teng and John King Fairbank.

1.5 'Commentary on the Suicide of Miss Zhao', translation copyright © 1992 by The John King Fairbank Center for East Asian Research. In Stuart R. Schram, ed., *Mao's Road to Power: Revolutionary Writings, 1912–1949*. Vol. I. *The Pre-Marxist Period, 1912–1920* (Armonk, New York: M. E. Sharpe, 1992), pp. 421–2. Reprinted with permission.

1.6 'The Politics of Gender in the Making of the Party,' copyright © 1995 by M. E. Sharpe, Inc. From Tony Saich and Hans van de Ven, eds, *New Perspectives on the Chinese Communist Revolution* (Armonk, New York: M. E. Sharpe, 1995), pp. 34–6. Reprinted with permission.

1.8 Hu Shih, *The Chinese Renaissance* (Chicago: University of Chicago Press, 1934).

1.9 Lu Xun, 'Call to Arms', 1922, from *The Complete Stories of Lu Xun*, transl. Leo Ou-Fan Lee, Indiana University Press, 1981.

2.1 Extracts from *Mao Tsetung and I Were Beggars* by Siao Yu, Souvenir Press Ltd, 1974 and Syracuse University Press, New York, 1959.

2.4 Excerpt from J. N. Wasserstrom, *Student Protests in Twentieth-century China: The View from Shanghai*, © 1991 by the Board of Trustees of the Leland Stanford Jr University, with the permission of Stanford University Press, www.sup.org.

2.9 Extracts from A. H. Rasmussen, *China Trader* (London: Constable, 1954).

3.2 'An Example of the Chinese Tenant-Peasant's Life (March 1927)'. In Stuart R. Schram, ed., *Mao's Road to Power: Revolutionary Writings, 1912–1949*. Vol. II. *National Revolution and Social Revolution, December 1920–June 1927* (Armonk, New York: M. E. Sharpe, 1994), pp. 478, 482–3. Reprinted with permission.

3.4 Translation copyright © 1995 by The John King Fairbank Center for East Asian Research. From 'An Official Fundraising Letter (February 13, 1929)'. In Stuart R. Schram, ed., *Mao's Road to Power: Revolutionary Writings, 1912–1949*. Vol. III. *From the Jinggangshan to the Establishment of the Jiangxi Soviets, July 1927–December 1930* (Armonk, New York: M. E. Sharpe, 1995), p. 139. Reprinted with permission.

3.5a and b   Translation copyright © 1996 by The John King Fairbank Center for East Asian Research. From Tony Saich, ed., *The Rise to Power of the Chinese Communist Party* (Armonk, New York: M.E. Sharpe, 1996), pp. 472–6. Reprinted with permission.

3.6 Translation copyright © 1995 by The John King Fairbank Center for East Asian Research. From 'Draft Resolution of the Ninth Congress of the Chinese Communist Party in the Fourth Red Army (December 1929)'. In Stuart. R. Schram, ed., *Mao's Road to Power: Revolutionary Writings, 1912–1949*. Volume III. *From the Jinggangshan to the Establishment of the Jiangxi Soviets, July 1927–December 1930* (Armonk, New York: M. E. Sharpe, 1995), p. 220. Reprinted with permission.

3.7   Translation copyright © 1995 by The John King Fairbank Center for East Asian Research. From 'Letter from the Fouth Army of the Chinese Red Army (the Red Army of Zhu and Mao) to the Soldiers of the Guomindang Army (January 1930)'. In Stuart R. Schram, ed., *Mao's Road to Power: Revolutionary Writings, 1912–1949*. Vol. III. *From the Jinggangshan to the Establishment of the Jiangxi Soviets, July 1927–December 1930* (Armonk, New York: M. E. Sharpe, 1995), pp. 247–54. Reprinted with permission.

3.9   Extracts from Otto Braun, *A Comintern Agent in China, 1932–1939* (London: Hurst, 1982).

4.2   From 'Communications Regarding the Xian Incident'. In Stuart R. Schram, ed., *Mao's Road to Power: Revolutionary Writings, 1912–1949*. Vol. V. *Toward the Second United Front, January 1935–July 1937* (Armonk, New York: M. E. Sharpe, 1999), pp. 458–9, 539–40, 547–9, 566, 569–72. Reprinted with permission.

4.4   From Agnes Smedley, *The Great Road: The Life and Times of Chu Teh* (London: John Calder Publications Ltd, 1958).

4.5c   © The Asahi Shimbun Company, from *Asahi Evening News* (Tokyo), 5 March 2001, pp. 1–2.

4.6   From *China Memoirs: Chiang Kai-Shek and the War Against Japan*, by Owen Lattimore (compiled by Fujiko Isono) © 1990 University of Tokyo Press. Reprinted by permission of the publisher.

4.8, 6.3   © 1970 MR Press. Reprinted by permission of Monthly Review Foundation.

5.1   From Edgar Snow, *Red Star over China*, © Lois Wheeler Snow.

5.3   Copyright © 1995 by M. E. Sharpe, Inc. From Mark Selden, *China in Revolution: The Yenan Way Revisited* (Armonk, New York: M. E. Sharpe, 1995), pp. 212–13, 250–2. Reprinted with permission.

5.4a   Translation copyright © 1999 by The John King Fairbank Center for East Asian Research. From 'For Comrade Ding Ling (December 1936)'. In Stuart R. Schram, ed., *Mao's Road to Power: Revolutionary Writings, 1912–1949*. Vol. V. *Toward the Second United Front, January 1935–July 1937* (Armonk, New York: M. E. Sharpe, 1999), p.573. Reprinted with permission.

5.4b, 5.5a and b   From *Dai Qing, Wang Shiwei and 'Wild Lilies': Rectification and Purges in the Chinese Communist Party, 1942–1944*, ed. David E. Apter and Timothy Check (Armonk, NY: H. E. Sharpe, 1994).

5.7   Copyright © 1995 by M. E. Sharpe, Inc. From Tony Saich and Hans van de Ven, eds, *New Perspectives on the Chinese Communist Revolution* (Armonk, New York: M. E. Sharpe, 1995), pp. 263–4, 271–3, 290–1. Reprinted with permission.

6.2   Courtesy of the George C. Marshall Foundation.

6.4   From Hua Qingzhao, *From Yalta to Panmunjom: Truman's Diplomacy and the Four Powers, 1945–1953*. Cornell East Asia Series No. 64 (Ithaca: Cornell University East Asia Program, 1993).

6.6, 7.11a, 12.8a and b   Reprinted by permission of Westview Press, a member of Perseus Books, L.L.C.

6.10   Lloyd Eastman, 'Who Lost China? Chiang Kai-Shek Testifies', *China Quarterly*, No. 88, 1981, pp. 658–62, © School of Oriental and African Studies.

7.1, 7.2, 9.14, 11.1a and b   By permission of the Cold War International History Project, Woodrow Wilson International Center for Scholars.

7.5, 14.3   By permission of Oxford University Press (China) Ltd.

7.9b   Frank Dikötter, 'Research Note: Crime and Punishment in Post-Liberation China', *China Quarterly*, No 149, 1997, pp. 148–9, © School of Oriental and African Studies.

8.2, 8.5a   © 1992 by M. E. Sharpe, Inc. From Michael Y. M. Kau and John K. Leung, eds., *The Writings of Mao Zedong, 1949–1976*. Vol. II. *January 1956-December 1957* (Armonk, New York: M. E. Sharpe, 1992). Used with permission.

8.3   Elizabeth J. Perry, 'Shanghai's Strike Wave of 1957', *China Quarterly*, No 137, 1994, pp. 1–27 © School of Oriental and African Studies.

8.5b   Reprinted by permission of Oxford University Press.

9.5   Reprinted from Roderick MacFarquhar, Timothy Cheek, and Eugene Wu, eds, *The Secret Speeches of Chairman Mao: From the Hundred Flowers to the Great Leap Forward* (Cambridge, Massachusetts: Council on East Asian Studies, 1989), pp. 490–8, 507. © The President and Fellows of Harvard College, 1989. Reprinted by permission of the Harvard University Asia Center.

9.6   From *The Private Life of Chairman Mao* by Dr Zhi-Sui Li, © 1995 by Dr Zhi-Sui Li. Used by permission of Random House, Inc. and Random House Group Ltd.

9.7   © 1983 Columbia University Press.

9.8a   © Sirin Pathanothai, 1994. Reprinted by permission of Simon & Schuster, UK and Georges Borchardt, Inc.

9.11   By permission of Blackwell Publishing.

9.12   By permission of John Murray and Simon & Schuster.

10.5   English translation copyright © 1996 by M. E. Sharpe, Inc. From Michael Schoenhals, ed., *China's Cultural Revolution, 1966–1969: Not a Dinner Party* (Armonk, New York: M. E. Sharpe, 1996), pp. 48–9. Reprinted with permission.

10.7   English translation copyright © 1996 by M. E. Sharpe, Inc. From Michael Schoenhals, ed., *China's Cultural Revolution, 1966–1969: Not a Dinner Party* (Armonk, New York: M. E. Sharpe, 1996), pp. 331–3. Reprinted with permission.

10.8   Copyright 1997 The Regent of the University of California. From Rae Yang *Spider Eaters: A Memoir* (Berkeley, California, University of California Press).

11.2   Copyright 1999. *The Kissinger Transcripts: The Top Secret Talks with Beijing and Moscow*, edited by William Burr. Reprinted with permission of The New Press (800) 233-4830.

11.3b   © 1991 by the Board of Trustees of the Leland Stanford Jr University. With the permission of Stanford University Press, www.sup.org.

12.1a   'Appendix I' from *The Courage to Stand Alone* by Wei Jingsheng, translated by Kristina M. Torgeson, © 1997 by Wei Jingsheng. Used by permission of Viking Penguin, a division of Penguin Putnam Inc. and The Penguin Group (UK).

12.4   By permission of Pacific Affairs, Institute of Asian Research, The University of British Columbia.

12.5   From *Bringing Down the Great Wall* by Fang Lizhi, translated by J. Williams, © 1991 by Fang Lizhi. Used by permission of Alfred A. Knopf, a division of Random House, Inc.

12.7   From *China's Search for Democracy: The Student and the Mass Movement of 1989*, ed. Suzanne Ogden, Kathleen Hartford, Lawrence Sullivan and David Zweig (Armonk, NY: M.E. Sharpe, 1992). Used with permission.

12.8a and b   © 2001 by Zhang Liang, Andrew J. Nathan, and E. Perry Link. Reprinted by permission of Public Affairs, a member of Perseus Book, L.L.C.

12.7, 12.9   From *China's Search for Democracy: The Student and the Mass Movement of 1989*, ed. Suzanne Ogden, Kathleen Hartford, Lawrence Sullivan and David Zweig (Armonk, NY: M.E. Sharpe, 1992). Used with permission.

13.3, 14.9   © *Guardian*.

13.4, 14.11   By permission of *New Left Review*.

14.4   © 2002, *The Washington Post*. Reprinted with permission.

The Writings of Mao Zedong © 1986 by M. E. Sharpe, Inc. From Michael Y. M. Kau and John K. Leung, eds.

Every effort has been made to obtain permission to reprint copyright material. If any proper acknowledgement has not been made, we would invite copyright holders to inform us of the oversight.

Romanization of Chinese names

There are two systems for transcribing Chinese names: Wade-Giles which was generally used in the West until 1979 and therefore occurs in many of the documents in this book; and *pinyin* which has been widely (but not universally) adopted since 1979 and has been used for all authorial comments, headings, etc.

Some key figures in Chinese history since 1919 and well-known authors of documents in this book whose names may occur in both *pinyin* and Wade-Giles are listed below. So are major place names. Diacritical marks have been omitted.

Individual names

Pinyin	Wade-Giles	Pinyin	Wade-Giles
Bo Yibo	Po Yi-po	Lu Xun	Lu Hsun
Chen Boda	Chen Po-ta	Mao Zedong	Mao Tse-tung
Chen Duxiu	Chen Tu-hsiu	Nie Yuanzi	Nieh Yuan-tzu
Chen Yi	Chen I	Peng Dehuai	Peng Teh-huai
Deng Xiaoping	Teng Hsiao-ping	Peng Zhen	Peng Chen
Ding Ling	Ting Ling	Wang Guangmei	Wang Kuang-mei
Fei Xiaotong	Fei Hsiao-tung	Wang Shiwei	Wang Shih-wei
Hu Feng	Hu Feng	Wei Jingsheng	Wei Ching-sheng
Hu Shi	Hu Shih	Wu Han	Wu Han
Hu Yaobang	Hu Yao-pang	Xiao Yu	Siao Yu
Hua Guofeng	Hua Kuo-feng	Zhang Xiruo	Chang Hsi-jo
Jiang Qing	Chiang Ching	Zhang Xueliang	Chang Hsueh-liang
Li Dazhao	Li Ta-chao	Zhao Ziyang	Chao Tzu-yang
Lin Biao	Lin Piao	Zhou Enlai	Chou En-lai
Liu Bocheng	Liu Po-cheng	Zhu De	Chu Teh
Liu Shaoqi	Liu Shao-chi		

Place names

Pinyin	Wade-Giles	Pinyin	Wade-Giles
Baoan	Paoan	Shaoshan	Shaoshan
Beijing	Peking	Tiananmen	Tien An Men
Changsha	Changsha	Tianjin	Tientsin
Guangzhou	Canton	Wuhan	Wuhan
Jiangxi	Kiangsi	Xian	Sian
Jingang	Chingkang	Xinjiang	Sinjiang
Lushan	Lu Shan	Yanan	Yenan
Nanjing	Nanking	Yangzi	Yangtse
Shanghai	Shanghai	Zhenbao	Chenpao
Shanxi	Shansi	Zunyi	Tsunyi
Shaanxi	Shensi		

Abbreviations

ACFTU	All-China Federation of Trade Unions
APC	Agricultural Producers' Cooperative
CC	Central Committee
CCP	Chinese Communist Party
CPSU	Communist Party of the Soviet Union
GMD	Guomindang – Nationalist Party (*pinyin* version)
KMT	Kuomintang – Nationalist Party (Wade-Giles version)
NPC	National People's Congress
PLA	People's Liberation Army
PRC	People's Republic of China
RMB	Renminbi – People's Currency
SOE	State-owned enterprise
TASS	The Soviet Press Agency
TVE	Township and village enterprise

Chronology

Republican China

1911   Rebellions against Manchu (Qing) Dynasty (October–December). Sun Yat-sen returns to China.
1912   Sun Yat-sen becomes Acting President of the Republic of China (January). The Qing Emperor abdicates; Sun Yat-sen resigns in favour of General Yuan Shikai (February). The Guomindang (GMD) (previously the Tong Meng Hui) becomes a legitimate political party and contests August general elections.
1913   Yuan Shikai orders dissolution of GMD (November).
1915   Japan presents '21 Demands' for territorial, mining, and railway concessions and appointment of Japanese advisers to government (January). The modified demands accepted by Yuan Shikai (May). Chen Duxiu founds *New Youth*, key journal of the cultural renaissance. Yuan Shikai proclaimed Emperor (December).
1916   Death of Yuan Shikai (June). Disintegration of central power and rise of the warlords.
1917   Hu Shi promotes literary renaissance. China declares war on Germany (August). Sun Yat-sen becomes Generalissimo of the 'Chinese National Military Government' in Guangdong province (September). October Revolution in Russia.
1919   Versailles Peace Conference. Chinese delegation unsuccessfully requests reversal of Japanese '21 Demands' and the unequal treaties with other powers. The May 4th demonstrations against foreign imperialism. China refuses to sign Versailles Treaty.
1921   Sun Yat-sen becomes President of a government based in Guangdong (May). Founding Congress of Chinese Communist Party (CCP) in Shanghai (July).
1922   Sun Yat-sen orders start of Northern Expedition to extend power of his regime (February) but is forced out of Guangdong (June).
1923   Sun Yat-sen is restored to power in Guangdong, signs agreement with Soviet envoy Adolph Joffe agreeing to alliance between GMD and Communist Party of the Soviet Union (January). CCP at Third Congress supports United Front with GMD (June).
1924   First GMD Congress, which adopts Sun's 'Three People's Principles' (January). Sun appoints Chiang Kai-shek Commander of Whampoa Military Academy and Commander-in-Chief of Nationalist forces.
1925   Death of Sun Yat-sen (March). Strikes and demonstrations against imperialism in May 30th Movement in Shanghai, protests spread to other parts of China.
1926   Growing unrest among peasants in Hunan. Chiang Kai-shek orders new stage of Northern Expedition (July) and Wuchang and Nanchang fall to his forces (October–November).
1927   Mao Zedong's *Report of an Investigation into the Peasant Movement in Hunan* (March). Chiang Kai-shek organizes Nationalist government in Nanjing, takes Shanghai, and orders massacre of Communists and labour leaders (April). Executions spread to Wuhan, Comintern advisers and Communist leaders flee. Abortive Communist uprising in Nanchang (August), and Autumn Harvest Uprising in Hunan also fails (September). Guangzhou Commune leftist uprising crushed (December).
1928   Chiang's Nanjing government accorded diplomatic recognition. Mao Zedong and Zhu De establish Red Army base in Jinggang Mountains.
1929   Mao and Zhu move forces to new base at Ruijin, Jiangxi.

1930   Communists once more attempt unsuccessful urban insurrections in Changsha and Nanjing (July–August). Chiang launches unsuccessful First Encirclement Campaign against Communists in Jiangxi (November–December).

1931   Second Encirclement Campaign fails (May). Third Encirclement Campaign halted when Japanese army attacks Mukden, Manchuria (September). Japanese occupy all Manchuria (December).

1932   Japanese forces attack Shanghai, strongly resisted by 19th Route Army. The Communist Soviet Republic declares war on Japan (February). Chiang's Fourth Encirclement Campaign against Communists (June).

1933   CCP Central Committee leaves Shanghai for Jiangxi. Further Japanese advances in northern China and Mongolia lead Nanjing government to sign truce with Japan (May). Fifth Encirclement Campaign begins (October).

1934   Chiang initiates New Life Movement (February). Chiang's Fifth Campaign forces the Communists to leave their bases and begin the Long March (October).

1935   CCP Politburo meeting at Zunyi elects Mao as leader (January). Long March ends in Northern Shaanxi (October).

1936   Communist forces base themselves in Yanan (December). The 'Xian incident' – Young Marshal kidnaps Chiang hoping to promote a united front against Japanese (December).

1937   Incident at Marco Polo bridge sparks off Sino-Japanese War (July). Soviet Union signs non-aggression pact with GMD government and offers military aid (August). Second United Front between GMD and Communists announced (September). Japan forces advance in China. National Government moves capital to Chungking (November). Fall of Nanjing and Japanese atrocities (December).

1938   Japanese advances continue. Japan occupies Guangzhou and Wuhan (October).

1939   Nanchang falls to Japanese (March). Second World War in Europe begins (September).

1941   United States enters Pacific war after bombing of Pearl Harbour (December). Japanese occupy Hong Kong.

1942   Fall of Singapore and Rangoon to Japan (February–March). Mao promotes 'rectification movement' in Yanan. General Joseph Stilwell created US Commander of China–Burma–India theatre of war (November).

1943   Britain and the United States abandon claims to their former concessions in China (January). Cairo Conference Declaration promises return to China of Taiwan, Manchuria, and the Pescadores after the war (December).

1944   Stilwell relieved of his command at Chiang's request (October). Patrick Hurley sent as Roosevelt's representative to mend US relations with Chiang and unite GMD and Communists (November).

1945   Yalta Agreement recognizes restoration of former Russian rights in Manchuria and Port Arthur (February). USSR declares war on Japan. Atomic bombing of Hiroshima and Nagasaki, Japan surrenders. USSR occupies Manchuria (August). Mao negotiates unsuccessfully with Chiang on setting up a coalition government, but GMD and Communists agree to avoid civil war (September–October). CCP Seventh Party Congress (October). General George Marshall replaces Hurley with task of mediating between the two sides (November).

1946   Communist armies enter Manchuria after USSR evacuates its forces (January–March). Communists issue new directives on land reform (May). Civil War breaks out (July). Student protests in Beijing over rape of student by American marines (December).

1947   Communist People's Liberation Army (PLA) offensives early in year. GMD forces occupy Yanan and gain some military success (March). PLA offensives (April–June) and increasing military success. Growing popular disillusionment with Chiang's regime and rising inflation.

1948   Further PLA offensives. Anti-American student demonstrations. Economic shortages and spiralling inflation.

1949   PLA liberates Beijing in January, Nanjing in April, and Shanghai in May. Major part of mainland taken by Communists by September.

Communist China

1949 People's Republic of China (PRC) established (October). Chiang Kai-shek flees to Taiwan (December).

1950 Sino-Soviet Treaty (February). Marriage Law ends many forms of discrimination against women (April). Outbreak of Korean War; Land Reform Law (June). Chinese troops sent into Tibet; Chinese 'volunteers' sent to Korea (October).

1951 UN declares China an aggressor in Korea and decides that PRC should not be admitted to UN as representative of China. 'Three Antis' campaign launched nationally (December).

1952 'Five Antis' campaign launched (February).

1953 First Five Year Plan starts (January). Death of Stalin (March). Korean Armistice (July).

1954 National People's Congress adopts constitution (September). United States and Taiwan sign Defence Treaty (December).

1955 Campaign against writer Hu Feng ends in his arrest (February–July). Mao calls for faster progress to full cooperativization (July). Mao sets out policy on agricultural cooperatives and transformation of capitalist industry, adopted at Sixth Plenum of Seventh Central Committee (October).

1956 Khrushchev denounces Stalin (February). Mao's speech 'On the Ten Major Relationships' stresses Stalin's achievements (April). Mao's speech on 'Hundred Flowers' to Supreme State Congress (May). CPC Eighth Congress adopts new Party Constitution and limits Mao's role. Polish and Hungarian Uprisings (October–November).

1957 Mao's speech on 'The Correct Handling of Contradiction among the People' (February). Widespread worker strikes. Hundred Flowers taken up by intellectuals and students (May–June). Clampdown on Hundred Flowers policy and intellectuals from July. Mao criticizes Soviet policy of coexistence with West (November). Liu Shaoqi calls for China to overtake Britain in iron, steel, and major industrial production (December).

1958 Great Leap Forward announced (May). Formation of communes. Campaign to make steel in local blast furnaces. Wuchang Conference raises doubts about Great Leap targets (November).

1959 Dalai Lama leaves Tibet (March). Liu Shaoqi replaces Mao as Head of State (April). At Lushan Conference of Central Committee, Peng Dehuai criticizes Mao (July). Problems with harvests and food shortages. Lin Biao replaces Peng Dehuai as Minister of Defence. Khrushchev in Beijing visit quarrels with Mao over policy differences (September).

1960 Further natural disasters and famine in some areas. USSR withdraws technical experts and nuclear weapon technology from China (July). Central Committee promotes retreat from Great Leap (July–November). Heightening of tension between CCP and CPSU at Moscow meeting (November).

1961 Grain imports and further famine in some areas. Publication of Wu Han's play *The Dismissal of Hai Rui* (November).

1962 Socialist Education Movement launched (September)

1963 Open rift between CPSU and CCP. USSR signs Partial Test Ban Treaty in August.

1964 Lin Biao compiles pocket book of Mao's thoughts for troops, later dubbed the Little Red Book (May). China tests atom bomb (October).

1965 Attacks on Wu Han's play *The Dismissal of Hai Rui* signal start of Cultural Revolution (November).

1966 Mao's letter to Lin Biao gives PLA central role in Cultural Revolution; Politburo creates Cultural Revolution Group (May). Mao's poster 'Bombard the Headquarters' published; Central Committee issues Sixteen-Point Decision; emergence of Red Guards (August).

1967 Education reforms and abolition of exams (January). Attacks on Liu Shaoqi and his wife (March–April). China tests first H bomb (June). Zhou Enlai calls on Red Guards to end violence and stop attacking foreign embassies (September).

1968 Increasing violence and moves to restore order with the 'three in one' committees (April). Liu Shaoqi expelled from Party (October).

1969 Clashes with USSR forces on Ussuri River (March). CPC Ninth Party Congress adopts new Party Constitution. Lin Biao confirmed as Mao's successor (April). After further clashes, talks between USSR and China on settling border dispute (October)

1971 Launch of fourth five-year plan (January). Kissinger arranges for Nixon to visit China (July). Lin Biao dies in plane crash, accused of attempting to assassinate Mao (September). UN votes for China to replace Taiwan in UN bodies (October).

1972 President Nixon visits China and signs Shanghai Communiqué (February).

1973 CPC Tenth Party Congress. Jiang Qing and other three members of Shanghai Group promoting Cultural Revolution policies (the Gang of Four) enter Politburo; Deng Xiaoping rehabilitated and restored to Central Committee (August).

1975 Fourth National People's Congress agrees new Constitution and approves 'four modernizations' promoted by Zhou Enlai and Deng Xiaoping (January). Death of Chiang Kai-shek in Taiwan (April). President Ford visits China (December).

1976 Zhou Enlai dies (January). Tiananmen demonstration in memory of Zhou Enlai (April). Deng Xiaoping removed from all his posts. Mao Zedong dies (September). Gang of Four arrested. Hua Guofeng, acting Premier since February, becomes Chairman of Party (October).

1977 Deng Xiaoping returns to Politburo and becomes Vice Premier (July). CPC Eleventh Congress reflects struggle between Hua (defending Maoist policies) and Deng (urging radical economic reforms and ties with the West) (August). Exams restored for entry to higher education (October).

1978 Deng speech to PLA launches his slogan 'seek truth from facts' (June). Beginning of 'Democracy Wall' and Wei Jingsheng poster on 'Fifth Modernization' (November–December). The Third Plenum of Eleventh Central Committee endorses economic reforms, including the 'responsibility system' in agriculture, and rehabilitates Peng Dehuai and others (December).

1979 Deng visits United States (January–February). Wei Jingshen arrested and clampdown on Democracy Wall (March–April). Proposal to set up special economic zones (April). Democracy Wall closed (December).

1980 Sino-American trade agreement; Fifth Plenum of Central Commitee rehabilitates Liu Shaoqi (February). China admitted to International Monetary Fund and World Bank (April–May). 'One child' policy launched; trial of Gang of Four begins (November).

1981 Sentencing of Gang of Four and 'Lin Biao clique' (January). Resolution on Party history agrees line on Cultural Revolution; Hua Guofeng resigns, succeeded by Hu Yaobang as Party Secretary, but Deng Xiaoping already recognized as the 'paramount leader' (June).

1982 CPC Twelfth Congress passes new Party Constitution requiring Party to act 'within the limits permitted by the Constitution and the laws of the state'.

1984 Deng Xiaoping statement on principles for resolving problems of Hong Kong and Taiwan 'One Country, Two Systems' (January). Sino-British Agreement on Hong Kong handover (September).

1986 Fang Lizhi calls for complete modernization, and students at his university in Hefei demonstrate (November–December).

1987 Student protests culminate in burning of *Beijing Daily*. Hu Yaobang dismissed as Party General Secretary, replaced by Zhao Ziyang (January). CCP Thirteenth Party Congress (October–November).

1989 Death of Hu Yaobang prompts popular demonstrations of grief and student protests against corruption and lack of funds for education; they demand removal of Prime Minister Li Peng (April). Gorbachev visits Beijing at time of mounting protest across country. Imposition of martial law. Resignation of Zhao Ziyang (May). Growing signs of worker unrest. Troops suppress students in Tiananmen Square and kill protesters in Beijing (June). Jiang Zemin becomes Party General Secretary.

1991 Anti-Gorbachev coup in USSR fails, but USSR disintegrates.

1992 Deng tours Shenzen economic zone and Guangdong province, supporting foreign economic investment (January–February).

1997 Deng dies (February). Jiang Zemin visits Moscow to endorse new bilateral relationship (April). Hong Kong returns to China (June). CCP Fifteenth Party Congress reaffirms 'building socialism with Chinese characteristics', confirms Jiang Zemin as General Secretary, and Jiang introduces 'Deng Xiaoping Theory' as a pillar of party ideology (September). President Yeltsin visits Beijing and signs trade agreements and pact defining Russian–Chinese border (November).

1998 Li Peng steps down as Premier, succeeded by Zhu Rongji (March).

2001 Jiang Zemin speech 'The Three Represents' reformulates the Party line (July). Jiang calls for businessmen to enter Party, criticized by leftists (August). China enters the World Trade Organization (November).

Preface

This selection of readings – political, economic, social, and cultural – is intended to illuminate the history of China from the May 4th Movement to the present. The items have been selected for their historical importance, for variety, to show contrasting views, and for their readability. There are a few very well-known documents, but I have sought to include a diverse range, including material that has not been easily accessible. Chinese sources include not only political statements and resolutions but also memoirs, letters, and speeches of political and military leaders, literary figures, and dissidents. Alongside famous people there are lesser-known individuals. The great majority of sources are primary. Recent publication of previously unpublished primary sources, for example the Cold War International History Project, has made it possible to include up-to-date revisionist materials. Selections from western visitors, journalists, military advisors, and diplomats include some classic accounts and provide another dimension. The limited number of secondary sources provide informed academic comment on key and contentious issues.

Given the limitations of space, the focus is on internal affairs. Foreign relations are not specifically covered except where they are of crucial importance to internal developments – for example, the changing relationships with both the Soviet Union and the United States.

Each chapter has an introduction which sets out the main events and characteristics of the period. In addition, where necessary some documents are prefaced by a brief explanatory note (in italics).

The documents are presented in the form in which they were originally transcribed. Thus, most of the earlier ones have names according to the Wade-Giles system, while the later documents are in the modern *pinyin* version (introduced in 1979). In my commentary and notes I have used *pinyin* throughout, with the exception of a few well-known people and places such as Chiang Kai-shek, Sun Yat-sen, Hong Kong, and Tibet which are given in their familiar form. Spelling (both British and American) follows the original documents.

Second preface

Alan Lawrance died unexpectedly of a heart attack in November 2002, after he had delivered this book to Routledge, but before he could see it through the press. Routledge wished to publish a valuable sourcebook for students and therefore asked me, as someone who had already helped editorially with the book, to assist in the final stages of publication. Alan Lawrance's family and wide circle of friends also wanted to see the book published as a memorial to him.

Alan Lawrance studied history at Trinity College, Cambridge, and the University of Minnesota, and taught modern history at schools, colleges, and universities in the United States, Canada, and Britain for nearly 40 years. He continued to lecture part-time for five years after his retirement, and is remembered with affection by many of his students and colleagues as a committed, lively, and often inspirational teacher.

He was also an enthusiastic traveller, with a special interest in the Communist world after he went to Yugoslavia as a student in 1952; subsequently he visited the Soviet Union, much of Eastern Europe, Cuba, and North Korea, and was in the Baltic States in 1991 at the time of the disintegration of the Soviet Union. A year later he sailed round the Baltic and developed a particular interest in the history of Estonia's struggle for independence.

However, from 1970 his greatest commitment was to studying China, and he spent a sabbatical year at the Department of Chinese Studies at the University of Leeds (1971–2). He went to China twice on official delegations in 1972 and 1981, experiencing the contrast between Cultural Revolution policies and their impact on education and the early stages of Deng Xiaoping's reforms. He also travelled there several times independently, getting closer to 'the real China'. He made a number of contacts, visiting the Tianjin Academy of Social Sciences and discussing academic exchanges in Beijing.

Alan published three earlier books on China: a reader on *China's Foreign Relations Since 1949* (1975), *Mao Zedong. A Bibliography* (1991), covering works by and on Mao, and a concise student textbook *China Under Communism* (1998). He was also active in promoting links between Britain and China through the Quaker China Group and the Society for Anglo-Chinese Understanding, made friends with Chinese students in Britain, and chaired the editorial board of the magazine *China in Focus* from its foundation in 1996 until his death. However, probably his greatest contribution to promoting an interest in contemporary China was in introducing undergraduate courses on China from the Opium Wars to the present. He taught these courses at the Hertfordshire College of Higher Education and the University of Hertfordshire for 30 years, often introducing his students to old China hands, academic experts on China, and Chinese students. The documents he prepared for his students were the starting point for the selection in this book.

In getting advice on the contents, Alan drew on friends with diverse interests in modern China: Sybille van den Sprenkel, Sadayoshi Itoh, Professor Alan Jenkins, Poppy Sebag-Montefiore, and Neil Taylor. Professor Robert Benewick and John Gittings gave their expert consideration to a proposed list of contents. M. F. Chen provided some translation, and Marella Buckley advised on presentation. Ruth Grillo processed the text through many drafts with great efficiency and good humour.

Alan also wished to express his thanks to staff at the Cambridge University Library, the library of the School of Oriental and African Studies, and the Hertfordshire University Library.

Since Alan's death, I have been greatly indebted to Ruth Grillo for further typing, to Paul Wingrove and Poppy Sebag-Montefiore for helping to tie up some loose ends, and to Christina Reedyk for proofreading.

Alan especially wished to thank Professor Hua Qingzhao, a history research professor in the Tianjin Academy of Social Sciences, for providing an indispensable Chinese viewpoint and for reading and commenting in detail on the text. I am also most grateful to him for his continued assistance.

I invited Professor Hua to be co-author of this preface, but he suggested that instead I should incorporate the following:

'I first met Alan in October 1987 in a London gathering for Chinese National Day when I was a British Council Visitor doing short-term research. Alan suggested that I look up certain documents at the Public Records Office. When I failed to find the important document, he provided me with a copy from his own collection and I used that source in my book on Truman's diplomacy. For the next fifteen years Alan and I kept close contact and he became a good friend of my family. He helped me to find placement in a British university so that I could pursue my research and was my advisor when I worked on a book on British life and society, which was published in China in 2000. On issues pertaining to Britain, Alan was my mentor, and I was glad to reciprocate by offering advice on his previous book, *China Under Communism*, and on this book.

'From his association with the Society for Anglo-Chinese Understanding and *China in Focus* and from his teaching and writings, it is clear that Alan contributed the second half of his life to the cause of enhancing Anglo-Chinese understanding. As an English liberal, Alan might not see eye-to-eye on every Chinese issue with some people in China, or even with me, but it is beyond any doubt that he was supportive of the People's Republic of China and was a true friend of the Chinese people'.

April Carter

I

The cultural renaissance

May 4th 1919 is a key date in China. It is the day on which both Chinese and Western historians agree that Contemporary History begins. In Beijing, three thousand students took to the streets to protest at the terms of the Versailles Peace Treaty by which former German concessions were given to Japan rather than restored to China. It was a patriotic protest against the role in which China had been cast ever since the Opium War of 1839–42.

Although the Chinese Empire came to an end with the fall of the Qing dynasty in 1911–12, the insubstantial foundations for a republic at that time led no further than dictatorship. An attempt to revive the empire by Yuan Shikai was followed by political disintegration during the period of the warlords.

If China was to escape from its subordination to the foreign powers and transform its traditional society, a cultural renaissance was necessary. How much of the old had to be thrown out to make way for the new? Thoughtful Chinese had been agonizing over this since the nineteenth century. One famous slogan was 'Chinese learning as the essence, Western learning for use.' But which Western learning and how could it be used effectively?

May 4th was rightly called an incident. It was soon recognized as an event in the 'May 4th Movement' which began several years earlier and continued into the 1920s. Some sought Western liberal models and were influenced by the American philosopher and educationalist, John Dewey, and the English thinker, Bertrand Russell, while others admired the new way forward provided by the example of the Russian revolution. Leading Chinese Marxists at that time were Chen Duxiu and Li Dazhao.

Men and women marched side by side. The anti-imperialist movement broadened to include calls for social reform and criticism of the current status of women. In contrast to the traditional Confucian respect for the old, the reformers called on younger people to rejuvenate China. The exhortations of Chen Duxiu's 'Call to Youth' were taken up by magazines such as *Morning Bell* (edited at first by Li Dazhao) and *Young China*. Students were prominent in the campaign.

The central feature of this intellectual movement was that a growing number of journals were written in the vernacular. Previously, Chinese writing had been in the classical style only understood by scholars. Now, reformist writers such as Hu Shi and Lu Xun addressed themselves to a much wider audience.

1.1 Chen Duxiu's 'Call to Youth', 1915

Chen Duxiu, the editor of New Youth, *was one of the most influential writers and subsequently a founder of the Chinese Communist Party.*

The Chinese compliment others by saying: 'He acts like an old man although still young.' Englishmen and Americans encourage one another by saying: 'Keep young while growing old.' Such is one respect in which the different ways of thought of the East and West are manifested …

What is needed is for one or two youths, who are quick in self-consciousness and brave in a struggle, to use to the full the natural intellect of man, and judge and choose all the thoughts of mankind, distinguishing which are fresh and vital and suitable for the present struggle for survival, and which are old and rotten and unworthy to be retained in the mind. Treat this problem as a sharp tool cleaves iron, or a sharp knife cuts hemp. Resolutely make no compromises and entertain no hesitations …

1 BE INDEPENDENT, NOT SERVILE

All men are equal. Each has his right to be independent, but absolutely no right to enslave others nor any obligation to make himself servile. By slavery we mean that in ancient times the ignorant and the weak lost their right of freedom, which was savagely usurped by tyrants. Since the rise of the theories of the rights of Man and of equality, no red-blooded person can endure [the name of slave]. The history of modern Europe is commonly referred to as a 'history of emancipation': the destruction of monarchical power aimed at political emancipation; the denial of Church authority aimed at religious emancipation; the rise of the theory of equal property aimed at economic emancipation; and the suffragist movement aimed at emancipation from male authority.

Emancipation means freeing oneself from the bondage of slavery and achieving a completely independent and free personality … For once the independent personality is recognized, all matters of conduct, all rights and privileges, and all belief should be left to the natural ability of each person; there is definitely no reason why one should blindly follow others. On the other hand, loyalty, filial piety, chastity, and righteousness are a slavish morality …

2 BE PROGRESSIVE, NOT CONSERVATIVE

Now our country still has not awakened from its long dream and isolates itself by going down the old rut … All our traditional ethics, law, scholarship, rites, and customs are survivals of feudalism. When compared with the achievement of the white race, there is a difference of a thousand years in thought, although we live in the same period. Revering only the history of the twenty-four dynasties and making no plans for progress and improvement, our people will be turned out of this twentieth-century world and be lodged in the dark ditches fit only for slaves, cattle, and horses. What more need be said? I really do not know what sort of institutions and culture are adequate for our survival in the present world if in such circumstances conservatism is still advocated. I would much rather see the past culture of our nation disappear than see our race die out now because of its unfitness for living in the modern world …

3 BE AGGRESSIVE, NOT RETIRING

While the tide of evil is now rushing onward, would it not be rare virtue for one or two self-respecting scholars to retire from the world, to keep themselves clean? But if your aim is to influence the people and establish a new tradition, I suggest that you make further progress from your present high position. It is impossible to avoid the struggle for survival, and so long as one draws breath there can be no place where one can retire for a tranquil hermit's life. It is our natural obligation in life to advance in spite of numerous difficulties. Stated in kindly terms, retirement is an action of the superior man in order to get away from the vulgar world. Stated in hostile terms, it is a phenomenon of the weak who are unable to struggle for survival ... Alas! The war steeds of Europe are intruding into your house. Where can you quietly repose under a white cloud? I wish that our youth would become Confucius and Mo-tzu and not [the hermits] Ts'ao-fu and Hsu Yu ...

4 BE COSMOPOLITAN, NOT ISOLATIONIST

Any change in the economic or political life of one nation will usually have repercussions over the whole world, just as the whole body is affected when one hair is pulled. The prosperity or decline, rise or fall of a nation of today depends half on domestic administration and half on influences from outside the country. Take the recent events of our country as evidence: Japan suddenly rose in power and stimulated our revolutionary and reform movements; the European War broke out, and then Japan presented her demands to us – is this not clear proof? When a nation is thrown into the currents of the world, traditionalists will certainly hasten the day of its fall, but those capable of change will take this opportunity to compete and progress. According to the pessimists, since the opening of the treaty ports, our country has been losing territory and paying indemnities to the point of exhaustion. But according to the optimists, we would still be in the age of the eight-legged essay [the most notorious part of the traditional examination system] and the queue were it not for the blessings of the Sino-Japanese War of 1895 and the Boxer Uprising of 1900. Not only are we unable to support an isolationist and closed-door policy, but circumstances also are unfavorable to it ... If at this point one still hopes thereby to resist the current, then this still indicates the spirit of an isolationist country and a lack of knowledge of the world. When its citizens lack knowledge of the world, how can a nation expect to survive in it? A proverb says: 'He who builds his cart behind closed gates will find it not suited to the tracks outside the gates.' The cart-builders of today not only close their gates, but even want to use the methods contained in the chapter on technology in the Rites of Chou for use on the highways of Europe and America. The trouble will be more than not fitting the tracks.

Source: Chen Tu-hsiu, 'Call to Youth', *New Youth*.
In S. Y. Teng and J. K. Fairbank, *China's Response to the West*
(Cambridge, Massachusetts: Harvard University Press, 1954), pp. 240–3

1.2 A clarion call. Extract from the first issue of the *Morning Bell*, 15 August 1916

The day has its dawn and so has the year, the individual has his youth and so has the nation. Today, grey-haired China has one foot in the grave, while a youthful China is not yet conceived. The twilight of the old year is fading and the dawn of the New Year is approaching. Now, when things are dying, yet being born, when they are being ruined, yet being completed, destroyed, yet constructed, decaying, yet blossoming, we ring this morning bell, so that, together with our heroic and energetic young people, we can welcome every day anew the uplifting spirit of the morning, and make the efforts worthy of the new light of the twentieth century. Everyone filled with the vitality of youth should send forth the morning ray of the new youthful China. Every sound evokes an echo, and every echo awakes a dream, so that the self-awakening of each individual leads to the self-awakening of an entire people. Let everyone arise resolutely and march forward courageously without looking back, to demand from the goddess of liberty an ideal China, a youthful China ...

Source: *Morning Bell*. In *Selected Works of Li Ta-chao*
(Beijing: People's Publishing House, 1959), p. 58

1.3 Official statement of the Chinese delegation at Versailles, 28 June 1919

The Chinese delegation at the Peace Conference issued the following official statement to the press.

Feeling the injustice of the settlement of the Shantung question made by the Conference, the Chinese delegation sent a formal protest to the Council of Prime Ministers on May 4th 1919 and made a reservation at the Plenary Session of May 6th last vis-à-vis the clauses concerning that question in the Conditions of Peace which, taking that settlement for their basis, purport to transfer German rights in the Chinese Province of Shantung to Japan instead of restoring them to China, the rightful sovereign over the territory and a loyal copartner in the war on the side of the Allied and Associated Powers.

The announcement of the settlement evoked a nationwide protest in China, which was participated in by the Chinese people in every part of the world. In view of the united opposition of public opinion, the Chinese government had no course open to them except to accept the clauses in question. To this effect they instructed the Chinese delegates in Paris, who accordingly notified the President of the Peace Conference on May 26th last in a formal communication that they would sign the treaty of peace with Germany subject to the reservation made on May 6th last.

On May 28th last, the Secretary General of the Conference acknowledged the receipt of the notification and stated that it had been transmitted to the delegations of the Principal Allied and Associated Powers represented in the Supreme Council. From that time on, the Chinese delegation received no word from the Conference on the matter of reservation.

It was not until the 24th inst. that the Chinese delegation was informed by the Secretary General on behalf of the President of the Conference that reservations in the text of the treaty of peace were not permissible, for want of precedent, though there is a notable precedent in the Treaty of Vienna, of June 9th 1815, which was signed by the Swedish pleni-potentiary with a reservation made under his signature on three articles in the treaty.

What the Chinese delegates first proposed to do was merely to write in the treaty over their signatures the words 'Subject to the reservation made at the Plenary Session of May 6th 1919 relative to the question of Shantung (Articles 156, 157, and 158).' When this insertion was refused, the Chinese delegation proposed to make the reservation an annex to the treaty. On this being refused, they proposed to send to the President of the Conference, before proceeding to Versailles, a separate declaration in writing to the effect that the Chinese plenipotentiaries would sign the treaty subject to the reservation of May 6th, which was intended to enable China, after the signing of the treaty, to ask for the reconsideration of the Shantung question. This, again, was refused, and the refusal was explained on the ground that the Supreme Council had decided to admit no reservation of any kind in the text of the treaty or separately, before it was signed, but that the delegation could send him a declaration after its signature.

As the validity of a declaration made after the signing of the treaty would be doubtful, the delegation urged the right of making one in advance of it; but, out of deference to the decision of the Council to admit no reservations whatever, it suggested a further modification of the wording, so that the signing of the treaty by the Chinese plenipotentiaries might not be under-stood as precluding China from asking at a suitable moment for the reconsideration of the Shantung question. This proposal, to the surprise of the delegation, was once again refused.

After failing in all their earnest attempts at conciliation and after seeing every honourable compromise rejected, the Chinese delegation had no course open to them except to adhere to the path of duty to their country. Rather than accepting by their signature Articles 156, 157, and 158 in the treaty against which their sense of right and justice militated, they refrained from signing the treaty altogether.

The Chinese plenipotentiaries regret having had to take a course that appears to mar the soli-darity of the Allied and Associated Powers; but they are firmly of the opinion that the responsi-bility for this step rests, not with themselves, who had no other honourable course to pursue, but rather with those who, it is felt, unjustly and unnecessarily deprived them of the right to make a declaration to safeguard against any interpretation that might preclude China from asking for a reconsideration of the Shantung question at a suitable moment in the future, in the hope that the injustice to China might be rectified later in the interest of permanent peace in the Far East.

The Peace Conference having denied China justice in the settlement of the Shantung ques-tion and having today in effect prevented them from signing the treaty without sacrificing their sense of right, justice, and patriotic duty, the Chinese delegates submit their case to the impartial judgement of the world.

Source: *China Treaties and Agreements 1894–1919*
(New York: Oxford University Press, 1921), pp. 1497–8

1.4 Impressions of the student protests, May–June 1919

John and Alice Dewey, extracts from *Letters from China and Japan*

John Dewey, Professor of Philosophy in Columbia University, left early in 1919 for a trip to Japan. In May, he and his wife decided to go to China for a few weeks before returning to the United States. They changed their plans in the summer of 1919, when Professor Dewey applied to Columbia University for a year's leave of absence and stayed on in China. There he delivered a series of lectures on the philosophy of pragmatism. These letters were written to their children in America.

SHANGHAI, MONDAY MAY 12

The Peking tempest seems to have subsided for the present, the Chancellor still holding the fort, and the students being released. The subsidized press said this was due in part to the request of the Japanese that the schoolboy pranks be looked upon indulgently. According to the papers, the Japanese boycott is spreading, but the ones we see doubt if the people will hold out long enough – meanwhile Japanese money is refused here.

SHANGHAI, MAY 13

The students' committees met yesterday and voted to inform the government by telegraph that they would strike next Monday if their four famous demands were not granted – or else five – including, of course, refusal to sign the peace treaty, punishment of traitors who made the secret treaties with Japan because they were bribed, etc. But the committee seemed to me more conservative than the students, for the rumour this a.m. is that they are going to strike today anyway. They are especially angered because the police have forbidden them to hold open-air meetings – that's now the subject of one of their demands – and because the provincial legislature, after promising to help in education, raised their own salaries ... out of the small educational fund ... the students are mad and want action ...

Some of the teachers, as far as I can judge, quite sympathize with the boys not only in their ends but in their methods; some think it their moral duty to urge deliberate action and try to make the students as organized and systematic as possible, and some take the good old Chinese ground that there is no certainty that anything will come of it. To the outsider it looks as if the babes and sucklings who have no experience and no precedents would have to save China – if. And it's an awful if. It's not surprising that the Japanese with their energy and punitiveness feel they are predestined to govern China.

NANKING, MAY 23

I don't believe anybody knows what the political prospects are; this students' movement has introduced a new and incalculable factor – and all in the three weeks we have been here. You hear nothing but gloom about political China at first, corrupt and traitorous officials, soldiers only paid banditti, the officers getting the money from Japan to pay them with, no organizing power or cohesion among the Chinese; and then the students take things into their hands, and there is animation and a sudden buzz. There are a hundred students being coached here to go out and make speeches, they will have a hundred different stations scattered through the city. It is also said the soldiers are responding to the patriotic propaganda; a man told us that the soldiers wept when some students talked to them about the troubles of China, and the soldiers of Shantung, the province turned over to Japan, have taken the lead in telegraphing the soldiers in the other provinces to resist the corrupt traitors. Of course, what they all are afraid of is that this is a flash in the pan, but they are already planning to make the student movement permanent and to find something for them to do after this is settled. Their idea here is to reorganize them for popular propaganda for education, more schools, teaching adults, social service, etc.

It is very interesting to compare the men who have been abroad with those who haven't – I mean students and teachers. Those who haven't are sort of helpless, practically; the height of literary and academic minds. Those who have studied abroad, even in Japan, have more go to them.

PEKING, JUNE 1

We have just seen a few hundred girls march from the American Board Mission school to go to see the President to ask him to release the boy students who are in prison for making speeches on the street. To say that life in China is exciting is to put it fairly. We are witnessing the birth of a nation, and birth always comes hard. I may as well begin at the right end and tell you what has happened while things have been moving so fast I could not get time to write. Yesterday we went to see the temples of Western Hills, conducted by one of the members of the Ministry of Education. As we were running along the big street that passes the city wall, we saw students speaking to groups of people. This was the first time the students had appeared for several days. We asked the official if they would not be arrested, and he said: 'No, not if they keep within the law and do not make any trouble among the people'. This morning when we got the paper it was full of nothing else. The worst thing is that the University has been turned into a prison with military tents all around it and a notice on the outside that this is a prison for students who disturb the peace by making speeches. As this is all illegal, it amounts to a military seizure of the University and therefore all the faculty will have to resign. They are to have a meeting this afternoon to discuss the matter. After that is over, we will probably know what has happened again. The other thing we heard was that, in addition to the two hundred students locked up in the Law Building, two students were taken to the Police rooms and flogged on the back. Those two students were making a speech and were arrested and taken before the officers of the gendarmerie. Instead of shutting up as they were expected to do, the boys asked some questions of these officers that were embarrassing to answer. The officers then had them flogged ... We saw the students making speeches this morning about eleven, when we started to look for houses, and heard later that they had been arrested, that they carried toothbrushes and towels in their pockets. Some stories say that not two hundred but a thousand have been arrested. There are about ten thousand striking in Peking alone. The marching out of those girls was evidently a shock to their teachers, and many mothers were there to see them off. The girls were going to walk to the palace of the President, which is some long distance from the school. If he does not see them, they will remain standing ...

JUNE 5

This is Thursday morning, and last night we heard that about one thousand students were arrested the day before. Yesterday afternoon a friend got a pass which permitted him to enter the building where the students were confined. They have filled up the building of Law, and have begun on the Science building, in consequence of which the faculty have to go to the Missionary buildings today to hold their faculty meeting. At four yesterday afternoon, the prisoners who had been put in that day at ten had had no food. One of our friends went out and got the University to appropriate some money and they ordered a carload of bread sent in … On the whole, the checkmate of the police seems surely impending. They will soon have the buildings full, as the students are getting more and more in earnest, and the most incredible part of it is that the police are surprised. They really thought the arrests would frighten the others from going on. So everybody is getting an education …

PEKING, JUNE 10

The students have taken the trick and won the game at the present moment – I decline to predict the morrow when it comes to China. Sunday morning I lectured at the auditorium of the Board of Education and at that time the officials there didn't know what had happened. But the government sent what is called a pacification delegate to the self-imprisoned students to say that the government recognized that it had made a mistake and apologized. Consequently the students marched triumphantly out, and yesterday their street meetings were bigger and more enthusiastic than ever. The day before they had hooted at four unofficial delegates who had asked them to please come out of jail, but who hadn't apologized. But the biggest victory is that it is now reported that the government will today issue a mandate dismissing the three men who are always called traitors – yesterday they had got to the point of offering to dismiss one, the one whose house was attacked by the students on the fourth of May, but they were told that that wouldn't be enough, so now they have surrendered still more. Whether this will satisfy the striking merchants or whether they will make further demands, having won the first round, doesn't yet appear. There are lots of rumours, of course. One is that the backdown is not only due to the strike of merchants, but to a fear that the soldiers could no longer be counted upon. There was even a rumour that a regiment at Western Hills was going to start for Peking to side with the students. Rumours are one of China's strong suits. When you realize that we have been here less than six weeks, you will have to admit that we have been seeing life. For a country that is regarded at home as stagnant and unchanging, there is certainly something doing.

Source: John and Alice Dewey, *Letters from China and Japan*
(London: Dent and Sons, 1920), pp. 161, 177–8, 193–4, 209–11, 219–20, 231–2, 235–6

1.5 Commentary on the suicide of Miss Zhao

Mao Zedong, 16 November 1919

The parents of Miss Zhao arranged for her to marry a wealthy widower, the son of an antiques dealer. Miss Zhao objected to the proposed match and also complained that the groom was old and ugly. Seated in the bridal sedan chair, she slit her throat with a razor on 14 November 1919. Within two days Mao published the following.

When something happens in society, we should not underrate its importance. The background of any event contains the multiple causes of its occurrence. For example, the event of a 'person's death' can be explained in two ways. One is biological and physical, as in the case of 'passing away in ripe old age.' The other goes against biological and physical factors, as in the case of 'premature death' or 'unnatural death.' The death of Miss Zhao by suicide belongs to the latter category of 'unnatural death.'

A person's suicide is determined entirely by circumstances. Was it Miss Zhao's original intent to seek death? No, it was to seek life. If, in the end, Miss Zhao chose death, it was because circumstances drove her to this. The circumstances in which Miss Zhao found herself included: (1) Chinese society, (2) the family living in the Zhao residence on Nanyang Street in Changsha, (3) the Wu family of the Orange Garden in Changsha, the family of the husband she did not want. These three factors constituted three iron nets, which we can imagine as a kind of triangular construction. Within these triangular nets, however much Miss Zhao sought life, there was no way for her to go on living. The opposite of life is death, and so Miss Zhao was obliged to die.

If one of these three factors had not been an iron net, or if one of the iron nets had opened, Miss Zhao would certainly not have died. (1) If Miss Zhao's parents had not used excessive compulsion, but had acceded to her own free will, she would certainly not have died. (2) If, while exercising compulsion, Miss Zhao's parents had allowed her to put her point of view to her fiancé's family, and to explain the reasons for her refusal, and if in the end her fiancé's family had accepted her point of view, and respected her individual freedom, Miss Zhao would certainly not have died. (3) If, even though neither her own parents nor her husband's family could accept her free will, there had been in society a powerful segment of public opinion to back her, and if there had been an entirely new world to which she could flee, in which her act of flight would be considered honourable and not dishonourable, Miss Zhao again would certainly not have died. If Miss Zhao is dead today, it is because she was solidly enclosed by the three iron nets (society, her own family, her fiancé's family); she sought life in vain, and finally was led to seek death.

Source: Mao Zedong, 'Miss Chao's Suicide'.
In S. R. Schram, ed., *Mao's Road to Power: Revolutionary Writings*, 1912–1949, Vol. 1
(Armonk, New York: M. E. Sharpe, 1992), pp. 421–2

1.6 The politics of gender in the making of the Party

Christina Gilmartin

Engels' materialist analysis of the family as the prime locus of female oppression resonated well with the antifamily orientation of many Chinese Communists. They found in this materialist interpretation a theoretical framework for their May 4th critique of the family as a despotic institution that perpetuated the odious practices of footbinding, concubinage, arranged marriages, women's illiteracy, seclusion, and female submission to male authority. Thus, Engels' theory not only justified the continuing condemnation of the family in Chinese communist writings, but also facilitated the retention of other May 4th feminist issues in the communist gender discourse, at least until 1927. A brief review of a few representative titles by Communists exemplifies this phenomenon: 'Sadness about the Sin of the Marriage System,' 'The Event of Ms Xi Shangzhen's Suicide in the Office of the Commercial Press,' 'Women's Consciousness,' 'The Relationship between Love and Virginity,' 'An Admonition to New Gentlemen Who Denigrate Social Contact between Men and Women,' 'Social Contact between Men and Women and Old Ethics,' 'The Tragedy of the Old Style of Marriage,' 'The Issue of a Love Triangle,' 'A Discussion of the Co-Educational School Issue,' 'The Problem of Preventing Women Students from Getting a Divorce,' and 'How to Solve the Dilemma of Social Contact between Men and Women' ...

The [Engelsian] notion that the difference between a wife and a streetwalker was only the length of time that her sexual services were secured seemed to capture the inhumanity of the arranged marriage system and strip it of any lingering legitimacy for radical intellectuals. Shen Zemin, the younger brother of the well-known writer Mao Dun, published one of the most impassioned indictments of the marriage system that adhered to this mode of interpretation. He charged:

> The present system has a tendency to turn women into prostitutes. This is because the system is alive and expanding, purposely and incessantly swallowing innocent people into its bloody mouth. The present number of people who have fallen victims will increase. In such a social reality, this system noiselessly forces upper class women to sell unconsciously their most precious 'sex.' It forces working class women who can barely subsist to turn directly into prostitutes ...
>
> Money, of course, is not the only reason why women degenerate into this deplorable status, as women do not necessarily always demand money. Women have their own reasons for exchanging their only possession – their sexual services. In order to avoid the isolation of remaining single, or to fulfil a desire to become a mother, or to have their vanity indulged, women often marry men they do not love. Emotionally their predicament is similar to the experiences of prostitutes, for they have painfully to submit to their husbands and put up with fondling caresses in the absence of love.

The natural progression of this argument led Shen and other Communists of his era to call for the abolition of marriage. They believed that family-controlled marriages served only family interests and often resulted in unhappy unions for the individuals involved. In this respect, they were revealing certain anarchist inclinations. Such traits, for example, can be identified in the writings of Shi Cuntong, who was more candid than most budding

Communists in acknowledging his anarchist inclinations. In several articles on marriage that he published in May 1920, when he joined the Shanghai Marxist Research Society, he argued that marriage was the main instrument shackling individuals to the family system. Moreover, in Shi's view, marriage essentially required the subordination of one individual's emotions and sexuality to those of another person – a situation that no one should be forced to tolerate.

Source: Christina Gilmartin, 'The Politics of Gender in the Making of the Party'.
In T. Saich, ed., *New Perspectives on the Chinese Communist Revolution*
(Armonk, New York: M. E. Sharpe, 1995), pp. 34–6

1.7 Li Dazhao compares the French and Russian revolutions 1918

Li Dazhao

Li promoted Marxism at Beijing University, became a founder member of China's Communist Party, and was murdered in 1927.

The present situation of the Russian revolution is that political power belongs entirely to the Radical Socialist Party, which has overthrown fundamentally the traditional and political social organizations. The appearance of temporary confusion is likely to provoke the pessimism of those who follow developments there. Also, many of our countrymen are secretly and groundlessly worried about the situation. I have gone into the matter. In any age, the foundations of a new life and of a new civilization are often laid in hardship and terror; examples of this can easily be found throughout history. The birth pangs of a new creation often frighten conventional people who regard basic change as a catastrophe, without realizing that, in the course of the evolution of human history, the greatest success invariably comes in the wake of the greatest sacrifice and suffering. The Russian revolution today, like the French revolution in the past, is an unprecedented upheaval that will influence the civilization of the coming age. Did not France at that time give cause for fear and apprehension on the part of people throughout the world and make them deeply pessimistic about her? But the foundations of the later freedom and happiness of the French people were laid in that revolution. Not only that, but the entire world civilization of the nineteenth century, as expressed in political or social organizations, was wholly conceived in the bloody tide of the French revolution. The civilization following upon the early period of the twentieth century will inevitably undergo an unparalleled change; who knows but that its seed will germinate in the bloody tide of the Russian revolution just as it did in the eighteenth-century French revolution? Do not those people who are now pessimistic about the Russian revolution resemble those who were pessimistic about France?

It may be said that what the French advocated and fought for was 'freedom', whereas what Russians struggle for is 'bread'. Therefore, the demands of the French were directed at the liberation of reason whereas the demands of the Russians today concern the satisfaction of material needs and desires. The motivation of the Russian revolution is therefore inferior to that of the French revolution … This reasoning fails to discern that the French revolution was an eighteenth-century revolution, based on nationalism, and that it was a political revolution with social connotations. On the other hand, the Russian revolution is an early twentieth-century revolution, based on socialism, and it is a social revolution tinted with the colours of world revolution. The spirits of the ages differ, so do the natures of the revolutions; the two cannot be compared under the same sun. It is true that the French had the French patriotic spirit to uplift the hearts of the whole nation; but does Russia today have no Russian humanist spirit to awaken the mind of the people within and to swim with the world's current without? Otherwise it would have been impossible for the whole country to rise in revolution under the flowing red banners. Furthermore, nowhere on earth has the penetration of humanism into the hearts of the people been as deep as it has been in Russia. For many decades, writers have risen continually to fight tyrannical religious and political systems with their humanist and social literature. The difference is, then, that the French spirit was the spirit of patriotism, whereas the Russian spirit is the spirit of universal love. The former has its root in nationalism, the latter inclines to internationalism; the former often becomes the source of war, while the latter is likely to become the herald of peace …

The French revolution was not only a symptom of the awakening of the French mind, but was in fact the clear symptom of the awakening of the universal mind of humanity in the nineteenth century. The revolution of Russia is not only a clear symptom of the awakening of the Russian mind, but is in fact the clear symptom of the awakening of the universal mind of humanity in the twentieth century …

Our attitude towards the Russian revolution can only be to welcome it as the dawn of a New World civilization, and to lend our ears to the tidings of a new Russia based on freedom and humanity, so that we adapt ourselves to this new world current. There is no need to be pessimistic just because of the present temporary confusion.

Source: Li Ta-chao, 'A Comparative View of the French and Russian Revolutions',
Yen Chih **(Quarterly), vol 3, 1 July 1918. Reprinted in** *Selected Works of Li Ta-chao*
(Beijing: People's Publishing House, 1959), pp. 101–4

1.8 The literary revolution

Hu Shi, from *The Chinese Renaissance*, 1934

A lecture delivered by Hu Shi in 1933.

The Renaissance was the name given by a group of Peking University students to a new monthly magazine which they published in 1918. They were mature students well trained in the old cultural tradition of the country, and they readily recognized in the new movement then led by some of their professors a striking similarity to the Renaissance in Europe. Three prominent features in the movement reminded them of the European movement. First, it was a conscious movement to promote a new literature in the living language of the people to take the place of the classical literature of old. Second, it was a movement of conscious protest against many of the ideas and institutions in the traditional culture, and of conscious emancipation of the individual man and woman from the bondage of the forces of tradition. It was a movement of reason versus tradition, freedom versus authority, and glorification of life and human values versus their suppression. And lastly, strangely enough, this new movement was led by men who knew their cultural heritage and tried to study it with the new methodology of modern historical criticism and research. In that sense it was also a humanist movement. In all these directions, the new movement which began in 1917 and which was sometimes called the 'New Culture Movement,' the 'New Thought' movement, or 'The New Tide' was capturing the imagination and sympathy of the youth of the nation as something that promised and pointed to the new birth of an old people and an old civilization ...

The Renaissance movement of the last two decades differs from all the early movements in being a fully conscious and studied movement. Its leaders know what they want, and they know what they must destroy in order to achieve what they want. They want a new language, a new literature, a new outlook on life and society, and a new scholarship. They want a new language, not only as an effective instrumentality for popular education but also as an effective medium for the development of the literature of new China. They want a literature that shall be written in the living tongue of a living people and shall be capable of expressing the real feelings, thoughts, inspirations, and aspirations of a growing nation ...

Let me first state the problem for which the literary revolution offers the solution. The problem was first seen by all early reformers as the problem of finding a suitable language that could serve as an effective means of educating the vast millions of children and of illiterate adults. They admitted that the classical language, which was difficult to write and learn, and for thousands of years incapable of being spoken or verbally understood, was not suited for the education of children and the masses. But they never thought of giving up the classical language in which was written and preserved all the cultural tradition of the race. Moreover, the classical language was the only linguistic medium for written communication between the various regions with different dialects, just as Latin was the universal medium of communication and publication for the whole of medieval Europe ...

There was much serious talk about devising an alphabet for transcribing Chinese sounds and for publishing useful information for the enlightenment of the masses. The Christian missionaries had devised a number of alphabets for translating the Bible into the local dialects for the benefit of illiterate men and women. Some Chinese scholars also worked out several alphabetical systems for the mandarin dialect, and publicly preached their adoption for the education of illiterate adults. Other scholars advocated the use of the pei-hua, that is, the spoken tongue of the people, for publishing periodicals and newspapers in order to inculcate useful information and patriotic ideas in the people who could not read the literary language of the scholars.

But these scholar-reformers all agreed that such expedient measures as the use of the vulgar tongue or the adoption of an alphabet were only necessary for those adults who had had no chance to go to the regular schools. They never for a moment would consider the idea that these expedients should be so universally used as to replace the classical language altogether ...

All such attempts at reform were bound to fail, because nobody wanted to learn a language that was despised by those who advocated it, and that had no more use than the reading of a few cheap magazines and pamphlets that the reformers were kind enough to condescend to publish for the benefit of the ignorant and the lowly ... The schools continued to teach the language of the classics which had been dead for over two thousand years; the newspapers continued to be written and printed in it; and the scholars and authors continued to produce their books and essays and poems in it. The language problem remained unsolved and insoluble.

The solution of this problem came from the dormitories of the American universities. In the year 1915 a series of trivial incidents led some Chinese students in Cornell University to take up the question of reforming the Chinese language. My classmate, Mr Chao Yuen-ren and I prepared a series of articles on this question ... published in the Chinese Students Monthly. They attracted no comment and were soon forgotten.

But other disputes arose among some of my literary friends in the United States ... The original dispute was one of poetic diction. I was led to see that the problem was really one of a suitable medium for all branches of Chinese literature ... My answer was: The classical language, so long dead, can never be the medium of a living literature of a living nation; the future literature of China must be written in the living language of the people ... I resolved to write no more poems in the classical language, and to begin my experiments in writing poetry in the so-called vulgar tongue of the people ...

Then, an unexpected event occurred that suddenly carried the literary movement to a rapid success ... the 'May 4th Movement' ... In this political struggle, Peking University suddenly rose to the position of national leadership in the eyes of the students. The literary and intellectual movements led by some of the professors and students of the university ... were now openly acknowledged ... as new and welcome forces for national emancipation. During the years 1919–20, there appeared about 400 small periodicals, almost all of them published by the students in different localities ... all of them published in the spoken language of the people – the literary medium which the Peking University professors had advocated ... In the course of a few years, the literary revolution had succeeded in giving to the people a national language, and had brought about a new age of literary expression.

Source: Hu Shih, *The Chinese Renaissance*
(Chicago: University of Chicago Press, 1934), pp. 44, 46, 48–9, 50–2, 55–6

1.9 Lu Xun's preface to 'Call to Arms' 1922

Lu Xun

One of China's most distinguished story writers, Lu Xun, was famous for his satirical attacks on the old regime in, for example, The Madman's Diary *and* The Story of Ah Q. *Mao Zedong often cited his stories to point a moral. This was Lu's first collection of short stories (1918–22).*

When I was young, I, too, had many dreams. Most of them I later forgot, but I see nothing in this to regret. For, although recalling the past may bring happiness, at times it cannot but bring loneliness, and what is the point of clinging in spirit to lonely bygone days? However, my trouble is that I cannot forget completely, and these stories stem from those things that I have been unable to forget.

For more than four years I frequented, almost daily, a pawnshop and pharmacy. I cannot remember how old I was at the time, but the pharmacy counter was exactly my height, and that in the pawnshop twice my height. I used to hand clothes and trinkets up to the counter twice my height, then take the money given to me with contempt to the counter my own height to buy the medicine for my father, a chronic invalid ...

It is my belief that those who come down in the world will probably learn in the process what society is really like. My eagerness to go to N and study in the K Academy [N refers to Nanjing, and K to the Kiangnan (Jiangnan) Naval Academy where the author studied in 1898] seems to have shown a desire to strike out for myself, escape, and find people of a different kind. My mother had no choice but to raise eight dollars for my travelling expenses and say I might do as I pleased. That she cried was only natural, for at that time the proper thing was to study the classics and take the official examinations. Anyone who studied 'foreign subjects' was a social outcast regarded as someone who could find no way out and was forced to sell his soul to foreign devils. Besides, she was sorry to part with me. But in spite of all this, I went to N and entered the K Academy; and it was there that I learned of the existence of physics, arithmetic, geography, history, drawing, and physical training. They had no physiology course, but we saw woodblock editions of such works as *A New Course on the Human Body* and *Essays on Chemistry and Hygiene*. Recalling the talk and prescriptions of physicians I had known and comparing them with what I now knew, I came to the conclusion that those physicians must be either unwitting or deliberate charlatans; and I began to feel great sympathy for the invalids and families who suffered at their hands. From translated histories I also learned that the Japanese Reformation owed its rise, to a great extent, to the introduction of Western medical science to Japan.

These inklings took me to a medical college in the Japanese countryside. It was my fine dream that on my return to China I would cure patients like my father who had suffered from the wrong treatment, while if war broke out I would serve as an army doctor, at the same time promoting my countrymen's faith in reform.

I have no idea what improved methods are now used to teach microbiology, but in those days we were shown lantern slides of microbes; and if the lecture ended early, the instructor might show slides of natural scenery or news to fill up the time. Since this was during the Russo-Japanese War, there were many war slides, and I had to join in the clapping and cheering in the lecture hall along with the other students. It was a long time since I had seen any compatriots, but one day I saw a newsreel slide of a number of Chinese, one of them bound and the rest standing around him. They were all sturdy fellows but appeared completely apathetic. According to the commentary, the one with his hands bound was a spy working for the Russians who was to be beheaded by the Japanese military as a warning to others, while the Chinese beside him had come to enjoy the spectacle.

Before the term was over I had left for Tokyo, because this slide convinced me that medical science was not so important after all. The people of a weak and backward country, however strong and healthy they might be, could only serve to be made examples of or as witnesses of such futile spectacles; and it was not necessarily deplorable if many of them died of illness. The most important thing, therefore, was to change their spirit; and since at that time I felt that literature was the best means to this end, I decided to promote a literary movement. There were many Chinese students in Tokyo studying law, political science, physics, and chemistry, even police work and engineering, but not one studying literature and art. However, even in this uncongenial atmosphere I was fortunate enough to find some kindred spirits. We gathered the few others we needed and after discussion our first step, of course, was to publish a magazine, the title of which denoted that this was a new birth. ... [This magazine failed and Lu Xun lost his youthful fervour.]

In S [Shaoxing] Hostel was a three-roomed house with a courtyard in which grew a locust tree, and it was said that a woman had hanged herself there. Although the tree had grown so tall that its branches were now out of reach, the rooms remained deserted. For some years I stayed here, copying ancient inscriptions ...

The only visitor to drop in occasionally for a talk was my old friend Jin Xinyi. Having put his big portfolio on the rickety table, he would take off his long gown and sit down opposite me, looking as if his heart was still beating fast because he was afraid of dogs.

'What's the use of copying these?' One night, while leafing through the inscriptions I had copied, he asked me for enlightenment on this point.

'There isn't any use.'

'What's the point, then, of copying them?'

'There isn't any point.'

'Why don't you write something?' ...

I understood. They were bringing out *New Youth*, but since there did not seem to have been any reaction, favourable or otherwise, no doubt they felt lonely ...

I finally agreed to write, and the result was my first story 'A Madman's Diary.' And, once started, I could not give up but would write some sort of short story from time to time to humour my friends, until I had written more than a dozen of them.

As far as I am concerned, I no longer feel any great urge to express myself; yet, perhaps because I have not forgotten the grief of my past loneliness, I sometimes call out to encourage those fighters who are galloping on in loneliness, so that they do not lose heart. Whether my cry is brave or sad, repellent or ridiculous, I do not care. However, since this is a call to arms I must naturally obey my general's orders. This is why I often resort to innuendoes, as when I made a wreath appear from nowhere at the son's grave in 'Medicine,' while in 'Tomorrow' I did not say that Fourth Shan's Wife never dreamed of her little boy. For our chiefs in those days were against pessimism. And I, for my part, did not want to infect with the loneliness that I had found so bitter those young people who were still dreaming pleasant dreams, just as I had done when young.

It is clear, then, that my stories fall far short of being works of art; hence, I must at least count myself fortunate that they are still known as stories and are even being brought out in one volume. Although such good fortune makes me uneasy, it still pleases me to think that they have readers in the world of men, for the time being at any rate.

So now that these stories of mine are being reprinted in one collection, for the reasons given above I have chosen to entitle it *Call to Arms*.

Source: Lu Xun, *Call to Arms*, 1922. Reprinted in *The Complete Stories of Lu Xun* (Bloomington: Indiana University Press; Beijing, Foreign Languages Press, 1981), pp. v–x. Translated by Yang Xianyi and Gladys Yang

1.10 The problem of China

Bertrand Russell, 1922

The intelligentsia in China has a very peculiar position, unlike that which it has in any other country. Hereditary aristocracy has been practically extinct in China for about 2,000 years, and for many centuries the country has been governed by the successful candidates in competitive examinations. This has given to the educated the kind of prestige elsewhere belonging to a governing aristocracy. Although the old traditional education is fast dying out, and higher education now teaches modern subjects, the prestige of education has survived, and public opinion is still ready to be influenced by those who have intellectual qualifications. The Tuchuns [warlords], many of whom, including Chang-tso-lin, have begun by being brigands, are, of course, mostly too stupid and ignorant to share this attitude, but that in itself makes their regime weak and unstable. The influence of Young China – i.e. of those who have been educated either abroad or in modern colleges at home – is far greater than it would be in a country with less respect for learning. This is, perhaps, the most hopeful feature in the situation, because the number of modern students is rapidly increasing, and their outlook and aims are admirable. In another ten years or so they will probably be strong enough to regenerate China – if only the Powers will allow ten years to elapse without taking any drastic action.

It is important to try to understand the outlook and potentialities of Young China. Most of my time was spent among those Chinese who had had a modern education, and I should like to give some idea of their mentality. It seemed to me that one could already distinguish two generations: the older men who had fought their way with great difficulty and almost in soli- tude out of the traditional Confucian prejudices; and the younger men, who had found modern schools and colleges waiting for them, containing a whole world of modern-minded people ready to give sympathy and encouragement in the inevitable fight against the family. The older men – men varying in age from 30 to 50 – have gone through an inward and outward struggle resembling that of the rationalists of Darwin's and Mill's generation. They have had, painfully and with infinite difficulty, to free their minds from the beliefs instilled in youth, and to turn their thoughts to a new science and a new ethic ...

The younger men, however, have something more than the first generation of modern intellectuals. Having had less of a struggle, they have retained more energy and self-confi- dence. The candour and honesty of the pioneers survive, with more determination to be socially effective. This may be merely the natural character of youth, but I think it is more than that. Young men under thirty have often come in contact with Western ideas at a suffi- ciently early age to have assimilated them without a great struggle, so that they can acquire knowledge without being torn by spiritual conflicts. And they have been able to learn Western knowledge from Chinese teachers to begin with, which has made the process less difficult. Even the youngest students, of course, still have reactionary families, but they find less difficulty than their predecessors in resisting the claims of the family, and in realizing practically, not only theoretically, that the traditional Chinese reverence for the old may well be carried too far. In these young men I see the hope of China. When a little experience has taught them practical wisdom, I believe they will be able to lead Chinese opinion in the direc- tions in which it ought to move.

Source: Bertrand Russell, *The Problem of China*
(London: Allen and Unwin, 1922), pp. 76–8

2

The United Front and its breakdown

The First World War stimulated the Chinese economy. By the beginning of 1917 there were a million industrial workers in China; by 1922 there were nearly two million. Two hundred thousand Chinese had been sent to provide labour for the Allies in Europe. Some learned to read and write and came home to play a role in new labour organizations. At this time the embryo Communist party was founded under Chen Duxiu and Li Dazhao. At the first conference near Shanghai in 1921, Mao Zedong was in attendance.

Sun Yat-sen, respected in both Nationalist and Communist historiography as the founder of republican China, had been campaigning since 1885. In 1912 he became the first President of China, but was soon politically eclipsed by Yuan Shikai, who dispensed with democratic forms as he strove to become Emperor. After Yuan's death in June 1916, power fell into the hands of regional warlords.

Meanwhile, Sun Yat-sen's Guomingdang Party (GMD) had been ineffectual and was in decline. The post-war economic stimulus, together with the May 4th Movement, brought it to life. In Canton in 1920 the local warlord Chen Jiongming allowed Sun to set up a government, while Sun also made contact with the new labour unions. However, within two years Sun had fallen foul of Chen and went into exile to Shanghai.

Despairing of the treatment by the West in the Washington Conference of 1922, Sun was susceptible to approaches by the Comintern envoy, Maring. Maring recommended that, rather than trying to capture Canton by force of arms, Sun should embark on a campaign of propaganda. On the basis of Maring's report, the Comintern decided to work in cooperation with Sun Yat-sen. So it was that the Soviet government sent a key diplomat, Adolph Joffe, to negotiate with Sun. They both agreed that current circumstances in China were not right for Communism. Meanwhile, the Russian government offered to renounce all the treaties imposed on China by the Tsardom. Representing the Soviet Communist Party, Michael Borodin became personal adviser to Sun and political adviser to the GMD. The GMD was transformed into an approximate copy of the Bolshevik model, a move that was approved at a First National Congress in January 1924. In May 1924 the Russians paid for and staffed a Military Academy (Whampoa near Canton). So the small Chinese Communist Party was conscripted to the cause of the GMD. Individual Communists were to cooperate as card-carrying members. This was the beginning of the (First) United Front.

In the 1920s the groundswell of student discontent continued to be linked to anti-imperialism (British and Japanese). A campaign of Anti-Christian agitation in 1924 led to 'people's night schools' and joint student–workers' strikes and other actions. In Shanghai on 30 May 1925 protest marchers were fired on by British police who killed eleven Chinese and wounded many others. The Labour Association and Student Federation were joined by the

Chamber of Commerce in demanding redress and calling for wide-ranging reforms including the end of extraterritoriality and the removal of British and Japanese gunboats. Sympathetic protests elsewhere led to further bloodshed, notably on 23 June in Canton. In the Shameen massacre fifty-two Chinese were killed. Chinese opinion was united in condemning the foreign imperialist forces.

After Sun Yat-sen died in 1925, Chiang Kai-shek eventually succeeded as head of the GMD+. Although he had military training in Moscow, he had no trust in the Communist members of his party. By 1927 the United Front had the strength to mount a military expedition driving north and north-east in order to subdue the warlords and unite the country. By April, the United Front forces had gained support in cities and countryside up to the gates of Shanghai. In the city the organized workers, stiffened by Communists, were ready to welcome them. Then, Chiang struck. He ordered the systematic butchery of all left-wing sympathizers in Shanghai. Some Communist leaders were lucky enough to flee for their lives. The leaders of the Communist Party at its headquarters in Wuhan were traumatized and had to adjust to strained relations with Stalin, who in June 1927 was still urging cooperation with the GMD. The remnants of the CCP were driven underground, and by late 1927 Borodin and other Soviet advisers returned to the Soviet Union.

2.1 The Chinese Communist Party is born

Xiao Yu

Mao Zedong's friend describes how the two young men avoided the Secret Police in Shanghai in 1921. These recollections were compiled in 1950, and first published in the United States in 1959. Xiao Yu, who held top university posts in Nationalist China, lived in Europe and America after 1933. Apart from Mao's own writings, and recollections by Xiao Yu's brother, Emi Xiao, who stayed in Communist China, this is one of the main sources for Mao's early days.

In the spring of 1921, I lived in Changsha for about three months because I had many things to do before I returned to Peking … Some days before I was to leave Changsha, Mao Tse-tung suggested that he would accompany me, saying: 'I want to tell you, in the very strictest confidence, that in Peking, Kwangtung, Shanghai, and in fact everywhere, Communist groups have been formed and over a dozen delegates are due to gather in Shanghai for a secret meeting. The purpose of this meeting is formally to establish the Chinese Communist Party. I am the delegate for Changsha and I would very much like to have you go with me to this meeting.'

I told him: 'We can go to Shanghai on the same boat, but I do not want to attend your meeting.'

He insisted: 'Go on! You go there and meet these colleagues. Listen to their ideas. Talk with them!'

However, I asked: 'What's the good? Your meeting is not a discussion group. Everything has already been decided and now the Chinese Communist Party is to be established. If I were to attend that meeting, I should then be one of the founders of the Chinese Communism! I should then be responsible in the eyes of the Chinese people for a hundred, a thousand years, and I should be responsible before humanity for ten thousand years. I tell you, I am not prepared to have any part in the formation of the Communist Party!'

Mao replied: 'If we work hard, in about thirty to fifty years' time the Communist Party may be able to rule China.'

'That all depends upon how you go about it,' I said. 'I also believe that, after a long period of struggle, it may be possible for the Communists to dominate China. But it will not be for the good of the Chinese people; and their domination cannot last forever.'

'But if we manage to become the rulers of our country, don't you think that's a great achievement?' Mao asked.

'No, I don't,' I replied. 'I can best answer your question with a quotation from Lao Tzu: "Ruling a big country is like cooking a small fish".'

Mao laughed loudly at that. He thought I was joking. He did not know, and he never will be able to realize, that I was speaking very seriously. As a matter of fact, I wholeheartedly agree with Lao Tzu's philosophy, so aptly expressed in the sentence I had quoted.

That afternoon, Mao and I left Changsha by the West Gate on the river boat. We occupied the same cabin; I took the upper berth and he the lower. Many friends came down to see me off, as they knew I would soon be returning to France; so we were very busy talking with them all afternoon. In the evening, when the boat sailed, we had a sound sleep. When we entered Lake Tungting, it seemed as if we were on the ocean with a boundless expanse of water all around us. Mao was up first and went to sit on deck. Later I joined him and noticed a small thin book in his pocket. When I asked what it was, he took it out to show me the title, 'An Outline of the Capitalist System.' I said jokingly, 'Do you have to study capitalism to be able to form a Communist Party?' Mao smiled a little and said nothing. To break the silence, I continued, 'I understand you didn't have to study to be a Communist; so you shouldn't need to read books like that. The most important thing is to believe. That's why Communism is like a religion.' Mao just smiled again and still did not answer. Finally to break the spell, I asked if he had eaten his breakfast. 'No,' he replied, 'I was waiting for you, so we could eat together.'

Soon the boat reached Hankow and we parted. I went ashore while Mao went on to Shanghai, where we arranged to meet. He gave the secret address where I could find him after I had completed my business in Hupeh and Kiangsi.

When I arrived in Shanghai, I went directly to Valon Street in the French Concession and found the house number he had given me. In the room were two beds, one of which was undoubtedly for me, but Mao was not there. In the evening when he returned, he told me that they had had trouble with the secret police who had held them for some lengthy interrogations. Since the schools were on holiday, they had, after some difficulty, obtained the use of a classroom in a girls' college. Although they had locked all the doors for the meeting, the police had traced them and now it would be impossible to meet there again. These French Concession secret police were very smart and now they followed the delegates wherever they went; so they dared not meet again as a whole group. Though they scattered widely and maintained contact only by means of one or two delegates who acted as messengers, after several days' inactivity the police still maintained a close vigilance.

'We've hit on a new plan,' Mao announced one day, looking a bit happier than usual. 'One of the delegates has a girlfriend from Chiahsing in Chekiang Province and she says that on the way from Shanghai to West Lake you pass through Chiahsing. Just outside that city is another lake call Nan Hu (South Lake), and we are going to visit it as if we were tourists on the train, and when we get to Chiahsing we shall get off as if we were going to walk up and down the platform. We shall mix with the crowd till the train leaves. If the police follow us from Shanghai, they will not think of this. Besides, they are not so particular about what happens outside Shanghai City. I want you to come to Chiahsing with me and after the meeting we'll go and visit West Lake. Since I was a very small boy I have been told about the beautiful scenery there, and now, thanks to the Shanghai secret police, I'll see it.'

'Very well,' I consented. 'Tomorrow we shall go and visit West Lake.'

Next morning at seven, Mao and I left our room for the station where we bought third-class tickets for Hangchow. As we entered the station about nine o'clock, we saw the name 'Chiahsing' in large characters on a big white signboard. When the train stopped, we jumped down and mixed with the crowd on the platform … The other delegates had also left the train, but when they met, they gave no sign of recognition. Mao and I kept a sharp lookout as we walked, but no one was following us. We found a little hotel on a side street where we engaged a small room for the night …

As soon as we were settled, Mao set off for the meeting place …

'I expect to return late in the evening. We shall eat on the boat, so don't wait for me for supper' …

After supper there was still no sign of Mao Tse-tung … When Mao arrived two or three hours later, he held open the net and asked, 'Mr Siao, are you asleep already?'

'Yes,' I replied, 'I was asleep. But please don't hold open the net. The mosquitoes are terrible in here and they'll come in! Are you satisfied with the day's work?'

'Yes, very satisfied,' Mao replied. 'We were able to talk quite freely in the boat, at long last! It's too bad you didn't go.'

I answered quickly, 'You see you appreciated the "Freedom"! In Shanghai you were not free to talk with your colleagues. You were not free to hold your meeting. The police followed you everywhere. You didn't like that, yet that situation lasted only a few days: whereas in Russia it's like that night and day, every day, wherever one goes! Where could a group find a 'South Lake' in Russia? How is it that you like your freedom so much and yet you deliberately decide to destroy the freedom of your fellow countrymen, to make China a second Russia? What did you decide at the meeting? What action are you planning to take?'

Mao replied quietly, 'We decided that we must make China into a second Russia! We must organize ourselves and fight to the end.'

'How are you going to organize?' I asked.

'The delegates are not a bad lot,' Mao explained. 'Some of them are very well educated and they can read either Japanese or English. We decided that we must first form a nucleus. This nucleus is to be the Chinese Communist Party. Afterwards we shall arrange details of the propaganda to be carried out and the specific plan of action. The main idea is to start off by converting the laboring classes and the younger students to Communism. Then, too, we must be certain to have a sound economic basis. That explains why we must belong to the Third International.'

'But,' I protested, 'the Third International is Russian. Why don't you organize the Fourth International?'

'What is that?' asked Mao.

'The Fourth International,' I explained, 'is the idealist part of Communism. It is a combination of the ideals of Karl Marx and Prudhon [sic]. It is *free* Communism. You remember what I said about the two wheels of the rickshaw? The rickshaw of free Communism has both wheels; it needs no force to support it! If you agree to organize your movement along the lines of the Fourth International, I shall dedicate my whole life to it!'

'Let's talk about that again in a thousand years,' said Mao sadly, as he opened the mosquito net and got into bed.

Source: Siao Yu, *Mao Tsetung and I Were Beggars* (London: Souvenir Press, 1974), pp. 196–9 and 201–2. Originally published by Syracuse University Press, 1959

2.2 Joint statement of Sun Yat-sen and Joffe, 26 January 1923

China Yearbook, 1924–25

Dr Sun Yat-sen and Mr A.A. Joffe, Russian Envoy Extraordinary and Plenipotentiary to China, have authorized the publication of the following statement:

During his stay in Shanghai, Mr Joffe has had several conversations with Dr Sun Yat-sen, which have revealed the identity of their views on matters relating to Chinese–Russian relations, more especially on the following points:

1   Dr Sun Yat-sen holds that the communistic order or even the Soviet system cannot actually be introduced into China because there do not exist here the conditions for the successful establishment of either Communism or Sovietism. This view is entirely shared by Mr Joffe, who is further of the opinion that China's paramount and most pressing problem is to achieve national unification and attain full national independence, and regarding this great task, he has assured Dr Sun Yat-sen that China has the warmest sympathy of the Russian people and can count on the support of Russia.

2   In order to clarify the situation, Dr Sun Yat-sen has requested from Mr Joffe a reaffirmation of the principles defined in the Russian Note to the Chinese government, dated 27 September 1920. Mr Joffe has accordingly reaffirmed these principles and categorically declared to Dr Sun Yat-sen that the Russian government is ready and willing to enter into negotiations with China on the basis of the renunciation by Russia of all the treaties and exactions that the Tsardom imposed on China, including the treaty or treaties and agreements relating to the Chinese Eastern Railway (the management of which being the subject of a specific reference in Article VII of the said Note).

3   Recognizing that the Chinese Eastern Railway Question in its entirety can be satisfactorily settled only at a competent Russo-Chinese Conference, Dr Sun Yat-sen is of the opinion that the realities of the situation point to the desirability of a modus vivendi in the matter of the present management of the Railway. And he agrees with Mr Joffe that the existing Railway management should be temporarily reorganized by agreement between the Chinese and the Russian governments without prejudice, but to the true rights and special interests of either party. At the same time, Dr Sun Yat-sen considers that General Chang Tso-lin should be consulted on the point.

4   Mr Joffe has categorically declared to Dr Sun Yat-sen (who has fully satisfied himself as to this) that it is not and has never been the intention or purpose of the present Russian Government to pursue an imperialistic policy in Outer Mongolia or to cause it to secede from China. Dr Sun Yat-sen, therefore, does not view an immediate evacuation of Russian troops from Outer Mongolia as either imperative or in the real interest of China, the more so on account of the inability of the present government in Peking to prevent such an evacuation being followed by a recrudescence of intrigues and hostile activities by White Guardists against Russia and the creation of a graver situation than that which now exists.

Mr Joffe has parted from Dr Sun Yat-sen on the most cordial and friendly terms. On leaving Japan, to which he is now proceeding, he will again visit the south of China before finally returning to Peking.

Source: 'Joint Statement of Sun Yat-sen and Joffe', *China Yearbook, 1924–25*
(Tientsin, 1924), p. 863

2.3 The Three People's Principles. From the manifesto of the First National Congress of the Guomindang, 30 January 1924

Western-educated Sun Yat-sen had been propagating a republican solution to China's problems since 1885. At the time of the First National Congress of the Guomingdang in 1924, Sun Yat-sen's programme for the Three People's Principles was defined in the party's manifesto.

The Principles of the Kuomintang are no other than the three principles of the people. Our platform is based on these principles, and we firmly believe that there is no other way of saving the country. Every step of the National Revolution should be guided by these fundamental principles.

1   *The Principle of Nationalism.* There are two aspects to this principle, namely self-emancipation of the Chinese nation and equality of all races within Chinese territory:

   • The principle of nationalism seeks to make China a free and independent nation. Before 1911 this principle was directed against the dictatorship of the Manchus and the foreign Powers' policy of partitioning China. After the Manchus had been overthrown, the 'divide and govern' policy of the Powers was supplanted by one of international control. The militarists conspired with the imperialists and the capitalists, and since the condition of China was going from bad to worse, the Kuomintang members could not but continue to struggle for the emancipation of the Chinese race. However, they have to rely on the support of the majority of the people, namely the intellectual class, the peasants, the labourers, and the merchants. Only when the impact of the nationalist movement has weakened the strength of imperialism will our people be able to develop their ability. When the Kuomintang and the people are united, real freedom and independence for the Chinese race may then be achieved.

   • The government of China after 1911 being still in the hands of the militarists, the different races within the country began to entertain doubts regarding the sincerity of the Kuomintang policies. From now on we must try to secure the sympathy of these races, and explain their common interest in the success of the national revolutionary movement. The *Kuomintang* solemnly declares that it recognizes the right of self-determination of all races within the country; and that, after the completion of the National Revolution, a free and united Republic of China, based on the voluntary union of all races, will be established.

2   *The Principle of Popular Sovereignty.* This principle envisages a system of direct popular authority in addition to that of indirect popular authority; that is to say, the people will enjoy the rights of election, initiative, referendum, and recall. The procedure for wielding these powers will be elaborated in the Five-Power Constitution, namely

legislative, judicial, executive, examination, and control. The so-called modern system of popular government is often a monopoly of the property class, to be used as an instrument of oppression, whereas the principle of popular sovereignty is for the masses and not for the few. Citizens of the Republic will be allowed to participate in the exercise of the people's political rights, and the Party shall see to it that this power will not fall into the hands of those opposed to the Republic, be they individuals or organizations, to be used as an instrument against it.

3   *The Principle of the People's Livelihood.* This principle contains two fundamental aspects – equalization of land and regulation of capital. Since the right of owning land is controlled by a few, the State should enact a land law, a law for the utilization of land, a land expropriation law, and a land taxation law. Private landowners shall declare the value of their land to the government. It shall be taxed according to the values so declared, and the government may buy it at that price in case of necessity. Private industries, whether belonging to the Chinese or foreign nationals, that are either monopolistic in character or beyond the capacity of private individuals to develop – such as banking, railways, and navigation – shall be undertaken by the State, so that private-owned capital shall not control the economic life of the people.

China is an agricultural country, and the peasants are the class that have suffered most. The *Kuomintang* stands for the policy that those peasants owning no land should be given land by the State for cultivation. The State shall also undertake to irrigate and develop the waste land so as to increase the capacity of productivity. Those peasants that have no capital and are compelled to incur heavy indebtedness through borrowing on usurious terms should be supplied with credit by the State, for example, by the establishment of rural banks, cooperative societies, etc. The livelihood of Chinese labourers being unprotected by any sort of guarantee, the State should find remedies for the unemployed and enact labour laws to improve their livelihood. Other auxiliary measures such as those relating to the support of the aged, care of the young, relief of the sick and disabled, and the dissemination of knowledge shall be prosecuted until they are carried into effect.

In China today, from north to south, from the commercial centres to the villages and hamlets, poor peasants and overworked labourers are to be found everywhere. Because of the sufferings that they have undergone and their aspirations for liberation, there is in both of them a powerful will to revolt against imperialism. Therefore, the success of the National Revolution depends upon the participation of the peasants and the labourers of the whole country. The *Kuomintang* is now engaged upon a determined struggle against imperialism and militarism, against the classes opposed to the interests of the peasants and labourers. It is a struggle for the peasants and the labourers, one in which the peasants and labourers also struggle for themselves.

Such is the real meaning of the Three [People's] Principles. Our Party has been reorganized, and now we will enforce strict discipline to consolidate its foundation. Our members should be properly trained to preach the Kuomintang principles, to lead the people, and to organize a political revolution. At the same time, the Party will exert all its efforts to carry on a campaign of education among the people, so that they may actively cooperate in the revolutionary movement, recover their political power, and exterminate the people's enemy. After the political power has been wrested back and the government has been established, the *Kuomintang* must serve as the central organ for the administration of such political power, so that all counter-revolutionary movements will be suppressed, the designs of the imperialists to injure our people will be frustrated, and all obstacles in the way of executing the principles of the *Kuomintang* will be swept away. Only an organized party, and one with authority, can serve as the foundation of the revolutionary masses; only such a body can render this duty loyally to the people of the whole country.

Source: *The Teachings of Sun Yat-sen* (London: Sylvan Press, 1945), pp. 95–8

2.4 May 4th 1919 and May 30th 1925 student demonstrators compared

J. N. Wasserstrom

THE LABOR UPSURGE OF FEBRUARY 1925

There are several places one can logically begin the story of the May 30th Movement. For example, one can start with the anti-Christian agitation of 1924, since this struggle to regain control of China's educational system helped pave the way for the fight in 1925 to force the foreign community to return the concessions to Chinese rule. Some leaders of the May 30th Movement, such as Gao Erbai and Lui Yiqing, gained their first real experience as organizers and publicists during the anti-Christian agitation. Many of the propaganda pamphlets of the May 30th Movement were similar in form to tracts published in December 1924 as part of Anti-Christian Propaganda Week. The May 30th writers simply emphasized economic and political as opposed to cultural imperialism and substituted stories of foreign bosses mistreating native workers or accounts of members of the foreign-run police forces killing unarmed protesters for tales of missionary teachers misleading their Chinese pupils.

The roots of the May 30th Movement can also be traced to attempts, contemporaneous with the anti-Christian agitation, by Shanghai students to organize and form alliances with local workers by volunteering to teach at 'people's night schools' and helping to establish recreational clubs for laborers. The alliances that students from Shangda and other schools established through these activities helped lay the foundation for the various joint worker–student actions of spring 1925 that were so central to the success of the May 30th Movement. These alliance-building activities are important for another reason: many of the youths who led the mass movement of 1925 – such as the printer Liu Hua (a *gangong, banxue,* or part-time work, part-time study, student at Shangda Middle School) and Zhu Yiquan (a sociology student who became principal of a Shangda-run worker night school) – served their political apprenticeship teaching laborers to read and write in 1924.

The idea behind the people's night schools that sprang up throughout the city in 1924 was nothing new. The notion that intellectuals had a special mission to educate the untutored masses dates back at least to the late 1910s, when youths in Shanghai and other cities formed 'popular lecture corps' to spread new ideas to illiterate and semiliterate members of the community. The May 4th Movement stimulated new efforts, and in its aftermath groups of progressive students and professors established a number of special schools for workers, which, like their counterparts of 1924, emphasized literacy training. Other New Culture intellectuals organized mass literacy campaigns directed at the inhabitants of nearby towns and villages. The YMCA and other religious organizations sponsored similar schools and campaigns in the late 1910s and early 1920s, and the successes of foreign-run organizations in this field probably inspired the renewed efforts at mass education of 1924, by convincing non-Christian intellectuals that inaction would soon give missionary groups a monopoly of popular education in addition to their virtual monopoly of higher education in China.

However, the proliferation in 1924 of institutions promoting the welfare of the lower classes was rooted in more than simple altruism or a desire to compete with Christian organizations. Some intellectuals had a more explicitly political purpose in mind when they founded night schools and recreational clubs: they intended to use these organizations to promote class and national consciousness and thereby lay the foundation for a revolutionary labor movement ...

The workers in the Japanese-owned mills of the western section of the city – exploited by both imperialism and capitalist economic relationships – seemed an ideal target group for these young organizers. Several Shangda students focused exclusively upon this special population, taking an active role in the newly established West Shanghai Workers' Club. This club, which sponsored a special night school, began as a gathering place where the textile workers of the district came to relax, practice martial arts, and occasionally listen to lectures on economics or contemporary events. However, thanks in large part to the efforts of Liu Hua – who not only lectured at the club's night school but also was one of the organization's chief officers – and of other students from Shangda and Southern University, it quickly evolved into something much more akin to a labor union.

The mill strike of February 1925 served as the catalyst for the transformation of the club into a fully functional union and of students such as Liu Hua (who withdrew from Shangda to devote all his time to the labor movement) from night-school teachers and social workers into fully fledged organizers. The strike grew out of the early February firing by Japanese managers at the Nagai Wata Company's Cotton Mill No. 8 of 40 Chinese adult male employees without warning. Allegedly dismissed for 'disobedience of orders,' these men were replaced immediately by *yangchenggong* (youths trained by the company who would accept a lower wage and be more docile), an act that angered many of the mill's employees. This dissatisfaction increased when on February 4th the police arrested six of the laborers in question on a charge of 'intimidation,' after attempts to collect their final wages ended in a fracas with company officials. The workers at Mill No. 8 walked off their jobs that very day and were soon joined by the employees at ten other Nagai Wata factories, in a strike that lasted for almost a month and ultimately affected somewhere between 17,000 and 40,000 workers. The strike was accompanied by outbreaks of *dachang* (literally 'hitting the factory,' a traditional term for machine-breaking riots) and daily mass meetings, as well as a series of militant demonstrations aimed at preventing scabs from entering the factories. The *North China Herald* criticized the Chinese-controlled police force in western Shanghai for its laxness in suppressing these activities, but before workers returned to their jobs during the final week of February and the first week of March the police had arrested more than 50 people for strike-related activities ...

The February strike gave students the chance to deepen their alliances with workers at Japanese mills and to refine the propaganda themes, organizational skills, and protest techniques they would use in the May 30th Movement three months later. Views of the role students played in the events of February vary considerably: some praise student involvement as an act of patriotism; others condemn it as inappropriate youthful meddling. All sources agree, however, that the role was an important one: police reports, newspaper accounts, and memoirs alike testify that educated youths took an active part in unionizing workers, raising funds to support the strike, publicizing the strikers' grievances, and working to gain the release of arrested laborers. Shanghai Municipal Police (SMP) reports claim, in addition, that many participants in the 'worker' demonstrations that accompanied the dispute – parades by 'strikers' with flags threatening violence to scabs – were in fact members of what the SMP calls the 'student class' …

A wide range of student groups became involved in the February strike, either by issuing statements criticizing the Nagai Wata management for its treatment of workers or by joining the consortium of clubs and societies in the Strikers Support Committee. Some of these youth groups were admittedly closely tied to the CCP or its affiliated Youth League. Others – such as the National Student Union, which issued a proclamation calling the Nagai Wata strikes a response to the same kinds of indignities that had inspired the May 4th Movement – contained at least some members committed to Marxism–Leninism. Most of the dozens of youth groups that came to the aid of the strikers, however, were not directly controlled by Communists …

Despite these contrasts, however, the May 30th student protesters had much in common with their predecessors of 1919. Some new factors had begun to shape student political action by the mid-1920s, but the events of 1925 are so clearly recognizable as variations upon May 4th themes that it is fitting to end this chapter with a brief recap of some of the things the two generations of protesters had in common. The most basic point of similarity has to do with motivation: the youths of the May 4th and May 30th Movements took to the streets to protest against attacks on the dignity of their country and the bodies of their comrades, and both saw themselves as fulfilling a moral role as the conscience of a nation. Once on the streets, moreover, they acted in identical or almost identical ways. The May 30th Movement may have had fewer victory parades, and street fights between protesters and police may have been more common. Nonetheless, the May 4th 'repertoire' remained essentially intact: the student protesters of 1925 relied heavily upon the same basic mix of tightly organized mass rallies, colorful processions, streetside speechmaking drives, boycotts, and the like, that their predecessors had turned to in 1919.

In addition, both groups of Shanghai students performed the same set of protest roles, acting as agitators and allies, mourners and martyrs, organization builders and strikers, 'law' enforcers and keepers of order. The specific ways these roles were performed varied. In 1925, for example, rather than building a protest league from the ground up, students merely had to reorganize the extant but atrophying Shanghai Student Union. May 30th youths added some new twists to May 4th 'law' enforcement roles: along with organizing inspection teams to go from store to store to prevent the sale of boycotted goods, some youths began policing the waterways as well, and in several notorious cases of 'piracy' or 'customs inspection' (depending on one's point of view), they boarded ships and seized 'illegal' cargo. Through these and comparable innovations, the students of 1925 demonstrated their capacity for improvization. More often than not, however, they found themselves following quite closely in the footsteps of their predecessors, adapting the same kinds of script, performing the same kinds of role, and posing the same kinds of challenge to established order as their heroes – the student protesters of 1919.

Source: J. N. Wasserstrom, *Student Protests in Twentieth Century China* (Stanford, California: Stanford University Press, 1991), pp. 96–9, 99–100, 124

2.5 Document relating to the May 30th affair

China Yearbook, 1926–27

DEMANDS OF STUDENTS AND STREET UNIONS

The following is the list of demands framed at a meeting of the Shanghai Commercial and Labour Association, the Shanghai Street Unions, the National Chinese Students' Federation, and the Shanghai Chinese Students' Union, held on Sunday, June 7th:

PRELIMINARY DEMANDS

1 The Council should issue a proclamation forthwith for the cancellation of the state of emergency.
2 That landing parties from the different gunboats should be withdrawn forthwith, and the volunteers and special police should be demobilized.
3 All persons arrested should be released forthwith and sent back to their homes.
4 All schools, colleges, and other places seized by the Council or sealed should be reopened at once and returned to their rightful owners.

FORMAL DEMANDS

1 The officer who gave the order to fire, and the police who fired and shot and killed the labourers and students, must be handed over to the Chinese Government at once for detention, trial, and punishment.
2 Suitable indemnity must be paid by the Council to the families of the dead and wounded, the labourers who have gone on strike, the merchants who have gone on strike, and the schools and other places seized and sealed by the subordinates and servants of the Council.
3 Formal apologies shall be tendered to the Chinese government, the local officials, and those who have suffered.
4 The secretary of the Council, Mr E. S. Benbow Rowe, must be dismissed and replaced.
5 Chinese in the settlement shall have absolute freedom of speech.
6 Better treatment shall be afforded to the labouring classes, who shall have liberty to form unions and declare strikes, and who shall not be dismissed as a result of the present strike, and further, rules for the protection of labourers to be drawn up jointly by the Council and the Chinese Advisory Board shall be observed by foreign and Chinese mill owners alike.
7 A Chinese Commissioner of police must be appointed and all of his subordinates must be Chinese.
8 The proposed by-laws for the registration of the Press and Stock Exchanges, and the increase in wharfage dues, shall be cancelled forthwith.
9 The Council shall stop building roads into Chinese territory and the Council must not present any demands for the return of the existing roads, which shall be returned to the Chinese government forthwith.
10 The mixed Court shall be returned to China forthwith; in cases in which Chinese are the only parties concerned the Assessors shall not be empowered to sit or watch the

proceedings, and in cases where foreigners sue Chinese the Assessors shall be permitted to sit, but they shall not be empowered to interfere in the judgements; Chinese criminals shall be indicted according to the Chinese Criminal Code or the Municipal By-laws, but not by both; all the affairs of the Court shall be administered entirely by Chinese, including the work of the Registrar and the prosecuting solicitor, and all officials of the Court must be appointed to their places only by the Chinese government.

11 Chinese shall be eligible for election to the Shanghai Municipal Council, and foreigners in whose names Chinese land is registered shall not be permitted to stand for election.

12 Extraterritoriality must be abolished forthwith.

13 British and Japanese gunboats must be withdrawn from Shanghai permanently.

On 15 June the Chinese Chamber of Commerce presented thirteen very similar demands.

Source: 'Documents Relating to the May 30th Affair', *China Yearbook, 1926–27*
(Tientsin, 1926), pp. 928–9

2.6 Joining the army in 1926

Xie Bingying

I believe that all the girl students who wanted to join the Army had as their motive, in nine cases out of ten, to get away from their families, by whom they were suppressed. They all wanted to find their own way out. But the moment they put on their uniform and shouldered their guns, their ideas became less selfish. By that time a girl began to think of [all the] oppressed people, the responsibility for whom she was taking on her shoulders. Most of our schoolmates who enlisted did so unknown to their families but not unknown to the school – for our headmaster, Mr Shu, was the only person who was in favour of our joining the Army. All the schools forbade their student girls to enlist, so they secretly went to enlist as candidates for the military school. Those who passed the examination were happy and overjoyed, and it is impossible to describe their cheerfulness in words. I still remember very clearly how, on an afternoon when it was pouring in torrents, 250 brave young soldiers, both male and female, gathered in the East Station at Changsha waiting for the train to carry them away. Many elderly ladies and young girls came to bid us farewell, and then they secretly wiped away their tears with their handkerchiefs. But we were not sorry, at least I myself was not. I said: 'You people mustn't cry. You should encourage us to go and kill our enemies'.

Just then a young man unexpectedly came running towards me in the pouring rain and, panting for breath, handed me a pink envelope. He was the editor of *Flame*, a man utterly unknown to me. I was very sorry for him because I had no time to read the letter, and it was put aside for a very long time. Since I had decided to discard that image from my mind, anybody who came to offer me his warm feelings only received a douche of cold water.

We, the fifty girl soldier students, were all crowded into one car, and there was no room to sit down. We were rather like refugees, taking our small suitcases and bundles of clothes with us. This car had originally been meant for goods, so, but for two iron doors, there was not even a small window, and as we were miserable in the dark we began to sing loudly:

Arise, ye starvelings, from your slumbers,
Arise, ye criminals of want!

The moment we began to sing we felt happier, and we thought that we could really congratulate ourselves on the beginning of our new life and on our bright future. Every one of us was crazy, intoxicated, singing and jumping about.

Source: Hsieh Ping-Ying, *Autobiography of a Chinese Girl*
(London: Allen and Unwin, 1943), pp. 93–4

2.7 The rise and fall of the United Front

Chiang Kai-shek, from *A Summing-up at Seventy: Soviet Russia in China*, 1957

The Russian Communists, in the first flush of victory following upon their capture of political power, offered to join hands with all the proletariat in the Western countries in revolutions and promised to help Oriental nations achieve independence. On hearing this news, those working for our National Revolution welcomed it as a godsend and regarded its authors as saviors of mankind. That was why Russia's assistance was accepted without any reservations. This was no doubt an important factor in Dr Sun's decision to align the Kuomintang with Russia.

Before I went to Russia, I, too, had believed that the offer of the Russian Communist Party to help our National Revolution was motivated by a sincere desire to treat us as an equal and not with ulterior motives. As a result of my visit to Russia, however, I was completely disillusioned. I came to the conclusion that our policy of aligning with Russia and admitting Chinese Communists into our ranks, though it might prove to be useful in fighting Western colonialism for the time being, could not in the long run bring us to our goal of national independence and freedom. Furthermore, I felt that Soviet Russia's stratagem and the objective of her World Revolution program were even more dangerous to national independence movements in the Orient than the old colonialism.

After listening to my report, Dr Sun considered my views on the future of Sino-Russian relations overcautious and unsuitable, particularly in view of the revolutionary realities of the moment. He was of the firm belief that in the circumstances the only way to deter the Chinese Communists from inciting class conflicts and sabotaging our National Revolution was to place them under the leadership of the Kuomintang and to subject them to our Party's unified direction. He thought that the moment the Northward Expedition came to its successful conclusion the Three People's Principles could be implemented according to schedule, and that by that time it would be too late for the Chinese Communists to disrupt our National Revolution even if they should so try. Besides, was it not a fact that Soviet Russia recognized our Party as the only political party to lead China in her National Revolution, and was it also not a fact that Soviet Russia had asked members of the Chinese Communist Party to join our Party, and to obey its leadership, and in the meantime had admitted the impracticability of Communism for China? For these reasons, Dr Sun stuck to his policy of alignment with Soviet Russia and the admission of Chinese Communists into the Kuomintang.

During the First National Congress of our Party, I discovered how the Chinese Communists both in words and in actions tried to increase their own importance by playing up Soviet Russia, and how some of our own Party members had been swayed by Communist doctrines.

I was full of misgivings regarding our Party's ability to carry out the task entrusted to it by Dr Sun. In consequence, at the end of the Congress I declined my appointment as commandant of the Military Academy ... It was not until April of that year, and only after having been repeatedly urged by Dr Sun through letters and telegrams to obey orders as a member of a revolutionary party, that I returned once more to Canton, this time as commandant of the Whampoa Military Academy.

LI TA-CHAO'S MEMORANDUM

Li Ta-chao was the first Chinese Communist to join the Kuomintang following the Sun–Joffe statement of 26 January 1923. Many others followed shortly afterwards. The Kuomintang's First National Congress, convened on 20 January 1924, adopted a new constitution and elected members of the Central Executive and Supervisory Committees ... On behalf of the Communists, Li Ta-chao submitted a memorandum in which he gave reasons for their joining the Kuomintang. He said, in part:

> We believe that China today is a 'semicolony' of the Western powers, or a 'subcolony' as Dr Sun has well called it. It will be impossible for China to remove the double oppression imposed by foreign Imperialism and our own warlords, who curry favor with foreign powers, unless we throw the strength of the entire nation into the National Revolution. In order to bring the revolution to a successful conclusion, it is essential to have a national revolutionary party that is united and comprehensive in scope. We feel that at this moment we should not allow the forces of revolution to be dissipated through disunity because this would result in weakening them and hindering their progress. It is absolutely necessary to put the nation's heart and strength together in a single party.
>
> Looking around the country, we find that the Kuomintang is the only revolutionary party that has history, principles, and leadership. It is also the only one that can be developed into a great and comprehensive national revolutionary party to assume the responsiblility of liberating the people, restoring to them their rights and assuring them a secure livelihood. For this reason, we have decided to join this Party ...
>
> We join this Party as individuals, not as a body. We may be said to have dual party membership. But it may not be said of the Kuomintang that there is a party within a party ...

Li Ta-chao's memorandum sounded as if he was being perfectly frank. This was because the Communists, in wishing to join our Party, had no alternative but to accept the conditions laid down by Dr Sun following serious and detailed discussions with Moscow's emissaries, including Voitinsky, Maring, Joffe, and Borodin. All Li Ta-chao did was to reiterate them openly. Nevertheless, toward the end of his statement he could not help revealing that the Chinese Communist Party's action was designed to facilitate those with dual membership in their plot ultimately to undermine our Party. For he said: 'It is my hope that since we have already been permitted to join this Party, our senior comrades will not entertain suspicions about us or take precautionary measures against us' ...

This appeal had its desired effect: our Party failed to take the necessary precautions. The Communists were allowed to work through their secret cells, and they met with no opposition whatever as they moved to seize control and to manipulate our Party by plotting internal dissension and disruption …

The Political Department of our armed forces became a principal object of Communist infiltration. Under the cloak of auxiliary political service, they did their best to strain relations between the various units. They even held up supplies and munitions from troops in south-east provinces and interfered with the movement of reinforcements from regions on the upper Yangtze to the Kiangsu and Chekiang fronts, their intention being to cut off our forces on the coast from the rear. Despite all these obstructions, units forming the right wing of our Revolutionary Forces pushed forward and successfully effected the occupation of Shanghai and Nanking according to the original timetable.

On 24 March 1927, following the entry of Revolutionary Forces into Nanking, some soldiers suddenly broke loose and began attacking European and American residences, including those of members of foreign consular staffs and missionaries. This resulted in the loss of several lives … Earlier, when our forces entered such cities as Changsha, Hankow, Kiukiang, and Hangchow, no harm was done to any foreigners. Now it happened in Nanking, of all places. Communists in the armed forces had created this incident in the hope of provoking a direct clash between the foreign powers and the Revolutionary Forces. I shall not enter into the details of their plot, the evidence of which was conclusive.

When our forces were moving toward Shanghai, workers led by the Party declared a general strike to signify their support for the revolutionary cause. The Communists again tried to capitalize on the situation by organizing labor pickets and supplying them with arms. Their scheme was to start uprisings so that they could set up a labor government in the city, or at least to cause conflicts between the Western powers and the Revolutionary Forces in Shanghai. It was in these chaotic circumstances that our forces occupied Shanghai. I hurried to Shanghai from Kiukiang on 26 March to take personal command of the situation in this international metropolis in the East, and to forestall a repetition of what had happened in Wuhan. On 12 April, to prevent Communist uprisings, the Revolutionary Forces, in cooper-ation with local labor unions and chambers of commerce, disarmed the Red labor pickets and kept Communist saboteurs under surveillance. Only then was the situation in Shanghai brought under control.

At an emergency meeting of the Kuomintang's Central Supervisory Committee, held in Shanghai on 2 April, more evidence of Communist subversion and treason was submitted by Wu Ching-heng. Other members made similar reports on happenings in Hunan, Hupeh, Kiangsi, Chekiang, Anhwei, and Shanghai, where the Communists, upon orders from the Communist International, had tried to sabotage the revolution by engineering disturbances. It was unanimously resolved to ask the Central Executive Committee to take emergency measures and place all Communist ringleaders under the surveillance of local security organs. The Political Council of the Central Executive Committee further recommended that the Party take steps to rid itself of Communists. On 5 May, principles guiding the implementation of the decision were passed by the Central Standing Committee. A special committee was set up to be in charge of the purge, which was resolutely carried out in Nanking, Shanghai, and Canton. In this way, law and order was maintained and our south-eastern provinces were spared the ordeal of serving as a proving ground for Communism and escaped the disastrous consequences resulting from intra-party disputes in Moscow.

On 18 April the Party's Central Standing Committee and the National Government's State Council, in accordance with Dr Sun's bequeathed wishes, resolved to make Nanking the national capital, and numerous organs of the National Government were set up in Nanking soon afterwards.

Source: Chiang Kai-shek, *A Summing-up at Seventy: Soviet Russia in China*
(London: Harrap, 1957), pp. 24–8, 46–51

2.8 Reports from the *China Yearbook* on the events of April 1927

NANKING OUTRAGES AND THE NANKING GOVERNMENT

Meanwhile, the fact remained that Nanking was occupied by Cheng Chien's pro-Communist Army, and Chapei and other industrial districts of Shanghai were in the hands of the Communist General Labour Union. Chiang Kai-shek had too few troops to handle both Nanking and Shanghai. From a strictly Chinese standpoint, Nanking was the more important place, as Chiang Kai-shek could not establish a government in Shanghai, actually under the protection of foreign troops and foreign gunboats. All available troops were therefore sent to Nanking, which they easily occupied and where, in due course, they managed to disarm and disband most of Cheng Chien's army. Cheng and Lin managed to escape to Kiukiang, leaders with but few troops.

The Shanghai problem was handled differently. Arrangements were made with the Green and Red Societies, so that one morning they as 'White' labourers fell upon and shot down the Communists. Hundreds of Communists were killed in Chapei, Nantao, Kiangwan, Jessfield, Wusih, Soochow, Changchow, and Nanking. The Communists made a last stand in the Library building of the Commercial Press, where they were besieged for a day, only to surrender when they were told that heavy artillery would be brought up from Woosung and used against them. Since that day (26 March) there has not been a serious strike or lock-out in Shanghai, although the labourers are still organized in government-controlled unions. Cooperating to a very great extent with the police of the French Concessions, but to only a limited extent with the International Settlement, Chiang Kai-shek's officials were enabled to establish order in Shanghai ...

The establishment of a National Government was at no stage without major impediments. Actually, Chiang Kai-shek's armies controlled only southern Kiangsu, Chekiang, part of Anhwei, and the politically valueless province of Fukien. Kwuangtung and Kwangsi were broadly autonomous, although they recognized the political authority of Nanking. Opposite Nanking, on the north bank of the Yangtze, Chang Tsung-chang maintained a Shantung-Chihli force, which daily teasingly bombed Chiang's capital or sent their aeroplanes over his Yamen. At Yangchow, opposite Chinkiang, Sun Chuan-fang's troops were attempting to reorganize and to recover the rich Shanghai area. Thirty thousand British, American, Japanese, Italian, Spanish, and Dutch troops and sailors held the Shanghai areas, and British aeroplanes daily flew over Chinese territory, to Chiang Kai-shek's chagrin and mortification. For, in the eyes of the Chinese, Eugene Chen and the Hankow Communists had scored signal diplomatic victories, while Nanking could not keep British aeroplanes from flying over their Bureau of Foreign Affairs and the garrison at Lunghua ...

Finances were turned over to the bankers, but they, lacking experience as tax officers, resorted to loans, voluntary or forced, which did not quite serve the purpose. The tax machinery was confused and disorganized, and the tragedy of it was that there was not time to work out plans and to select good and able men … Money was desperately needed to send soldiers into the field – China's greatest curse, the need to spend all revenues on mere defences.

As regards party questions, the Nanking group was slightly more successful. Having expelled all Communists and having readmitted members of the Party who had not registered after Mr Borodin's reorganization of the Party in 1923, the party personnel was brought back to a sheer Kuomintang basis. The test was the actual acceptance of Dr Sun's 'Three People's Principles', a denunciation of Communism, Imperialism, and Tuchunism. New bourgeois elements were brought into the Party, which materially strengthened it. The local Chinese press solidly favoured the new government and the reconstruction of the Party.

Canton responded to Chiang Kai-shek's appeal and immediately announced its support of the new government in Nanking. Large mass meetings were held denouncing the Communists and supporting General Chiang's interpretation of the 'Three People's Principles'.

THE SOVIET EMBASSY RAID (*AND CHIANG KAI-SHEK'S MANIFESTO*)

On 6 April, under the direction of Marshal Chang Tso-lin, the Peking police raided the Soviet Embassy in Peking and seized a large number of incriminating documents. Because of the raid, a number of Communists were arrested and Li Ta-chao, who, with Chen Tu-hsiu, headed the Communist Party of China, was strangled together with a number of others. The effect of this raid was to give the widest publicity to the relations of Kuomintang and Communist leaders with the Soviet Embassy. The complete control that Borodin exercised over the Kuomintang was amply proved. These disclosures strengthened the Nanking Government with the Kuomintang rank and file, who seemed to take from that moment the view that the day of the Russian was over. In his 'Manifesto to the People' (April 1927), General Chiang Kai-shek deals with this problem as follows:

> The Communist Party has been spreading abroad all sorts of rumours such as 'oppression of the toiling masses by the Kuomintang' and 'Chiang Kai-shek the new militarist'. These are due to my opposition to its horrible policies. You must not be deceived and we should investigate the rumours in detail. The temporary surveillance of the Communists was ordered because they were hampering military operations, this fact being exposed by the Kuomintang Central Censor Committee. For the safety of our soldiers and of the people, it was imperative that their activities should be somewhat restricted during the time of war. This is a military necessity. We detain them only until military operations are completed, but we have no wish to endanger their lives. This gave rise to the so-called 'Party imprisonment'. With regard to reorganizing the Peasant and Labour unions controlled by the Communists, this is based on the same idea, and at the same time we should give real peasants and labourers the opportunity for free organization.
>
> We disarmed the Shanghai Labour Union Corps because it attacked our army with rifles and machine guns. On 13 April 1927, the Labour Corps surrounded and attacked the headquarters of the 2nd Division of the 26th Army, but they were repulsed, and as a result we captured 90 prisoners, of which 40 were proved to be soldiers of Chang Tsung-chang under the orders of the Communist Party. This proves that the Communists will do anything possible to ruin the cause of the revolution, even though they conspire with the northern militarists.

It was from documents of all sorts discovered in searching the Shanghai Labour Union that we ascertained their secret and dangerous plots. The talk of oppression of the toiling masses by the Kuomintang is entirely false. If that is true of us we are willing to be beheaded. It is a fact that the Kuomintang's opposition to Communism is not opposition to peasants and labourers. Now is the best opportunity for the real toiling masses to arise and organize. For your own interests your organization must not be neglected. If you do not organize yourselves, others will do it by falsely assuming your name. Free from the Communist Party's monopolized control, all of you have the opportunity of making your own organizations. Within the jurisdiction of our Nationalist Government, the emergency measures taken against the Communist Party would do you, the real peasants and labourers, no harm.

Source: 'Reports on the Events of April 1927',
China Yearbook, 1928–29 (Tientsin, 1928), pp. 1362–5

2.9 A Western trader has dealings with warlords and bandits, 1925

A. H. Rasmussen

I don't know whether one could call the wars in China at that time civil wars, because politics, ideology, and patriotism were not the causes. The wars were rather private ones between military leaders for the control of as large a slice of the country as they could grab, and for its extension as far as possible afterwards.

This period was called politely The Wars of the Tuchuns (military leaders), and was in full swing when I arrived in north China. The warlords had started in a desultory way in 1916 after Yuan Shikai's death, but the struggle spread and grew in intensity as time went on. The contenders seemed to follow a set formula. The first step was to grab a railway line, or part of one. This meant not only revenue but also cheap transportation; there was an unwritten law among the warlords that rail traffic should never be interfered with because without it they would be severely handicapped in a game of beggar-my-neighbour. Trains came and went through the opposing camps, the warlord in the north taking the revenue from all southbound trains, and vice versa.

When the railway was under control, every city was assessed at so much a contribution to 'war funds', and the money was invariably paid because failure to do so meant the looting of the city. Then the warlord's printing press started to turn out worthless paper money which was enforced as legal tender throughout his territory. The soldiers were paid in this paper currency, as were all supplies to the armies. The whole countryside swarmed with soldiers in dirty grey uniforms, living off the country like locusts.

We were very close to all this in Tientsin, where the warlords had their palatial houses and their harems and strutted about in their comic-opera uniforms. Yes, it was all very comic opera, for very little blood was shed. It was so much easier to buy small opponents over than to fight them, and the big rivals could be mastered by the simple expedient of buying over the high officers and their men who were holding strategic key positions when any real fighting had to be done. Some of the obscure officers rose to wealth and fame by changing sides several times, and were able to start in business on their own in a big way.

Every man was for sale at a price; and to simplify the problem of taking over large bodies of troops at the minimum cost and trouble, each man simply changed the calico armband he had fastened on to his sleeve by a safety pin and put on the band of his new master. This band was the only insignia the solders carried to show whose men they were, the uniforms being identical throughout the warring sections; cheap grey cotton cloth in the summer and the same stuff padded with wadding in the winter. This armband business was a very practical solution to the problem of changing sides quickly, but the Chinese are essentially a practical people.

The whole business would have been comic opera had it not been so tragic for the country people. Growing crops were trampled down by the armies, stocks of grain were seized as well as farm animals and carts for transport services, and as many men as were required. There can be few examples of man's inhumanity to equal the heartless and wicked exploitation that went on in north China during those years. The country was bled white, because, when one warlord retired from business or was defeated, his paper money automatically became valueless. A new one took his place and started to print his paper money, and so it went on. I shall never forget those pathetic queues of ruined Chinese waiting for hours outside the Chinese banks, only to be told that there were no funds to redeem the bank notes they had brought.

One could always predict the retirement or imminent fall of a warlord by watching his bank. The warlords invariably had their banks within the foreign Concessions because it was the only safe place for their money. Indeed, the main offices and vaults of the Chinese government bank, the Bank of China, were in the foreign Concessions and never in the adjoining native cities. Worst of all, the soldiers were never paid off but left to fend for themselves. The argument was that they had their rifles and ammunition, and what better equipment could a man have to make a fat living in a country where the people were at their mercy?

That was the beginning of the rapidly growing bandit menace in north China …

The eliminating bouts of the comic-opera armies were over by 1925, and the big fellows were now starting. The smaller fry had either retired to their palaces or had been eliminated, and the main contenders were the Big Three – Chang Tso Lin, Feng Yu Hsiang, and Yen Hsi Shan, Governor of Shansi.

The thunder of guns and rat-tatting of machine guns made sleep difficult. Refugees were pouring into the Concessions, and nearly every day, on my way home in the car, the Concession bridge was choked with defeated soldiers from one faction or another seeking sanctuary. They were being disarmed by British and French soldiers, as no armed men were allowed inside the Concessions.

To get through them in a car was slow work, crawling along foot by foot, steering with one hand and pushing men with rifles and Mauser pistols off the running-board with the other.

The Border Regiment was stationed in Tientsin then, and was later relieved by the Lancashires. Sunday church parade was one of the big events, when the men came swinging along Race Course Road to Gordon Hall, where the service was held, and the strains of 'John Peel' sent the blood tingling through your body …

Feng Yu Hsiang had a brief spell of lording it in Peking after stabbing Wu Pei Fu in the back. His hymn-singing troops often marched through the ex-Russian Concession to the strains of 'Onward Christian Soldiers', in spite of the fact that Feng was now rabidly anti-Christian.

His regime did not last very long. Once more, the guns were thundering around Tientsin as Chang Tso Lin advanced with a big and well-equipped army …

Chang defeated Feng thoroughly at Tientsin and later chased him out of Peking. Chang was now the new master in north China and had a very firm grip of affairs. With Feng's defeat, our difficulties really started for he was retreating along our main communications. He had made a stand at the Nankow Pass in the high mountain ranges beyond Peking and astride the railway line that carried wool supplies from the interior. He broke all precedents by refusing to allow trains to leave his territory, so that business was brought to a standstill. It was, in fact, no longer a gentlemen's war.

I had very large quantities of wool stored at Kalgan, Kweihuacheng, and Paotow, and a good deal more was expected by caravan from Chinese Turkestan and Tibet. The most serious part of the new development was that no forecast could be made as to how long the stoppage would last.

I had been looking for an opportunity of visiting our Chinese agents up-country, and this was my first chance. The difficulty was that, on account of Feng's rabid antiforeign policy, no passports were being issued to foreigners to cover interior districts; in fact, all foreigners in the interior had been warned to evacuate as their lives were in peril …

We were bound for the border country around the Mongolian plateau, which had always been notorious for banditry, and, at that particular time, Sun Mo Ling, the most dreaded of all bandit leaders, was very active. His speciality was kidnapping and demanding high ransoms. If the families of his captives were slow in meeting his demands, a finger joint or an ear would be sent to them as a reminder that his patience was at a low ebb …

I had not noticed, when boarding the train [from Kalgan], that all the windows but one in the compartment were broken … it had been a first-class compartment; now it was the most complete wreck I had ever seen …

The military-train guard of five men under a sergeant was quartered with us and squatted in a recess between our coach and the next. Their quarters were comparatively draught-free, and the men hospitably invited us to join them …

The train was crawling up a long steep ascent towards the Pingdichuen pass, the highest point on the railway, some five thousand feet up; snow came tearing through the windows with the rising wind and settled on the litter on the floor … After an eternity, the train came to a jerky stop at Pingdichuen station right on top of the pass … Finally, the sergeant went out to inquire and came back with the news that the military commander had taken our locomotive to move troops from the next station.

There had been a mutiny among the Shansi troops at Fengchen which, incidentally, was my destination before proceeding to Kweihuacheng.

We arrived at Fengchen during the forenoon. Mr Yu, the manager, met us. He looked very anxious. 'Come with me, quickly', he whispered, 'there is a short cut here' …

'It is far from safe for you here', he explained. 'The soldiers are in a very ugly mood and we may have trouble at any moment. They are shooting their general today'.

He told me about the revolt and subsequent looting of the shopping district. Many of the people had been bayoneted. Fortunately, the looting and murdering had been confined to the shopping and residential districts, and our compound, being in the outskirts, had escaped, but if they started again we might not be so lucky …

I stayed in Fengchen for a couple of weeks as there was a good deal to do. Rail transportation of goods from there to Kalgan had come to a stop a month or so before I arrived, and we were using camels. This sounds simple, but nothing is simple in China that can possibly be made complicated. Bandits had never been more active than they were since this great armed force had moved in, for the coalition of Chang Tso Lin and Yen Hsi Shan against Feng Yu Hsiang had brought nearly half a million men into the field ...

We had two thousand bales of camels' wool lying at various stations between Fengchen and Kweihuacheng, and, in all, we had eight thousand bales to move to Tientsin if I could find ways and means to get them through this maze of difficulties. There was only one hope – Dammuran Serang, the strong man of the border, and if I could secure his aid and a couple of hundred of his tough ex-bandits as escort, I could send the caravan through Sun Mo Ling's territory without undue risk.

Source: A. H. Rasmussen, *China Trader*
(London: Constable, 1954), pp. 184–6, 186–7, 188–9, 202–9

3

Mao–Zhu in the countryside and the Long March

By July 1927 the Communist leaders lacked any prospect of influencing policy in the GMD. While some dithered and debated, Mao considered 'going to the mountains'. Meanwhile, on 1 August a newly constituted Front Committee promoted insurrection in Nanchang, where several communist officers of the GMD's national revolutionary army were based. At about the same time, plans were approved for an Autumn Harvest Rising in Hunan, and an attack was mounted on Changsha, the central city of Hunan. Both enterprises failed: the Nanchang insurrection lost 13,000 out of 21,000 men in two weeks, while in Changsha half of a force of 3,000 men were lost in eight days; Mao himself, having been captured, was lucky to escape. He took refuge in the barely accessible heights on the border of Hunan and Jiangxi. Then, in April 1928, in what was to prove a turning point, Mao was joined by Zhu De. A one-time petty warlord and opium addict, he studied in Germany, joined the Communist Party, and returned to China during the GMD–CCP cooperation. He led the remainder of the Nanchang insurrection to support Mao in the mountains. Their combined armies were merged to form the 'Fourth Red Army', with Zhu as Military Commander and Mao as Party representative. The peasants referred to Mao–Zhu in the same breath.

The base area was small – about 35 miles in diameter. The 'army' comprised Mao's few hundred men plus 120 bandits already in residence. It was augmented by about 1,000 followers of Zhu De, and in autumn 1928 by a force led by Peng Dehuai. The Jinggangshan base did not long survive Nationalist attacks. In January–February 1929, Mao and Zhu repudiated the advice of the Party Central Committee that they should disperse. They moved east, settling in Ruijin on the border of Jiangxi and Fujian. There they controlled a larger area and created the Jiangxi Soviet.

Meanwhile, Chiang Kai-shek, who had succeeded in extending his authority to Peking and setting up a new capital in Nanjing, was determined to concentrate on the Communist enemies. He organized one extermination campaign after another. During the years 1927–34, the Red Army and the Jiangxi Soviet had much practice refining their strategy for survival. Mao already had the experience on which to build a new concept of Marxism–Leninism. His *Analysis of the Classes in Chinese Society* was written in 1926 when he was head of the Peasant Movement Training Institute, and his well-known work *The Peasant Movement in Hunan* was published in March 1927. Thus, the Red regime drew on the revolutionary potential of hired labourers, the poor and middle peasants, expropriating the landlords (the treatment of the richer peasants varied from time to time according to circumstances).

The distinctive strategy developed by the Red army was summarized in 16 characters:

Enemy advances, we withdraw,
Enemy rests, we harass,
Enemy retires, we attack,
Enemy withdraws, we pursue.

Guidelines for the treatment of the civilian population were laid down. Mao wanted the support of the peasants, a 'sea' in which the 'fish', the Red army, could swim. Captured soldiers were to be well treated, given the option of either joining the Communists or accepting travel expenses to go home. Political propaganda was directed to the GMD army.

The discipline was impressive, but the Jiangxi period was not always harmonious. Mao and Zhu De were far enough from the Communist centre to promote their independent style but nevertheless had to fend off repeated criticism. There were also purges and witch-hunts in which imaginary subversives were tortured and killed.

Meanwhile, Chiang was not to be distracted by the Japanese aggression that was launched in 1931 with the invasion of Manchuria. He preferred to attack Communists rather than Japanese on the grounds that the former were a disease of the heart rather than a disease of the skin. In 1934 the fifth campaign using a strategy of building block houses and with German advisers threatened to squeeze the Jiangxi Soviet to extinction. The Red Army set out on what was to be a tortuous Long March which ended up 6,000 miles later in Shaanxi.

Only one in ten of the 90,000 who started out from Jianxi survived. During a halt at Zunyi, Mao emerged as a dominant figure – a pre-eminence he was to retain until the day he died. However, the ultimate destination was disputed for a time by Zhang Guotao, leader of the Communist forces in western Sichuan, who was joined by Zhu De. When Zhang's forces were all but destroyed by Nationalist and Muslim forces, Mao led the remnants to Baoan in Shaanxi (moving on by January 1937 to Yanan). In spite of the heavy human losses, the Long March was a propaganda triumph – a legend to be forever exalted in the history of the Party.

3.1 Analysis of the classes in Chinese society, March 1926

Mao Zedong

In 1923, when the United Front was established, Mao opposed it, but he was elected to the Central Committee of the Communist Party and subsequently became the Propaganda Chief of the GMD. During the winter of 1925–6, when he was in charge of the Peasant Movement Training Institute, he wrote his first major analytical work. Some Party leaders objected to his emphasis on the peasantry, in particular Chen Duxin.

Who are our enemies? Who are our friends? This is a question of the first importance for the revolution. The basic reason why all previous revolutionary struggles in China achieved so little was their failure to unite with real friends in order to attack real enemies. A revolutionary party is the guide of the masses, and no revolution ever succeeds when the revolutionary party leads them astray … To distinguish real friends from real enemies, we must make a general analysis of the economic status of the various classes in Chinese society and of their respective attitudes towards the revolution.

The landlord class and the comprador class. In economically backward and semi-colonial China, the landlord class and the comprador class are wholly appendages of the international

bourgeoisie, depending upon imperialism for their survival and growth. These classes represent the most backward and most reactionary relations of production in China and hinder
the development of her productive forces … Their political representatives are the *Étatistes*
and the right wing of the Kuomintang.

The middle bourgeoisie. This class represents the capitalist relations of production in China
in town and country. The middle bourgeoisie, by which is meant chiefly the national bourgeoisie, is inconsistent in its attitude towards the Chinese revolution: they feel the need for
revolution and favour the revolutionary movement against imperialism and the warlords
when they are smarting under the blows of foreign capital and the oppression of the
warlords, but they become suspicious of the revolution when they sense that [it] is threatening the hope of their class to attain the status of a big bourgeoisie. Politically, they stand for
the establishment of a state under the rule of a single class, the national bourgeoisie … It is
against interpreting the Kuomintang's Principle of the People's Livelihood according to the
theory of class struggle, and it opposes the Kuomintang's alliance with Russia and the admission of Communists and left-wingers …

The petty bourgeoisie. Included in this category are the owner-peasants, the master handicraftsmen, the lower levels of the intellectuals – students, primary and secondary school
teachers, lower government functionaries, office clerks, small lawyers – and the small
traders. Both because of its size and class character, this class deserves very close attention.
The owner-peasants and the master handicraftsmen are both engaged in small-scale production. Although all strata of this class have the same petty-bourgeois economic status, they fall
into three different sections. The first section consists of those who have some surplus
money or grain, that is, those who, by manual or mental labour, earn more each year than
they consume for their own support. Such people very much want to get rich and are devout
worshippers of Marshal Chao [Zhao Gongming God of Wealth in Chinese tradition] … This
section is a minority among the petty bourgeoisie and constitutes its right wing. The second
section consists of those who in the main are economically self-supporting. They are quite
different from the people in the first section; they also want to get rich, but Marshal Chao
never lets them. In recent years, moreover, suffering from the oppression and exploitation of
the imperialists, the warlords, the feudal landlords, and the big comprador-bourgeoisie, they
have become aware that the world is no longer what it was. They feel they cannot earn
enough to live on by just putting in as much work as before … [they] prefer to be neutral, but
they never oppose the revolution. This section is very numerous, making up about one-half
of the petty bourgeoisie. The third section consists of those whose standard of living is falling
… Such people are quite important for the revolutionary movement; they form a mass of no
small proportions and are the left wing of the petty bourgeoisie. In normal times these three
sections of the petty bourgeoisie differ in their attitude to the revolution. But in times of war,
that is, when the tide of the revolution runs high and the dawn of victory is in sight, not only
will the left wing of the petty bourgeoisie join the revolution, but the middle section too may
join, and even right-wingers, swept forward by the great revolutionary tide of the proletariat
and of the left wing of the petty bourgeoisie, will have to go along with the revolution. We
can see from the experience of the May 30th Movement of 1925 and the peasant movement
in various places that this conclusion is correct.

The semi-proletariat. What is here called the semi-proletariat consists of five categories:
(1) the overwhelming majority of the semi-owner peasants, (2) the poor peasants, (3) the
small handicraftsmen, (4) the shop assistants, and (5) the pedlars. The overwhelming majority
of the semi-owner peasants, together with the poor peasants, constitute a very large part of

the rural masses. The peasant problem is essentially their problem. The semi-owner peasants, the poor peasants, and the small handicraftsmen are engaged in production on a still smaller scale than the owner-peasants and the master handicraftsmen ... The semi-owner peasants are worse off than the owner-peasants because every year they are short of about half the food they need, and have to make up this deficit by renting land from others, selling part of their labour power, or engaging in petty trading ... but they are better off than the poor peasants. For the poor peasants own no land, and receive only half the harvest or even less for their year's toil, while the semi-owner peasants, though receiving only half or less than half the harvest of land rented from others, can keep the entire crop from the land they own. The semi-owner peasants are therefore more revolutionary than the owner-peasants, but less revolutionary than the poor peasants. The poor peasants are tenant-peasants who are exploited by the landlords. They may again be divided into two categories according to their economic status. One category has comparatively adequate farm implements and some funds. Such peasants may retain half the product of their year's toil. To make up their deficit they cultivate side-crops, catch fish or shrimps, raise poulty or pigs, sell part of their labour power, and thus eke out a living, hoping in the midst of hardship and destitution to tide over the year. Thus, their life is harder than that of the semi-owner peasants, but they are better off than the other category of poor peasants. They are more revolutionary than the semi-owner peasants, but less revolutionary than the other category of poor peasants. As for the latter, they have neither adequate farm implements nor funds nor enough manure, their crops are poor, and, with little left after paying rent, they have even greater need to sell part of their labour power ... They are the worst off among the peasants and are highly receptive to revolutionary propaganda. The small handicraftsmen are called semi-proletarians because, though they own some simple means of production and moreover are self-employed, they too are often forced to sell part of their labour power and are somewhat similar to the poor peasants in economic status ... The shop assistants are employees of shops and stores, supporting their families on meagre pay and getting an increase perhaps only once in several years while prices rise every year ... The pedlars, whether they carry their wares around on a pole or set up stalls along the street, have tiny funds and very small earnings, and do not make enough to feed and clothe themselves. Their status is roughly the same as that of the poor peasants, and like the poor peasants they need a revolution to change the existing state of affairs.

The proletariat. The modern industrial proletariat numbers about two million. It is not large because China is economically backward. These two million industrial workers are mainly employed in five industries – railways, mining, maritime transport, textiles, and ship-building – and a great number are enslaved in enterprises owned by foreign capitalists. Though not very numerous, the industrial proletariat represents China's new productive forces, is the most progressive class in modern China, and has become the leading force in the revolutionary movement. We can see the important position of the industrial proletariat in the Chinese revolution from the strength it has displayed in the strikes of the last four years, such as the seamen's strikes, the railway strike, the strikes in the Kailan and Tsiaotso coal mines, the Shameen strike, and the general strikes in Shanghai and Hongkong after the May 30th incident. The first reason why the industrial workers hold this position is their concentration. No other section of the people is so concentrated. The second reason is their low economic status ... There is as yet little modern capitalist farming in China. By rural proletariat we mean farm labourers hired by the year, the month, or the day. Having neither land, farm implements, or funds, they can live only by selling their labour power. Of all the workers, they work the longest hours, for the lowest wages, under the worst conditions, and with the least security of employment …

Apart from all these, there is the fairly large lumpen-proletariat, made up of peasants who have lost their land and handicraftsmen who cannot get work. They lead the most precarious existence of all. In every part of the country they have their secret societies, which were origi-nally their mutual-aid organizations … One of China's difficult problems is how to handle these people. Brave fighters but apt to be destructive, they can become a revolutionary force if given proper guidance.

Source: Mao Tse-tung, 'Analysis of the Classes in Chinese Society'. In *Selected Works of Mao Tse-tung*, Vol. I (Beijing: Foreign Languages Press, 1965), pp. 13–19

3.2 The economic prospects of a tenant peasant in 1926

Data collected in 1926 and published in March 1927 by the Central Peasant Movement Training Institute.

Place: Xixiang, Xiangtan, Hunan
Time: The fifteenth year of the republic
A hypothetical case. A hard-working and capable tenant peasant in his prime rents 15 mu of land (the amount of land that can be tilled with the manpower of one tenant peasant) plus a sizeable vegetable plot, a hilly area in which to collect firewood, and a thatched hut to live in. Both of this tenant peasant's parents are dead and he has only a wife and a son. The wife cooks and raises pigs for him, and the son of twelve or thirteen looks after the oxen for him. This tenant peasant is able to till the 15 mu of fields he has rented without any hired help. Because he is poor, he rents the land from a dealer, so there is no rent deposit to be paid, and the rent, according to the general rule in this area, is 70 percent of the crops …

INCOME

1 Receipts from the land. Each mu yields 4 dan of grain (paddy rice) annually, and 15 mu yield a total of 60 dan of grain. Rent is paid with 42 dan (70 percent), leaving 18 dan for the peasant himself. At 4 yuan per dan, the total is 72 yuan.
2 Raising pigs. Forty yuan a year (a minimum of 3.30 yuan a month).
3 Cutting firewood or working as a porter during the winter season. Twenty yuan can be earned in the course of a winter.
4 Savings in wages and food money. Because the peasant goes out to cut firewood or to work as a porter during the months of September, October, and November and does not eat and work at home, food money and wages for one person should be deducted from the previous items of expenditure. The cost of food each month is 2.74 yuan (2.40 yuan for 6 dou of grain, 25 fen for 1 jin of oil, and 9 fen for 11 liang of salt). The total for 3 months is 8.22 yuan. Wages are 2.50 yuan a month, making a total of 7.50 yuan for three months. These two items add up to a total of 15.72 yuan.

The four items listed above add up to a total of 147.72 yuan.

CONCLUSION

Calculating income against expenditure [167.3655 yuan] leaves a shortfall of 19.6455 yuan.

Even an annual income of 147.72 yuan is possible only provided the following six conditions are met:

1   Absolutely no natural calamities of any kind such as flood, drought, wind storms, hail-storms, insect blight, or plant disease.
2   Robust health and absolutely no illness that would affect one's ability to work.
3   Being shrewd and good at adjusting (the local way of saying 'good at calculating' is 'good at adjusting').
4   No disease and death among the pigs and oxen raised.
5   Sunny days and no rain during the winter season.
6   Hard work all year round, with no holidays whatsoever.

Actually, it is very rare that all six conditions are met, especially numbers 3 and 5. There are always more simple and honest ones than shrewd ones among the poor tenant peasants.

In the countryside today, where the competition for survival is very fierce, this factor is of crucial importance to a peasant's rise or fall. Moreover, there is often an unbroken spell of wet and windy weather over the winter, which causes more suffering among poor tenant peasants, greatly reducing their income from cutting wood and working as a porter. As to the first condition of natural calamities, the second of illness, and the fourth of animal diseases, all of them are basically inevitable. The sixth condition shows that a Chinese tenant peasant lives a worse life than that of an ox, for an ox gets some rest during the year, while a man gets none at all. But in reality not every tenant peasant can work so hard all year with no rest, and, as soon as one so much as slacks off for a moment, a loss of income immediately follows. This is the real reason why, living a worse life than that of the tenant peasants in any other country in the world, many Chinese tenant peasants are being forced to leave the land and become soldiers, bandits, or vagrants.

Under the present system of heavy rents in China, such a life for the tenant peasant in which he earns a small amount of his income from his main occupation and the greater part of his income from sidelines, and at the end of the year suffers a large loss, is extremely wide-spread. It is only because the tenant peasants themselves frequently do not count their wages in their own calculations that many of them exert their utmost efforts all year to struggle for survival through what they earn from side jobs, yet they feel they are just managing to make ends meet and not suffering any great loss.

This article is based on an interview with Mr Zhang Lianchu, a tenant peasant.

Source: 'An Example of the Chinese Tenant-Peasant's Life', Central Peasant Movement Training Institute, March 1927. In S. Schram, ed., *Mao's Road to Power: Revolutionary Writings*, 1912–49, Vol. 2 (Armonk, New York, M. E. Sharpe, 1994), pp. 478, 482–3

3.3 The peasant movement in Hunan, March 1927

Mao Zedong

THE IMPORTANCE OF THE PEASANT PROBLEM

During my recent visit to Hunan I made a first-hand investigation of conditions in the five counties of Hsiangtan, Hsianghsiang, Hengshan, Liling, and Changsha. In the thirty-two days from 4 January to 5 February, I called together fact-finding conferences in villages and county towns which were attended by experienced peasants and by comrades working in the peasant movement, and I listened attentively to their reports and collected a great deal of material. Many of the hows and whys of the peasant movement were the exact opposite of what the gentry in Hankow and Changsha are saying. I saw and heard of many strange things of which I had hitherto been unaware. I believe the same is true of many other places, too. All talk directed against the peasant movement must be speedily set right. All the wrong measures taken by the revolutionary authorities concerning the peasant movement must be speedily changed. Only thus can the future of the revolution be benefited, for the present upsurge of the peasant movement is a colossal event. In a very short time, in China's central, southern, and northern provinces, several hundred million peasants will rise like a mighty storm, like a hurricane, a force so swift and violent that no power, however great, will be able to hold it back. They will smash all the trammels that bind them and rush forward along the road to liberation. They will sweep all the imperialists, warlords, corrupt officials, local tyrants, and evil gentry into their graves. Every revolutionary party and every revolutionary comrade will be put to the test, to be accepted or rejected as they decide. There are three alternatives. To march at their head and lead them? To trail behind them, gesticulating and criticizing? Or to stand in their way and oppose them? Every Chinese is free to choose, but events will force you to make the choice quickly.

GET ORGANIZED!

The development of the peasant movement in Hunan may be divided roughly into periods with respect to the counties in the province's central and southern parts where the movement has already made much headway. The first, from January to September of last year, was one of organization. In this period, January to June was a time of underground activity, and July to September, when the revolutionary army was driving out Chao Heng-ti, one of open activity. During this period, the membership of the peasant associations did not exceed 300,000–400,000, the masses directly under their leadership numbered little more than a million, there was as yet hardly any struggle in the rural areas, and consequently there was very little criticism of the associations in other circles. Since its members served as guides, scouts, and carriers of the Northern Expeditionary Army, even some of the officers had a good word to say for the peasant associations. The second period, from last October to January in this year was one of revolutionary actions. The membership of the associations jumped to two million and the masses directly under their leadership increased to ten million. Since the peasants generally enter only one name for the whole family on joining a peasant association, a membership of two million means a mass following of about ten million. Almost half the peasants in Hunan are now organized. In counties like

Hsiangtan, Hsianghsiang, Liuyang, Changsha, Leiyang, Chenhsien, and Anhua, nearly all the peasants have combined in the peasant associations or have come under their leadership. It was on the strength of their extensive organization that the peasants went into action and within four months brought about a great revolution in the countryside, a revolution without parallel in history.

DOWN WITH THE LOCAL TYRANTS AND EVIL GENTRY! ALL POWER TO THE PEASANT ASSOCIATIONS!

The main targets of attack by the peasants are the local tyrants, the evil gentry, and the lawless landlords, but in passing they also hit out against patriarchal ideas and institutions, against the corrupt officials in the cities, and against bad practices and customs in the rural areas. In force and momentum the attack is tempestuous; those who bow before it survive and those who resist perish. As a result, the privileges which the feudal landlords enjoyed for thousands of years are being shattered to pieces. Every bit of the dignity and prestige built up by the landlords is being swept into the dust. With the collapse of the power of the landlords, the peasant associations have now become the sole organs of authority, and the popular slogan 'All power to the peasant associations' has become a reality. Even trifles such as a quarrel between husband and wife are brought to the peasant association …

Many middle and small landlords and rich peasants and even some middle peasants, who were all formerly opposed to the peasant associations, are now vainly seeking admission. Visiting various places, I often came across such people who pleaded with me, 'Mr Committee-man from the provincial capital, please be my sponsor!' …

THE QUESTION OF 'GOING TOO FAR'

Then there is another section of people who say, 'Yes, peasant associations are necessary, but they are going too far'. This is the opinion of the middle-of-the-roaders. But what is the actual situation? True, the peasants are in a sense 'unruly' in the countryside. Supreme in authority, the peasant association allows the landlord no say and sweeps away his prestige. This amounts to striking the landlord down in the dust and keeping him there. The peasants threaten, 'We will put you in the other register!' They fine the local tyrants and evil gentry, they demand contributions from them, and they smash their sedan chairs. People swarm into the houses of local tyrants and evil gentry who are against the peasant association, slaughter their pigs, and consume their grain. They even loll for a minute or two on the ivory-inlaid beds belonging to the young ladies in the households of the local tyrants and evil gentry. At the slightest provocation they make arrests, crown the arrested with tall paper hats, and parade them through the villages, saying, 'You dirty landlords, now you know who we are!' Doing whatever they like and turning everything upside down, they have created a kind of terror in the countryside. This is what some people call 'going too far', or 'exceeding the proper limits in righting a wrong', or 'really too much'. Such talk may seem plausible, but in fact it is wrong. First, the local tyrants, evil gentry, and lawless landlords have themselves driven the peasants to this. For ages they have used their power to tyrannize over the peasants and trample them underfoot; that is why the peasants have reacted so strongly. The most violent revolts and the most serious disorders have invariably occurred in places where the local tyrants, evil gentry, and lawless landlords have perpetuated the worst outrages.

The peasants are clear-sighted. Who is bad and who is not, who is the worst and who is not quite so vicious, who deserves severe punishment and who deserves to be let off lightly – the peasants keep clear accounts, and very seldom has the punishment exceeded the crime. Second, a revolution is not a dinner party, or writing an essay, or painting a picture, or doing embroidery; it cannot be so refined, so leisurely and gentle, so temperate, kind, courteous, restrained, and magnanimous. A revolution is an insurrection, an act of violence by which one class overthrows the power of the feudal landlords which has lasted for thousands of years. The rural areas need a mighty revolutionary upsurge, for it alone can rouse the people in their millions to become a powerful force ...

With the increasing bankruptcy of the rural economy in recent years, the basis for men's domination over women has already been weakened. With the rise of the peasant movement, the women in many places have begun to organize rural women's associations. The opportunity has come for them to lift up their heads, and the authority of the husband is getting shakier every day. In a word, the whole feudal-patriarchal system and ideology is tottering with the growth of the peasants' power. At the present time, however, the peasants are concentrating on destroying the landlords' political authority. Wherever it has been wholly destroyed, they are beginning to press their attack in the other three spheres of clan, the gods, and male domination. But such attacks have only just begun, and there can be no thorough overthrow of all three until the peasants have won complete victory in the economic struggle. Therefore, our present task is to lead the peasants to put their greatest efforts into the political struggle, so that the landlords' authority is entirely overthrown. The economic struggle should follow immediately, so that the land problem and the other economic problems of the poor peasants may be fundamentally solved. As for the clan system, superstition, and inequality between men and women, their abolition will follow as a natural consequence of victory in the political and economic struggles ... It is for the peasants themselves to cast aside the idols and pull down the temples to the martyred virgins and the arches to chaste and faithful widows; it is wrong for anybody else to do it for them.

Source: Mao Tse-tung, 'Report on an Investigation of the Peasant Movement in Hunan'.
In *Selected Works of Mao Tse-tung*, Vol. I
(Beijing, Foreign Languages Press, 1965), pp. 45–7

3.4 An official fundraising letter, 13 February 1929

The Red Army is an army that strives for the well-being of the workers and peasants. It also makes every effort to protect the merchants. It exercises strict discipline and does not encroach upon anyone. Because of the current shortage of food supplies, we are writing to you now to request that you kindly collect on our behalf 5,000 big foreign dollars for the soldiers' pay, 7,000 pairs of straw sandals and 7,000 pairs of socks, 300 bolts of white cloth, and 200 laborers. It is urgent that these be delivered to our headquarters before eight o'clock this evening. We hope that you will do as we request without delay. If you ignore our requests, it will be proof that the Ningdu merchants are collaborating with the reactionaries and are out to make things difficult for the Red Army. In that case we will be obliged to burn down all reactionary shops in Ningdu as a warning against your treachery. Do not say that we have not forewarned you. The above message is communicated to all the gentlemen in charge of the Ningdu *Xian* Reception Center.

N.B. It is reported that this demand was met on time.

Source: 'An Official Fundraising Letter'. In S. R. Schram, ed.
Mao's Road to Power: Revolutionary Writings, 1912–49, Vol. 3
(Armonk, New York, M. E. Sharpe, 1995), p. 139

3.5 Conflict over strategy

3.5a Letter from the Party Centre to Mao and Zhu De, 7 February 1929

This letter, drafted by Zhou Enlai, suggested they leave the Fourth Red Army and that it be broken into small units.

The Sixth Congress decided that our Party's central task at present is to win the support of the people. The Party's major task at present is to establish and develop bases among the proletariat, mainly to establish branches among the industrial workers and to mobilize the masses. This does not mean that we will not expand the rural revolution or direct spontaneous peasant uprisings or ignore guerrilla warfare. Indeed, these should be adjusted to fit with the central work of the Party.

In view of this background, the armed forces under your direction should also reconsider their present task and act in accordance with the political situation throughout the country as a whole and with the Party's task. In line with the decision of the Sixth Congress, the CC has said for a long time that you must make plans gradually to divide the Red Army troops into small detachments and scatter them over the countryside of the Hunan–Jiangxi border area to carry out the rural revolution. The CC asks you to follow this instruction because the current political situation in China demands us to wage an extensive struggle in the countryside. This strategy can also help divert the enemy's attention, solve the supply problem, and prepare for protracted warfare. However, either you did not receive this instruction or you are not willing to follow it. In your current operations, you have continued to adopt the tactics of concentrating forces. Of course, being surrounded by the enemy, you certainly have to amass the troops. However, the CC holds that you must clearly understand the current situation and the Party's tasks and firmly carry out the plan to disperse the forces in an orderly way. At the same time, you must also realize that the CC by no means orders you to take the pessimistic attitude to send the Red Army soldiers back home. What we ask you to do is to scatter our armed forces into villages when the time and conditions are favourable; that is, when there is no serious threat of the enemy's attack …

Under current conditions, we have decided to transfer Comrade Zhu De and Comrade Mao Zedong to the CC. The two comrades might feel reluctant to leave the army since they have worked in it for over a year. However, taking into consideration both the needs of the situation and the demands of our work, the CC believes that it is necessary for them to leave the army now. Zhu and Mao's departure will not cause the army any losses and will help it implement the plan to disperse its forces. If Zhu and Mao stay with the army, their activities will draw the enemy's attention, thus making it more difficult for us to disperse the troops. When Zhu and Mao come to the CC, they can introduce to our comrades all over the country their precious experience in leading a 10,000-strong armed force in dealing with the enemy for more than a year. This will make a greater contribution to the whole revolutionary cause. Therefore, as soon as comrades Zhu and Mao receive the CC decision, they should leave the army and come to the CC immediately. They must not neglect more important and difficult duties because of an emotional attachment to the soldiers in the army.

Source: 'Letter from the Party Center to Mao and Zhu De',
7 February 1929. In Tony Saich, ed., *The Rise to Power of the Chinese Communist Party*
(Armonk, New York: M. E. Sharpe, 1996), pp. 472, 473–4

3.5b Letter from the Front Committee to the Party Centre, 5 April 1929

The uncompromising reply by Mao and Zhu De.

The Fujian Provincial Committee passed on your letter of 7 February to us at Ruijin on 3 April. We are afraid that your estimate in the letter of both the situation and our strength is rather pessimistic. The campaign of the three offensives launched by the Nationalist troops on the Jianggang Mountains represented the climax of the reactionary forces, but it was also a turning point. The reactionary forces are at a low ebb, while the revolutionary tide has gradually risen. Although the fighting power and the organizational capacity of our party are as weak as you have pointed out, they will surely grow strong again, and the pessimistic atmosphere inside the Party will soon disappear because the reactionaries will be at a low ebb. The broad masses support us unreservedly. The enemy's policy of harsh suppression and massacre is just like driving fish into deeper water, and the promise of reformism can no longer win support from the masses. The people's illusions about the GMD are bound to vanish before too long …

Proletarian leadership is the only guarantee of victory of the revolution. At present, the Party's vital organizational task is to form a proletarian basis within the Party and found industrial branches in cities. Nevertheless, the development of our struggle in the countryside, the establishment of revolutionary regimes in rural areas, and the creation and strengthening of the Red Army are also important. They are of great significance in promoting our struggle in the cities and in paving the way for the revolutionary climax. While it is wrong to abandon the struggle in the cities, it would be incorrect for some Party members to fear that the growth of peasant strength might surpass that of the workers, and that such a development would not be so good for the progress of the revolutionary cause if the struggle grows more powerful than that of the workers. Our Party's Sixth Congress has pointed out the mistake of neglecting the peasant struggle, and the Party Center has mentioned again in its letter the necessity to 'wage a massive and universal struggle in the countryside.' We think this is a correct attitude.

The Party Center says that to preserve the Red Army and mobilize the masses we should break up our troops into very small units, disperse them throughout the countryside, stay away from any big targets, and that Zhu [De] and Mao [Zedong] should leave the army. This is not a practical idea. Since the winter of 1927 we have not only planned but also tried many times the tactic of dispersing troops throughout the countryside, operating separately on the basis of a company or a battalion, using the tactics of guerrilla warfare to mobilize the masses, and staying away from big targets. Unfortunately, all those tactics failed. They failed because first, unlike the militia forces, the majority of the main force of the Red Army is not made up of local people but of members of the former National Revolutionary Army, the peasant troops from Liu, Ping, and south Hunan, and previous prisoners of war. There are hardly any peasants from the Hunan–Jiangxi border area in the Red Army because peasants there are not willing to join the Red Army but only the militia forces of their own counties. Second, once the troops are dispersed, the leading organ is also broken up. Hence, it is difficult for us to handle the dangerous environment and it is easy to fail. Third, it will allow the enemy to defeat us separately. (The Fifth Army in Ping and Liu and the Fourth Army in the border area and in south Hunan were defeated five times by the enemy because they divided their forces.) Fourth, the more adverse the circumstances are, the more concentrated the troops should be and the more firmly the leaders must act. Only in this way can we maintain morale and deal with the enemy. In fact, the tactics to disperse the troops for guerrilla warfare can only be used when there are favourable circumstances that enable the leaders to leave the troops.

Source: 'Letter from Front Committee to Party Center', 5 April 1929.
In Tony Saich, ed., *The Rise to Power of the Chinese Communist Party*
(Armonk, New York: M. E. Sharpe, 1996), pp. 474–6

3.6 Extracts from the Red Army resolution on the treatment of captured soldiers, December 1929

Considerate treatment of captured enemy soldiers is an extremely effective method for conducting propaganda directed at enemy troops. Methods of considerate treatment of captured soldiers include the following. First, there should be no body searches for money and other objects. The past practice of body searches of captured soldiers for money and goods by Red Army soldiers should be resolutely abolished. Second, captured soldiers should be warmly and enthusiastically welcomed, to make them feel happy in their minds. Any humiliation of the captured soldiers by word or deed should be opposed. Third, captured soldiers should enjoy the same material treatment as the old soldiers. Fourth, if they do not want to stay, they will be let go with travel expenses after they have been exposed to propaganda, so that they may spread the influence of the Red Army in the White Army. The practice of forcibly keeping those who are unwilling to stay in order to satisfy the greed for more soldiers should be opposed. All the above points are entirely applicable to captured officers, except in special circumstances.

Providing medical treatment for wounded enemy soldiers is also a very effective method for conducting propaganda directed toward the enemy troops. The medical treatment of wounded enemy soldiers and the money issued to them should be exactly the same as those of the wounded soldiers of the Red Army. Advantage should be taken of all possible circumstances to send the enemy wounded back to the enemy army after they are given medicine and money. The treatment of the wounded enemy officers is also the same.

Source: 'Draft Resolution of the Ninth Congress of the Chinese Communist Party in
the Fourth Red Army (December 1929)'. In S. R. Schram, ed., *Mao's Road to Power*,
Vol. 3, p. 220

3.7 Letter from the Fourth Army of the Chinese Red Army (the Red Army of Zhu and Mao) to the soldiers of the Guomindang army, January 1930

Brother soldiers of the Guomindang army!

1 THE WARLORDS ARE NOW OPENING FIRE AGAIN!

The warlords are now fighting again. On the one hand, the imperialist allies are attacking the Soviet Union (Russia), and the Chinese warlord Chiang Kai-shek is their loyal running dog; on the other hand, Chiang Kai-shek, having usurped all power over the central government, has aroused the opposition of warlords big and small throughout the nation. The outbreak of both these wars has aggravated the suffering of the workers, peasants, and soldiers, especially our brothers who are soldiers, who are tragically sacrificed directly for the warlords and imperialists. Since the situation has become this serious, you must absolutely think, brothers, about what is the way out for us soldiers!

2 LISTEN TO THE VIEWS OF THE RED ARMY

We are China's Red Army. Two years ago a portion of our comrades fighting to the death for the National Revolution, struggling bitterly, saw with their own eyes old brothers and new brothers, one group after another, become cannon fodder for the army commanders and division commanders of the Guomindang high command … We are people who have been deceived by the Guomindang, and as the day of this battle approaches we think of the suffering of our brothers, and we specially and very sincerely offer an opinion to our brothers!

3 WHY DO WE WANT TO SUPPORT THE SOVIET UNION?

Brothers! First we must realize the danger that the imperialist attacks on the Soviet Union pose to those of us who are soldiers. Today, the entire world is divided into two fronts, one of which is the front of imperialist capitalism, of countries such as Great Britain, the United States, Japan, and France, which specialize in oppressing the proletariat and the weak and small nations. Since coming to power in Nanjing, Chiang Kai-shek has shamelessly surrendered to the imperialists, because he is both a capitalist and a warlord and, therefore, acts as a running dog of the imperialists. The other is the front of the proletariat, of those like the Soviet Union and the impoverished workers, peasants, and soldiers of various countries … We must defend the Soviet Union, defend the state of the proletariat, and turn our rifles around and shoot at the Chinese warlords!

4 WE MUST RISE UP AND OVERTHROW THE WARLORDS

Brothers! Second, we must realize that the senseless wars of the Chinese warlords add to the sufferings of those of us who are soldiers and to those of the workers and peasants … Every time they go to war, we soldiers must die by the hundreds of thousands, while the warlords, whether they win or lose, always strip the land to the extent of hundreds of thousands and into the millions in some cases ...

5 WHAT ARE THE SUFFERINGS OF US SOLDIERS?

Brothers! Third, we must realize the source of our own suffering and also our way out. Brothers! We were not born soldiers, nor was it fated that we should be soldiers. It's just that at home we had no clothes to wear, no food to eat, so we had no choice but to run off and become soldiers ... After we joined the army, we first entered an army camp, where every day we had three drills and two lectures, seven beatings and eight scoldings ... And the soldier's clothing? At most two sets of clothing to wear, too long, too short, clothes that don't fit at all, so that when we go out people laugh at us. Bedding? Just a bed or two of old blankets, too heavy in summer and too light in winter, full of big holes ... The money for food is never given out, and the warlords skimp on food by providing terrible meals of rice gruel and cabbage every day, all with no oil and no salt. This is the clothing, food, and housing for soldiers.

6 WHAT ALTERNATIVE DO WE HAVE?

Brothers! In the past, some of our brothers in the Red Army were, like you, very obedient to the warlord officers, and did not understand that the warlords are detestable. Afterwards, the facts allowed them to see through the dark curtain of the warlords' oppression of the soldiers ... Brothers! Do you want to know what the advantages of the Red Army are?

7 THE RED ARMY IS THE ARMY OF THE REVOLUTION OF THE WORKERS AND PEASANTS

First of all, the Red Army is the army of the worker and peasant revolution ... Worker and peasant comrades, shouldering rifles and making up the ranks – these are the Red Army. Red Army comrades, putting down their rifles and going out into the fields and into the factories – these are the workers and peasants. This is why, when the Red Army reaches a location, the workers and peasants form a crowd to welcome us, cook rice and make tea, kill pigs and slaughter sheep, to welcome us. Those local bullies and bad gentry ... who are caught are fined, or else they are brought to trial and sentenced by a meeting of the workers, peasants, and soldiers. All their lands and property are disposed of by decision of a big meeting of the workers, peasants, and soldiers ...

8 THE RED ARMY IS AN ARMY OF SOLDIERS THEMSELVES

Second, the Red Army is an army of soldiers themselves. The Guomindang army hangs out the label 'National Revolutionary Army,' but in its bones it is an army of the warlords. The officers have authority, the soldiers have no authority ... In the Red Army the officers, the soldiers, and the laborers all dress, eat, and are paid the same. In the Red Army, there are only different tasks; there are no class distinctions. The commanding officer does not beat the soldiers; the soldiers respect the commanding officer; finances are open and public; and the representatives of the soldiers have the right to ask questions ...

9 THE RED ARMY SUPPORTS THE COMMUNIST PARTY IN UNITING THE FORCES OF THE WORLD REVOLUTION

The Red Army supports the Communist Party in uniting the forces of the world revolution. The forces of imperialism and of the warlords are extremely great and they have, moreover, a worldwide union. Our revolution of the workers, peasants, and soldiers must assuredly also have a worldwide union if we are to be able to overthrow them. The Communist Party is the guiding organ of the worldwide revolution and has very good organizations in various countries ...

10 COME OVER TO THE SIDE OF THE RED ARMY!

Brothers! Rise up! Be no longer the beasts of burden, the slaves, of the warlords. Quickly bring your rifles and join the Red Army. The broad masses of the workers and peasants, and of the Red Army throughout the nation, warmly welcome you ... Leave hell, rise up to heaven. Come quickly!

> **Source: 3.7. 'Letter from Red Army Leaders to Soldiers of the Guomindang Army'.**
> **In S. R. Schram, ed., *Mao's Road to Power: Revolutionary Writings*, 1912–49, Vol. 3**
> **(Armonk, New York, M. E. Sharpe, 1995), pp. 247–54**

3.8 On the Long March with Chairman Mao

Chen Changfeng, Mao's bodyguard

One of several heroic versions of the Long March.

ON LIUPAN MOUNTAIN

At dusk in the middle of September, we arrived at the village close to Latzukou. I spread the Chairman's pallet so that he could get some rest. But when I went into the next room, he was already in conference with Lin Piao and other leaders. The table was spread with maps.

Latzukou was known as the 'dangerous pass'. It connects the provinces of Szechuan and Kansu, and was one of the major passes we had to get through to reach northern Shensi. I was sure this was what the Chairman and the others were discussing, so I withdrew without a word. The Chairman didn't get to sleep until very late that night.

But we attacked the pass the next morning at dawn. After taking it, we didn't linger but pushed on.

At the end of September, we crossed the Weishui River blockade line and headed for Luipan Mountain.

Luipan Mountain, a spur of the Lungshan Range, is the highest peak in western Kanshu. It was also the last big mountain we had to cross to get to northern Shensi.

The sky was cloudy and a cold wind blew the day we set out to climb it. Soon it started to rain. But although we were soaked by the time we reached the foothills, nothing could dampen our determination ... I was still weak from the malaria. The trail was about 15 kilometres to the top and very uneven. By the time we were halfway up, I was gasping for breath. My heart was pumping hard and I was drenched with sweat.

Chairman Mao quickly noticed the shape I was in. Whenever we came to a difficult stretch, he extended his big strong hand and pulled me along ... 'Are you cold?' the Chairman asked.

'Chilled to the bone'. 'Here, put this coat on and drink some more hot water. You'll feel better when you warm up a bit'. The Chairman took off his overcoat.

All he had on underneath was a grey cotton army uniform that had been made for him when we were in Tsunyi ...

WE ARE HOME!

After we passed Liupan Mountain, we entered the Hui region of Kansu. The Hui people were very warm to us. Wherever we went they streamed out to welcome us along the roadside, handing us bowls of hot water and saying 'You must be tired comrades. Please drink some hot water'. We were beyond words when we heard them call us 'comrades'. We gathered from them that our Red 25th Army, which had passed through here in July, had left them a very good impression with its rigorous discipline.

As we were getting nearer to northern Shensi, our excitement made us forget all our fatigue and ailments. We wished we could step onto the soil of Shensi at once.

One day soon after we started out from Huanhsien County in Kansu, we found ourselves on a small path skirting a mountain. Suddenly we saw five men on horseback galloping toward us. They carried Mausers on their hips and wore white towels on their heads. They were sturdy, young chaps in their twenties. When they reached the foot of the mountain, they dismounted and walked toward us. 'Where's Chairman Mao?' they called.

I went to meet them and asked them what they wanted.

An older man among them, breathing heavily and with sweat all over his face, said in a warm voice, 'We're sent by Old Liu to deliver a letter to Chairman Mao. Where is he?' Old Liu! 'Is that Comrade Liu Chih-tan?' I asked. 'Exactly', they said in one voice. Meanwhile, the older man handed me the letter. I hurried with it to the Chairman. When the Chairman read it he smiled and said to the newcomers: 'Comrades, you've done good work!' Then they knew it was he – Chairman Mao – whom the people of northern Shensi had expected for so long. They crowded around, smiling and jostling to shake hands with him.

The Chairman walked over to our resting troops. Standing in their midst, he spoke loudly, 'Comrades, we are about to reach the Soviet area in northern Shensi! Our 25th and 26th Armies have defeated the enemy's second encirclement campaign and sent men to meet us'.

Tumultuous cheers broke out. People were shouting, laughing, and flinging their arms around each other. Many were crying for joy. Never before had I seen such a moving scene!

The five comrades who had come to meet us acted as our guides, leading us into a village called Sanchachen. That evening, the Chairman talked with them for a long while and wrote a letter for them. He did not even have time to eat.

The following day we stopped at a small village whose name we did not know. There was no rice to be bought, only golden-coloured millet. Being all southerners, we bodyguards had never seen millet before, let alone cooked it. What to do? Since there were plenty of sheep, we bought a big one and prepared a mutton dinner.

'Why only meat?' the Chairman wanted to know when the leg of mutton we had reserved for him was brought in.

'We couldn't get any rice in this village or any flour', said Little Tseng quickly. 'There's only millet but we don't know how to cook it'.

'Learn to do it; it isn't difficult', said the Chairman. 'We have to learn new ways of living when we come to a new place. Otherwise, we'll starve to death'.

We started out to cook the millet. 'There's no hurry', said the Chairman. 'Let's have the mutton on its own this time!'

During the 40 kilometre march between Chuchih and the dividing ridge on the Kansu–Shensi border, we fought some 18 battles with cavalry units of the Kuomintang warlord Ma Hung-kuei. But as soon as we made contact, Ma's horsemen would gallop away. We laughed at them and said they did not even measure up to 'bean-curd' troops of Kweichow warlord Wang Chia-lieh – they were only the refuse from the beans after making the curd!

The Chairman's wry comments on these troops tickled our sense of humour. 'They don't dare fight when they learn it's the Chinese Workers' and Peasants' Red Army', he remarked. 'They're only "expert" at running away!'

On the top of the ridge stood a large tablet which read 'Dividing Ridge', marking the border between Kansu and Shensi provinces. We sat down for a rest under a chestnut tree near the tablet.

The Chairman was reading the words on the back of the tablet. 'We have crossed ten provinces', he told us in high spirits. 'When we go down this mountain, we'll be in the eleventh – Shensi, our base and "home"!'

A day and a half's march from the ridge brought us to Wuchi where we stayed in cave rooms cut in the side of the loess hills. It was the first time in our lives we had seen such caves. We were now in the Soviet area.

Source: *China Reconstructs*, October 1971, pp. 18–23

3.9 A Comintern agent on the Long March, 1935

Otto Braun

Otto Braun, the key military adviser sent to the Red Army by the Comintern, provides the only European eyewitness account of the Long March. However, he did not speak Chinese and lost his diary during the March. His account is also influenced by his declared hostility to Maoism. Nevertheless, he provides an interesting contrast to the later mythologizing of the Long March.

Mao Tse-tung persisted in his plan to cross the Yangtze and link up with the 4th Corps. He and Lin Piao decided to turn westwards, overrun the Yunnan troops, who they considered to be the weak link in the chain, and look for a good crossing point further upstream between the riverports of Lu-chou and Yi-pin.

Accordingly, the 1st Corps crossed the Ch'hi-shui River and advanced from the south-west corner of Szechwan to the border of Yunnan without meeting serious resistance. But, since they were repulsed by Szechwanese troops north of this point, they then turned south in a time- and energy-consuming manoeuvre as Lin Piao tried to avoid major battles. The same happened to other corps, especially the 3rd ...

In their retreat ... the 3rd, 5th and 9th Corps, ... not far from Tsunyi, made a surprise attack on General Chou's army. The 1st Corps arrived at just the right time to thrust into the enemy's flank. According to the situation report of General Headquarters, two or three enemy divisions were badly beaten, several thousand prisoners were taken, and large stores of weapons and urgently needed ammunition were captured ...

In Tsunyi I rejoined the central command column. The city presented a desolate sight. Shops and warehouses were empty; the homes of the rich landlords and merchants, including the governor's summer residence, were boarded up or half-destroyed and plundered. Here and there, shreds of posters and defaced slogans of our political workers hung on house walls. These were the only traces of the Sovietization that had been so ambitiously started at the beginning of the year.

The Politburo and the Military Council were going to have to make some quick decisions, for General Chou, despite his partial defeat, was quickly regrouping his forces and receiving reinforcements from the north. Their meeting was not without definite, if guarded, criticism of Mao's north operation. Lo Fu, who had by now replaced Po Ku as General Secretary of the Central Committee, characterized it as an imprudent and ill-conceived undertaking and said that, under more favourable conditions, a victory over Chou's troops could have been achieved earlier and a new Soviet base established in Kweichow ...

The strategic plan of crossing the Yangtze and linking up with the 4th Corps was ratified ...

For all of March and April 1935 the Central Army Group marched through southern Kweichow and eastern Yunnan, constantly harassed both by provincial armies waging a sort of 'pin-prick' war against our flank and rear guard, and especially by strong Kuomintang forces operating in three groupings ...

Obsessed with the idea of finding a place to cross the river, Mao Tse-tung and his Command Panel avoided larger battles, although there were many promising opportunities. There was no fortifications system to inhibit our mobility, except for the high and ancient city walls frequently encountered in Inner China. And the extremely mountainous terrain rendered it more difficult for the enemy to concentrate his numerically superior forces ...

This brief operational outline might give the impression that this segment of the march proceeded according to plan and was purely and simply a victory campaign for the Red Army. It is certainly portrayed as such by Maoist historiography. In reality, it was nearly the opposite. The march increasingly resembled a retreat and eventually degenerated into outright flight. In its effort to avoid battle, the Army group pursued a zigzag route with endless parallel, forward, and backward marches, diversionary movements, and even circles. Forced marches of 40–50 km were the rule. The command column, which followed relatively few detours, once covered 70 km. Marching was done at night because the Kuomintang air force flew incessant sorties during the day, bombing and strafing us. Especially insidious were the low-flying planes. Hugging the ground, they would rise up from behind an elevation without a sound, and immediately machine-gun fire would be raining down upon us. The advance, flank, and rear guards endured dozens of attacks, occasionally on all sides at once.

The situation worsened when we crossed the jagged mountains on the Kweichow–Yunnan border. The narrow path led up and down sheer cliffs. Many horses fell and broke their legs; only the mules kept their footing. Rations were becoming an ever more critical problem as we advanced into Yunnan. There was hardly anything to eat in the mountains. Soldiers sliced flesh from dead horses until nothing but the skeletons remained. Even in the plains, few vegetables and little rice were found. But everywhere the eye looked, poppies swayed in the wind. High rents, oppressive taxes, and inland duties had made opium cultivation the only possibility for the peasants to eke out a semi-endurable existence. Even we used confiscated raw opium as our chief means of exchange. With its good durability and easy divisibility, it was willingly accepted everywhere as money. There was no alternative but to tolerate opium smoking among the locally recruited pack-carriers and soldiers. It was otherwise strictly prohibited in the Red Army.

The troops were showing increasing symptoms of fatigue …

The number of deaths, more from disease and exhaustion than battle wounds, increased daily. Although several thousand volunteers had been enlisted since the beginning of the year, the ranks had visibly dwindled. What was most admirable – and I want to emphasize this – is that, despite everything, the self-discipline and fighting morale of the soldiers remained unbroken. But the mood of the leading cadres, who had an overall view of the predicament, darkened as the Army moved westward. Dissatisfaction with Mao Tse-tung's leadership assumed such proportions that a new power struggle was a real possibility. Mao's harshest critics were his erstwhile most ardent and reliable supporters: Lo Fu and Lin Piao. They openly blamed him and his Command Panel for 'flight before the enemy' and 'military bankruptcy'. P'eng Te-huai and his political commissar, Yang Shang-k'un, basically agreed with this. Chou En-lai and Wang Chia-hsiang, who were affected by the criticism as much as Mao himself, let matters take their course. They adopted more of a passive 'wait and see' attitude. Chu Te behaved similarly and refrained from attacking Mao. Po Ku mentioned to me his fear that a renewed power struggle would fracture the Party and Army leadership. This would have to be prevented by any possible means, for otherwise the Central Army Group was doomed.

This was a genuine crisis, and it sharpened dangerously over the next weeks …

One day, Lo Fu, with whom I normally had little contact, joined me during a march and began talking of what he termed the catastrophic military predicament engendered by Mao's reckless strategy and tactics ever since Tsunyi. Although the failure of the Northern Operation was compensated in part by the victory near Tsunyi, the present westward flight could destroy the Army … Recognizing his honest concern, but not judging the situation quite so pessimistically, I answered that everything depended on whether or not we succeeded in crossing the Chin-sha …

A few days later, Mao Tse-tung invited me to talk to him. He touched on two main points. The military situation was serious, he admitted, but he insisted that somewhere and some time we would succeed in crossing the Chin-sha and effect a juncture with the 4th Corps. The possibility that the Red Army might be forced to march very far upstream before finding a place to cross did not seem to frighten him. He even revealed a plan – for the first time, I believe – to lead the Central Army Group over Sikang and Tsinghai into Sinkiang. From there he would try to contact the Soviet Union and request immediate assistance … Finally, he invited me to join his marching group so that we could consult, to win my support. A little later, when Mao was sitting somewhat more firmly in the saddle, he lost interest in my advice. …

Surprisingly, there was never an open confrontation between Mao Tse-tung and Lo Fu in the Military Council. It was agreed that the crossing of Chin-sha was imperative. A change in the leadership was never mentioned. Mao apparently succeeded in persuading a majority in the Politburo and Military Council that any alteration in the command structure would negatively affect our combat performance. Lo Fu would have to acquiesce – for the common welfare. This was hardly a solution to the question of Mao's leadership. Ultimately, this position hung on the success of the Chin-sha operation.

The crossing of the Chin-sha, which marked the border between Yunnan and Szechwan, succeeded thanks to a stratagem. The 9th Corps moved upstream and began preparation for rafts and a bridge. Our main forces followed. Informed by air reconnaissance of these movements, Chiang Kai-shek threw all available troops at this point. Meanwhile, a vanguard battalion under the command of Liu Po-ch'eng marched in the opposite direction towards Chiao-ch'e Ferry, north-east of Yüan-mou. Liu, a native of Szechwan who had served there many years after the 1911 revolution, was an expert on local conditions. The south bank of the Chin-sha was flat here and no problem to occupy. But on the north side towered a cliff wall that had been converted into the formidable stronghold of a Szechwan garrison.

There were also a few boats. Liu Po-ch'eng fitted his men out with the highly visible blue and white insignia of the Kuomintang and dressed himself in the uniform of a senior Nationalist officer. He then forced some local dignitaries to accompany him. The enemy mistook them for reinforcements, and, at Liu's request, sent a boat big enough for a platoon to the south bank. Liu crossed over, conferred with the fortress commandant and managed to have more boats sent to the south bank. His deception resulted in the almost immediate and bloodless surrender of the Szechwan troops. This took place a few days after 1 May 1935.

Our main forces followed in forced march. Although passage over the 200 m wide and turbulent river went on day and night, it took nearly a week. Just as the last platoon of our rearguard set out, the advance troops of Chiang Kai-shek's troops appeared on the south bank ...

Mao Tse-tung praised the crossing of the Chin-sha as a decisive strategic victory. At his prompting, a meeting of the Politburo was convened in mid-May not far from Hui-li. This time there were no 'outsiders', that is, non-Politburo members. Not even Lin Piao and P'eng Te-huai were present. I was invited at the last moment, but without my interpreter ...

Lo Fu opened with a short briefing in which he largely withdrew his earlier criticism and request for a change in the military leadership. Mao then spoke, moving to the offence. He accused Lo Fu, Lin Piao, and others of sectarian activity and lack of faith in the revolution. This manifestation of right opportunism would have to be fought. His strategy had been proved correct by the crossing of the Chin-sha River. It was now imperative that the second part of the problem be solved, namely, the juncture with the 4th Corps. Chou En-lai and Wang Chia-hsiang seconded this, although in moderate tones and with an absence of political labelling ...

Without a formal vote it was eventually agreed that we should continue into north-west Szechwan to link up with the 4th Corps, which was supposedly out there somewhere, and establish a large base. All pledged themselves to preserve the solidarity of the existing political and military leadership and to oppose deviations ...

Source: Otto Braun, *A Comintern Agent in China, 1932–1939*
(London: Hurst, 1982), pp. 109–18

3.10 Loushan Pass

Poem on Long March by Mao Zedong, 28 February 1935

The Red Army recaptured Loushan Pass on 26 February 1935, after holding the Zunyi Conference. Mao is using here one of the classical forms of Chinese poetry – the ci pattern of Yi Qin E.

Fierce, the westerly wind howls,
Echoing of wild geese in a moonlit frosty dawn.
In a moonlit frosty dawn.

Fading away is the clattering sound of horses,
While the bugle moans.

Don't say that the stronghold in the pass is iron wrought,
We nevertheless swing over it in strides.
Like the sea are the dark mountains,
And like blood the setting sun.

Translated for this book by Professor Hua Qingzhao.

**Source: Mao Zedong, 'Loushan Pass'. In *Ten Poems and Lyrics by Chairman Mao*
(Shanghai: Tung Fang Hung Press, 1969).**

4

The Nanjing decade (1927–37) and World War Two (1937–45)

Within a couple of years of the Shanghai massacre, Chiang Kai-shek had reached Beijing, had come to an agreement with the warlords, and set up his new capital in Nanjing. In the following decade, despite great economic difficulties and the need for structural reforms, his policies had some successes. Manifestations of social reform and indoctrination appeared in the Blue Shirts organization and in the New Life Movement designed to regenerate Chinese society by moral commitment and social responsibility. It was launched on 19 February 1934.

As Mao's forces settled in Shaanxi at the end of the Long March, Chiang Kai-shek was anxious to encourage his military leader in the north-west, the Young Marshall, Zhang Xueliang (son of the Old Marshall of Manchuria who had been assassinated by the Japanese), to destroy the Communists. Chiang flew to Xian to press his point. Then, in a bizarre episode, Chiang was captured by patriotic officers under the Young Marshall, held prisoner, and only released on the understanding that he would turn his attention to the Japanese invaders. This 'Xian incident' in December 1936 was followed by proposals for a Second United Front, which was finally agreed in September 1937 after the Japanese invasion in the summer of 1937.

The blatant Japanese aggression was accompanied by appalling atrocities. Although most of the Western world sympathized with China, there was no prospect of intervention by the League of Nations. Chiang Kai-shek chose the relatively safe option of retreating to a new headquarters in Chongqing. For their part, the Communists gained a national reputation by harassing the Japanese behind the lines while evolving their own philosophy in Yanan (see Chapter 5). Cooperation in the United Front was less than satisfactory. In any case, after Pearl Harbour (December 1941), with the extension of the war to America and Britain, Chiang Kai-shek could afford to wait for a successful outcome of the anti-Japanese war and preferred to preserve his forces for a later show-down with the Communists. He resisted the blandishments of General Stilwell and others to take a more significant part in the World War. This outward sign of antipatriotism was to be joined with charges of corruption and incompetence in the eventual tally of Chiang's downfall.

In contrast, during the same period, the Communist forces used the war against the Japanese invaders to increase the bases of their power. In 1937 the Communists controlled only a million and a half people in the north-west. By 1945 their fiat extended to over 140 million people.

However, when World War Two ended suddenly, the Nationalists, recognized by both the Americans and the Soviet Union and strongly supported by American arms, seemed to be in an invincible position.

4.1 The New Life Movement

Madame Chiang Kai-shek

New Life was launched at Nanchang in 1934. It was designed, on the basis of a revival of certain virtues of ancient China, to provide the people in the province of Kiangsi with something spiritual and practical to guide them at a time when they needed help to recover from a long period of warfare. It is estimated that they had lost a million lives, had suffered the destruction of the homes of more than a million people, and had sustained property losses valued at a total of a billion and a half dollars. The survivors emerged benumbed, impoverished, and reduced to beggary.

Something more than mere military protection was necessary to restore to mental and physical fitness the people in such a state of mind and health. Four of the cardinal virtues of Old China were recalled as a possible source of reviviscence, and it was determined to essay a practical application of them to present-day conditions. They were 'Li', 'I', 'Lien', and 'Chih', the four principles which, in ancient China, governed personal behavior and relations, assured justice for all classes, inspired integrity in official and business life, and demanded respect for the rights of others.

They were adopted because of our belief that these principles could be successfully employed to satisfy both psychological and physical needs. Practical application of them manifested itself in the teaching of hygiene, the care of homes and children, the cleanliness of the environment, the betterment of means of livelihood, the promotion of communal help, and the worthwhileness and advantages of cooperation. Their ultimate aim was the awakening of the people to a full sense of their individual and collective rights, duties, and responsibilities as citizens, and the offsetting of the inertia caused by hundreds of years of Manchu misrule which, by excluding the masses from participation in state affairs and administration, killed national consciousness and produced an apathy calamitous to national progress and well-being.

The nation at large only became aware of the real significance of New Life after demonstrations of its usefulness in Kiangsi conclusively proved that the interests and well-being of the people constituted the mainspring of national reform. Not only did the province of Kiangsi welcome the progress and prosperity that New Life envisaged and seemed capable of ensuring, but, as soon as its work became known and appreciated by the people of other provinces, the whole nation began to adopt its principles and procedure.

New organizations had to be created to give impetus to a spiritual revival in the devastated areas and to help the unfortunate millions to rebuild their homes and recover a footing for themselves. This initial step having been taken, social centres and schools, cooperative societies, and rural reconstruction agencies soon sprang to life and began to march together in bettering the lot of the struggling people. Each cooperative began its existence as a preparatory society. When it matured, after a year of apprenticeship, it became a fully fledged cooperative; and in due course there grew up credit cooperatives, utility cooperatives, supply cooperatives, marketing cooperatives, and others with mixed functions. Then there developed unions of cooperatives for the improvement of the enterprises and interests of all …

By the summer of 1937 … more than 300 senior secretaries of the New Life Movement, representing important city and provincial branches, assembled at Lushan (Kuling) to undergo a course of rigid training and draw up a programme to be carried out systematically on a nationwide scale. Out of China's 2000-odd Hsien (Counties), more than 1400 formed local New Life organizations. At that time there were 400,000 volunteer workers under the New Life service corps.

Since the beginning of the war, many organizations have, of course, participated in the work of resistance and reconstruction. But New Life has had to help them all, and has consequently been able to exert a beneficial influence through the ever-widening channels ...

A shining example of efficiency is the work done by the War Area Service Corps. It was organized by the Military Council when resistance began, and it was staffed by men trained by New Life ... In 1939, with 168 workers, the Corps established 31 stations covering important military and strategic points and rendered services to 1,445,460 men in uniform. Out of this number 58,601 were given first-aid dressings, 60,799 fed with congee (rice gruel), 725,853 served with tea, 29,305 provided with sleeping accommodation, 13,148 letters were written for the disabled, and other forms of service, such as entertainments, etc., were given to 557,754 wounded.

Another service that reflects the New Life spirit is the Wounded Soldiers League. Its chief duty is the distribution of the Generalissimo's cash awards to the wounded. The Generalissimo, with a deep sympathy and consideration for those of his men who were wounded during the heroic fight against Japanese aggression, issued an order on 25 September 1937 to distribute awards to all wounded officers and men ...

A third kind of service sponsored by New Life is the Friends of the Wounded. Its very name caught the imagination and heart of Chinese patriots. A campaign held in Chungking in commemoration of the 6th anniversary of New Life met with surprising results. Figuring on the basis of 100,000 wounded soldiers in various army hospitals, the movement aimed at soliciting 100,000 'friends'. The goal of the campaign was to provide a 'friend' for each wounded soldier. To become a 'friend', one paid a friendship fee of $1 (Chinese), or more, and pledged service to the wounded. By the end of a month, the campaign had brought in no less than 654,741 'friends', with a total of $1,332,505.74 in cash, which was 554 per cent over the top. Names of more friends and more funds are still coming in.

**Source: Madame Chiang Kai-shek, *China Shall Rise Again*
(London: Hurst and Blackett, 1941), pp. 209–15**

4.2 Communications regarding the Xian incident December 1936

FOR THE PERUSAL OF THE HONORABLE MR KAI-SHEK, I DECEMBER 1936

The Communist Party, the Soviet, and the Red Army have, since August of last year, repeatedly asked you to end the civil war and reunite to resist Japan. Since the publication of this proposal, all social groups, regardless of party affiliation, have responded favorably. Yet you, sir, have insisted on your own views from beginning to end, first ordering a campaign of 'encirclement and suppression,' which led to the Battle of Zhiluozhen last winter. This spring the Red Army crossed the Yellow River in the east for the purpose of going to the Hebei–Chahar front, but again you stopped us in the valley of the Fen River. Since we were unwilling to see our national defence forces make meaningless sacrifices, we commanded the army to cross the river to the west to seek alternative routes to fighting the Japanese while, at the same time, issuing a declaration calling on you to come to your senses … Although we have ordered forces to suspend any attacks against your forces and continued to retreat step by step, even this failed to modify your long-standing sentiments of hostility. For the sake of our self-defence and the preservation of the armed forces fighting the Japanese and the anti-Japanese base areas, we had no choice but to fight the Battle of Xhanchengbao in Dingbin on 21 November. Now, the people of the whole country have demonstrated their utmost fury toward the Japanese bandits and the keenest support for the officers and soldiers fighting the Japanese in Suiyuan, but you, sir, devote all your energies to the civil war of mutual slaughter. As we face them on the battlefield, we know full well the emotions of the officers and soldiers of your forces in the north-west. Their feelings are no different from ours; they urgently want to end the suicidal civil war and go to the front to fight the Japanese as soon as possible … At the moment, the determination of the national strategy needs only one word from you. If the civil war is ended today, the Red Army and the massive force sent here to destroy the Communists would leave the battlefield of mutual butchery tomorrow to go to the front to fight the Japanese. The forces defending our country in Suiyuan will increase by 10 times instantly. All it requires is a change of mind and a change of heart on your part, and our country can be avenged; our country's territory can be defended; our lost land can be recovered. You will also become a glorious hero in the resistance against Japan, respected by all and honored forever by history … We are genuinely reluctant to see our future generations tell one another that it was Chiang Kai-shek and no one else who destroyed China. Instead, we want to see our future generations look upon you, sir, as a hero, who, after amending his errors in time, saved the country and its people. It is often said that those who have sinned should not try to make amends by praying. It is also said that one must put down the butcher's knife to become a Buddha. We hope that you, sir, understand clearly which alternative to choose. The enemy has driven deep into our country and brought the most devastating calamity upon us. Our words are as strong as our hearts are heavy. Having made this appeal, we eagerly await your instructions.

Respectfully submitted by Mao Zedong, Zhu De, Zhang Guotao, Zhou Enlai, Wang Jiaxiang, Peng Dehuai, He Long, Ren Bishi, Lin Biao, Liu Bocheng, Ye Jianging, Zhang Yunyu, Xu Xiangqian, Chen Changhao, Xu Haidong, Dong Zhentang, Luo Binghui, Shao Shiping, and Guo Hongtao, on behalf of the Chinese People's Red Army.

TELEGRAM FROM MAO ZEDONG AND ZHOU ENLAI TO ZHANG XUELIANG, 13 DECEMBER 1936, AT NOON

FOR THE PERUSAL OF ELDER BROTHER LI YI

We are in receipt of your telegram dated in the early morning of the 12th day of the month.

The fact that the prime culprit has been arrested makes for happiness shared far and wide. As for the current tasks, in terms of the whole country they have been expressed in the telegram to (Pan) Hannian, which we had the honor of submitting to you yesterday, and beg that you transmit to Shanghai; in terms of the north-west, we herewith describe them briefly, and respectfully request that you consider the matter:

1   Deploy the main forces in Tongguan, Fengxiang, and Pingliang, the most important being Tongguan, and firmly resist Fan Songfu.

2   Call upon the popular masses of Xi'an and the north-west to rise up in support of this magnanimous act for the public good and do the same throughout the country. Your younger brothers and the rest of us believe that only by basing all actions on the popular masses will the Xi'an uprising firmly develop toward victory.

3   It would be best to place under arrest immediately or to drive out the fascist elements within the armed forces, and carry out broad and thoroughgoing political mobilization throughout the army, proclaim to all officers and soldiers Mr Chiang's crimes in selling out the country and harming the people, and politically unite the whole army. This is one of the most pressing tasks at the moment.

4   When the troops of Hu (Zongnan), Zeng (Wanzhong), and Guan (Linzheng) press towards the south, the Red Army has decided to act in concert with the forces of our elder brother, from the side and the rear, and to destroy them resolutely. Please inform us by telegram at any time as to how we should proceed ... Enlai plans to come to Xi'an to discuss with our elder brothers the plans for the future and would like to request that you send a plane to Yan'an to fetch him, and that elder brother Yang Hucheng secretly inform by telegram the troops in Yan'an for protection. We eagerly await your reply as to how this can be arranged. Please order your radio station to maintain contact with us at all times.

Your younger brothers, [Mao Ze] Dong and [Zhou En] lai, bow respectively.

TELEGRAM FROM THE RED ARMY COMMAND TO THE GUOMINDANG AND TO THE NATIONAL GOVERNMENT ON THE XIAN INCIDENT, 15 DECEMBER 1936

To the gentlemen of the Guomindang and of the National Government in Nanjing, for their perusal.

The Xi'an incident and the startling news of Mr Chiang's detention were quite unexpected. This was, however, the result of Mr Chiang's three grossly erroneous policies of capitulation in foreign affairs, use of military force in domestic affairs, and oppressing the people. Zhang (Xueliang) and Yang (Hucheng), both of whom are members of the Central Executive Committee of your honorable party and leaders of the 'Suppress-the-Communists' Army, have also firmly requested that the campaign to 'suppress the Communists' be halted, and that everyone join together to resist Japan. Looking at the eight articles of their proclamation, these are indeed the words of the people of the whole country ... Consequently, if you gentlemen should wish to disassociate yourselves from Mr Chiang and from the pro-Japanese clique, you need only say that you have summoned up your resolve and decided to ... remove Mr Chiang from office, and hand him over to the judgment of the citizens. Unite all parties, all factions, all walks of life, and all armies; organize a united front government ... Let freedom of speech blossom, unban patriotic publications, release patriotic prisoners, order all the armies engaged in civil war to go immediately to Shanxi and Suiyuan to resist the Japanese bandits. Turn darkness into light, and change misfortune into great good fortune. If this is done, then all of us, incapable as we are, shall be willing to lead the 200,000-strong masses of the People's Red Army to join hands with the armed forces of your honorable party, and march forward together to the battlefield of the National Revolution, to fight in a bloody battle for the freedom and liberation of our motherland. Otherwise, not only will it be impossible for the people of an entire nation, including the patriots within your honorable party, merely to sit and watch the loss of the country and the extinction of the race, we as well shall certainly not watch from the sidelines with arms folded. Having submitted this telegram, we look forward to receiving enlightened instruction from you.

Mao Zedong, Zhu De, Zhou Enlai, Zhang Guotaong, Lin Zuhan, Xu Teli, Wang Jiase, Peng Dehuai, He Long, Ye Jianying, Ren Bishi, Lin Biao, Xu Xiangqian, Chen Changhao, Xu Haidong (other names deleted).

REGARDING THE CIRCUMSTANCES SURROUNDING THE RELEASE OF CHIANG KAI-SHEK, 25 DECEMBER 1936, AT MIDNIGHT

Peng [Dehuai] and Ren [Bishi]
The principle of restoring Chiang's freedom, under five conditions, for the purpose of transforming the orientation of the whole situation, is the result of negotiations we proposed. This has been completely accepted by Chiang and Nanjing's left-wing representatives. Last night I sent a telegram to Enlai to the effect that Chiang should not be let go before they make sure that the prerequisite conditions are met and that the situation has developed to the point that there would be no wavering after his release. But they have already released Chiang Kai-shek today, and Song Ziwen, Zhang Xueliang, and Song Meiling flew today to Luoyang on the same plane. Judging from the circumstances, there are advantages to releasing Chiang, but whether or not the advantages have been realized is a matter that remains to be confirmed subsequently according to the evidence.

The field army should still concentrate its forces in Xianyang immediately.

Mao Zedong.

A STATEMENT ON CHIANG KAI-SHEK'S PROCLAMATION OF THE 26TH, 28 DECEMBER 1936

According to a telegram from the Hongse Zhonghua agency, yesterday the Communist Party organ, Douzheng, published a statement by Comrade Mao Zedong commenting on the proclamation made by Chiang Kai-shek in Luoyang on the 26th (that is, the so-called admonition to Zhang and Yang), the main idea of which is as follows:

In Xi'an Mr Chiang Kai-shek accepted the demand for resistance to Japan put forward by Zhang (Xueliang) and Yang (Hucheng) and the people of the north-west, and he has ordered his troops conducting the civil war to withdraw from the provinces of Shaanxi and Gansu. This marks the beginning of Mr Chiang's reversal of his erroneous policy of the last decade.

N.B. Chiang Kai-shek always denied making this commitment.

Source: 'Communications regarding the Xian Incident'.
In S. R. Schram, ed., *Mao's Road to Power: Revolutionary Writings*, 1912–49, Vol. 5
(Armonk, New York, M. E. Sharpe, 2000), pp. 458–9, 539–40, 547–9, 566, 569–72

4.3 Chiang Kai-shek on the Xian incident

Chiang Kai-shek

Chiang Kai-shek's version of the events, published in 1957.

To go back to the time when war with Japan seemed inevitable, the Chinese Government tried to reach a settlement with the Chinese Communists at home. My view was that the Communist armed forces must be disbanded before the Communist problem could be considered as a political issue and solved as such ...

On 5 May 1936, the Chinese Communists issued a circular telegram calling for 'cessation of hostilities and holding of peace negotiations'. Whereupon, Chou, as a representative of the Chinese Communist Party, and Pan Han-nien, as a representative of the Communist International, came to Shanghai ... The government put up to the Chinese Communists the following four points:

1   Abide by the Three People's Principles.
2   Obey Generalissimo Chiang Kai-shek's orders
3   Abolish the 'Red Army' and integrate it into the National Army.
4   Abrogate the Soviets and reorganize them as local governments.

After protracted discussions, they finally accepted these four points. Understanding had been reached on practically all the issues. I was then in Sian. All that remained to be done was to get my final approval as soon as I returned to Nanking.

During this period, the Communists had started a propaganda offensive for 'peace', and made Shensi province their first objective. They had established contact with Chang Hsueh-liang and Yang Hu-cheng, two military commanders in Shensi. Leaflets advocating 'Fight the Japanese instead of the Communists' had made their appearance among the Manchurian army under Chang ... Unless timely measures were taken, the situation could lead to a rebellion. Therefore, I went to Sian in the hope that my presence there would constitute a stabilizing factor. It was also my plan to call all officers to a conference at the end of the year, at which I would announce the government's policies on the continued prosecution of the military campaign against the Communists and on the question of armed resistance against Japan. I had every intention to expose the Communists' peace offensive so that these officers would not be taken in.

On 12 December, in the dead of the night, I was suddenly seized in Sian by men under Chang Hsueh-liang and Yang Hu-cheng. I instantly realized that these two men must have acted under the strong influence of the Chinese Communists. Therefore, when Chang came to see me in the quarters where I was detained, I simply admonished him by saying: 'Either for your own sake or for the sake of the nation, the only thing for you to do is to repent at once and escort me back to Nanking. You must not fall into the trap set by the Communists. Repent now before it is too late'.

In these circumstances, Chang did not dare to bring up the eight demands that they had prepared. All he said was that the situation was complicated and that it was not as simple as I had put it. He begged me to control my anger and hear him through. I cut him short and forbade him from touching on any political subjects. It was not until the third day that Chang finally mumbled, partly to persuade and partly to implore, the so-called eight demands he and the others had previously agreed upon among themselves. He also said that all I had to do was sign my name and he would at once escort me back to Nanking. In reply, I said: 'So long as I am a captive, there can be absolutely no discussion'. At the time I thought that, even if Chang and the others should come to their senses, the Communists would seize upon this rare opportunity either to force me to accept the demands or to kill me. For to the Communists this meant life or death. As I was prepared to sacrifice myself if necessary, I flatly refused to discuss any political conditions with the rebels. The government likewise ignored the preposterous demands made by Chang and Yang and promptly decided to send an army against them.

On 22 December my wife suddenly arrived in Sian. The first thing I said to her when we met was: 'For the past ten days the rebels have been putting all kinds of pressure on me. Were I to accept their terms they would send me back to Nanking. You have come to be with me in my hour of peril. I believe you have done this out of consideration for our national interests and not for personal reasons alone. National interests must come first. If the rebels should ask you to persuade me to sign any terms you must absolutely refuse. We would rather die than accede to these demands'. I am proud to say my wife was equally and similarly determined. She would never persuade me to do anything against my principles. 'I am here to share your fate', she avowed. Three days later, on Christmas Day, we safely returned to Nanking without having to subscribe to any conditions ...

Communist front organizations, namely, 'Third Party', the 'National Salvation Association', and the 'Students' Federation', carried out the initial reactionary propaganda to instigate rebellious actions by Chang Hsueh-liang and Yang Hu-cheng ... Not being Communists, these people were able openly to spread rumours not only among the civilians but also among the armed forces. They even subjected Chang Hsueh-liang and the troops under him to an intensive propaganda, and they kept on provoking Chang, who, being torn between 'suppression of the Communists' and 'resistance against Japan', finally succumbed to this incessant offensive by the neutralists. Chang Hsueh-liang, on his part, would never admit that he had been influenced by Communist instigations. He said he was merely anxious to fight Japan so as to avenge the loss of Manchuria, and his original idea was to make use of the strength of the Communists to fight Japan.

Chang Hsueh-liang, in his own account of the events leading up to this Sian incident, said that he had fallen for the Communist intrigue not because it was particularly effective but because of the existence of internal contradictions in our own midst. This had created an opening for Communist infiltration. Chang recalled how he had assumed military command when he was still in his twenties, how he had taken part in civil wars, and how he had succeeded in turning erstwhile foes into friends. He himself originally had fought the government, but finally, for the sake of national unity, he had declared his allegiance to the government. He thought the Communists could be dealt with in the same way, since they were also Chinese.

**Source: Chiang Kai-shek, *A Summing-up at Seventy: Soviet Russia in China*
(London: Harrap, 1957), pp. 72–9**

4.4 Zhu De's comments on the United Front

Agnes Smedley

Agnes Smedley was a left-wing American journalist who wrote for the Manchester Guardian *and the* Frankfurter Zeitung. *She visited Communist headquarters in Yanan. In this extract from her book, Ms Smedley explains Communist proposals for the United Front and records Zhu De's comments on the situation.*

General Chu, Mao Tse-tung, and their staffs were in almost continuous conference in Yenan. In February 1937, when Chou Enlai headed a Communist delegation to Nanking, Chu and Mao, representing the Red Army and the Communist Party respectively, addressed a long telegram to the Central Committee of the Kuomintang, then in session in Nanking, in which they appealed for a national united front and offered to make important concessions provided the Kuomintang introduced democratic reforms throughout the country. If the united front were formed, they wired, the Red Army would change its name and place itself under the command of the Central Military Council, provided it were given the same treatment as other armies. In order to draw every element of the country into the anti-Japanese struggle, they offered to stop the confiscation of landlord estates and transform the north-western Soviet regions into a Special Administrative District administered by the Communists but under the direction of the central government. They declared their intention to carry out fully the principles and policies of Sun Yat-sen in this region.

In return for these concessions, the Communist Party and the Red Army urged the Kuomintang to give the masses something worth fighting and dying for by restoring civil liberties to them. They should also release all political prisoners and grant the people the right to organize and arm themselves for the anti-Japanese struggle.

However, it was months before the united front began to take concrete form. Interpreting the Communist offers as surrender, the Kuomintang tried to use the situation to destroy the Red Army, insisting that four of its seven divisions be disbanded and the other three reorganized into a new army staffed by Kuomintang officers. The Communists argued against the disbandment of any of their troops, and suggested a brotherly exchange of officers between the Red and Kuomintang armies – a suggestion that caused the Kuomintang to drop the subject like a hot potato.

Talking with me about these Kuomintang manoeuvres, General Chu declared:

> Our army would be destroyed and there would be no resistance to the Japanese at all if we accepted the Kuomintang proposals. Chiang and his clique do not really want to fight the Japanese, yet Chiang realizes that, if he does not, he will be swept from the stage of history by our own and other anti-Japanese armies, and by the Chinese people. Our army may have to accept subsidies and ammunition for only three of our divisions, but we will not disband the other four because war with Japan will most certainly start soon and all manpower and national resources of the country must be mobilized for victory. The Kuomintang has refused us new guns of any calibre, and we will get no clothing, blankets, or medicine; at best we will get ammunition and money for three divisions.
>
> After the war begins, however, all our troops will go to the front. We will root ourselves in the people as we have always done, and mobilize, train, arm, and educate them. We will survive and fight.

Shortly after this conversation, a Kuomintang military delegation arrived in the north-west to inspect the Red Army, then came on to Yenan where I also had gone when the army of Hu Tsung-nan took over Sian.

During the week's stay of the Kuomintang military delegation in Yenan, I saw General Chu in the role of host to generals and colonels who had fought him for ten years. Instead of the blunt, simple soldier I had learnt to know, he now appeared with all the graces of the old social order, yet without any of its indirectness and obsequiousness. Through his graciousness ran a cold stream of dignity, gravity, and self-confidence. At the first breakfast of welcome to the Kuomintang officers, which I also attended, he welcomed them in these unadorned words:

> This is a historic moment marking the end of the decade of bloody fratricide in which millions of the best sons and daughters of our country have died. Had this national united front been formed years ago, China's manpower and national resources would have been preserved, none of our territory would have been lost, and we would today be strong enough to meet the Japanese on equal terms …

When I asked General Chu later what the Red Army troops thought of the united front, he spoke with the utmost frankness:

> Our troops are workers and peasants. They're not intellectual, cultured men. Their ideology is Red Army ideology. As peasants and workers they have hated landlords and militarists all their lives. They knew how to work before, but it is now very difficult for them to be called upon to work with every person willing to fight Japanese imperialism. To retrain them, we have called hundreds of cadres to Yenan to pass through special training courses in Kangta (the Red Army College) on the principles and tactics of the united front. After completing their courses, they will return to the army and others will be trained. Our army must be a model in carrying out the united front.

**Source: Agnes Smedley, *The Great Road: The Life and Times of Chu Teh*
(London: John Calder, 1958), pp. 354–6**

4.5 Japanese atrocities

4.5a Extract from the documents of the Nanking safety zone, 16–19 December 1937

When the Japanese overran Nanjing in the winter of 1937, an International Committee of Westerners (British, American, German, and Danish) initially thanked the Japanese commander for sparing the safety zone. The Committee took responsibility for Chinese civilians within the zone. As the Japanese soldiers ran amok, the Committee recorded the atrocities and forwarded their record to the Japanese.

57. On 16 December, seven girls (whose ages ranged from 16 to 21) were taken away from the Military College. Five returned. Each girl was raped six or seven times daily (reported 18 December). On 17 December at 11 p.m. the soldiers climbed over the wall and took away two girls but they returned in 30 minutes. (Tsan Yuen-kwan)

On 17 December Mr Rabe reports his house was visited by about 15 Japanese soldiers. Some of them scaled the wall and came in with drawn bayonets, robbing his submanager Mr

Han Siang-lin of his money and some business passports. The money was taken out of the inside pocket of his coat. A complete list of what had been stolen was given to Major Y. Nagai. In spite of Major Nagai's being kind enough to write a big poster forbidding Japanese soldiers to enter Mr Rabe's house, which poster was stuck on the door of his house, and in spite of the fact that Mr Rabe is a German subject and has four German swastika flags flying on his property, two Japanese soldiers came in at about 6 o'clock just when Mr Rabe returned to his home. He found one of the soldiers partly undressed just about to rape a girl. Both these soldiers were ordered to get out and disappeared the same way they came – over the wall. A motor car was removed from Mr Rabe's house against a receipt reading as follows: 'I thank you present, Japanese army, K. Sato.' A proper receipt which was asked for was refused. Value of motor car $300. (Rabe)

While Major Y. Nagai was kind enough to call on our Chairman Mr Rabe at his house at Siao Tao Yuen, a neighbor right opposite called for help because four Japanese soldiers had entered his house and one of them was raping one of the women. Major Nagai caught the man and slapped his face and ordered him out. The other three soldiers ran when they saw the Major coming. (Rabe)

December 19 at 11.30 a.m. Mr Hatz reports that he found two Japanese soldiers in a dugout at the house next door to our headquarters on Ninghai Road, who were trying to rape some of the women. There were about 20 women in the dugout. Hearing the women yelling for help, Mr Hatz went into the dugout and chased these honorable soldiers out. (Hatz)

61. December 19th. About 10 o'clock this morning Dr Bates, Mr Fitch and I went from interviewing Mr Tanaka about these disorders to the University Middle School to see how they had fared during the night. We found that three girls had been taken during the night and one raped by three soldiers in the gatehouse. As we came towards the gate to leave, but still in the compound, Miss Pearl Wu-Bromley came in the gate followed by three Japanese soldiers on foot and one lower officer on horseback. We tried to stop the soldiers and told Miss Bromley to get in our car. The officer objected and pushed his horse in the way of our leaving, but his horse became frightened at the car so we got out the gate and took Miss Bromley to the Japanese Embassy to ask where she would be safe in this city today. Miss Bromley is a returned student from America with the Phi Beta Kappa key. She decided to go to the University Hospital to help them. (Smythe)

62. On 18 December the Refugee Home at the Military College reports: on the 16th, 200 men were taken away and only five returned; 17th, 26 men were taken away; 18th, 30 men were taken away. Looting: money, luggage, and one bag of rice, over 400 sheets of hospital bedding. Besides, one man was killed (aged 25), and one old woman was pushed down and died after 20 minutes. (Tsan Yuen-kwan)

On Ninghai Road, half a tin of kerosene oil was taken away from a boy by force and the boy bitterly beaten when asked to carry the same. At Yin Yang Ying at about 8 a.m. a Japanese grasped at food freely. At Pin Chen Shan No. 6, one pig was taken away by Japanese soldiers. A number of ponies have been taken away by five Japanese soldiers. Several girls living in No. 121 Ho Lu were raped after all the men who live together with them as refugees were chased away. One tea house master's daughter, aged 17 years, was raped by seven Japanese soldiers and died on the 18th. Last night, three Japanese soldiers raped four girls between six and ten o'clock. In No. 5 Moh Kan Lu, one old man reported his daughter was raped badly by several Japanese soldiers. Three girls were taken away by Japanese soldiers last night from the Girls' College and returned to No. 8 Tao Ku Hsin Tsun in bad condition this morning. In

Pin An Shan, a girl was raped by three Japanese soldiers and died. Raping, robbery, and searching are happening along the Yin Yang Ying. (Reported on 18 December, Ma Sie-hwa)

There are about 540 refugees crowded in Nos 83 and 85 on the Canton Road. Since 13 inst. up to the 17th, those houses have been searched and robbed many many times a day by Japanese soldiers in groups of three to five. Today, the soldiers are looting the places mentioned above continually, and all the jewelry, money, watches, and clothes of any sort are taken away. At present, women of younger ages are forced to go with the soldiers every night who send motor trucks to take them and release them the next morning. More than 30 women and girls have been raped. The women and children are crying all the night. Conditions inside the compound are worse than we can describe. Please give us help. Yours truly, *All the refugees*. (Translation signed by Han Siang-Lin)

65. One motor car of Ford make belonging to Mr Zeimssen, of German nationality, has been taken by three Japanese soldiers soon after 6.00 p.m. on 18 December 1937 from Lang Yah Lu No. 11. (Signed by Kung Ching-fah)

**Source: Shuhsi Hsu, ed., *Documents of the Nanking Safety Zone*
(Shanghai: Kelly and Walsh Ltd, 1939), pp. 34–7**

4.5b Japanese atrocities described

Madame Chiang Kai-shek

Wherever the Japanese army has gone, it has left behind it charred and mutilated bodies, ruined homes, and blood-soaked earth. It has demolished by bomb and fire every school and college it has come across. Because it says they are hotbeds of resistance, its first objective is always the annihilation of institutes of learning. This picture is no figment of the imagination; no usual wartime atrocity story. It is stark and terrible reality – vouched for and verified by many of your own missionaries who have been eyewitnesses of these ghastly deeds. One American missionary told me that he saw with his own eyes Japanese soldiers line up hundreds of our able-bodied peasants who had taken refuge in the safety zone at Nanking, tie them together by the wrists in groups of 50, and march them off to face firing squads manning machine guns and bayonets.

Another missionary told me that women and young girls who had taken refuge in missionary compounds were dragged out again and again by the Japanese military to be violated. In one compound, in one night, thirty-five different parties of Japanese soldiers entered the buildings and did their nefarious deeds. What happened to the women and girls in outlying country districts, where they could not even have the protection of a foreign mission compound, beggars imagination ...

The higher authorities of the Japanese army are not guiltless of what is now happening, because not only are they fully aware of the shocking horrors, but they themselves are actually participants in amazing organized national gangsterism, which they naturally find vastly profitable. Everything with any intrinsic value has been taken, including furniture, iron and metalware, bedclothing, and even warm garments from the backs of the people. They have deliberately deprived the survivors of these terror-stricken regions of every means of livelihood in the hope that China will perish. Consequently, we now have millions of refugees fleeing from one section of the country to another, with their pitiful belongings under their arms or on their backs, dragging their children with them or losing them in the continuous assaults made upon them in their flight. Thousands of our children have been deported to Korea, Formosa, and Japan, to be brought up as future enemies of the Chinese race. The Japanese aim to train these children to hate everything Chinese, and to glorify only the Emperor of the Rising Sun. Tens of thousands of other children have been mercilessly slaughtered as part of Japan's criminal effort to destroy the future manpower of China.

Swept by flames, deluged by blood, stripped by looters – you have a panorama of a ravaged, bleeding country. And what is the purpose of this mass massacring, this meticulous marauding of China by the Japanese? Why this barbarism – this unleashing of unparalleled terror? It is inspired by the hope that they will be able to erect on the ashes of what was China a Japanese continental empire. An empire to dominate the Pacific, to have a determining voice in the foreign policies of Western nations, and to be, indeed, the overlord of the world.

Source: Madame Chiang Kai-shek, *China in Peace and War*
(London: Hurst and Blackett, 1940), pp. 170–2

4.5c Criticizing a Japanese history textbook

The Asahi Evening News, 5 March 2001, reports on 137 revisions to history text after protests from China and South Korea.

Authors of a history textbook that infuriated Asian neighbors for passages that justified Japan's wartime aggression have rewritten 137 sections on the basis of government recommendations, sources said Sunday.

The Ministry of Education, Culture, Sports, Science, and Technology requested the 137 revisions ...

Most of the revisions of the textbook involved depictions of modern history that have raised criticism from the Republic of Korea (South Korea) and China, the sources said.

The revised draft of the textbook will undergo a final screening by the Ministry's Textbook Authorization Research Council this month, and is likely to be given the go-ahead for publication by the Education Minister, the sources said.

The textbook, to be used in junior high schools, was compiled by a group called Atarashii Rekishi Kyokasho wo Tsukuru-kai (Society to Make a New History Textbook). The group is headed by Professor Kanji Nishio of the University of Electrocommunications.

Ministry officials said they requested the revisions to 'balance' the contents of the textbook in line with a clause in the criteria for textbook screening. The clause requires the contents to 'make considerations from the standpoint of international understanding and harmony in depictions of modern history concerning neighboring Asian nations.'

Although the textbook's publisher, Fuso-sha, declined to comment on details of the revisions, a spokesman acknowledged that the changes were made in light of the clause.

'The textbook's contents are now different from those that came under fire from South Korea and China,' the spokesman said.

Nishio, who is known for his nationalistic views, said: 'We went along with requests for revisions in parts that could be described as humiliating. But our ideas, which are different from the Marxist view of history, still remain in the textbook.'

Fuso-sha first submitted the draft to the Ministry for screening in April last year and was told about the requested revisions in December. Of those, about 100 involved passages on modern history, the sources said.

The publisher submitted a revised version to the Ministry and was again told to change the sections that drew heavy criticism from Japan's neighbors.

In February, the publisher submitted the final version with all revisions according to Ministry specifications, sources said.

Nishio and his group have contended that history textbooks currently in use are 'masochistic.' Criticism soared and protests were arranged, particularly in South Korea and China, when reports surfaced about plans to publish the textbook.

Critics said that the group's textbook 'distorted history' and justified and romanticized Japan's wartime aggression.

Concerning the Nanking Massacre in China, the original draft said: 'Because it was war there could have been some killings. But they were not of a similar sort to the Holocaust.'

This passage does not appear in the revised version, the sources said.

Source: *Asahi Evening News*, (Tokyo) 5 March 2001, pp. 1–2

4.6 The Generalissimo and Madame Chiang Kai-shek

Owen Lattimore

Chiang Kai-shek asked Roosevelt for a personal adviser. Owen Lattimore was recommended as a China expert who was anti-Japanese and also, as Chiang requested, had no previous Washington connections.

Having known Chiang Kai-shek personally, I still think that he was a great man. He certainly was no saint, but neither was he a total villain. He was a man who was not only patriotic, but, according to his own lights, revolutionary. He wanted to change Chinese society. He had a mixed career of great success and important mistakes, such as the 1927 coup d'etat against the Communists. Because of this there was not in fact a united China to resist the Japanese aggression when the invasion of the north-east came about in 1931. In spite of all this, Chiang Kai-shek was the rallying point in the war against the Japanese. In one of my conversations with Chou En-lai in Chungking, Chou himself said very emphatically that Chiang was essential to the resistance against Japan. While the Communists wanted him to be more effective in the national front, that in no way implied that they wanted Chiang removed from power.

It was not simply that Chiang sat back when he should have been active in resistance. He thought the way to save China was to create a trained, organized elite; and through his educated elite he intended to give the right orders to the common people and see to it that these orders were carried out. He did not show to the peasantry that he was offering them something of personal advantage to fight for. A part of his mistake was in the structure and the nature of his own background. He had been trained first in the old Military Academy in Paotingfu, then in Japan, and later he became the military head of the revolutionary, or semi-revolutionary, Whampoa Military Academy in Canton. He wound up with an army of professional officers, mainly from the landlord class, in command of troops who were badly paid, forced conscripts ...

He also once said to me, however, that, after the war, China's agriculture would have to be collectivized in order to set free manpower for a planned new industrialization. Because of China's shortage of capital, land would have to be taken from the landlords without compensation. 'Just the same as in the Soviet Union,' he concluded, 'only *I* shall be doing it, not Stalin' ...

The relationship between Chiang Kai-shek and Madame Chiang was something like that of political allies who do not entirely trust each other. I think that it was also for political reasons that Chiang converted to Christianity. He refused to be converted in advance, however, in order to marry a Christian wife, so it was some time after their marriage before he announced his conversion. They were Christian enough to maintain liaison with missionaries, especially the kind of missionaries who were influential in the United States. Madame Chiang very quickly realized the political usefulness of showing off their Christianity to get the support of US voters ...

The value and importance of Madame Chiang has been greatly exaggerated, especially by Americans. They took her as the symbol of modern China, and there were those who were simple-minded enough to say that, after all, Chiang Kai-shek was just a warlord by origin and did not even speak English, while his wife had an American education and spoke English brilliantly; therefore, she must be the real brains of Chiang Kai-shek's government. Nothing of the kind. The two were united more politically than affectionately, I should say. While Madame Chiang did not do anything to stop the people from believing that *she* was the clever one, in fact Chiang was able to make good use of her because of her standing in the United States. She did have a high standing, but it had only limited value.

It is true that, for a man like Chiang Kai-shek, half-feudal and militaristic and half-modern in his mentality, and in the China of that day with its mixture of modern and archaic elements, his wife and her relatives automatically formed political factions among themselves – competing factions, each with its own allies and rivals. Nevertheless, she certainly never controlled the planning or execution of either his international policy or his policy inside China, though such tasks as drafting cables to Currie [Roosevelt's assistant] were, of course, handled by her because they were in English and the code was in her hands ...

Chiang's attitude towards the Communists was very different from that of his wife. Madame Chiang had a simple-minded American anti-Communist and anti-Soviet attitude. It was after she had retired to bed that, to my great astonishment, Chiang said: 'After the war the question of the Chinese Communists will have to be settled by military force, but the Soviet Union is different. We cannot negotiate with the Chinese Communists because the same words have different meanings to us and them. But we can rely on Stalin. He keeps his word.'

In fact, the Soviet Union never supplied the Chinese Communists with so much as a revolver. All airplanes, guns, and ammunition went to Chiang. The Soviet line was that they were supporting China as a nation against the Japanese imperialists, and in this situation it would be totally improper for them to do anything that could be regarded as playing Chinese domestic politics. Later, Chiang may have changed what he had to say about the Soviet Union and Stalin, and in his memoirs, which I have not read, I am told that he attributed the whole story of Chinese Communism to the Soviet Union. He was by that time totally dependent on Washington. I am only repeating what he told me in one of our tête-à-tête evening conversations in Chungking, quite soon after my arrival ...

CHIANG KAI-SHEK AND HIS GOVERNMENT

Though in the West there is an exaggerated impression even to this day that Chiang Kai-shek was a dictator, he never really was one. Being a Chinese military politician who had come up on top, he had to keep balancing one faction against another. He had also to bear in mind the geography of China: 'In which province did each important general have his power base in money and manpower and how had his interests been affected by the Japanese invasion?' When he gave an order to a general, he had to think first: 'Is this an order this man will obey, or will he sabotage it?' ...

For Chiang Kai-shek, there was also the problem of getting the right kind of information. I have already mentioned that Madame Chiang had no confidence in the Soviet advisers in Chungking. The opinions of the Soviet advisers had to be filtered to Chiang Kai-shek through reports from his own general staff, and the latter did not like to admit that they were militarily inferior to the Soviets and had to rely on Soviet advisers. Therefore, they always depreciated the Soviet advisers in their reports to the Generalissimo ... In the Chinese manner, each general who rose to a high position tried to create his own power base by appointing his own men, largely his own relatives or people who had been disciples at Whampoa Military Academy. Therefore, they were jealous of one another and jealous of the Soviets. In these conditions, how could Chiang Kai-shek get realistic reports?

As there were so many competing factions in Chungking, it was Chiang's canny practice to use several channels of communication to guide his own Washington policy. One was his own Foreign Office; the second was his ambassador Hu Shih and also TV Soong in Washington; and the third channel was myself. He always, and not only in an emergency situation, used more than one channel so that he could play off one faction against another ...

Like perhaps all dictators or would-be dictators, Chiang Kai-shek relied very heavily on secret intelligence. Also, as in all such situations, he kept several intelligence services going in rivalry with one another in order to avoid becoming captive of his own intelligence services. They would leak information on one another, and in that way he would get to know what they were really up to ...

Parallel with this, he developed his political Intelligence Service, through which he organized a youth movement within the Kuomintang, and placed his own men in key positions in his intelligence service. In this way he would know very quickly if any faction was developing in the Kuomintang that might challenge the ascendancy of Chiang Kai-shek ...

In Chungking you had the paradox that on the one hand there was Chiang Kai-shek's secret services, such as Tai Li and the Ch'en brothers who were persecuting and tracking down leftists, and on the other hand you had a significant number of leftists who were being protected by highly placed people in the Kuomintang administration. I did not fully realize this at the time I was in Chungking, but looking back it seems to me much clearer what was going on. The general assumption of the top Kuomintang people, even before Pearl Harbor, was that sooner or later the United States would be in the war. Then the primary work of defeating Japan would be done by the Americans. China must get ready for post-war planning. In every ministry that dealt with the United States and with economic matters of post-war development, there was somebody who was either a Marxist or a follower of Marxism ...

What it is essential to understand about the Communists in 'sensitive' positions under Chiang Kai-shek, the great anti-Communist, is that the Generalissimo and his most trusted supporters assumed that, after the war, China would be dependent on the United States not only for capitalist economic support but also for capitalist expertise. That made it imperative to have experts who knew what made American capitalism tick ... Who had studied that side of the world? Principally the Marxists, who were for ever talking about 'capitalist contradictions' ...

I would say that, in spite of everything, Chiang Kai-shek was a genuine patriot. He was highly nationalistic and certainly responsible for holding China together at the critical moment, for example, of the defection of Wang Ching-wei to the Japanese in 1938. At that time, the defeatist pressure on him was very strong, and, if he had not stood out against them, a considerable number of influential generals and politicians might have made their peace with the Japanese.

Source: Owen Lattimore, China Memoirs
(Tokyo: University of Tokyo Press, 1990), pp. 135–6, 137–40, 143–9

4.7 Excerpts from the diary of Joseph Stilwell, 1942 and 1944

General Joseph W. Stilwell was Commander of the United States Forces in China.

April 7 1942 Chiang Kai-shek at 12.30. Tu (Yu-ming), Lo (Cho-ying), Madame Chiang Kai-shek, and I (photos with the Chiang Kai-sheks). Then talk with the boys, who were told in plain words that I was the boss – that they would take orders without question – that I would handle the British, that I had full power to promote, relieve, and punish any officer in the Chinese Expeditionary Force. (Jesus.) This is a new note in Chinese history. Chiang Kai-shek has come around to my contention: i.e., it is necessary to fight where we are, to hold the oil and food; we *must* fight the decisive battle now. Lo Cho-ying and Tu Yu-Ming [Nationalist Generals] are all for it now.

Madame told them that this is just what I've been telling them from the beginning, and if they'd done as I said, we'd have been better off. 96th to go at once to Gathwa. British to hold till we get there. When we get set, ATTACK.

Well, a month ago, this would have seemed incredible and I wouldn't have believed it would ever come out. Now, Tu and Lo say they don't want to go home if we don't beat the Japs. Baloney, maybe, but they have committed themselves. Pumped by Mrs Luce for *Life* article. (Chiang Kai-shek wore his teeth for lunch.) Deathly afraid of this damn publicity; what a flop I'll look like if the Japs just run me up in the hills. Why can't they wait until after the event, and give me a chance to escape the fiasco I may be inviting?

SOLUTION IN CHINA [PROBABLY JULY 1944]

The cure for China's troubles is the elimination of Chiang Kai-shek. The only thing that keeps the country split is his fear of losing control. He hates the Reds and will not take any chances on giving them a toehold in the government. The result is that each side watches the other and neither gives a damn about the war [against Japan]. If this condition persists, China will have civil war immediately after Japan is out. If Russia enters the war before a united front is formed in China, the Reds, being immediately accessible, will naturally gravitate towards China's influence and control. The condition will directly affect the relations between China and Russia, and therefore indirectly those between Russia and US.

If we do not take action, our prestige in China will suffer seriously. China will contribute nothing to our effort against Japan, and the seed will be planted for chaos in China after the war.

SEPTEMBER 26 1944

Two years, eight months of struggle and then a slap in the puss as reward. Jap broadcast said I was plotting to oust Chiang Kai-shek and make myself czar of China. Clever. Just what would make Chiang Kai-shek suspicious. (Or was it manufactured in Chungking to make his action plausible?)

SEPTEMBER 30 1944, LETTER TO MRS STILWELL

Tomorrow it is October. 1944 is three-quarters gone and we are still floundering around with a gang of morons who can't see beyond their noses. You can see by the papers what is happening in South China. The pity of that is that it could all have been avoided if certain men of genius and amateur strategists had kept their hands off. Right now we don't know where we are, and the whole structure is tottering in the breeze. There may possibly (be) a loud bang out here before you get this, and if you look carefully in the debris which will be flying through the air you may see yours truly with his pants blown entirely off.

OCTOBER 1 1944, LETTER TO MRS STILWELL

It looks very much as though they have gotten me at last. The Peanut has gone off his rocker and Roosevelt has apparently let me down completely. If old softy gives in on this, as he apparently has, the Peanut will be out of control from now on. A proper fizzle. My conscience is clear. I have carried out my orders I have no regrets. Except to see the USA sold down the river. So be ready, in case the news isn't out sooner, to have me thrown out on the garbage pile. At least, I'll probably get home and tell you all about it. God help the next man.

It hasn't happened yet, but it is a thousand to one that it will soon.

[UNDATED]

Chaing Kai-shek is the head of a one-party government supported by a Gestapo and a party secret service. He is now organizing an S.S. of 100,000 members.

[He] hates the so-called Communists. He intends to crush them by keeping any munitions furnished him and by occupying their territory as the Japs retire.

[He] will not make an effort to fight seriously. He wants to finish the war coasting, with a big supply of material, so as to perpetuate his regime. He has blocked us for three years and will continue to do so. He has failed to keep his agreements.

[He] has spoken contemptuously of American efforts and has never said one word to express gratitude for our help, except in one message to the President, in which he attacked me.

[He] is responsible for major disasters of the war. Nanking. Lan Fang. Changsha and Hengyang. Kweilin and Liuchow. Red blockade.

But [he] is the titular head of China and has marked me as *persona non grata*.

Therefore, I cannot operate in the China theatre while he is in power — unless it is made clear to him that I was not responsible for the September 19 note, and that the US will pull out unless he will play ball.

Ignored, insulted, double-crossed, delayed, obstructed for three years. Orders to [my] subordinates during operations. False charges of disobedience and non-cooperation. Constant attempts to put the screw on US. Use our air force. Borrow our money. Refuse us men for the equipment we hauled. Attempts to get the munitions at Ichang and Sian, and let Y [force] and Z [force] starve.

Source: General Joseph W. Stilwell, *The Stilwell Papers*
(London: MacDonald, 1949), pp. 97, 296, 308–312

4.8 The Eighth Route Army fighting the Japanese

Jack Belden, from *China Shakes the World*, 1949

The American war reporter Jack Belden covered the early stages of the Japanese invasion of China. In this extract he visits the Communist border region of Shanxi, Hebei, Shandong, and Henan where the divisional commander was General Liu Bocheng, and looks back to the guerrilla campaign against the Japanese in this region by Liu's Eighth Route Army.

General Liu Po-cheng was not only one of the ablest but also one of the most colorful of the Red commanders. A former associate of Dr Sun Yat-sen, he had revolted against Chiang Kai-shek after 1927 and joined Mao Tze-tung in the first Chinese Soviet on the mountain of Chikanshan in South China. At one time he had been Chief-of-Staff of the Red Army. At another time, he had attended the highest military schools in the Soviet Union. He had been in the vanguard of the Red Army's six-thousand-mile Long March in 1934 and had eaten the blood of a chicken with a Lolo tribal chieftain so that the Reds could obtain safe passage through the land of those savage tribesmen. During years of combat, a hand grenade had blown out one of his eyes so that he had acquired the nickname of Blind Liu, the One-Eyed General, etc. Sometimes he was referred to as the One-Eyed Dragon, as, according to Chinese lore, a dragon symbolizes power and cunning ...

It was rather breathtaking to come into the small mountain village of Yehtao (population about two thousand) and find hardly any signs that an army of three hundred thousand regulars and one million partisans was directed from inside its stone walls. Except for a radio aerial over one building, you could not have told this was a headquarters town, for no areas in the villages were restricted and there were no sentries at all outside any of the various military departments ...

Yet these informal officers, dressed so poorly in cotton-cloth uniform, were the same men that had directed a war against the Japanese for eight years from these self-same Taihang Mountains ...

It was more than a reporter's normal curiosity that made me inquire into these events; I also had a personal interest in finding out how the Reds had lived behind the Japanese lines. In August 1937, after the Japanese captured Peiping, I had sneaked through their lines and, after a somewhat adventurous journey, joined the troops of Chiang Kai-shek then gathering in North China to do battle. All through the summer of 1937 I had retreated with Chiang's soldiers both across the

North China Plain and through the mountains of Shansi. In one terrible retreat through Shansi I had seen the armies of Chiang almost completely collapse, soldiers throw away their weapons, and officers grab all available transportation, abandon their troops, and rush to the rear. At that time it had seemed as if China could not possibly resist and as if North China had been completely abandoned into the hands of the enemy. Chiang's soldiers had been driven from the area, and all organized resistance in the north seemed at an end. Yet even while Chiang's troops and I were fleeing the north, the Communists were infiltrating into position behind the Japanese lines where it had appeared to me no Chinese soldiers could possibly operate.

How had they survived?

It seemed to me that here was not only a great story, but a profound human experience. Here also was the answer to the riddle of why Communism was having such great successes in China today. From the epic fight of the people of North China behind the Japanese lines, one also could gain many clues as to who was going to win the war in China – the Communists or Chiang Kai-shek. Finally, it seemed to me that, in the history of these years, there were many lessons to be learned, not only political and military, but human and philosophical as well.

To find an answer to these questions, I went to Commissar Po Yi-po who had led a band of students into the Shansi Mountains in 1937 and organized the first guerrilla resistance in the region against the Japanese. Not only had Po fought in these parts for ten years, but he was also a native of Shansi Province and consequently familiar with the country and its people …

INTERVIEW WITH PO YI-PO

'Even before the Eighth Route Army appeared in North China, underground Communist workers had organized their own guerrilla units under various names, such as the Hopei Militia or the Dare to Die Corps. Only the leaders of such units were Communists and such groups were primarily of patriotic origin.

'In addition, there were also student groups who took up guerrilla warfare. Some of these groups had been organized before the war because of Warlord Yen Hsi-shan's dissatisfaction with Chiang Kai-shek's continued appeasement of Japan …

'When the Japanese invaded Shansi in 1937, Yen tried to attract them to follow him to the south. But I issued a countercall, saying: "Follow me into the mountains."

'Most came with me. In the summer of 1937 I led five columns of these students into the Taihang and Taiyueh mountains. Each column was led by a Communist worker, all of whom had only just been released from Chiang Kai-shek's prisons.

'Besides this student army, small groups of railway workers and labor defence units who had spontaneously organized themselves to fight the Japanese followed me into the mountains.

'These bands – you could hardly call them troops – had a United Front complexion and were composed of all those who did not wish to run away and cross the Yellow River with Chiang Kai-shek's forces. As a slogan, I used the words: "Better to sacrifice to Shansi than be refugees." Except for the big officials, the big landlords, and the government of Yen Hsi-shan, most of the people stayed behind to fight.

'While this movement was going on in the mountains, a parallel movement sprang up on the plains. In Hopei, for example, militia were organized by professors and teachers of North China. Soon a local government, composed of students, a few underground members of the Communist party, and liberals, was organized under the leadership of Professor Yang Hsuifeng who was later to become head of the Border Region government. Similar governments came into being in Honan and in western Shantung.

'Besides these, there sprang up more or less spontaneously nearly a hundred self-defence corps. At this time, all organizations were motivated by a spirit of patriotism, a feeling of horror at Japanese atrocities, and an anger at the Kuomintang for retreating so quickly without putting up much of a fight. Altogether, there were perhaps one hundred thousand men.

'This force had little to do with the Communist party and no connexion at all with the Eighth Route Army. Its strong point was its close relations with the people; its weak point, its lack of unity, central leadership, and military experience. Such a force, composed of students who hardly knew how to fire rifles, professors who knew nothing of tactics, and farmers who knew neither tactics nor politics, was in danger of disintegrating for lack of a directing head and of being wiped out for lack of technique.

'Such was the condition of resistance in North China when, in November 1937, General Liu Po-cheng led three regiments of the 129th Division of the Eighth Route Army from the loess country of Shensi Province on the west, across the Yellow river, and into the Taihang Mountains. Here was the military leader we had been waiting for.

'Although Liu had only six thousand men, they were some of the best soldiers in China. All of them had been on the Long March. They were technically skilful, well trained, especially in guerrilla warfare, and politically highly conscious … "From smallness to bigness; from nothing to something."

'These regulars of Liu's were combined with my five student columns and then later sent among the various people's units. The combination of these forces enabled North China to mould a front against the Japanese.

'The force of the people can be compared to water,' Po concluded, adopting a famous saying of General Peng Teh-hwai's: 'The force of General Liu to fish. Only in the water could the fish swim.'

BUILDING RESISTANCE

To mould a front against the Japanese, however, was a task of Herculean proportions.

With only six thousand troops to face an enemy fifteen times the size of his own in fire power and number, Liu appeared in a position of almost checkmate. If he elected to attack the Japanese, on the theory that the best defence is an offence, he courted almost certain defeat and annihilation. If he decided to remain in the mountains and conserve his forces, the enemy would consolidate their gains on the plain, raise a puppet army for garrison duty, and come after him in the mountains at their leisure. Finally, if he scattered his regular army among the people's bands, he would almost certainly destroy his only striking force, he would ruin the unity of the only professional body of troops under his command, and, by mixing trained fighters with people's rabble, that is, mixing blood with water, he would run the risk of lowering his soldiers' morale and spoiling the high traditions of the old Red Army.

Liu chose this latter course …

Perhaps another army, split apart like this behind the enemy's lines, would have become demoralized and disintegrated. But these were no ordinary soldiers. Many years before when they had revolted against the landlords in their own villages, these former tenants had disinherited themselves from the protection of established society. They were used to acting on their own …

Across dusty Hopei into the crowded villages and green hills of Shantung, the soldiers of Liu and other Communist commanders continued on, marching for many days until they reached the shores of the Pacific Ocean, several hundred miles from their starting point. Everywhere behind them had been left companies, squads, and platoons to organize guerrilla warfare. And out of every squad had come one or two soldiers to join the various bands that farmers, teachers, and even patriotic landlords had raised to fight the Japanese.

Cordially embracing these professional companions in arms, the people soon elevated Liu's erstwhile soldiers to staff positions in their various bands. Even cooks and donkeymen from the old Red Army became company commanders among people's units. The students of Po Yi-po followed where the soldiers had led and before long became political directors in guerrilla organs.

By dispersing his forces and spreading the war Liu had gained a much greater victory than if he had directly attacked and defeated a large Japanese force. For even if he had defeated the Japanese in battle and diminished their forces, he would at the same time have diminished his own. But by adopting the strategy he did, Liu was able to expand to an extent that even he had not thought likely.

The Japanese used both ingenious and brutal tactics to quell the guerillas, including surrounding a specific area prior to attack with deep ditches and mud walls and a policy of looting, burning, and killing. The Chinese Communists responded by creating a network of spies and informers to provide advance intelligence, by moving people out of areas where the Japanese advanced, by building 'a vast system of tunnels beneath the fields where units could hide in time of danger and directing organs could carry on work' (Belden, pp. 93–4).

Source: Jack Belden, *China Shakes the World*, first published New York 1949.
Reprinted Harmondsworth: Penguin, 1973, pp. 37, 74–87

5

Yanan

The formative years, 1936–44

The survivors of the Long March reached a remote area of northern Shaanxi and merged with the local Red Army forces. Around the small city of Yanan the soil is yellow and dry, and many of the inhabitants dwell in caves hollowed out of the steep hillsides. This is loess country. The sun obscured by the fine particles of yellow dust hanging in the air is rarely if ever seen, but the ambient glow is not unpleasant. Yanan became a Communist capital in December 1936 and, with the exception of a short period in 1947, when they were driven out by Chiang Kai-shek's forces, Yanan remained the headquarters and spiritual and symbolic home of Chinese Communism in its most formative years.

Yanan was also a mecca for a handful of Western journalists. Most notable was the American Edgar Snow who went there in 1937 to 'discover' Mao and present him to the world in a heroic light in *Red Star over China*.

When the Japanese occupied the cities of north and east China, the Communists, relatively safe in their remote base, and having agreed to a (second) united front with the Nationalists, were able to play a dual role. They fought the Japanese, most effectively by guerrilla methods behind the lines. In contrast, Chiang Kai-shek, fighting a conventional war, withdrew westwards to set up his capital in Chongqing. Since much of the countryside between the Japanese-held cities was controlled by the Communists, they also had scope to extend their political ideas and to practise some measure of land reform. When cadres and soldiers took leave from organizing the peasants and harassing the enemy, they would return to the anti-Japanese military and political university of Yanan. There they would mix with recent recruits who had travelled from all over the country to join the resistance movement.

Later, Mao was to say that the Japanese invasion had proved invaluable. The circumstances of the United Front and the American entry into the war in December 1941 gave time for him to confirm his position as leader, to bring rivals – including a group of Moscow-trained Chinese Communists – to conformity with his ideas, and to indoctrinate all his followers, including newcomers from the cities, with his interpretation of the mass line. In his key philosophical works, Mao stressed the importance of applying the ideas of Marxism–Leninism to the actual conditions of China. In the rectification movement 1942–4, Mao demonstrated the importance of moulding and, as necessary, remoulding a correct ideological consciousness. One of Mao's critics at Yanan, Ding Ling, condemned for being 'narrowly feminist', recanted and survived. Another, Wang Shiwei, was imprisoned and shot and has only recently been rehabilitated posthumously.

Pioneering interpretations of the Yanan model, by, for example, Mark Selden are open to political and economic reassessment. (Selden has now noted the repressive as well as the democratic tendencies in the Yanan Way.) How did the Yanan regime survive financially?

Selden suggested the 'mass line' provided the formula, but recent research reveals also the importance of the opium trade.

5.1 Red Star over China, 1937

Edgar Snow

Pao An was once a frontier stronghold, during the China and T'ang dynasties, against the nomadic invaders to the north. Remains of its fortifications, flame struck in that afternoon sun, could be seen flanking the narrow pass which once emptied into this valley the conquering legions of the Mongols. There was an inner city, still, where garrisons were once quartered; and a high defensive masonry, lately improved by the Reds, embraced about a square mile in which the present town was located.

Here at last I found the Red leader whom Nanking had been fighting for ten years – Mao Tse-tung, Chairman of the 'Chinese People's Soviet Republic', to employ the official title that had recently been adopted. The old cognomen, Chinese Workers' and Peasants' Soviet Republic, was dropped when the Reds began their new policy of struggle for a united front ...

I met Mao soon after my arrival: a gaunt, rather Lincolnesque figure, above average height for a Chinese, somewhat stooped, with a head of thick black hair grown very long, and with large searching eyes, a high-bridged nose, and prominent cheekbones. My fleeting impression was of an intellectual face with great shrewdness, but I had no opportunity to verify this for several days ...

There would never be any one 'saviour' of China, yet undeniably one felt a certain force of destiny in Mao. It was nothing quick or flashy, but a kind of solid elemental vitality. One felt that whatever there was extraordinary in this man grew out of the uncanny degree to which he synthesized and expressed the urgent demands of millions of Chinese, and especially the peasantry. If their 'demands' and the movement which was pressing them forward were the dynamics that could regenerate China, then in that deeply historical sense Mao Tse-tung might possibly become a very great man. Meanwhile, Mao was also of interest as a person-ality, and apart from his political life, because, although his name was as familiar to many Chinese as that of Chiang Kai-shek, very little was known about him, and all sorts of strange legends existed about him. I was the first foreign newspaperman to interview him ...

Mao Tse-tung was forty-three years old when I met him in 1936. He was elected Chairman of the provincial Central Soviet Government at the second All-China Soviet Congress, attended by delegates representing approximately 9,000,000 people then living under Red laws. Here, incidentally, it may be inserted that Mao Tse-tung estimated the maximum popula-tion of the various districts under the direct control of the Central Soviet Government in 1934 as follows: Kiangsi Soviet, 3,000,000; Hupeh–Anhui–Honan Soviet, 2,000,000; Hunan–Kiangsi–Hupeh Soviet, 1,000,000; Kiangsi–Hunan Soviet, 1,000,000; Chekiang–Fukien Soviet, 1,000,000; Hunan–Hupeh Soviet, 1,000,000; total, 9,000,000. Fantastic estimates ranging as high as ten times that figure were evidently achieved by adding up the entire population in every area in which the Red Army or Red partisans had been reported as operating. Mao laughed when I quoted him the figure of 180,000,000 people living under the Chinese Soviets, and said that when they had that big an area the revolution would be practically won ...

The influence of Mao Tse-tung throughout the Communist world of China was probably greater than that of anyone else. He was a member of nearly everything – the revolutionary military committee, the political bureau of the Central Committee, the finance commission, the organization committee, the public health commission, and others. His real influence was asserted through his domination of the political bureau, which had decisive power in the policies of the Party, the government, and the army. Yet, while everyone knew and respected him, there was – as yet, at least – no ritual of hero worship built up around him. I never met a Chinese Red who drooled 'our great leader' phrases, I did not hear Mao's name used as a synonym for the Chinese people, but still I never met one who did not like 'the Chairman' – as everyone called him – and admire him. The role of his personality in the movement was clearly immense.

Mao seemed to me a very interesting and complex man. He had the simplicity and naturalness of the Chinese peasant, with a lively sense of humour and a love of rustic laughter. His laughter was even active on the subject of himself and the shortcomings of the Soviets – a boyish sort of laughter that never in the least shook his inner faith in his purpose. He was plain-speaking and plain-living, and some people might have considered him rather coarse and vulgar. Yet he combined curious qualities of naivete and incisive wit and worldly sophistication.

I think my first impression – predominantly one of native shrewdness – was probably correct. And yet Mao was an accomplished scholar of Classical Chinese, an omnivorous reader, a deep student of philosophy and history, a good speaker, a man with an unusual memory and extraordinary powers of concentration, an able writer, careless in his personal habits and appearance but astonishingly meticulous about details of duty, a man of tireless energy, and a political strategist of considerable genius. It was interesting that many Japanese regarded him as the ablest Chinese strategist alive ...

Mao's food was the same as everybody's, but being Hunanese he had the southerner's *ai-la*, or 'love of pepper'. He even had pepper cooked into his bread. Except for this passion, he scarcely seemed to notice what he ate. One night at dinner I heard him expand on the theory of pepper-loving peoples being revolutionaries. He first submitted his own province, Hunan, famous for the revolutionaries it has produced. Then he listed Spain, Mexico, Russia, and France to support his contention, but laughingly had to admit defeat when somebody mentioned the well-known Italian love of red pepper and garlic, in refutation of his theory ...

I often wondered about Mao's own sense of responsibility over the question of force, violence, and the 'necessity of killing'. He had in his youth had strongly liberal and humanistic tendencies, and the transition from idealism to realism evidently had first been made philosophically. Although he was peasant-born, he did not as a youth personally suffer much from oppression of the landlords, as did many Reds, and, although Marxism was the core of his thought, I deduced that class hatred was for him probably an intellectually acquired mechanism in the bulwark of his philosophy rather than an instinctive impulse to action ...

I was able to check up on many of Mao's assertions, and usually found them to be correct. He subjected me to mild doses of political propaganda, but it was interesting compared with what I had received in non-bandit quarters. He never imposed any censorship on me, in either my writing or my photography, courtesies for which I was grateful. He did his best to see that I got facts to explain various aspects of Soviet life.

Source: Edgar Snow, *Red Star Over China* (London: Victor Gollancz, 1937).
Revised and enlarged edition, Harmondsworth: Penguin, 1972, pp. 105–11, 113

5.2 Documents on the Cheng-Feng (Rectification) Movement

5.2a Rectify the Party's style of work, 1 February 1942

Mao Zedong

Why must there be a revolutionary Party? There must be a revolutionary Party because the world contains enemies who oppress the people and the people want to throw off enemy oppression ... Without such a Party it is simply impossible for the people to throw off enemy oppression. We are Communists, we want to lead the people in overthrowing the enemy, and so we must keep our ranks in good order, we must march in step, our troops must be picked troops and our weapons good weapons. Without these conditions the enemy cannot be overthrown.

What is the problem now facing our Party? The general line of the Party is correct and presents no problem and the Party's work has been fruitful. The Party has several hundred thousand members who are leading the people in extremely hard and bitter struggles against the enemy. This is plain to everybody and beyond all doubt.

Then is there or is there not any problem still facing our Party? I say there is and, in a certain sense, the problem is quite serious.

What is the problem? It is the fact that there is something in the minds of a number of our comrades that strikes one as not quite right, not quite proper.

In other words, there is still something wrong with our style of study, with our style in the Party's internal and external relations and with our style of writing. By something wrong with the style of study we mean the malady of subjectivism. By something wrong with our style in Party relations we mean the malady of sectarianism. By something wrong with the style of writing we mean the malady of stereotyped Party writing. All these are wrong, they are ill winds, but they are not like the wintry north winds that sweep across the whole sky. Subjectivism, sectarianism, and stereotyped Party writing are no longer the dominant styles, but merely gusts of contrary wind, ill winds from the air-raid tunnels. (*Laughter*) ... Although no longer dominant in the whole Party, they still constantly create trouble and assail us. Therefore, it is necessary to resist them and to study, analyse, and elucidate them ...

To accomplish the task of overthrowing the enemy, we must accomplish the task of rectifying these styles within the Party. The style of study and the style of writing are also the Party's style of work. Once our Party's style of work is put completely right, the people all over the country will learn from our example. Those outside the Party who have the same kind of bad style will, if they are good and honest people, learn from our example and correct their mistakes, and thus the whole nation will be influenced ...

Our comrades in the Party School should not regard Marxist theory as lifeless dogma. It is necessary to master Marxist theory and apply it, master it for the sole purpose of applying it. If you can apply the Marxist-Leninist viewpoint in elucidating one or two practical problems, you should be commended and credited with some achievement. The more problems you elucidate and the more comprehensively and profoundly you do so, the greater will be your achievement. Our Party School should also lay down the rule to grade students good or poor according to how they look at China's problems after they have studied Marxism–Leninism, according to whether or not they see the problems clearly and whether or not they see them at all.

Finally, in opposing subjectivism, sectarianism, and stereotyped Party writing, we must have in mind two purposes: first, 'learn from past mistakes to avoid future ones', and second, 'cure the sickness to save the patient'. The mistakes of the past must be exposed without sparing anyone's sensibilities ... But our aim in exposing errors and criticizing shortcomings, like that of a doctor curing a sickness, is solely to save the patient and not to doctor him to death. A person with appendicitis is saved when the surgeon removes his appendix. So long as a person who has made mistakes does not hide his sickness for fear of treatment or persist in his mistakes until he is beyond cure, so long as he honestly and sincerely wishes to be cured and to mend his ways, we should welcome him and cure his sickness so that he can become a good comrade ...

I have taken this occasion of the opening of the Party School to speak at length, and I hope comrades will think over what I have said. (*Enthusiastic applause*)

**Source: 'Rectify the Party's Style of Work'. In *Selected Works of Mao Tse-tung*, Vol. 3
(Beijing: Foreign Languages Press, 1965), pp. 35–6**

5.2b For whom are our literature and art? Talks at the Yanan Forum on Literature and Art: Conclusion, 23 May 1942

Mao Zedong

The first problem is: literature and art for whom? ...

We have said that China's new culture at the present stage is an anti-imperialist, antifeudal culture of the masses of the people under the leadership of the proletariat. Today, anything that is truly of the masses must necessarily be led by the proletariat. Whatever is under the leadership of the bourgeoisie cannot possibly be of the masses. Naturally, the same applies to the new literature and art which are part of the new culture. We should take over the rich legacy and the good traditions in literature and art that have been handed down from past ages in China and foreign countries, but the aim must still be to serve the masses of the people. Nor do we refuse to utilize the literary and artistic form of the past, but in our hands these old forms, remoulded and infused with new content, also become something revolutionary in the service of the people.

Who, then, are the masses of the people? The broadest sections of the people, constituting more than 90 per cent of our total population, are the workers, peasants, soldiers, and urban petty bourgeoisie. Therefore, our literature and art are first for the workers, the class that leads the revolution. Second, they are for the peasants, the most numerous and most steadfast of our allies in the revolution. Third, they are for the armed workers and peasants, namely the Eighth Route and New Fourth Armies and the other armed units of the people, which are the main forces of the revolutionary war. Fourth, they are for the labouring masses of the urban petty bourgeoisie and for the petty-bourgeois intellectuals, both of whom are also our allies in the revolution and capable of long-term cooperation with us. These four kinds of people constitute the overwhelming majority of the Chinese nation, the broadest masses of the people.

Our literature and art should be for the four kinds of people we have enumerated. To serve them, we must take the class stand of the proletariat and not that of the petty bourgeoisie ... Many comrades concern themselves with studying the petty-bourgeois intellectuals and analysing their psychology, and they concentrate on portraying these intellectuals and excusing or defending their shortcomings, instead of guiding the intellectuals to join with them in getting closer to the masses of workers, peasants, and soldiers, taking part in the practical struggles of the masses, portraying and educating the masses. Coming from the petty bourgeoisie and being themselves intellectuals, many comrades seek friends only among intellectuals and concentrate on studying and describing them …

We encourage revolutionary writers and artists to be active in forming intimate contacts with the workers, peasants, and soldiers, giving them complete freedom to go among the masses and to create a genuinely revolutionary literature and art. Therefore, here among us the problem is nearing solution. But nearing solution is not the same as a complete and thorough solution. We must study Marxism and study society, as we have been saying, precisely in order to achieve a complete and thorough solution. By Marxism we mean living Marxism which plays an effective role in the life and struggle of the masses, not Marxism in words. With Marxism in words transformed into Marxism in real life, there will be no more sectarianism. Not only will the problem of sectarianism be solved, but many other problems as well.

> Source: 'Talks at the Yenan Forum on Literature and Art: Conclusion'.
> In *Selected Works of Mao Tse-tung*, Vol. 3,
> (Beijing: Foreign Languages Press, 1965), pp. 76–7, 79

5.3 Assessing the Rectification Campaign – the Yanan Way revisited, 1995

Mark Selden

Selden's book on the Yanan Way was first published in 1971.

THE MASS LINE

The radical departures in Party policy developed during the *cheng-feng* movement led beyond economic development to a broad vision of man and society in revolution. At this time the principles of the mass line were fully articulated to define the relationship between leaders and the people in any society that was taking shape in the base areas. Mao Tse-tung's Polit-buro resolution of 1 June 1943, 'The Methods of Leadership,' represents the earliest as well as the classic statement of mass line principles:

> The two methods that we Communists should employ in carrying out any tasks are, first, the linking of the general with the specific, and, second, the linking of the lead-ership with the masses … In all practical work of our Party, correct leadership can only be developed on the principle of 'from the masses, to the masses' … The basic method of leadership is to sum up the views of the masses, take the results back to the masses so that the masses can give them their firm support, and so work out sound ideas for leading the work on hand.

The mass line emphasis on forging close links between leadership and the people represents a synthesis of major insights drawn from guerrilla experience. In the final years of the resistance war, these principles were applied to the development and transformation of China's peasant society ...

The mass line was geared to the problems and limitations of a peasant society. But it was also attuned to a realization of the creative potential of peasant activists and community action at the grassroots level – a potential abundantly realized during the resistance struggle and in the economic and social movements of 1943.

During the ratification and production movements of 1942 and 1943, a new conception of the communist ideal man emerged. This ideal transcended barriers of specialization and status to combine in a single individual the values and accomplishments of the laborer, the leader, the soldier, and the student. These qualities were exemplified by the local activist who not only introduced and propagated new values and methods in his own village or factory but played a key role in the guerrilla resistance and struggled to educate himself and others in his 'spare time.' The gulf that separated leaders from those whom they led as well as mental from manual labor was thus appreciably narrowed. In war and in production, tight bonds of common struggle were formed at the community level. The labor hero or outstanding local activist was an informal intermediary between high levels of leadership and the village, at once actively committed to the creation of community ties and action leading to the transformation of rural life.

The great contribution of the Yenan period was the discovery of concrete methods for linking popular participation in the guerrilla struggle with a wide-ranging community attack on rural problems. In the people's war, community action penetrated every village and every family, and involved every individual. This required new approaches to leadership which were eventually raised to the level of theory as the mass line. In the final triumphant years of the war of resistance against Japan, the mass line took root in base areas and on battlefields throughout China ...

This Epilogue has explored questions of democracy and power in the base areas from several angles. *The Yenan Way* highlighted egalitarian, participatory, and cooperative achievements of the wartime resistance. In the course of the resistance, the Party challenged landlord power, strengthened the position of the poor and of independent cultivators through rent and tax reform, and initiated fruitful forms of mutual aid, all within the context of a mixed economy resting on foundations of the family farm and market access. At the same time the movement promoted literacy and education, and it introduced a mobilization politics that embraced the rural poor and women. These were among the factors that seemed to me to constitute foundations for a socialist transition that could expand villagers' political roles and ultimately empower them.

Writing in the mid-1990s, I see this approach as inadequate. The appropriate question is why, given promising beginnings conducive to a democratic transition, particularly the strengthening of an independent cultivator majority, was subsequent development of a democratic polity so meager? Why did the reformist and democratic elements of the Party's New Democracy wither and die in subsequent decades? Why were important gains reversed as the Party exercised a tight monopoly on power that it retains at this writing? And why did villagers who provided the core of the wartime revolutionary force and were in many ways beneficiaries of Party policies framed in the course of the resistance experience such hardship in the era of mobilizational collectivism associated with the final decades of Mao's rule? Part of the answer, but only a part, lies in more explicitly recognizing the limits of democratic progress of the resistance era. In particular, it is necessary to grasp the ways in which democratic impulses remained subordinated to Party–army mobilization. In the course of the resistance, the popular gains associated with the revolutionary movement coincided with growing Party hegemony. We can trace the origins of subsequent conflicts between Party and people and between city and countryside to tendencies that can already be discerned in Yenan.

In *The Yenan Way* I rightly noted the significance of sprouts of democracy associated with the introduction of forms of electoral politics, the growth of an independent cultivator majority, and the emergence of a cooperative economy. But I insufficiently grasped that these were part of a package associated with a Party-dominated mass line and a conception of mobilization that could pose formidable obstacles to further democratic advance and economic and political empowerment of rural producers in the years ahead.

Reflecting anew on *The Yenan Way* in the 1990s leads me to the following conclusions:

1   The Yenan Way, as the summation of the Chinese Communist Party's experience in the resistance, constituted an important moment in history of anticolonial resistance and revolutionary change in the periphery. It also offered hints applicable to the political economy of development, including the contributions of policies empowering an owner-cultivator majority through rent and tax reforms that constituted a 'silent revolution' and preliminary steps towards mutual aid, cooperation, and democracy. This central thesis of the original work remains intact.

2   The Yenan Way also, however, encapsulated repressive and regressive tendencies that I insufficiently appreciated in my initial study. When carried to extremes in the People's Republic, notably in the Great Leap Forward, the Cultural Revolution, and the repression of democratic aspirations and movements from 1957 to 1979 to 1989 and beyond, the results were frequently tragic and certainly conflict with the revolution's finest proclivities, including those towards democracy, equality, and the uplifting of a poverty-stricken countryside.

We can trace these and other unresolved tensions in Chinese political economy back to the synthesis I have called the Yenan Way. It is worth appreciating in all its complexity so as to keep alive its most humane possibilities while identifying the repressive forces detrimental to further progress towards social and economic development and human liberation.

Source: Mark Selden, *China in Revolution: The Yenan Way Revisited*
(Armonk, New York: M. E. Sharpe, 1995), pp. 212–13, 250–2

5.4   The role of women

5.4a For Comrade Ding Ling

A poem by Mao Zedong, December 1936

Ding Ling (1904–86), a writer who joined the Communist Party in 1932, was imprisoned for a time in Shanghai before going to Baoan in the summer of 1936. She was sent to work in the Red Army in the Political Department.

Red flags on the walls flutter in the glow of the setting sun,
Waving idly in the West wind above the isolated town.
New figures come to Bao'an for a time.

A banquet is held in a cave,
To honor one just out of prison.
Who can compare with a pen so fine?
Three thousand crack troops armed with Mausers.
Battle plans lead to the East of the Gansu mountains.
Yesterday a literary young lady,
Today a warlike general.

**Source: Mao Zedong, 'For Comrade Ding Ling (December 1936)'.
In S. Schram, ed., *Mao's Road to Power: Revolutionary Writings*, 1912–49, Vol. 5
(Armonk, New York, M. E. Sharpe, 2000), p. 573**

5.4b Thoughts on March 8 (Women's Day) 1942

Ding Ling

When will it no longer be necessary to attach special weight to the word 'woman' and to raise it specially?

Each year this day comes around. Every year on this day meetings are held all over the world where women muster their forces. Even though things have not been as lively these last two years in Yan'an as they were in previous years, it appears that at least a few people are busy at work here. And there will certainly be a congress, speeches, circular telegrams, and articles.

Women in Yan'an are happier than women elsewhere in China. So much so that many people ask enviously: 'How come the women comrades get so rosy and fat on millet?' It doesn't seem to surprise anyone that women make up a big proportion of the staff in hospitals, sanatoria, and clinics, but they are inevitably the subject of conversation, as a fascinating problem, on every conceivable occasion …

People are always interested when women comrades get married, but that is not enough for them. It is impossible for women comrades to get onto friendly terms with a man comrade, even more so with more than one. Cartoonists ridicule them: 'A departmental head getting married too?' The poets say: 'All the leaders in Yan'an are horsemen, and none of them artists. In Yan'an it's impossible for an artist to find a pretty sweetheart.' In other situations they are lectured at: 'Damn it, you look down on us old cadres and say we're country bumpkins. But if it wasn't for us country bumpkins, you wouldn't be coming to Yan'an to eat millet!' Yet women invariably want to get married. (It's even more of a sin not to marry, and single women are even more of a target for rumours and slanderous gossip.) So they can't afford to be choosy, anyone will do: whether he rides horses or wears straw sandals, whether he's an artist or supervisor. After marriage, they inevitably have children. The fate of such children is various. Some are wrapped in soft baby wool and patterned felt and looked after by governesses. Others are wrapped in soiled cloth and left crying in their parents' bed, while their parents consume much of the child's allowance. But for this allowance (25 yuan a month, equivalent to just over three pounds of pork), many would probably never get a taste of meat. Whoever they marry, those women who were compelled to bear children will probably be publicly derided as the 'Noras returned home.' Those women comrades in a position to employ governesses can go out once a week to a prim get-together and dance. Behind their backs there will also be the most incredible gossip and whispering campaigns, but wherever they go they cause a great stir and all eyes are glued to them. This has nothing to do with our theories or doctrines or the speeches we make at meetings. We all know this to be a fact, a fact that is right before our eyes, but it is never mentioned.

It is the same with divorce. In general there are three conditions to observe when getting married. These are (1) political purity, (2) similar age and comparable looks, and (3) mutual help. Even though everyone is said to fulfill these conditions – as for (1), there are no open traitors in Yan'an; as for (3), you can call anything 'mutual help,' including darning socks, patching shoes, and even feminine comfort – everyone nevertheless makes a great show of giving thoughtful attention to them. And yet the pretext for divorce is invariably the wife's political backwardness. I am the first to admit that it is a shame when a man's wife is not progressive and retards his progress. But let us consider how backward they really are. Before marrying, they were inspired by the desire to soar in the heavenly heights and lead a life of bitter struggle. They got married partly through physiological necessity and partly as a response to sweet talk about 'mutual help.' After that they are forced to toil away and become the 'Noras returned home.' Afraid of being thought 'backward,' those who are a bit more daring dash around begging nurseries to take the children. They ask for abortions and risk punishment and even death by secretly swallowing potions to induce them. But the answer comes back: 'Isn't giving birth to children also work? You're just after an easy life, you want to be in the limelight. After all, what indispensable political work have you performed? Since you are so frightened of having children and so unwilling to take responsibility once you have had them, why did you get married in the first place? No one forced you to.' Under these conditions how can women escape the destiny of 'backwardness'? When women capable of working sacrifice their careers for the joys of motherhood, people always sing their praises. But after ten years or so, they inevitably pay the tragic price (i.e., divorce) of 'backwardness' … In the great majority of cases it is the husband who petitions for divorce. If the wife does so, she must be leading an immoral life, so of course she deserves to be cursed!

I myself am a woman, so I understand the failings of women better than others. But I also have a deeper understanding of what they suffer. Women are incapable of transcending the age they live in, of being perfect, or of being hard as steel. They are incapable of resisting all the temptations of society or all the silent repression they suffer here in Yan'an. They each have their own past written in blood and tears, they have experienced great emotions – in elation as in depression, in the lone battle of life or in the humdrum stream of life. This is even truer of the women comrades who come to Yan'an, and so I have much sympathy for those fallen and classed as criminals. What's more, I hope that men, especially those in top positions, and women themselves will consider women's mistakes in the social context. It would be better if there were less empty theorizing and more talk about real problems, so theory and practice are not divorced, and if each Communist Party member were more responsible for his own moral conduct.

But we must also hope for a little more from our woman comrades, especially those in Yan'an. We must urge ourselves on and develop our comradely feeling.

People without ability have never been in position to seize all. So if women want equality, they must first strengthen themselves.

Source: Ding Ling, 'Thoughts on March 8 (Women's Day) 1942'. From Dai Qing, *Wang Shiwei and 'Wild Lilies': Rectification and Purges in the Chinese Communist Party 1942–1944* (Armonk, New York: M. E. Sharpe, 1994), pp. 78–81

5.5   Dissidence at Yanan

5.5a Wild Lily, March 1942

Wang Shiwei

A Yanan dissident expresses criticism which leads to his arrest and execution.

While I was walking alone along a riverbank, I saw a comrade wearing a pair of old-style padded cotton shoes. I immediately fell into thinking of comrade Li Fen, who also wore such shoes. Li Fen, my dearest and very first friend. As usual my blood began to race. Li Fen was a student in 1926 on the preparatory course in literature at Beijing University. In the same year she joined the Party. In the spring of 1928 she sacrificed her life in her home district of Baoqing in Hunan province. Her own uncle tied her up and sent her to the local garrison – a good illustration of the barbarity of old China. Before going to her death, she put on all her three sets of underclothes and sewed them tightly together at the top and at the bottom. This was because the troops in Baoqing often incited riff-raff to defile the corpses of the young women Communists they had shot – yet another example of the brutality, the evil, the filth, and the darkness of the old society.

On scores of occasions I have drawn strength from the memory of Li Fen – vital and militant strength. Thinking back on her on this occasion, I was moved to write a *zawen* under the title 'Wild Lily'. This name has a twofold significance. First, the wild lily is the most beautiful of the wild flowers in the hills and countryside around Yan'an, and is therefore a fitting dedication to her memory. Second, although its bulbs are similar to those of other lilies, they are said to be slightly bitter to the taste, and of greater medicinal value, but I myself am not sure of this.

What is lacking in our lives?

Recently, young people here in Yan'an seem to have lost some of their enthusiasm, and have become inwardly ill-at-ease.

Why is this? What is lacking in our lives? Some would answer that it is because we are badly nourished and short of vitamins, others that it is because the ratio of men to women is eighteen to one, and many young men are unable to find girlfriends. Or because life in Yan'an is dreary and lacks amusements.

There is some truth in all these answers. It is true that there is need for better food, for partners of the opposite sex, and for more interest in life. That is only natural. But one must also recognize that young people here in Yan'an came with the spirit of sacrifice to make revolution, and not for food, sex, and an enjoyable life. I cannot agree with those who say that their lack of enthusiasm, their inward disquiet even, are a result of our inability to resolve these problems. So what is lacking in our lives? Perhaps the following conversation holds some clues.

During the New Year holiday I was walking home in the dark one evening from a friend's place. Ahead of me were two women comrades talking in animated whispers. We were some way apart so I quietly moved closer to hear what they were saying.

'He keeps talking about other people's petty-bourgeois egalitarianism; but the truth is that he thinks he's something special. He always looks after his own interests. As for the comrades underneath him, he doesn't care whether they are sick or well, he doesn't even care if they die, he hardly gives a damn! ... Crows are black wherever they are. Even Comrade XXX acts like that'.

'You're right! All this bullshit about loving your own class. They don't even show ordinary human sympathy! You often see people pretending to smile and be friendly, but it's all on the surface, it doesn't mean anything. And if you offend them, they glare at you, pull their rank and start lecturing you.'

'It's not only the big shots who act that way, even small-fry are just the same. Our section leader XXX crawls when he's talking to his superiors, but he behaves very arrogantly towards us. Often comrades have been ill and he hasn't even dropped in to see how they are. But when an eagle stole one of his chickens, you should have seen the fuss he made! After that, every time he saw an eagle he'd start screaming and throwing clods of earth at it – the self-seeking bastard!' ...

In the winter of 1938, our Party carried out a large-scale investigation of our work and summoned comrades to 'unfold a lively criticism' and to 'give full vent to their criticisms, no matter whether they are right or wrong'. I hope we have another such investigation, and listen to the 'grumbles' of the youth ...

EGALITARIANISM AND THE SYSTEM OF RANKS

According to what I heard, one comrade wrote an article with a similar title for his departmental wall newspaper, and as a result was criticized and attacked by his department 'head' and driven half-mad. I hope this story is untrue. But since there have been genuine cases of madness even among the 'little devils' (orphaned children who acted as personal assistants to the Communist cadres), I fear there may be some madness among adults. Even though the state of my nerves is not as 'healthy' as some people's, I still have enough life in me not to go mad under any circumstances. I therefore intend to follow in the footsteps of that comrade and discussed the question of equality and the ranking system.

Communism is not the same as egalitarianism, and we are not at present at the stage of Communist revolution. There is no need for me to write an eight-legged essay [the most notorious part of the traditional examination system] on that question, since there is no cook crazy enough to want to live in the same style as one of the 'heads'. (I don't dare write 'kitchen operative', since it sounds like a caricature; but, whenever I speak to cooks, I always address them in the warmest possible way as 'comrade kitchen operatives' – what a pitiful example of warmth!) The question of the system of ranks is rather more difficult.

Those who say that a system of ranks is reasonable use roughly the following arguments: (1) they base themselves on the principle of 'from each according to their ability, to each according to their worth', which means that those with more responsibilities should consume more; (2) in the near future, the three-thirds government [the 'tripartite system' under which the Communists nominally shared power with other 'petty bourgeoisie and the enlightened and gentry' in the areas under their control] intends to carry out a new salary system, and naturally there will be pay differentials; and (3) the Soviet Union also has a system of ranks.

In my opinion all these arguments are open to debate. As for (1), we are still in the midst of revolution, with all its hardships and difficulties: all of us, despite fatigue, are laboring to surmount the present crisis, and many comrades have ruined their precious health. Because of this it does not yet seem the right time for any one, no matter who, to start talking about 'to each according to their worth.' On the contrary, all the more reason why those with greater responsibilities should show themselves willing to share weal and woe with the rank and file ... It goes without saying that it is not only reasonable but necessary that those with big responsibilities who need special treatment for their health should get such treatment. The same goes for those with medium positions of responsibility. As for (2), the pay system of the three-thirds government should also avoid excessive differentials; it is right that non-Party officials should get slightly better treatment, but those officials who are Party members should uphold our excellent traditions of frugal struggle so that we are in a position to mobilize even more non-Party people to join us and cooperate with us. As for (3), excuse my rudeness, but I would beg those 'great masters' who can't open their mouths without talking about 'Ancient Greece' to hold their tongues.

I am not an egalitarian, but to divide clothing into three and food into five grades is neither necessary nor rational, especially with regard to clothes. (I myself am graded as 'cadres' clothes and private kitchen', so this is not just a case of sour grapes.) All such problems should be resolved on the basis of need and reason. At present there is no noodle soup for sick comrades to eat and young students only get two meals of thin congee a day (when they are asked whether they have had enough to eat, Party members are expected to lead the rest in a chorus of 'Yes, we are full'). Relatively healthy 'big shots' get far more than they need to eat and drink, with the results that their subordinates look upon them as a race apart ... This makes me most uneasy. But perhaps it is a 'petty-bourgeois emotion' to always be talking about 'love' and 'warmth'? I await your verdict.

> **Source: Wang Shiwei, 'Wild Lily'. From Dai Qing, *Wang Shiwei and 'Wild Lilies'*:**
> ***Rectification and Purges in the Chinese Communist Party 1942–1944***
> **(Armonk, New York: M. E. Sharpe, 1994), pp. 69–71, 72, 73–5**

5.5b The rehabilitation of Wang Shiwei

From the *Literary Journal*, 20 February 1992

After the Public Security Department publicized last year the document 'Concerning The Decision To Reinvestigate The Trotskyite Problem Of Wang Shiwei', having been wrongly accused forty-nine years ago, Wang Shiwei was finally rehabilitated.

Wang Shiwei, original name Shu Han, began as a translator and writer in 1930. In 1937, he travelled to Yan'an and became involved in translating Marx and Lenin's works as well as writing critical essays. During the Yan'an rectification, he published a series of critical essays titled 'Wild Lilies'. In 1942, Wang Shiwei was wrongly accused of three crimes: 'counter-revolutionary', 'Trotskyite spy', 'hidden KMT spy', and 'member of the Five-Member Anti-Party Gang'. Afterwards, he was wrongly executed.

Following the [1978] Third Plenum, the CCP organization department rendered a decision in February 1982 that denied the existence of the so-called Five-Member Anti-Party

Gang. The August 1986 version of the *Mao Zedong Reader* publicly acknowledged that, regarding the [original] footnote on Wang Shiwei, 'the accusation that Wang Shiwei was a hidden KMT spy was untrue'. The document issued on 7 February 1991, 'Concerning the Decision to Reinvestigate the Trotskyite Problem of Wang Shiwei', stated:

> Upon reinvestigation, it is clear that comrade Wang Shiwei accepted and sympathized with some Trotskyite views and helped translate some of Trotsky's work as a result of his contact with former Beida schoolmates Wang Fanxi and Chen Qingchen (both were Trotskyites) and during his stay in Shanghai. In some of the materials containing Wang Shiwei's confession, Wang kept changing his story regarding whether he participated in the Trotskyite organization. No evidence turned up during the reinvestigation to prove that Wang Shiwei was ever involved with the Trotskyite organization. Thus, the conclusion against Wang Shiwei as a counter-revolutionary spy should be rectified, and therefore Wang, who was wrongly executed during the [civil] war, should be rehabilitated.

Wang Shiwei's wife, comrade Liu Ying, is now 85 years old. Two comrades from the Public Security Department delivered this decision on Wang Shiwei to her, together with 10,000 yuan as consolation money (*weiwen jin*). Upon reading the decision restoring the appellation 'comrade' to Wang Shiwei, tears streamed down Liu Ying's face. However, she absolutely refused to accept the money. Later, to memorialize Wang Shiwei, she decided to contribute the funds to the literary and artistic association in her resident town (Shiyan, Hubei province) as part of its award to young writers.

Source: 'The Rehabilitation of Wang Shiwei', *Literary Journal,* **20 February 1992,**
Wang Shiwei and 'Wild Lilies', pp. 189–90

5.6 'Labour Heroes' and 'Living Newspaper'

Harrison Forman, an American journalist

There are Labor Heroes in every field. During a visit to a spinning and weaving mill, I talked with Li Chih-hwa, the blacksmith Labor Hero – a tall, quiet-spoken, intelligent man. They had made him a Labor Hero for doubling his work output by keeping two forges going at the same time, thus avoiding the waste of time entailed by waiting for metal to heat up between spells of pounding and shaping. An apprentice stood by each forge as the metal was being reheated, while Li Chih-hwa moved back and forth from the one anvil to the other, devoting his full energies to the working of the metal. During the little spare time he has available, he teaches his apprentices three new Chinese characters daily. These he writes on a little blackboard set atop the two forges. As I talked with him, his three apprentices smiled broadly behind his back and stuck up their thumbs, meaning 'He's tops!'

The fireman Labor Hero is Tung Yu-hsin. He works for *Giefang Ribao* (*Chiehfang Jihpao*), the Communists' official newspaper. Tung was a Manchurian puppet soldier captured by the Paluchun back in 1938, who decided to remain with the Communists after being offered his freedom; and now he tends the fires that boil the water for the newspaper's staff of 500 workers. By a simple reduction in the size of the firehole, and by improving the air-draft of the stove, he was able to reduce daily coal consumption from 325 catties to 25 catties. For this he was elected a Labor Hero and generously rewarded.

Li Wei, the soldier Labor Hero, is one of Wang Cheng's squad leaders. He had a sad tale to tell me of his life before he joined the army. His father, a hired laborer, was so badly treated by his employer that he died while Li Wei was still a boy. His mother tried to get a living by begging, but eventually she married again, and Li Wei was given to a distant relative to work as a goatherd with no pay and little food. When the Eighth Route Army came to his Shansi home in 1939, he promptly joined them. He worked hard, was exemplary in his behavior, and was promoted to squad leader. When Weng Cheng brought his brigade to Nanniwan, Li Wei started the 'cultivate one *mou* a day' movement, himself setting a goal for his fellows by cultivating almost two *mou* a day, and often pitching in to help a lagging member in order to maintain the squad's high average.

Li Wei is the true peasant type: slow of speech but inherently friendly and hospitable. He was proud of the spick-and-span cave in which he and his buddies lived. 'When he joined the army he could neither read nor write,' said one of them, adding proudly, 'Now his articles, which are posted in our company's wall newspaper, are among the best written and are read by all of us.'

There are women Labor Heroes too, such as Kuo Feng-ying, a sturdy, self-possessed woman of thirty-six. She was married at fifteen and led a hard life until, when she was twenty-four, her husband died, leaving her only nine *mou* of land, a picul of black beans for food reserves, and the care of two children, aged nine and seven. Kuo Feng-ying did not sit down to bewail her fate, nor did she become dependent on others. She unbound her feet, put cotton into the tips of her shoes for support, and diligently set out to get the utmost from her tiny patch of land. By dint of sheer hard work she gradually prospered. Last year, when she harvested a bumper crop, her neighbors called a meeting and recommended her as their representative to the Labor Heroes' Convention, at which she was elected a National Labor Hero.

The Labor Heroes they are most proud of are the ex-*erh liu* tze Labor Heroes. The worst thing you can call one in the Border Region today is an *erh liu* tze – a loafer. In their struggle for self-sufficiency – almost a matter of life and death – these blockaded people have little patience with *erh liu* tze. Loafers are not merely parasites. Their wayward habits, their laziness, gambling, cheating, lying, and stealing, are sources of demoralization for others, and they have no place in the vigorous society for which the Communists are striving.

Of an estimated 70,000 loafers in the Border Region when the Communists arrived in 1935, all but 9,554 were reformed by the beginning of 1943, and these were particularly hardened cases. But the government was determined to solve the problem completely. An intensive reform campaign was instituted; and by the beginning of 1944 all but 3,967 loafers were reformed, these diehards, resisting all pressure directed against them. When pleas, bribes, even threats proved of no avail, the people decided to take the law more or less into their own hands: every loafer had to wear a big white badge inscribed 'erh liu tze' – to be jeered and hooted at and incessantly humiliated in the campaign to shame him into reform.

The government, meanwhile, was employing subtler methods. At a recent convention for Labor Heroes, five hardened loafers were chosen by the government and invited to attend. Suspecting that they were in for some sort of punishment or public humiliation, these five at first declined – only to yield when their neighbors insisted. On their arrival at Yenan, the five loafers were astonished to find themselves accorded the same courtesies extended to the heroes. As they entered the big auditorium, they were applauded loudly and ushered to the platform to be seated with the honored guests. They were served with wine, cakes, and sweetmeats, and were called on to participate in all discussions on an equal footing with the

Labor Heroes. By the end of the convention they were vigorously acclaimed by the Labor Heroes and offered liberal advice and assistance in drawing up their own production plans. The government, on its part, offered them grants of land and loaned them farm implements, seeds, and animals. By this time the five loafers declared 'If we fail in this reform, we shall no longer consider ourselves human beings!' ...

Also rooted in the original Yang Ko of the peasantry is the 'Living Newspaper,' a rather special form of Yang Ko drama, not yet a year old. As the name suggests, it has a message to transmit. It is a far cry form the stilted, formalized Chinese drama of long beards, falsetto voices, and exaggerated dialogue. The Communists' Living Newspaper is vivid and actual, designed primarily to bring the news of the day to the illiterate masses, to enlarge their vision, and to make them conscious of the greater world in which circumstances have made them an integral part. In some respects the Living Newspaper might be compared to some of our popular radio programs, such as 'The March of Time' or 'Five-Star Final.' Performances are given in the open with no stage and the minimum of props. Plentifully seasoned with lusty burlesque and humor, they are certainly to the liking of the fascinated spectators. A mixture of Western and Chinese instruments provides an orchestral accompaniment, skilfully employed to accentuate dialogue and to heighten dramatic suspense. Living Newspaper performances are full of propaganda, but propaganda specifically calculated to encourage the people and mobilize their resistance to Japan. For example, the performance entitled *Second Front*, given just three days after Eisenhower's landing in France, opened with Tojo brandishing a broken blood-tipped sword. He staggered about the scene trying to console a caricatured Hitler who moaned about his failure in Russia ...

The finale was a victory celebration. The ensemble of fifty or more lustily sang Shostakovitch's *Song of the United Nations* as they danced around huge flags of China, America, Britain, and the Soviet. Each girl flag-bearer was in national dress. The girls' Western costumes – of America, Britain, and the Soviet – were characteristically stuffed out with padded breasts; they also wore long artificial noses, the more clearly to indicate the Occidental roles they were playing.

Yang Ko dramas and Living Newspapers are performed irregularly. But Saturday night dancing – modern dancing – is a social event in which almost everyone participates ...

Typical of these Saturday night dances was the one given in the apple orchard at military headquarters. Soft lights from candles or pressure lamps, covered with red, blue, green, and yellow paper and hung from spreading branches, flooded the plain earthen dance floor. It was not a good floor to dance on, to be sure; but since every man, woman, and child wore ordinary cloth slippers or rope sandals, no one cared. The girls all wore a pajama-like belted blouse and slacks, skirts being impracticable for this rough frontier life. Moreover, to assert their emancipated status, the girls did most of the choosing of partners; there was no hesitation or embarrassment over this. The orchestra was composed of a weird blend of ancient Chinese fiddles, modern violins, mouth organs, native banjos, a Cantonese zither, a musical saw, and a missionary-type pedal organ. The music? They played sentimental Chinese ballads, French minuets, and Viennese waltzes such as *The Blue Danube*. Occasionally the orchestra gave out with something really hot and modern – like *Jingle Bells*, or *Yankee Doodle* – in honor of their foreign guests.

But don't think that worried them. They danced foxtrots, waltzes, and onestep with total indifference to what the orchestra might be playing. And all enjoyed themselves immensely.

On any evening you might see bushy-haired, shirtsleeved Mao Tze-tung, venerated leader of ninety million under the Communists' protection, having a grand time dancing a fast onestep with a cute co-ed from Yenta, while a truck-driver might be swinging buxom Madame Chu Teh. Roly-poly Chu Teh himself, commander-in-chief of over half a million Jap-killers, who looks like a fatherly old cowpuncher, was having the time of his life dancing with a bright young thing one-half his size and one-third his age. Battle-scarred generals Lin Piao, Nieh Yung-chien, Yeh Chien-ying, and a dozen others – for each of whom the Japanese would gladly sacrifice a full division of crack troops – would be seen flitting about like jitterbugging college kids.

Source: Harrison Forman, *Report from Red China*
(London: Robert Hale, 1946), pp. 68–71, 94–7

5.7 The blooming poppy under the red sun: The Yanan Way and the opium trade

Cheng Yung-fa

I have discovered that profits from opium production and sales by the CCP made a substantial contribution to the economic development of the Shaan-Gan-Ning [Shaanxi Gansu-Ningxia] base area and the financing of its government. Documentation of this finding and an account of the CCP's evolving policies toward the opium trade are provided in the pages that follow. In this chapter, I make no attempt to deny entirely the validity of Mark Selden's account of the 'Yan'an Way,' but I do argue that the omission of the opium revenues from accounts of the Yan'an Way is a serious mistake. For, without the opium trade, the economic improvements Mark Selden found in Shaan-Gan-Ning would have been simply impossible. In studying the problem of economic development, Selden stressed dedication, voluntarism, and the human spirit, but failed to realize how important financial subsidies were to the production campaigns and other economic ventures of the time. The Party considered various options in handling the fiscal problems of the base area, but in the end opium revenues emerged as its most important financial resource. After the civil war of the late 1940s, when the opium trade ended and the CCP refocussed its attentions on the Beijing-centered nationwide economy, the Shaan-Gan-Ning economy stagnated and even began to lose ground because of the lack of development capital formerly supplied by opium revenues.

OVERCOMING THE CRISIS

How did the CCP overcome the financial crisis? The current scholarly literature gives only one answer: the 'Yan'an Way.' By the 'Yan'an Way,' Mark Selden meant the mass line and the policies embodying that political principle. New evidence enables us to move beyond this magic formula. First, let me cite a set of 1943 statistics to facilitate our discussion of possible answers. I cite it only because of the lack of similar material for the two other years ...

First, the famous production campaign, which peaked in 1943, still fell short of expectations, although many state units did produce enough to meet their daily needs other than grain. Second, the frugality campaign, including the much praised policy of 'crack forces and simplified administration,' helped offset the deficit, but the Party was still left with a sizable deficit amounting to at least 30.4 percent of the base area annual budget. Where could the Party find the resources to fill the gap?

The Party tried three other means: taxation, printing money, and expanding 'foreign trade.' In the end, considerable extra endeavour was needed to make all the efforts worthwhile.

The Yan'an authorities intensified their extraction efforts drastically. The 'national salvation public grain' previously amounted to no more than 100,000 dan; in 1941, the quota was doubled ... As a result, the average burden for Yan'an County amounted to 35.03 percent of the annual yield, at least five times the tax burden imposed on Nationalist Huainan. The peasants of Qinghua district paid an average of 43.7 percent of their harvest to the Party; we can imagine that their discontent increased.

To indicate the mood of the discontented peasants, one need only refer to a story widely circulated around this time. In a storm, a cadre was 'struck' by lightning and killed. On hearing the news, peasants were overheard to have wondered why lightning did not strike Chairman Mao. In the face of such discontent the Party reduced the quota for the tax grain in 1942, but the next year it had to raise the quota again ... Only in 1944 could the Party reduce the extraction significantly. Under these circumstances, the Party had to try other solutions.

The printing machine of the Communist State bank also helped tremendously. But unless the Party could assure the supply of commodities in the domestic market, issuing unbacked currency would inevitably reignite inflation. This is exactly what happened in 1943, when the Party pumped an additional 276 million yuan (bianbi) without solid backing into the economy. ... In terms of price, millet rose 1400 percent in the year, cotton textiles 1900 percent ... As a result, the Party eventually ... decided to stop further printing and tighten the money supply.

To expand 'foreign trade' (i.e., export earnings) of the base area was a sensible answer to the problem of inflation, but to expand it at a time of economic blockade was surely an uphill struggle. However, the Party did not spare on the attempt ... Salt had been mined [along the Nangxia–Shaanxi border] for hundreds of years, but because of high transportation costs it could not compete with sea salt. The Japanese occupation of the coastal areas eliminated this competition; the Nationalist territory in eastern Gansu and central Shaanxi needed a new source of salt.

Indeed, the Party placed high hopes on salt production and trade. It enlisted peasants to transport the salt. As they saw no profit in the work, they began to complain loudly and eventually forced the Party to commute the corvée into taxes. The Party also mobilized soldiers for production. In any case, in 1943, the Party exported 727. 09 million yuan (bianbi) of salt. Though the total value (not the total profit) exceeded the Party's budget for the year, salt accounted for only 13.59 percent of total trade. I cannot explain the basis on which the Party calculated the value of the salt trade, but I feel quite safe in concluding that the export of local products could not solve the deficit of the Shaan-Gan-Ning government ...

THE OPIUM TRADE AND CORRUPTION

In 1941, the Party urged all units to engage in profit-making businesses in order to pull through the period of economic difficulty. To meet the Party's expectations, many state units found it necessary to engage in smuggling. Needless to say, greed also accounted for this phenomenon. Many smuggled salt in and cotton out, but others were bold enough to smuggle opium. In fact, smuggling by these publicly owned businesses overshadowed smuggling by private citizens. For example, the transportation team of the Third Garrison Brigade was caught trading 'special product' in Inner Mongolia and Shanxi. For another example, the transportation team of the First Garrison Brigade went to Dingbian, nominally to carry salt but actually to trade in opium. To combat the contraband trade, the Party therefore set up the Bureau of Trade first and the Bureau of Commodity Supply later.

Concerning opium smuggling in Shaan-Gan-Ning, we have only the fragmentary materials noted above. The case of Huainan might help us imagine it. In 1941, the central China base area followed the example of Yan'an and encouraged the army, government, and other organizational units to form cooperatives and engage in commerce. These publicly owned ventures immediately began to smuggle contraband, including opium. The seriousness of the problem even forced a newly-appointed commissar to call a meeting, in which the commander of the local garrison faced charges of corruption. The commander, a Long March veteran, had joined Mao's Red Army immediately after the collapse of the first United Front in 1927. He was accused of allowing the cooperative of the garrison command to engage in opium smuggling and dividing the high profits among members. Yet even faced with the accusation, he refused to reveal any details. The charge against the local Public Security Office was more concrete; it engaged in 'attacking local gentry,' but kept no detailed records of confiscated opium. The cooperative of this unit also smuggled opium. It even burned the accounting book after learning of the charge and denied any wrongdoing during the interrogation …

At any rate, the corruption problem brought about by opium seemed less serious in Yan'an than in Huainan. Compared with the situation in Nationalist areas, it also seemed under control. In Nationalist territory, the Bureau of Opium Prohibition was legendary for its corruption; in the Yan'an region, I have found one case of opium-related corruption. A district-level Party cadre of eastern Gansu was found in 1945 to have been an opium addict; he had been ordered go to the countryside to handle a murder case, but instead used the opportunity to obtain the drug …

After 1941, the Nationalist government constantly accused its foes of growing opium in the Yan'an area and elsewhere. But the charge stirred up little emotional response. In sharp contrast to the effective Communist propaganda, the Nationalists' accusation was dismissed mostly as exaggeration, if not complete fabrication. Forty years later, the Communists' own data forced us to accept the Nationalist charge as a fact. How can we explain the lengthy disbelief? Here I would like to propose two plausible explanations. First, the Nationalist government had by this time lost credibility … Second, the Communists were very effective in eradicating opium smoking in areas under their rule. Unable to find an opium den in the Communist areas, observers naturally believed the Communist insistance on innocence. Furthermore, the Party matched its propaganda with deeds. When it decided to open the Shaan-Gan-Ning territory to outside scrutiny, it first moved the opium fields into the neighboring Jin-Sui base area, so that outsiders could not find opium fields in the Yan'an area after they actually arrived en masse in 1944.

Put in historical context, what Mark Selden calls the Yan'an Way appears problematic. No one can deny the Communists' achievement in developing the Shaan-Gan-Ning border region through the mass line in the 1940s. But ignorance of the role played by opium revenues led Selden to exaggerate the economic accomplishments and overlook the internal constraints imposed by the poverty and backwardness of the border region. In fact, self-reliance was both a myth and an ideal. It was a myth because the border region could never have survived without external trade. It was an ideal because, in its pursuit, the Party succeeded in increasing agricultural production and creating some light industry. But as the size of the opium trade testifies, the border region never achieved the goal of genuine self-reliance ...

In reviving the opium trade, however, Mao Zedong never allowed himself to degenerate to the level of the warlords. He insisted on banning opium smoking within his jurisdiction and on the use of opium profits for the development of the Shaan-Gan-Ning economy. Although we are doubtful of the lasting effect of his economic policy in the 1940s, we cannot deny that he used the opium trade revenues to build a viable and integrated programme of economic development. Moreover, unlike his warlord predecessors, he had a firm grip over the cadres and officers and, through rectification, developed an effective mechanism of behavior control, in which ideological commitment played a vital role. Mao's problem lay in his inability to make idealism work over the long term, but idealism was precisely what made his rectification programme effective in the short run.

The predicament in which Mao Zedong found himself in the 1940s should alert us to the need to reassess the Maoist emphasis on such values as dedication, sacrifice, and voluntarism. Regardless of the means he used to mobilize the peasants and intellectuals through the mass line, Mao also understood the necessity of financing his development projects. In this sense, he was as realistic as he was romantic. And no matter how much he believed in human perfectibility, he also understood the necessity of fighting against the lure of corruption. We should not overlook this realism in characterizing Maoism as a belief in human transcendence.

Source: Cheng Yung-Fa, 'The Blooming Poppy under the Red Sun:
The Yan'an Way and the Opium Trade'. In T. Saich and H. Van der Ven, eds,
New Perspectives on the Chinese Communist Revolution
(Armonk, New York: M. E. Sharpe, 1995), pp. 263–4, 271–3, 290–4

6

The civil war and communist victory

Only the day before the capitulation of Japan, VJ Day, 15 August 1945, the Soviet Union signed a Treaty of Friendship and Alliance with the Chinese Nationalist Government. This confirmed the agreement made at Yalta in February 1945 by the Big Three, in the absence of the Chinese, for the restoration of Russian interests in Manchuria which had been lost in 1905, specifically control of the Chinese Eastern and South Manchurian railways and the use of Port Arthur and Darien.

The unexpectedly quick surrender by the Japanese saved both Nationalists and Communists the hard slog of reconquering occupied territory. Chiang Kai-shek was well placed. He had been harbouring his resources in World War Two. The United States was backing him, notably by supplying the airforce that lifted his troops back into the areas occupied by the Japanese.

American mediators sent by Roosevelt and, after 1945, Truman failed to reconcile the Nationalists and the Communists. Negotiations begun in Chongqing in August 1945 soon faltered. US ambassador Patrick Hurley resigned and was followed by special envoy General George Marshall, who appeared momentarily to integrate the two sides into a national army, theoretically a step further than they had reached during World War Two. In fact, the agreement broke down almost immediately.

There were soon to be wider international forces at work. By March 1947 the 'cold war' had been identified by Churchill in his Fulton speech. The Americans were easily persuaded to perceive the threat of Soviet-backed Communism to their interests in China. In fact the USSR, after a momentary incursion into Manchuria, withdrew and conducted the cold war confrontation in Europe. However, the Americans were not easily convinced that Stalin had washed his hands of Mao's Communists.

In the first clash of forces in the Civil War from 1946 to 1947 the outcome was far from clear. Even with less than 100 per cent American support for the Nationalist advance into Manchuria, Chiang Kai-shek enjoyed some successes. For a time in 1947 he had driven Mao out of his Yanan base. But by spring and summer 1948. the Red forces were successfully adjusting from guerrilla tactics to the use of large mobile formations.

The morale of the Communist armies in the floodtide of victory is legendary. Nevertheless, Chiang had some well-equipped troops. The defeat of the Guomingdang was the combined consequence of corruption, flawed strategy, poor military intelligence – the PLA had many sympathizers – and the growing disaffection of the civil population. In particular, the chronic hyperinflation in the cities demoralized the Nationalists' middle-class supporters.

But not all peasants rejoiced in the cause of Communism. The better-off and middle peasants had doubts about the processes of redistribution. In the middle of the Civil War

(12 January 1948), the Communists, fearing that harming the interests of the middle peasants would lead to defeat in the war, made a statement of policy in favour of more lenient treatment for middle peasants.

By April 1949, the Communists were anticipating victory and laying down the immediate principles for the unification of the country. They called for those in the GMD government, in business, and in the police to stay at their posts. Many Nationalist forces still in the field quickly came to terms with the Communists.

By summer 1949, the issue of diplomatic relations with foreign powers had to be clarified. Communist intentions still had to be reconciled to the anticipations of the Powers by 1 October 1949, when Mao Zedong proclaimed the inauguration of the People's Republic of China.

6.1 Mao on the foolish old man who removed the mountains, 11 June 1945

Mao Zedong

There is an ancient Chinese fable called 'The Foolish Old Man Who Removed the Mountains'. It tells of an old man who lived in northern China long, long ago and was known as the Foolish Old Man of North Mountain. His house faced south, and beyond his doorway stood the two great peaks, Taihang and Wangwu, obstructing the way. He called his sons, and hoe in hand they began to dig up these mountains with great determination. Another greybeard, known as the Wise Old Man, saw them and said derisively, 'How silly of you to do this! It is quite impossible for you few to dig up these two huge mountains'. The Foolish Old Man replied, 'When I die, my sons will carry on; when they die, there will be my grandsons, and then their sons and grandsons, and so on to infinity. High as they are, the mountains cannot grow any higher and with every bit we dig, they will be that much lower. Why can't we clear them away?' Having refuted the Wise Old Man's wrong view, he went on digging every day, unshaken in his conviction. God was moved by this, and he sent down two angels, who carried the mountains away on their backs. Today, two big mountains lie like a dead weight on the Chinese people. One is imperialism, the other is feudalism. The Chinese Communist Party has long made up its mind to dig them up. We must persevere and work unceasingly, and we, too, will touch God's heart. Our God is none other than the masses of the Chinese people. If they stand up and dig together with us, why can't these two mountains be cleared away? ...

The US government's policy of supporting Chiang Kai-shek against the Communists shows the brazenness of the US reactionaries. But all the scheming of the reactionaries, whether Chinese or foreign, to prevent the Chinese people from achieving victory is doomed to failure. The democratic forces are the main current in the world today, while reaction is only a countercurrent. The reactionary countercurrent is trying to swamp the main current of national independence and people's democracy, but it can never become the main current. Today, there are still three major contradictions in the old world, as Stalin pointed out long ago: first, the contradiction between the proletariat and the bourgeoisie in the imperialist countries; second, the contradiction between the various imperialist powers; and third, the contradiction between the colonial and semi-colonial countries and the imperialist metropolitan countries. Not only do these three contradictions continue to exist, but they are becoming more acute and widespread. Because of their existence and growth, the time will come when the reactionary anti-Soviet, anti-Communist, and antidemocratic countercurrent still in existence today will be swept away.

Source: Mao Tse-tung, 'The Foolish Old Man Who Removed the Mountains'
In *Selected Works of Mao Tse-tung*, Vol. 3
(Beijing: Foreign Languages Press, 1965), pp. 322–3

6.2 General George Marshall's statement on leaving China, Nanjing, 5 January 1947

The President has recently given a summary of further developments in China during the past year and the position of the American government toward China.

In this intricate and confused situation, I shall merely endeavor here to touch upon some of the more important considerations – as they appeared to me – during my connection with the negotiations to bring about peace in China and a stable democratic form of government.

In the first place, the greatest obstacle to peace has been the complete, almost over-whelming suspicion with which the Chinese Communist Party and the Kuomintang regard each other.

On the one hand, the leaders of the government are strongly opposed to a Communistic form of government. On the other, the Communists frankly state that they are Marxists and intend to work toward establishing a Communistic form of government in China, though first advancing through the medium of a democratic form of government of the American or British type ...

I think the most important factors involved in the recent breakdown of negotiations are these: on the side of the National Government, which is in effect the Kuomintang Party, there is a dominant group of reactionaries who have been opposed, in my opinion, to almost every effort I have made to influence the formation of a genuine coalition government. This has usually been under the cover of political or Party action, but since the Party was the government, this action, though subtle or indirect, has been devastating in its effect. They were quite frank in publicly stating their belief that cooperation by the Chinese Communist Party in the government was inconceivable and that only a policy of force could definitely settle the issue. This group includes military as well as political leaders.

On the side of the Chinese Communist Party there are, I believe, liberals as well as radi-cals, though this view is vigorously opposed by many who believe that the Chinese Commu-nist Party discipline is too rigidly enforced to admit of such differences of viewpoint. Nevertheless, it has appeared to me that there is a definite liberal group among Communists, especially of young men who have turned to the Communists in disgust at the corruption evident in the local governments – men who would put the interest of the Chinese people above ruthless measures to establish a Communistic ideology in the immediate future. The dyed-in-the-wool Communists do not hesitate at the most drastic measures to gain their end, as, for instance, the destruction of communications in order to wreck the economy of China and produce a situation that would facilitate the overthrow or collapse of the govern-ment, without any regard to the immediate suffering of the people involved. They completely distrust the leaders of the Kuomintang Party and appear convinced that every government proposal is designed to crush the Chinese Communist Party. I must say that the quite evidently inspired mob actions of last February and March, some within a few blocks of where I was then engaged in completing negotiations, gave the Communists good excuse for such suspicions ...

Sincere efforts to achieve settlement have been frustrated time and again by extremist elements of both sides. The agreements reached by the Political Consultative Conference a year ago were a liberal and forward-looking charter which then offered China a basis for peace and reconstruction. However, irreconcilable groups within the Kuomintang Party, interested in the preservation of their own feudal control of China, evidently had no real intention of implementing them. Though I speak as a soldier, I must here also deplore the dominating influence of the military. Their dominance accentuates the weakness of civil government in China. At the same time, in pondering the situation in China, one must have clearly in mind not the workings of small Communist groups or committees to which we are accustomed in America, but rather of millions of people and an army of more than a million men ...

Between the dominant reactionary group in the government and the irreconcilable Communists, who, I must state, did not so appear last February, lies the problem of how peace and well-being are to be brought to the long-suffering and presently inarticulate mass of the people of China. The reactionaries in the government have evidently counted on substantial American support regardless of their actions. The Communists by their unwillingness to compromise in the national interest are evidently counting on an economic collapse to bring about the fall of the government, accelerated by extensive guerrilla action against the long lines of rail communications – regardless of the cost in suffering to the Chinese people.

The salvation of the situation – as I see it – would be the assumption of leadership by the liberals in the government and in the minority parties, a splendid group of men, but who as yet lack the political power to exercise a controlling influence. Successful action on their part under the leadership of the Generalissimo Chiang Kai-shek would, I believe, lead to unity through good government.

In fact, the National Assembly has adopted a democratic constitution that in all major respects is in accordance with the principles laid down by the all-party Political Consultative Conference of last January. It is unfortunate that the Communists did not see fit to participate in the Assembly since the Constitution that has been adopted seems to include every major point that they wanted.

Soon the government in China will undergo major reorganization pending the coming into force of the Constitution following elections to be completed before Christmas Day 1947. Now that the form for a democratic China has been laid down by the newly adopted constitution, practical measures will be the test. It remains to be seen to what extent the government will give substance to the form by a genuine welcome of all groups actively to share in the responsibility of government.

The first step will be the reorganization of the State Council and the executive branch of government to carry on administration pending the enforcement of the Constitution. The manner in which this is done and the amount of representation accorded to liberals and to non-Kuomintang members will be significant. It is also to be hoped that during this interim period the door will remain open for Communists or other groups to participate if they see fit to assume their share of responsibility for the future of China.

It has been stated officially and categorically that the period of political tutelage under the Kuomingtang is at an end. If the termination of one-party rule is to be a reality, the Kuomingtang should cease to receive financial support from the [American] government.

I have spoken very frankly because in no other way can I hope to bring the people of the United States to even a partial understanding of this complex problem …

Source: *George C. Marshall's Mediation Mission to China between 1945–January 1947*
(Lexington, Virginia: George C. Marshall Foundation, 1998), pp. 555–9

6.3 How Guomingdang forces were persuaded to join the Communists

Jack Belden, from *China Shakes the World*, 1949

Since they were so weak in the cities and since the Chinese proletariat was such an effective force, the Communists could not stimulate Chiang's troops to revolt by mass strikes. In fact, their best method of directly contacting Chiang's troops was on the field of battle. It was principally through contact in combat that the Kuomingtang soldiers and officers were roused to turn over to the Communists. This must be accounted one of the most ludicrous phenomena of the Chinese war. To beat the Communists, Chiang had to attack them, but every time he did so, his troops became infected with the revolutionary mood of the Eighth Route soldiers.

It seems that the first break in the army appeared among the provincial forces and former subordinates of the Christian General Feng Yu-hsiang, who had come to America and denounced Chiang Kai-shek. This does not mean that these troops were necessarily more revolutionary than the others. On the contrary, the regiments, close to the old China, had many elements of conservatism. But just for this reason the changes caused by the war were more noticeable in them. Besides, they were always being shifted around, watched by Chiang's spies, and given worse equipment than Chiang's favoured forces. They were sick of it, and wanted to make peace …

During the latter half of 1948, Kuomingtang commanders in Manchuria drew back into the cities, with orders, it was said, to hold on until Dewey was elected President of the United States and America poured forth her might in aid of Chiang Kai-shek. Some weeks before the presidential election, the 60th and the 7th Kuomingtang Armies retired to the city of Changchun with their heavy American equipment while a small force of the People's Liberation Army of General Lin Piao took up positions of siege around the city. Here, the Communists had an extraordinary opportunity to apply their methods of disintegrating Chiang's army by revolutionary propaganda.

Every squad in Lin Piao's forces organised an enemy work group. They discussed the misconceptions of the Kuomintang troops facing them. Then a programme of propaganda was decided upon and a shouting war began.

'Brothers!' the voices called across no man's land, 'lay down your arms which you never wanted to take up. Did you join the Kuomingtang army? No, you were dragged into it at the end of a rope. Come over to us. If you want we will send you home. Better still, you can join us and fight to free your homes as we have ours'.

A barrage of fire greeted these words. But the words themselves were a red-hot revolutionary medium, a high conductor of ideas, that the rifles could not still. Pretty soon, at scattered places along the front, the rifles ceased firing. At last a squad of seven men led by a soldier named Tang Kuo-hua crossed the lines. The Kuomintang commanders were frightened. They told their troops that the deserters had been disarmed by the Communists and buried alive. This lie was short lived. For squad commander Tang himself soon called across the 75 yards separating the two forces and begged his old comrades to follow him into the renewed China. From a handful, the number of desertions grew to a steady stream.

The Kuomintang tried countermeasures. It scoured Changchun for prostitutes and officers' wives and sent them into the front lines to sing obscene songs and invite the soldiers of the People's Liberation Army to cross over to them. 'Brother', called back Lin Piao's soldiers, how can your officers deceive us, when they can't even deceive you?'

Soon letters were exchanged between the opposing forces. One Kuomintang squad wrote saying its commander was sick and resting inside Changchun, but as soon as he came back, they would come over. Another wrote: 'Thanks for the cakes, but we are southerners and would like rice. We also can't understand your dialect, find a southerner to shout to us'.

Source: Jack Belden, *China Shakes the World*
(Harmondsworth: Penguin, 1973 [1949]), pp. 545–6, 546–7

6.4 US marines rape a Chinese student, 1946

Hua Qingzhao, *From Yalta to Panmunjom*, 1993

The student protests were generated by an incident in Beijing on the evening of 24 December [1946]. In Dongdan Park, about two hundred yards from what is now the Beijing Hotel, two US marines raped a Chinese girl; they were apprehended by passers-by when the girl cried out, and taken, with the victim, to a police station. The two marines, no doubt frustrated by having to stay in China after the war ended, probably did not fully understand the gravity of their offence or the hornet's nest it would overturn. As it happened, the victim was a student at Beijing University, one of the most prestigious institutions of higher education in China, and it was said that her father was a professor. The university had a long tradition of protest movements; its students and professors formed the nucleus of the famous May 4th Movement of 1919, and Mao Zedong himself was for some time an assistant in the university library.

By this time, sixteen months after World War II ended, GI Joe was no longer a war hero in Chinese eyes, but rather a symbol of occupation and corruption. Many American military personnel had forgotten an important lesson, captured in their own Chinese-language training manual: *Ru guo wen jin, ru jin wen su* [When entering a new country, inquire as to what is not allowed; when going to a new place, inquire as to the native customs]. But more important in the changing perception of the US military was the prolonged stay of US forces and their role in the civil war. Since the war's end, the KMT government had antagonized the Chinese people, who, after so many years of war, looked forward to peaceful lives with some degree of security in such basic needs as food and shelter. Instead, they were plunged again into chaos. Many KMT officials, on the other hand, were enthusiastically acquiring *wu zi deng ke* (the five most desirable possessions: gold, houses, status, women, and automobiles) by seizure from the Japanese and their collaborators. When the simmering conflict between the KMT and the CCP exploded, the Chinese people well understood that, without American aid, the KMT would not have had the strength to start a civil war. The CCP had been successfully popularizing the local slogan 'Fight hunger, oppose civil war', thereby winning popular support, and launched a propaganda war against

the United States, criticizing the 'support Chiang' policy and painting the Truman administration as a 'black hand' behind the KMT's mischief. Against this background, the two
marine culprits were looked upon by the citizens of Beijing as rats running in the street;
everyone shouted: 'Beat them!'

In the view of the US embassy in Nanjing:

> On the whole the recent anti-American demonstrations in China may be inter-
> preted as a manifestation of general discontent and unrest caused by the overall
> political and economic situation existing in China. Widespread resentment against
> the government which cannot be openly expressed is being turned almost entirely
> against the US ... [T]here exists in China a potentially explosive political situation
> and it is possible to foresee serious disturbances within the next few months ... [I]n
> such a situation, the position of the US is vulnerable so long as the presence of US
> troops in China offers an immediately available target for propagandists of any
> coloration and for normally latent Chinese xenophobia.

What a wonderful analysis! If only this had precipitated in the Truman administration a thorough review of its Chinese policy.

Under popular pressure, the local judiciary in Beijing decided that the two marines should
be tried by a Chinese court. But higher authorities yielded to US insistence that the two
marines should be court-martialled by the US Navy. This treatment of the case was obviously
extraterritorial, invoking a privilege which the United States, together with some Allied
nations, formally renounced during the war. A US Navy court set up in Beijing sentenced one
of the two marines to 15 years in prison, the other to a shorter term. These sentences were
approved by the commanding general of the First Division (reinforced), USMC, on 21
February 1947, even though two members of the court had recommended clemency. On
6 June, upon interference from Congressman Riley, the Judge Advocate General of the US
Navy reported to the Secretary of the Navy that the case should be 'set aside,' and copies of
his report were sent to President Truman and Secretary of State Marshall. ...

This incident in the relationship between the US government and the Chinese people was
of great importance, because it occurred just as the situation in China was reaching a critical
phase. It touched off a spectacular anti-American demonstration, with half a million students
in the Nationalist areas going out on strike and demonstrating against the United States and
the KMT from the end of December 1946. The students demanded the withdrawal of US
troops from China. The CCP was directing this campaign, as revealed by Zhou Enlai himself.
But it was the US military presence in China that stoked popular discontent, and it was the
crimes of two members of the US military that gave the CCP its opportunity to attack the
Truman administration.

This important episode in the American failure in China has not attracted much attention
among non-Chinese scholars. They seem to have underestimated its importance or to have
believed that the incident was misrepresented in Communist propaganda. Although the
struggles surrounding the Christmas Eve incident marked 'a new high tide' of the Chinese
Revolution, for one reason or another the file of this incident slept unremarked in the Marine
archives for some four decades.

Source: Hua Qingzhao, *From Yalta to Panmunjom*
(Ithaca, New York: Cornell University Press, 1993), pp. 132, 134

6.5 Denunciation of Chiang Kai-Shek, 13 January 1946

Speech by Professor Zhang Xiruo, Head of Department of Politics,
Southwest Associated University, Kuming

Professor Zhang was a leading non-partisan figure in the Chinese political scene. His speech delivered to about 7,000 students and visitors represents the widespread opposition among intellectuals to the Guomindang regime.

It is not easy to see through political difficulties. But it is the duty of all who study and teach in universities to stick to the truth. In discussing how China's problems can be resolved, I am going to state the truth without consideration for the vested interests of any party, or the 'face' of any person … China is suffering because political power has been monopolized by an extremely reactionary and exceedingly despotic political faction, dominated by a group of stupid, corrupt ignoramuses. This conglomeration is the Kuomingtang, the Nationalist Party. I do not say that the Kuomintang has always been such a body. It has developed into such a body, and today thinks only of its own interests. It shouts high-sounding slogans such as 'for the nation and the people'. It professes to 'bring happiness to the nation and welfare to the people'. But these are mere words, and it really plunges the nation into ruin and the people into misery.

The Kuomintang still claims that it is a 'revolutionary political party', but in reality it has long since become something to be revolted against. Its members still talk about revolution, but their words are mere parrot's mimicry. They do not know what they're talking about. How does this political faction continue to exist? The Kuomintang claims that it is the legal government. That is correct, but legality is not enough for a government. It must have the support of the people. Legally, the Kuomintang can be said to be a government. Morally, it is simply a bandit. The Kuomintang holds political power by force and guns … We honour Dr Sun Yat-sen as 'the Father of the Nation', but his principles have been exploited for selfish gain. How his spirit must protest this cruelty and shame!

The conclusions that I have drawn may be profoundly disturbing to some people. These conclusions are supported by facts, but some people see these facts and others do not. Still others see them and then, not liking them, turn away and pretend that they haven't seen them. I ask you to let the facts speak for themselves.

1   *The Three People's Principles*. The Kuomintang talks about these day and night. In the May 6th Draft Constitution [1936] it is provided that 'China shall be a Republic of the Three People's Principles'. The first of these principles is nationalism, which means to help each national group to obtain independence and freedom. But the only positive achievement of the Kuomintang has been to recognize the independence of Outer Mongolia. The second principle is that of the people's rights. But the people have no rights. The only right the people have is the right to attend the weekly memorial meetings, to bow to the Kuomintang flag, and to read Kuomintang principles. They have nothing else. I need not talk about the Principle of the People's Livelihood. The streets are filled with beggars. The soldiers live worse than the beggars. The streets are filled with them for everyone to see.

2   *Limitation of Capital and Equalization of Land Ownership*. The Kuomintang has been talking about this for twenty years. But look at the war profiteers! Did anyone ever try to limit

their capital? How do they propose to equalize ownership of land? Maybe they are waiting until the peasants can no longer afford to plant their crops because of the heavy land tax. Not only has nothing been done, but, when I asked the Chairman of the Kuomintang and other responsible people about it, they all said that they do not yet have any plan.

3 *The Period of Tutelage.* It has always been said that this period is intended to train the people for the assumption of their political rights. Who has heard of any training being done? The real purpose of 'tutelage' is to postpone constitutional government indefinitely.

4 *The People's Assembly.* So far we have heard only about the construction of buildings for the Assembly. Dr Sun's will, which called for the convocation of a People's Assembly 'in the shortest possible time', was written in 1925. 'The shortest possible time' is already twenty years. No wonder that foreigners complain that the Chinese idea of a unit of time is very long.

5 *Thought control.* This is the only thing that can be said to have been a really successful undertaking …

What can be done? First, we must abolish one-party rule so that the whole attitude of the government can be changed. I will suggest concrete steps that might be taken. For the sake of our country and for his own sake, I advise Chiang Kai-shek to resign … Not only should Chiang Kai-shek resign, but also all his lieutenants. They bear their share of responsibility and should be punished. A coalition government should be formed which might include enlightened and liberal-minded Kuomintang elements. When formed, the coalition government should call a convention to draft a constitution for the nation.

The above would be the ideal solution. However, I realize that it might not be practicable and so I suggest the following: to abolish one-party rule and tutelage, but to allow Chiang Kai-shek to stay. This does not mean that we want him, but merely that, since he will not get out, we will suffer him under certain conditions: (a) the 'Supreme Leader', 'Chief of State', or 'President' must come within the law. This means that Chiang Kai-shek must abide by the law, shall have no part in legislation, and cannot change laws at will. (b) Policy making must be removed from Chiang Kai-shek and given to the policy-making body. Chiang Kai-shek could participate, but he would have only one vote. If this is not done, the Political Consultative Council will be impotent. (c) The responsibility for putting agreed policies into practice must be vested in a group and not in one man. Only when this is done will ministers become responsible officials. (d) The number of posts held by Kuomintang members must be limited to twenty-five per cent of the total or at most thirty-three per cent. This is necessary because of the poor record of Kuomintang officials in the past, and because the Kuomintang is badly in need of a purge. If this were done, there would not be many members left qualified to hold official posts …

With regard to the National Assembly, delegates must be elected by the people under a coalition government. The present delegates were appointed by Chiang Kai-shek and the two Chen brothers and cannot be recognized. After the coalition government is formed, it should promulgate an electoral law, and the new delegates should be elected according to that law.

In conclusion, I want to tell you a story. General Kuan Lin-cheng once told me that Professor Ch'ien Tuan-sheng was a Communist. I asked him how he knew this. He replied that, in one of his speeches, Professor Ch'ien had referred to Chiang Kai-shek as Mr Chiang instead of 'The Leader' and had described him as 'senile'. If this makes Professor Ch'ien a

Communist, I do not know what I shall be called after this speech. But we who love our country and the truth, and who do not wish to be slaves, must not hesitate to speak up. Our consciences, our education, and all that our great teachers have taught us leave us no other course but to speak loudly in this time of serious national crisis.

Source: Speech by Professor Chang Hsi-jo, from Chiang Kai-shek,
China's Destiny, **edited by Philip Jaffe (London: Denis Dobson, 1947), pp. 312–20**

6.6 Attacking the landlords in Houhua village

Wang Fucheng

During the Civil War the Communists pursued their aims of destroying the landlord class and redistributing their land and other assets. The process was interrupted whenever the Guomindang regained territory.

Land reform began again after the Guomindang New Fifth Army left. A work team of two or three people from the district came to promote it. Some were Communist Party members and some were not, but all represented the Party. They reorganized a peasant association and held meetings where people were told about the landlords' crimes and taught how to criticize them.

There were two rich peasant households in the village, those of Wang Yinchun and Wang Xuewu, and two landlord households, headed by Wang Demao and Wang Zengduo, who we called Wu Laoda. There were about 40 middle peasant households, 100 poor peasant households, and 10 hired laborers. The total land area was about 4,000 mu; 2,500 was crop land and 1,500 was salt land. The landlords and rich peasants owned almost two-thirds of the crop land, about 1,600 mu. Middle peasant families owned between 5 and 20 mu each, and poor peasants owned almost none – 3.5 mu per family at most. Most earned their livelihood by making salt; 100 jin of salt was worth about 6 jin of grain. Some poor peasants and hired laborers worked long-term for rich peasants, and some worked only at harvest time; some begged …

During land reform I was not a Party member, but I was an activist working for the Party. I would do anything I was asked to do. I shouted slogans and went from house to house to collect people for meetings. I criticized the landlords, telling them to confess that their property came from us. I led people to their houses and brought their furniture to our office to be distributed to poor peasants. Sometimes we would go to the landlords' houses at night and beat them.

Wang Zengduo (Wu Loada) was the only person from this village who was killed during the land reform. He had left the village and come back with the Guomindang. He wasn't really even a landlord. He had about 100 mu of land that he farmed himself as well as hiring others to help him, so he was really just a rich peasant. We called him a landlord because people hated him. So, you see, we had two criteria for landlord status – one was based on land and labor, and the other was based on the attitude of the masses. Wang Zengduo was the kind of person commonly referred to as *eba* (evil tyrant). If the poor went to his fields to scavenge after harvest, he beat them, especially women and children. Once, he stripped naked a woman who was gleaning his field. This enraged the people. When the poor wanted to borrow anything, he would beat and curse them. His crimes were very serious. The poor peasants themselves decided he should be killed. We had an organization called the United Defense Brigade that approved it. He was shot.

There were other sharp struggles in the village. We struggled against Wang Zengduo's widow in the east of the village. We hung her from a big tree with a rope tied to her hands behind her body. I was the director of the meeting. Most people taking part were women and children. They beat her to find our where she had hidden family property.

Wang Xuewu's wife was also hung from a tree and beaten. I shouted 'Down with the landlords. If you don't confess, we'll hang you higher.'

Redistribution of land was based on the number of people in each household. In this village each person was to get 1.5 mu of crop land. The amount differed according to the quality of the land. There were many arguments and much bitterness over the division of property. One rich peasant family didn't talk to their neighbors for several decades after land reform.

Source: Peter J. Seybolt, *Throwing the Emperor from His Horse: Portrait of a Village Leader in China, 1923–1995* (Boulder, Colorado: Westview Press, 1996), pp. 35–6

6.7 The Communist Party reassesses its policy towards the peasants, 18 January 1948

1   The interests of the poor peasants and farm labourers and the forward role of the poor peasant leagues must be our first concern. Our Party must launch the land reform through the poor peasants and farm labourers and must enable them to play the forward role in the peasant associations and in the government organs of the rural districts. This forward role consists in forging unity with the middle peasants for common action and not in casting aside the middle peasants and monopolizing the work. The position of the middle peasant is especially important in the old liberated areas where the middle peasants are the majority and the poor peasants and farm labourers a minority. The slogan 'The poor peasants and farm labourers conquer the country and should rule the country' is wrong. In the villages it is the farm labourers, poor peasants, middle peasants, and other working people, united together under the leadership of the Chinese Communist Party, who conquer the country and should rule the country, and it is not the poor peasants and farm labourers alone who conquer the country and should rule the country. In the country as a whole, it is the workers, peasants (including the new rich peasants), small independent craftsmen and traders, middle and small capitalists oppressed and injured by the reactionary forces, students, teachers, professors and ordinary intellectuals, professionals, enlightened gentry, ordinary government employees, oppressed minority nationalities, and overseas Chinese, all united together under the leadership of the working class (through the Communist Party), who conquer the country and should rule the country, and it is not merely some of the people who conquer the country and should rule the country.

2   We must avoid adopting any adventurist policies towards the middle peasants. In the cases of middle peasants and persons of other strata whose class status has been wrongly determined, corrections should be made without fail, and any of their belongings that have been distributed should be returned, as far as that is possible. The tendency to exclude middle peasants from the ranks of the peasants' representatives

and from the peasants' committees and the tendency to counterpose them to the poor peasants and farm labourers in the land reform struggle must be corrected. Peasants with an income from exploitation should be classified as middle peasants if such income is less than 25 per cent of their total income, and classified as rich peasants if it is more. The land of well-to-do middle peasants must not be distributed without the owner's consent.

Source: 'Some Concrete Problems of Policy in the Land Reform and Mass Movements', 18 January 1948. In *Selected Works of Mao Tse-tung*, Vol. 3, (Beijing: Foreign Languages Press, 1965), pp. 182–3

6.8 Inflation and student protest in 1947

William Sewell

William Sewell, a British Quaker, taught Biology in Chengdu at the West China Union University. Inadvertently caught up by the Japanese invasion of Hong Kong, he was interned until 1945. He returned to the university at Chengdu (which he called Duliang to protect individuals) in 1947 and decided to stay on after some other Westerners had left.

The economic situation was beginning to dominate everything. Duliang is situated in fertile rice country, and the well-being of the people was indicated by the price and availability of rice. A teacher eats about a bushel of rice every month, though a manual worker needs more. In 1939 it cost two Chinese dollars a bushel, but, as a result of the Japanese occupation of part of China, it had risen to $45 before I left on my ill-fated trip to the coast in 1941. [Sewell was caught up in the occupation of Hong Kong and interned throughout the war.] When I returned to Duliang in 1947 it had risen to $50,000 a bushel, but already by the spring of the following year it was $110,000. Paper money was almost worthless; we were most of us millionaires, but quite unable to cope. We began to know the terror that comes from a galloping inflation, the lack of security when money received on Friday has lost half its value by Saturday, and is useless on Monday. We knew, moreover, that there was no end in sight.

Dr David Fan, the President of the University, was worried about his Chinese staff, as indeed we all were. In his long years of wise guidance he had never faced a problem like this. Only the previous month, salaries had been doubled. Although they were linked to the cost of living index, prices rose too quickly for the University to be able to keep up. When I asked my Chinese colleagues in the Department of Chemistry how they were managing, they looked blankly at one another. It was the youngest, Fu May-lan, who spoke up for all. 'When I must have a new pair of shoes, my salary is sufficient to buy one shoe and then I must trust to being able to buy the other shoe the following month' – and the bitter laugh from all who were gathered round the bench showed that they felt she had spoken well ...

In the days when students had paid their fees in silver, it was easy work for all; but with inflation came hardship. Parents of a student, living two days travel away, would sell a small piece of land or some produce to pay fees for a year; but by the time the student arrived two days later there was sufficient only for one term, or perhaps just for a month. Fees which had been $20 a term had increased to five million and were still rising. So it was agreed that fees should be paid in kind; and special stores were built for the rice that was brought, often from long distances away. But quality varied, and rice was soon infested with insects if not properly cared for …

Rice was frequently hard to get. The military men, who were becoming richer while the others got poorer, were buying it up, storing it, and then selling again only when the price was much higher. The government agreed to provide rice at a nominal price for the students to eat; but even then there was trickery. The students were given orders to collect rice at distances so great that there was no means of bringing it to Duliang even if the distant officials had been willing to give it.

At last the students, hungry and anxious, could stand it no longer. A demonstration was planned to ask the Governor to give the rice that he had promised on easier terms, and to provide transport if it had to come from a distance. A thousand strong, they marched to the headquarters of the Military Governor, placards lifted high, flags flying, and slogans shouted by voices that quickly grew hoarse.

The students arrived in the square, where all was hushed. Then, at a given signal, hundreds of soldiers and police, who had been hidden round about, ran out brandishing sticks and carrying ropes. Those students whom they caught they bound and drove indoors, some were trampled on and injured, but many escaped. The captured students were whipped and mostly set free; but some were confined overnight and kept without food until they were released. When they straggled back to the campus, President Fan was there to meet them, tears streaming down his face with emotion that students should have been treated in such a manner.

Thus the tide was turned. The situation was never the same again. 'Others have shed their blood. What about you?' was the question in blazing red characters that screamed from the walls of every building at Jen Dah. The Military Governor had kindled a torch.

Liu Lo-lah had shed blood – at least just a trifle. She and Min-lah had both been in the procession. Next day she had knocked at my door. I saw her face pressing against the glass as I went to open. 'Shien-sen', she cried, 'look what they have done', and, turning, she lifted her gown to show the red weals behind both her knees. They were the sign of a change in her life. I saw them again and again until they had faded, leaving no discernable mark, though the scar on her soul increased until it consumed her.

'Now I have hate', she spoke the words deliberately and so low that I could hardly hear them. 'Only those with great hate can have great love'. She told of her longing to love with ever greater intensity the poor of the land, the ignorant peasants, and all to whom privilege is denied. 'And the Chinese women especially I would love', she told me. 'You have heard from my brother of our misery. We are not born just for ourselves, but for the multitude who suffer. You can never know what Chinese women have suffered, the agonies and the humiliations they have endured. They are suffering now, as my mother suffered, and her mother's mother. But now is the time; now is the change. If we fail now, if we are weak, the chance will be lost, and misery will continue to my daughter, and my daughter's daughter. I am uneasy and ashamed that my home is rich; but I must become one of the people. I must hate what they hate; love what they love' …

In her present mood it seemed important simply to listen to her as she talked, yet her words about hatred troubled me. 'Only those who have greatly suffered are capable of deep love or indeed of bitter hate', I tried to persuade her, telling her that they were not of necessity dependent on each other. In the end I believe she has driven some of the bitterness from her. She agreed that if it lay in her heart it would cloud her mind, warp her judgement, and make it less easy to achieve her great purpose.

What this purpose was seemed clear to me. There was no need to ask her, for I knew the answer before she gave it. 'Apart from Communism', she said, 'there is now no hope for China or the masses of her people'. Though I argued against it, she would not agree.

'I must teach you to understand. You are too foreign yet to know. It is our only hope. Our present government must go', and she tightened her grasp on my hand with her short fingers as she sought for English words with which to express her meaning. 'They now serve only the rich and rob the poor, so that the few can live in ever greater luxury'.

Source: William Sewell, *I Stayed in China*
(London: George Allen and Unwin, 1966), pp. 21–2, 24–7

6.9 The Communist army enters Nanjing, April 1949

Seymour Topping, a reporter with Associated Press

During the upheaval of the civil war, most liberal students chose the Communists, attracted by their asceticism and dedication, and repelled by the corruption and police brutality of the Kuomintang. Thousands went into the 'liberated areas' to work for the Communist cause without any prior intellectual commitment to Marxism–Leninism. The students whom the Communist troops met on the morning of April 24 near the Northwest Gate had elected to remain in the Nationalist areas, to continue their schooling and agitate for peace and good government from within. This was not enough to elicit the trust of the Communists. Several weeks after the Communist entry, I saw a column of thousands of students escorted by soldiers being marched down to the river to strengthen the dykes against the spring floods. The students were being indoctrinated not only through political lectures by army commissars but also by participation in manual labor, from which the classical tradition exempted intellectuals and to which they were not accustomed. The Party would be ready to greet those who passed the ideological tests.

The orderly entry of the Communist army was marred by in incident at [US Ambassador] Stuart's residence. At 6.30 a.m., 12 peasant soldiers sightseeing round the big city chanced on the embassy, forced the night gatekeeper to open the iron gates, and several blundered into the ambassador's bedroom, awakening the 72 year old envoy. 'Who are you? What do you want?' the Ambassador shouted. The armed soldiers left muttering and returned with the others, one of them explaining that they were simply looking round and meant no harm …

The incident was widely publicized after the embassy reported to Washington, making the Communists appear provocative and belligerent …

I, too, became involved in an incident with the Communist soldiers at the Associated Press House. Upon my return from the Northwest Gate, three soldiers entered my office as I sat at a typewriter. They were accompanied by Liu, my number one servant. Pointedly addressing themselves to Liu, they asked what I did. 'Oh, he sends messages to the United States,' Liu said casually, not seeing he was arousing the ideological vigilance of our guests. 'What does he say in these messages?' the spokesman asked suspiciously of Liu. My spirits sank as Liu replied: 'He reports about everything.' That did it. With fixed bayonets, the delegation marched out, and within a few minutes the house was surrounded by sentries. I could not leave, nor could my cook go to the market for food. Ronning [at the Canadian Embassy], hearing of my plight, delivered food packages through the barbed wire fence. I telephoned the USIS officer at the embassy and gave him a message to be sent to Fred Hampson, the AP Bureau chief in Shanghai. The message, intended to describe my predicament, said: 'Boy Scouts posted at front door.' Hampson promptly included it in one of his dispatches. After two days the sentries vanished without explanation. Other incidents, almost always due to some misunderstanding, occurred at the French embassy and other foreign properties.

In celebration of their victory, Communist soldiers climbed onto the facades and roofs of government buildings and Chiang Kai-shek's former office in the T'ai P'ing Palace to plant their red flags. Some of the Communist soldiers camped in the looted and stripped residences of the former Nationalist officials, bringing their small shaggy ponies into the houses or turning them out to graze on the lawns.

A proclamation signed by Ch'en Yi told government employees they could keep their jobs if they were not on the war criminal list. All property of Chiang Kai-shek was ordered confiscated. Foreign property and nationals were assured protection if they did not engage in espionage, shelter war criminals, or otherwise 'impair the interests of the Chinese people' ...

The only newspaper to appear, filled with laudatory articles welcoming the Communists, was the Catholic *Yi Shih Pao*. The official Communist New China News Agency began functioning, staffed by journalists who two days earlier had been working for the official Nationalist Central News Agency. About 60 political prisoners were released from jail, including a number of Chinese newsmen. Into the prison went the crippled former Mayor Teng Cheih, Shen Ching-cheng, director of the Nationalist Social Affairs Bureau, and Hsu Hsin-nung, director of the City Health Bureau. Teng was charged with trying to make off with the City funds that had been allocated as severance pay for the municipal employees.

Most of the shops in the city remained closed because of uncertainty as to what currency to accept. Those open sold goods only for silver dollars. Water and electric utilities were restored, but service was erratic ...

Some of Ch'en Yi's troops remained in Nanking a few days as the bulk of the army wheeled to the east and thrust to Hangchow on the coast to cut off and envelop Shanghai. Liu Po-ch'eng was proclaimed Chairman of the Nanking Military Control Commission and later named Mayor. Not long after he assumed control of the city, apprehensive Chinese businessmen were reassured by the legendary one-eyed Szechwanese general who met with them. 'Members of the Communist Party announce unreservedly that we fight for Communism, that we plan eventually to materialize a Communist society,' the general told them. 'However, being believers in materialism, we realize that the revolution in its present stage belongs to the new democracy. Under these conditions we should make friends with over 90 percent of the people and we oppose only reactionaries who represent less than 10 percent.'

Liu said that, during the period of the 'new democracy,' the Communists wanted to concentrate on the development of production by promoting private as well as public enterprises, giving equal attention to capital and labor. In the past, he said, the Communists had espoused 'erroneous policies of excessively high wages and excessively high income tax.'

Liu's Control Commission administered the city through a secretariat and eight bureaus. These handled supplies, foreign affairs, real estate control, financial and economic affairs, military takeover, political takeover, cultural takeover, and public security. The bureaus were largely staffed by former Nationalist employees who were content with the new regime. Many of them had indulged previously in graft simply because they could not feed their families on the fixed government salaries during a rampant inflation. The Communists had converted the old Nationalists gold yuan into new Communist People's banknotes. Although the general price index was rising gradually, the government employees and the population generally were able for the first time in years to buy basic commodities at fairly stable prices. As in other Communist cities, the price of daily necessities was controlled by the Government Trading Corporation, dealing in such commodities as rice, flour, bean oil, pork, coarse cloth, and fuel.

After the first weeks of occupation, beggars disappeared from the streets, although there was considerable unemployment. Most shops reopened, but trade was slack. The Communists lifted the Kuomintang ban on dance halls. One did not hear from the people any more complaints of petty police corruption ...

During May there was no radical change in the cultural life of Nanking. The Communists extended their controls gradually. They took over the National Central University, but the foreign-assisted private schools such as Nanking University and Ginling College operated under the former presidents with no changes and curricula. At Nanking University a new board was set-up in which professors, instructors, administrative staff, students, and campus workers were represented.

Students generally greeted the establishment of Communist power with great enthusiasm. They formed speaking teams which toured the city explaining the 'new democracy' to the people. They sang Communist songs and performed the popular Yang Ko or rice planting song dances on the streets. Each dancer, arms akimbo, would take three short steps forwards, then three backwards, with a kick often added as an extra flourish, while symbols and drums gave the beat. Couples would weave in and out under a bridge of arms. Communist soldiers taught students the steps of the revolutionary reel, and newspapers published words of the songs. One popular song went:

Reactionaries who exploit the people deserve to be cut into thousands of pieces.
They totally ignore the affections of the common people and want only to be dictators.
Big landlords, big warlords, big compradors, big families – all conspire together, all
    conspire together, all conspire together.
And therefore, we poor people suffer.

Source: Seymour Topping, *Journey between Two Chinas*
(New York: Harper and Row, 1972), pp. 74–9

6.10 Who lost China? Chiang Kai-shek testifies

Lloyd E. Eastman

To tell the truth, never, in China or abroad, has there been a revolutionary party as decrepit (*tuitang*) and degenerate (*fubai*) as we (the Guomindang) are today; nor one as lacking spirit, lacking discipline, and, even more, lacking standards of right and wrong as we are today. This kind of party should long ago have been destroyed and swept away!

The time was January 1948; the speaker was Chiang Kai-shek. Frequently during 1947–50, the climactic years of struggle with the Communists for control of the Chinese mainland, Chiang addressed his military commanders and civilian cadres in similarly scathing, forthright language. His purpose, he asserted, was to identify the causes of Nationalist areas and weakness so that he could 'turn defeat to victory.' Chiang's speeches from that period – readily available in published form for years, but until now ignored by all – shed light from an entirely new direction on the controversial question of why the Nationalists were defeated by the Communists ...

Chiang Kai-shek was surprised and humiliated by the accumulating series of defeats. 'Regardless of what aspect we discuss,' he declared in June 1947, 'we hold an absolute superiority; in terms of troops, equipment, battle techniques, and experience, the Communists are not our equal ... And we are also 10 times richer than the Communist army in terms of military-supply replacements, such as food, fodder, and ammunition' ... During 1947 and 1948, Chiang examined this question repeatedly and from different perspectives. With regard to the military he observed the chief weaknesses were:

1   *Lack of military knowledge and skill.* The officers, Chiang declared, were utterly lacking in professional ability. Most commanders, from the top to the bottom level, 'fight muddle-headed battles' (*da hutu zhang*). 'No one studies theory or basic military manuals (*Dian fanling*); even less do they pay attention to reconnoitring the enemy's situation or the lie of the land; they indifferently draw up plans and casually issue orders, and are unable to study carefully or make thorough preparations' ...

2   *Poor conditions of the common soldiers.* Chiang scolded these officers for their indifference to the condition of their men. They so ignored such basic elements in their training as aiming, firing, reconnoitring, and liaison that 'the soldiers combat skills are so poor that they cannot fight.' Nor did they provide the troops with adequate food, clothing or medical care, even embezzling supplies meant for the men. Chiang's solution was that the officers should 'eat what the troops eat, wear what the troops wear, and live in the troops' barracks.' He added: 'We can say that the Communists' military cadres have already completely attained this' ...

3   *Moral and spiritual shortcomings.* 'It cannot be denied,' Chiang observed in June 1947, 'that the spirit of most commanders is broken and their morality is base.' High-level officers had become complacent in their high posts, encumbered by family members and acting like warlords. 'As a consequence, their revolutionary spirit is almost completely dissipated, and they are concerned only with preserving their *shi li* (military strength and resources)' ...

Chiang felt that his commanders deceived him in their reports from the battlefield. One of their most serious deceptions, he said, was that 'now, when many troops at first arrive at the front and still have not actually established contact with the enemy, they say that such-and-such an enemy troop column has arrived at their front, such-and-such a column at their flanks, and it seems as though the situation is absolutely critical. But if you go and investigate the actual situation, there are only a few of the enemy, and perhaps no such unit at all at their front. And after establishing contact, they often exaggerate victory, saying that they have killed so many thousands or tens-of-thousands of the enemy' ...

The civilian branches of the regime fared no better than the army in Chiang's assessment. Both the Guomindang and the Youth Corps, he said in September 1947, lacked organization, training, and discipline; they 'can be said to be mere empty shells, without any real strength.' Four months later, he observed that 'Our revolutionary work is conducted carelessly and perfunctorily so there is absolutely no progress.' And, because of the Party's mistakes, 'most people in society attack the Party unsparingly, even regarding Party members as offenders against the state and the nation.'

Amazingly, Chiang expressed unabashed admiration for the Communists. They represented everything he admired and everything the Nationalist regime lacked: organization, discipline, and morality ...

Despite his pessimism about the condition of the Guomindang and his army in 1947–8, Chiang Kai-shek was not, of course, prepared to abandon the field to Mao Zedong. 'Although [the Communist organization, training, propaganda techniques, etc.] are all superior to ours,' said Chiang in September 1947, 'our ideology, thought and [political] line are nevertheless definitely more correct than theirs and are, moreover, more suited to the needs of the nation. Therefore, if only we can study everything of theirs and comprehend everything of theirs, we can then have assurance of annihilating them.'

The march of events did not, however, allow the Nationalists the needed time to 'study everything of theirs and comprehend everything of theirs.' And on 21 January 1949 – with the economy nearing total collapse, with the army being pushed back to the Yangtze River, and with the people feeling disillusioned with, and even contempt for, the government in Nanjing – Chiang Kai-shek resigned the presidency ...

During the summer of 1949, Chiang again plunged into the maelstrom of Chinese politics. Using his post as Director-General of the Guomindang (which he had retained even though resigning as President) and control of the government's gold reserve (which he had secreted out of Shanghai to Taipei) as his chief weapons, he engaged in a bitter power struggle with Acting-President Li Tsung-jen. Finally, as Communist armies consolidated their control on the mainland, Li flew to the United States in December 1949, and Chiang Kai-shek, taking refuge in Taiwan, resumed the office of President of the National Government in March 1950.

Source: Lloyd Eastman, 'Who Lost China? Chiang Kai-shek Testifies',
China Quarterly, **No. 88, December 1981, pp. 658–62**

7

The Sino-Soviet Alliance, the Korean War, and the early years of the People's Republic, 1949–55

By the summer of 1949, with victory in sight, Mao Zedong stated that 'there could be no third road' and that China would 'lean to one side' in the cold war – the Soviet Union.

There was an obvious need to rewrite the Sino-Soviet relationship in the Yalta agreement, and the GMD–Soviet Treaty of August 1945, which had restored Russian interests in Manchuria. So, while the Communist forces were still rooting out Nationalist forces in the south west, Mao took the train to Moscow (6 December), arriving on 16 December. At the initial meeting, Stalin was loathe to jettison the Yalta accords and several weeks passed with Mao ignored, and fretting, in Stalin's personal dacha. Eventually, it was agreed that Zhou Enlai should come to Moscow, a harbinger of a new settlement. On 14 February the Sino-Soviet treaty was agreed. The parties contracted (1) to resist jointly any resumption of Japanese aggression, (2) not to join in any alliance against one another, (3) to work together for peace and security throughout the world, and (4) to develop and consolidate economic and cultural ties, and to render all other possible economic assistance and to carry out necessary economic cooperation. A few weeks later it was agreed to set up joint stock companies for the development of Xinjiang's mineral resources, and to establish a Sino-Soviet airline and a shipyard in Dalian. So, with the promise of technical and financial assistance loaned at one per cent interest, Soviet experts went out to help build the new China on the Soviet industrial model – with a few 'wedding cake' architectural monstrosities such as hotels and exhibition venues!

In 1945, Korea, occupied since 1910 by the Japanese, was liberated as a theoretically unified nation. Pending de facto unification, the peninsula was occupied by the Americans in the South under Syngman Rhee and by the Russians supporting their protégé Kim Il Sung in the North. Meanwhile, the People's Republic of China made no secret of its urgent objective – the pursuit of Chiang Kai-chek's fugitive regime now established on the island of Taiwan. With a confidence that soon proved to be unfounded, the Americans under President Truman and Secretary of State Acheson announced that they would not 'pursue a course that will lead to involvement in the civil conflict in China' and 'will not provide military aid or advice to Chinese forces on Formosa (Taiwan)'. What Acheson described as the dawning of a new and amicable relationship, rid of American paternalism, was taken by Kim Il Sung as a signal for reuniting Korea by force.

In June 1950, the North Koreans, after consultation with both Stalin and Mao, invaded South Korea. The United Nations (effectively the United States and its allies) intervened. As it became clear that the North Koreans could not sustain the war themselves, Stalin encouraged Mao to send in the People's Liberation Army in the guise of 'volunteers'. In the event, China bore the brunt of the conflict with appalling casualties (estimates vary from 366,000 to 920,000) but had the satisfaction of fighting the United States and its allies to a draw.

Any prospect of capturing Taiwan was set back indefinitely by a Mutual Security Pact on 2 December 1954 between the United States and the Nationalists. With the need to suppress treasonable activities at home, the People's Republic issued a stream of directives against counter-revolutionaries. This was followed at the end of 1951 by the 'three antis' campaign against corruption, waste, and bureaucratism, and the 'five antis' campaign against bribery, tax evasion, fraud, theft of government property, and economic secrets. Western visitors reported favourably on the absence of corruption and a range of reforms – notably a literacy campaign, and improved status for women. The first law proclaimed in the PRC was the Marriage Law of 1950. *Inter alia* this abolished concubinage and arranged marriages, gave women equal rights in family property, and provided new laws on divorce (In the first year there were almost one million divorces).

Although some entrepreneurs and other middle-class elements had fled on liberation, many had stayed. Many intellectuals were prepared to work in a new China. For the time being, private ownership had a role in industry. While the landlords were wiped out as a class, the reorganization of the countryside proceeded relatively gently for a few years.

7.1 Conversations between Stalin and Mao

With the Communists gaining ground in 1948–9, Stalin had ambivalent views. After all, it was the Guomingdang regime with which Stalin had made wartime agreements and the Sino-Soviet Treaty of August 1945. Although Mao had doubts about Stalin's commitment to the communist cause in China, he was preparing to lean to the Soviet side in the cold war. However, three times in 1947–8 and again early in 1949, Chinese proposals for Mao to go to Moscow were turned down. Eventually, the Soviets invited Liu Shaoqi, Mao's second in command, to visit Moscow in the summer of 1949. During this meeting and after further pressure, the Soviets agreed that Mao should go to Moscow in December, nominally for Stalin's 70th birthday.

7.1a Conversation between Stalin and Mao, Moscow, 16 December 1949

After an exchange of greetings and a discussion of general topics, the following conversation took place.

COMRADE MAO ZEDONG: The most important question at the present time is the question of establishing peace. China needs a period of 3–5 years of peace, which should be used to bring the economy back to prewar levels and to stabilize the country in general …

COMRADE STALIN: In China a war for peace, as it were, is taking place. The question of peace greatly preoccupies the Soviet Union as well, though we have already had peace for the past four years. With regards to China, there is no immediate threat at the present time: Japan has yet to stand up upon its feet and is thus not ready for war; America, though it screams war, is actually afraid of war more than anything; Europe is afraid of war; in essence, there is no one to fight with China, not unless Kim Il Sung decides to invade China? Peace will depend on our efforts. If we continue to be friendly, peace can last not only 5–10 years but 20–25 years and perhaps even longer.

COMRADE MAI ZEDONG: Since Liu Shaoqi's return to China, CC CPC has been discussing the treaty of friendship, alliance, and mutual assistance between China and the USSR.

COMRADE STALIN: This question we can discuss and decide. We must ascertain whether to declare the continuation of the current 1945 treaty of alliance and friendship between the USSR and China, to announce impending changes in the future, or to make these changes right now. As you know, this treaty was concluded between the USSR and China as a result of the Yalta agreement, which provided for the main points of the treaty (the question of the Kurile Islands, South Sakhalin, Port Arthur, etc.). This is why we searched to find a way to modify the current treaty in effect while formally maintaining its provisions, in this case by formally maintaining the Soviet Union's right to station its troops at Port Arthur while, at the request of the Chinese government, actually withdrawing the Soviet armed forces currently stationed there ... The withdrawal of troops does not mean the Soviet Union refuses to assist China, if such assistance is needed. The fact is that we, as Communists, are not altogether comfortable with stationing of forces on foreign soil, especially on the soil of a friendly nation. Given this situation, anyone could say that, if Soviet forces can be stationed on Chinese territory, then why could not the British, for example, station their forces in Hong Kong, or the Americans in Tokyo? We would gain much in the arena of international relations if, with mutual agreement, the Soviet forces were to be withdrawn from Port Arthur. In addition, the withdrawal of Soviet forces would provide a serious boost to Chinese Communists in their relations with the national bourgeoisie. Everyone would see that Communists have managed to achieve what [Nationalist Chinese leader] Jiang Jieshi [Chiang Kai-shek] could not. The Chinese Communists must take the national bourgeoisie into consideration ...

COMRADE MAO ZEDONG: In discussing the treaty in China we had not taken into account the American and English positions regarding the Yalta agreement. We must act in a way that is best for the common cause. This question merits further consideration. However, it is already becoming clear that the treaty should not be modified at the present time, nor should one rush to withdraw troops from Port Arthur.

> **Source: Conversation between Stalin and Mao on 16 December 1949,** *Cold War*
> *International History Project Bulletin,* **Winter 1995–6, pp.5–6**

7.1b Moscow, 22 January 1950

STALIN: There are two groups of questions that must be discussed: the first group of questions concerns the existing agreements between the USSR and China; the second group of questions concerns the current events in Manchuria, Xinjiang, etc. I think that it would be better to begin not with the current events but rather with a discussion of the existing agreements. We believe that these agreements need to be changed, though earlier we had thought that they could be left intact. The existing agreements, including the treaty, should be changed because war against Japan figures at the very heart of the treaty. Since the war is over and Japan has been crushed, the situation has been altered, and now the treaty has become an anachronism. I ask to hear your opinion regarding the treaty of friendship and alliance ...

MAO ZEDONG: We must act so as to take into account the interests of both sides, China and the Soviet Union.

STALIN: True. We believe that the agreement concerning Port Arthur is not equitable.

MAO ZEDONG: But changing this agreement goes against the decisions of the Yalta Conference?!

STALIN: True, it does – and to hell with it! Once we have taken up the position that the treaties must be changed, we must go all the way. It is true that for us this entails certain inconveniences, and we will have to struggle against the Americans. But we are already reconciled to that.

MAO ZEDONG: This question worries us only because it may have undesirable consequences for the USSR.

STALIN: As you know, we made the current agreement during the war with Japan. We did not know that Jiang Jieshi would be toppled. We acted under the premise that the presence of our troops in Port Arthur would be in the interests of the Soviet Union and democracy in China.

MAO ZEDONG: The matter is clear.

STALIN: In that case, would you deem the following scenario acceptable: declare that the agreement on Port Arthur shall remain in force until a peace treaty with Japan is signed, after which the Russian troops would be withdrawn from Port Arthur. Or perhaps one could propose another scenario: declare that the current agreement shall remain in place, while in effect withdrawing troops from Port Arthur. We will accept whichever of these scenarios is more suitable. We agree with both scenarios …

MAO ZEDONG: We believe that Port Arthur could serve as a base for our military collaboration, while Dalny could serve as a base for Sino-Soviet economic collaboration. In Dalny there is a whole array of enterprises that we are in no position to exploit without Soviet assistance. We should develop a closer economic collaboration there.

STALIN: In other words, the agreement on Port Arthur will remain in force until a peace treaty is signed with Japan. After the signing of the peace treaty the existing agreement shall become invalid and the Russians shall withdraw their troops. Did I sum up your thoughts correctly?

MAO ZEDONG: Yes, basically so, and it is exactly this that we would like to set forth in the new treaty.

STALIN: Let us continue the discussion of the KChZhD question [the Chinese Changchun Railroad]. Tell us, as an honest Communist, what doubts do you have here?

MAO ZEDONG: The principal point is that the new treaty should note that joint exploitation and administration will continue in the future. However, in the case of administration, China should take the lead role here. Furthermore, it is necessary to examine the question of shortening the duration of the agreement and to determine the amount of investment by each side …

STALIN: Let us discuss the credit agreement. We need to officially formalize that which has already been agreed to earlier. Do you have any observations to make?

MAO ZEDONG: Is the shipment of military arms considered a part of the monetary loan?

STALIN: This you can decide yourself: we can bill that towards the loan, or we can formalize it through trade agreements.

MAO ZEDONG: If the military shipments are billed towards the loan, then we will have little means left for industry. It appears that part of the military shipments will have to be billed towards the loan, while the other part will have to be paid with Chinese goods. Can't the period of delivery of industrial equipment and military arms be shortened from 5 to 3–4 years?

STALIN: We must examine our options. The matter rests in the requisition list for our industry. Nevertheless, we can move the date that the credit agreement goes into effect to 1 January 1950, since the shipments should begin just about now …

MAO ZEDONG: We believe that the conditions of the credit agreement are generally favourable to China. Under its terms we pay only one per cent interest.

STALIN: Our credit agreements with people's democracies provide for two per cent interest. We could, says Comrade Stalin jokingly, increase this interest for you as well, if you would like.

Of course, we acted under the premise that the Chinese economy was practically in ruins. As it is clear from the telegrams that we have received, the Chinese government intends to use its army in the reconstruction of its economy. That is very good. In our time we also made use of the army in our economic development and had very good results … Any other questions?

MAO ZEDONG: I would like to note that the air regiment that you sent to China was very helpful. They transported 10 thousand people. Let me thank you, comrade Stalin, for the help and ask you to allow it to stay a little longer, so it could help transport provisions to [CCP CC member and commander of the PLA's Second Field Army] Liu Bocheng's troops, currently preparing for an attack on Tibet.

STALIN: It's good that you are preparing to attack. The Tibetans need to be subdued. As for the air regiment, we shall talk this over with the military personnel and give you an answer.

The meeting took two hours.

Mao obtained a formal alliance that promised Soviet military aid against Japanese aggression or 'any other state that may collaborate in any way with Japan in acts of aggression'. In addition, China was given military aid for developing its air force and heavy artillery and a loan of $300 million at 1 per cent. China was to receive Soviet technicians and Chinese personnel were sent for training in the Soviet Union.

Source: Conversation between Stalin and Mao on 22 January 1950,
***Cold War International History Project Bulletin*, Winter 1995–6, pp. 7–9**

7.2 Selected ciphered telegrams on the beginning of the Korean War

The role of Stalin and Mao in approving the North Korean invasion of the South is the subject of these telegrams between Shtykov, the Soviet Ambassador to North Korea, and the Soviet Foreign Minister, and between Stalin and Shtykov, and Stalin and Mao.

FROM SHTYKOV TO VYSHINSKY, 19 JANUARY 1950

Strictly secret. I report about the frame of mind expressed by Kim Il Sung during a luncheon at the Ministry of Foreign Affairs of the DPRK. On January 17 the Minister of Foreign Affairs of the DPRK, Pak Hon-yong, held a lunch attended by a small circle of persons, on the occasion of the departure of the Korean ambassador Yi Chu-Yon to the Chinese People's Republic …

During the luncheon, Kim Il Sung and the Chinese trade representative, who was sitting next to him, many times enthusiastically conversed with each other in Chinese. From individual phrases it was possible to understand that they were speaking about the victory in China and about the situation in Korea. After the luncheon in the reception room, Kim Il Sung gave advice and orders to his ambassador to China, Yi Chu-Yon, about his work in China, and moreover, while speaking in Korean, Kim several times said phrases in Russian about how Yi would act boldly in China, since Mao Zedong is his friend and will always help Korea …

Further, Kim said that he himself cannot begin an attack, because he is a Communist, a disciplined person, and for him the order of Comrade Stalin is law. Then he stated that, if it is now possible to meet with Comrade Stalin, then he will try to meet with Mao Zedong, after his return from Moscow. Kim underscored that Mao Zedong promised to render him assistance after the conclusion of the war in China. (Apparently, Kim Il Sung has in mind the conversation of his representative Kim Il with Mao Zedong in June 1949, about which I reported by ciphered telegram.) Kim said that he also has other questions for Mao Zedong, in particular the question of the possibility of the creation of an eastern bureau of the Cominform …

Then Kim Il Sung came toward me, took me aside, and began the following conversation: can he meet with Comrade Stalin and discuss the question of the position in the south and the question of aggressive actions against the army of Rhee Syngmann, that their people's army now is significantly stronger than the army of Rhee Syngmann. Here he stated that, if it is impossible to meet with Comrade Stalin, then he wants to meet with Mao Zedong, since Mao after his visit to Moscow will have orders on all questions.

Then Kim Il Sung placed before me the question, why don't I allow him to attack the Ongjin peninsula, which the People's Army could take in three days, and with a general attack the People's Army could be in Seoul in several days.

I answered Kim that he has not raised the question of a meeting with Comrade Stalin and if he raises such a question then it is possible that Comrade Stalin will receive him. On the question of an attack on the Ongjin peninsula, I answered that it is impossible to do this. Then I tried to conclude the conversation on these questions and, alluding to a later time, proposed to go home. With that the conversation was concluded.

After the luncheon, Kim Il Sung was in a mood of some intoxication. It was obvious that he began this conversation not accidentally, but had thought it out earlier, with the goal of laying out his frame of mind and elucidating our attitude to these questions.

In the process of this conversation, Kim Il Sung repeatedly underscored his wish to get the advice of Comrade Stalin on the question of the situation in the south of Korea, since [Kim Il Sung] is constantly nurturing his idea about an attack.

STALIN TO SHTYKOV, 30 JANUARY 1950

I received your report. I understand the dissatisfaction of Comrade Kim Il Sung, but he must understand that such a large matter in regard to South Korea as he wants to undertake needs large preparation. The matter must be organized so that there would not be too great a risk. If he wants to discuss this matter with me, then I will always be ready to receive him and discuss with him. Transmit all this to Kim Il Sung and tell him that I am ready to help him in this matter.

HAVING MET KIM IL SUNG, MAO SEEKS CLARIFICATION OF STALIN'S POSITION

Ciphered telegram 13 May 1950. Strictly secret. Making copies is forbidden.
[Stamp: Declassified 14 December 1993]
From [Soviet Ambassador] Peking.
For immediate report to comrade Filippov [Stalin].
Today on May 13, at 23 hours 30 minutes, Chou En-lai paid a visit to me and, following the instructions of Mao Tse-tung, let me know the following:

1   Kim Il Sung and Minister of Foreign Affairs of the Korean People's Democratic Republic, Po Siang-Yung, arrived in Peking on May 13 this year.

2   In the evening, Comrade Mao Tse-tung has had a meeting with them. In the conversation with Comrade Mao Tse-tung, the Korean comrades informed about the directives of comrade Filippov that the present situation has changed from the situation in the past and that North Korea can move toward actions; however, this question should be discussed with China and personally with comrade Mao Tse-tung.

3   The Korean comrades will stay in Peking for 2 days. In connection with the above mentioned, Comrade Mao Tse-tung would like to have personal clarifications of Comrade Filippov on this question, which, according to the previous telegram from Comrade Filippov transferred by the [Soviet] Ambassador [to China] Comrade [N.V.] Roschin, were to follow in coming days. The Chinese comrades are requesting an urgent answer.

STALIN'S REPLY 14 MAY 1950

For Mao Tse-tung.
Comr. Mao Tse-tung!
In a conversation with the Korean comrades, Filippov [Stalin] and his friends expressed the opinion, that, in light of the changed international situation, they agree with the proposal of the Koreans to move toward reunification. In this regard, a qualification was made that the question should be decided finally by the Chinese and Korean comrades together, and, in case of disagreement by the Chinese comrades, the decision on the question should be postponed until a new discussion. The Korean comrades can tell you the details of the conversation.

Filippov
Telegraph the fulfilment
Vyshinsky

5 copies
14 May 1950
Copies:
1   Comr. Stalin
2   Comr. Molotov
3   Comr. Vyshinksy
4   Comr. 10th department
5   Comr. Copy

CIPHERED TELEGRAM, SHTYKOV TO FYN-SI [STALIN], TRANSMITTING LETTER FROM KIM IL SUNG TO STALIN, 8 JULY 1950

To Comrade Fyn-Si [Stalin].
I received the following letter from KIM IL SUNG addressed to us.
To the Chairman of the Council of Ministers of the USSR, Generalissimo Comrade Stalin, I.V.
I ask that you accept the expression of deepest respect and gratitude for the invaluable assistance that you, Comrade Stalin, continually render to our people in their struggle for independence.

Being confident of your desire to help the Korean people rid themselves of the American imperialists, I am obliged to appeal to you with a request to allow the use of 25–35 Soviet military advisers in the staff of the front of the Korean Army and the staffs of the 2nd Army Group, since the national military cadres have not yet sufficiently mastered the art of commanding modern troops.

Yours faithfully,

Kim Il Sung, Chairman of the Cabinet of Ministers DPRK.

Pyongyang, 8 July 1950.

Source: Ciphered Telegrams on the Beginning of the Korean War, *Cold War International History Project Bulletin,* **Spring 1995, pp. 8–9, and Winter 1995–6, pp. 43–4**

7.3 Mao Zedong reports to the Central Committee on the economic prospects for the next three years, 6 June 1950

He appears to be oblivious to the imminent danger of war in Korea.

China is a vast country and conditions are very complex; moreover, the revolution triumphed first in certain areas and only later throughout the country. Accordingly, in the old liberated areas (with a population of approximately 160 million), agrarian reform has been completed, public order has been established, the work of economic construction has started on the right track, the life of most of the working people has improved, and the problem of unemployed workers and intellectuals has been solved (as in the north-east) or is nearing solution (as in north China and Shantung Province). In particular, planned economic construction has begun in the north-east. On the other hand, in the new liberated areas (with a population of approximately 310 million), since liberation occurred only a few months ago, or half a year or one year ago, the more than 400,000 bandits scattered in remote regions have yet to be wiped out, the land problem has not been solved, industry and commerce have not been properly readjusted, unemployment has remained serious, and public order has not been established. In a word, the conditions for carrying out planned economic construction are still lacking. That is why I said some time ago that we had achieved a number of successes on the economic front, for example, budgetary revenues and expenditures were nearly balanced, inflation was being checked, and prices were tending towards stability – all this indicated that the financial and economic situation was beginning to take a turn for the better, but not yet a fundamental turn for the better. Three conditions are required for a fundamental turn for the better in the financial and economic situation, namely (1) completion of agrarian reform, (2) proper readjustment of existing industry and commerce, and (3) large-scale retrenchment in government expenditures. The fulfilment of these three conditions will take some time, say three years or a little longer. The whole Party and nation must strive to bring about these conditions. I believe, and so do you all, that we can surely do this in about three years. By that time, we shall be able to witness a fundamental turn for the better in the entire financial and economic situation of our country.

Source: Mao Zedong: Written Report to Central Committee 6th June 1950, *Selected Works of Mao Tse-tung,* **Vol. 5 (Beijing: Foreign Languages Press, 1977), pp. 28–9**

7.4 An eye-witness account of liberation and early days in the People's Republic

Sidney Shapiro

Administrative organizations were set up, a government was functioning – though it was characteristic of the new regime that it wasn't formally proclaimed until 1 October [1949], when most of China had been liberated, and more experience had been gained in governing a large country.

We stood that day with hundreds of thousands in the square before Tien An Men – the Gate of Heavenly Peace – massive entrance to what had once been called the Forbidden City, the palace where for 500 years China's Emperors had ruled. Now, on the magnificent gate house, topped with tiles of Imperial yellow, Mao Tsetung and his staunchest colleagues had gathered. Mao, the philosopher, poet, and historian, was surely profoundly conscious of the significance of that day as he ringingly proclaimed the establishment of the People's Republic of China.

Phoenix was in tears, and I was deeply moved. It wasn't my country, I was a foreigner. But in that sea of humanity I could feel the emotions sweeping through like an electric current. People in shabby patched clothes. Army men and women, sprucer, but whose uniforms showed signs of hard wear. The crowd had been silent at first, recalling years of suffering in fierce fighting. But now, at last, victory. A roar welled from thousands of throats, a heart cry of triumph and resolve.

We began to see changes almost immediately. Hills of uncollected refuse were removed in Peking, 200,000 tons in ninety days. Courtyards were swept, housewives organized to keep the lanes clean. Streets had their foreign names converted into Chinese.

On Wangfuching, formerly Morrison Street, the main shopping thoroughfare, for a time the black market dealers in currency continued to stand openly on street corners, jingling piles of silver dollars. Security police informed them that this was no longer allowed. A few days later, those still at it had their money confiscated. If, after another week, they persisted, they were arrested.

A new currency was issued, pegged to the value of a few essential commodities like grain, edible oil, and cotton goods, whose prices were kept strictly controlled. Gradually, the inflation subsided and prices stabilized.

There was a crackdown on crime. Phoenix took part in closing down the brothels. Peking's houses of joy were anything but. The girls were mostly peasant children who had been sold, often for a pittance, by their desperately poor parents to professional collectors who, in turn, sold them to brothels. Theoretically, if the girl earned enough, she could pay off her purchase price and regain her freedom. This, in fact, rarely happened. The girls told the raiders some shocking stories. They had been beaten, ill-fed, and treated with the most callous brutality by the owners of the establishment. A dying girl was nailed into a coffin even before she drew her last breath, because she was 'no longer of any use' ...

The worst of the monsters were arrested and tried, with the girls giving testimony. A few, after the details of their crimes had received full publicity, were shot, in the presence of their victims and the local citizenry.

Rehabilitation was not easy, at first. They couldn't conceive of anyone being genuinely interested in their welfare. But after several days of good food, rest, and medical treatment – nearly all had venereal disease – they relaxed and started talking openly with the women who had been sent to look after them. Then they aired their suffering at 'speak bitterness' meetings. The Women's Association and political workers helped them see that the root of their troubles, like the troubles of all China's poor, was class oppression. The girls were impressed by the arrest and punishment of the brothel keepers. They were finally convinced that the old days were not going to return.

Training programs were set up. They were taught to operate sewing machines and other useful trades. Those who wished were sent home all expenses paid. Those who preferred to start a new life were found jobs in other parts of the country, and their pasts were kept secret from the general public. Many of them subsequently married and had children ...

> Source: Sidney Shapiro: *An American in China*
> (Beijing: New World Press, 1979), pp. 37–9

7.5 Zhang Da looks back on his part in the Korean War

I was only 17 when I went to Korea. It all happened so quickly. Only the year before, I was still a student, dancing in the streets of Chengdu to welcome the liberating army. I was so drawn by the revolution, I gave up normal schooling to join the South West People's Revolutionary University. This Military Institute led by Marshall He Long offered short-term training to revolutionary cadres. I joined the Communist Youth League there, and after half a year was sent to work for the county government in my hometown, Meishan. Our main task was to clear-out the residual warlords and bandits and prepare for land reform.

The nationwide campaign 'Resist America, Aid Korea' had begun. I remember long reports in the newspapers, attacking the South for invading the North and the Americans for using North Korea as a stepping stone to invade China. The United States even sent a fleet to the Taiwan Strait in an open challenge to our territory. Today, with so much information coming to light, I know who invaded whom. But back then, I was so angry with America and badly wanted to join the army to fight for justice. When a high-ranking officer from Meishan was called up, he took me and another enthusiastic young man with him.

In October 1950, I joined the 539th Regiment of the 180th Division of the Sixtieth Army, then based in the outskirts of Chengdu. After only a month's military training, our Regiment was moved up north. We understood fighting had intensified. We were briefly stationed at Changzhou in Hebei, where we were given mobilization talks. And we were asked to write a statement saying we voluntarily went to war. In fact, few of us needed any persuasion. We were all more than willing to go and wrote many times asking to be sent. Some even wrote in their own blood to show their determination!

At the very beginning of 1951, we reached Dandong, on the Korean border. Our weapons were changed for better models made in the Soviet Union. The atmosphere of war at the border was already very strong. Whether or not America really intended to invade China, I saw with my own eyes US aeroplanes that flew over to the Chinese side and dropped bombs. As we crossed the bridge over the border, we too were bombed. We were mostly virgin soldiers with the barest training and no war experience. We also knew that the Americans were better equipped. But we had no fear of them. Chairman Mao called the American imperialists 'paper tigers', so that's what we thought of them. And there was just so many of us, maybe 200,000–300,000 sent there as the second batch of volunteers.

I had the nerve-racking experience of combat for the first time when we were caught in the middle of the fourth campaign, which took place in the North, near the thirty-eighth parallel. I know now that all new soldiers are frightened of the loud crash of artillery fire, while veteran soldiers fear gunshots. Luckily, we were not on the frontline and didn't engage the enemy at close range. That didn't mean we were spared any danger, though. The Americans had great aerial advantage over us and bombed us so heavily it made little difference where you were. They also used advanced artillery that could fire shells miles away. By this time, we understood what good equipment meant. Still, our regiment survived our first battle with limited casualties. We didn't enjoy such good luck in the fifth campaign.

In terms of equipment, we were luckier than the first batch of soldiers hurriedly called up and sent to the battlefield, where some suffered severe frostbite to their hands and feet. At least we received new uniforms, and soon after arrival the weather grew warm. As you can imagine, the food was poor: our main staple was baked dry flour with rice, sorghum, or ship biscuits. Canned food was an occasional treat …

The fourth campaign gave us the upper hand, the battle ground moved further south, and the first half of the fifth campaign, begun in late April 1951, also went in our favour. I remember we confiscated many trucks and asked the American prisoners to drive. But they firmly refused, even after death threats, as they knew driving such obvious targets was inviting trouble. The latter half of the battle was hard and bitter. Around 19 May, when the fifth campaign was declared over, our 180th Division was holed up at a hilly place around Chun Chon in the south. Our food and ammunition had run out …

Now, I fully understand the old saying, 'the rout of an army is as fast as a landslide'. Our soldiers were killed with such speed, or chased by the enemy out of their positions. They sent planes to circle over our heads, persuading us to surrender. The regiment leaders decided we should try to break out of the encirclement and march towards the north-west, from where reinforcements were expected. That decision was later considered a mistake, for if we had stuck together more of us might have escaped. Second, it was too difficult to determine the north-west, as none of us had a compass. I started off with the other soldiers, but at night we ran into some Americans. We scattered I was completely on my own for seven days before my capture.

Soon, I was transferred from a field hospital to a prisoner-of-war camp in Pusan, where I had the sad comfort of meeting numerous people from the same division. I later heard that about one-third of the 180th Division was captured, another third had survived, and the rest were dead.

I'm sure casualties in our regiment were the heaviest of all. After Pusan, we were moved to Koje Island. It took negotiators a long time to settle the repatriation of over 20,000 Chinese POWs. The Americans insisted only those willing to return would be sent back, but China demanded them all. In the end, 14,000 went to Taiwan and 6,000 of us returned to mainland China. Another couple of 1,000 died from illness or torture. I had a harder time in the camp than on the battlefield. For example, in order to celebrate the third anniversary of the founding of the People's Republic of China in October 1952, we raised the Red Flag. But our little uprising was brutally put down by the Americans and around 100 of us were killed.

Why did so many soldiers not want to come back to China? I don't think all of them were traitors. Though most worried they would be regarded as such, particularly after being warned or threatened by the Nationalists or real traitors. Yes, some did turn tables to oppose the Communists. When I made it clear that I didn't want to go to Taiwan, several traitors forced a tattoo on my left arm: 'oppose communism, fight the Soviet Union'. I had to scrape it off with a razor … I chose to come back basically because I was patriotic.

Looking back at the Korean War, I still don't understand why the top leaders decided to participate. It's a question far beyond a little character like me. But I do have some different views now. The war has always been regarded as a victory in China. Yet today, I tend to agree with one American general's view: 'You did not win and we did not lose'. More importantly, it was not worthwhile. We lost so many lives, the official figure was 30,000, but now I know the real figure is far greater. And the war planted such deep hatred between the ordinary people of China and the United States, creating a negative impact that is not over yet even today.

Source: Zhang Da, 'Resist America. Aid Korea'. In Zhang Lijia and Calum MacLeod, eds, *China Remembers* (Hong Kong: Oxford University Press, 1999), pp. 25–8, 29–31

7.6 Extracts from documents on suppressing and liquidating counter-revolutionaries

7.6a 27 September 1950

A selection of statements showing changing policy emphasis.

[The policy of] not executing a single [secret agent] and not arresting the majority of them is a policy to which we must adhere in the current struggle against secret agents. If not a single secret agent is to be executed, they will dare to make a clean breast of things; by not arresting the majority among them, only a small number [of cases] will have to be handled by the security organs, while the majority can be handled by the various [government offices] and schools themselves. We must make the Party committees in all the localities adhere to this policy.

Source: Directives on Suppressing and Liquidating Counter-revolutionaries September 27 1950–2 April 1951. J. K. Leung and Y. M. Kau, *The Writings of Mao Zedong 1949–1976*, Vol. 2 (Armonk, New York: M. E. Sharpe, 1992), pp. 136–7

7.6b 17 January 1951

A bunch of bandit chiefs, local ruffians and petty tyrants, and secret agents in the twenty-one *xian* of western Hunan [Province] have been executed, and preparations are being made to have another bunch executed by local authorities this year. I believe this arrangement is very necessary. Only in this way will we be able to quell the enemy's arrogance and give full play to the people's morale. If we are weak and indecisive, and excessively indulgent and protective of evil people, then we may well bring a disaster upon the people and divorce [ourselves] from the masses.

Source: Directives on Suppressing and Liquidating Counter-revolutionaries September 27 1950–2 April 1951. J. K. Leung and Y. M. Kau, *The Writings of Mao Zedong 1949–1976*, Vol.2 (Armonk, New York: M. E. Sharpe, 1992), p. 162

7.6c 24 March 1951

The suppression of counter-revolutionaries is a great struggle. Only after this is accomplished can political power be consolidated.

The suppression of the counter-revolutionaries consists of [the suppression of] (1) counter-revolutionaries in society, (2) counter-revolutionaries concealed among the old personnel and new intellectuals in the military and government systems, and (3) counter-revolutionaries concealed within the Party. In order to suppress the counter-revolutionaries in the three areas, we must, of course, proceed a step at a time, and we cannot do it simultaneously. However, with regard to certain crucial departments in the Party, in the government, and in the military, and in particular, with regard to the Public Security Department, it is necessary to clean out [counter-revolutionaries] promptly; it is absolutely essential that suspicious elements be dealt with so that these organs may be placed in the hands of reliable personnel.

> Source: Directives on Suppressing and Liquidating
> Counter-revolutionaries September 27 1950–2 April 1951.
> J. K. Leung and Y. M. Kau, *The Writings of Mao Zedong 1949–1976*, Vol. 2
> (Armonk, New York: M.E. Sharpe, 1992), p. 178

7.6d 30 March 1951

In some localities in Shandong there is a tendency toward insufficient fervor, and in some localities there is a tendency toward doing things carelessly. These are two kinds of tendency that generally exist in the provinces and municipalities in the country, and attention ought to be given to correcting them in all cases. In particular, the tendency towards doing things carelessly is the most dangerous one. [This is so] because, where there is insufficient fervor, it can always be brought up to a sufficient level through education and persuasion, and whether the counter-revolutionaries are executed a few days sooner or a few days later does not make much difference. But if things are done carelessly, and people are arrested and executed by mistake, there will be very bad repercussions. Please exercise strict control in your work of suppressing counter-revolutionaries; it is imperative for you to be cautious in doing things and to correct any tendency towards doing things carelessly. We absolutely must suppress all counter-revolutionaries, but we also must absolutely not make arrests or carry out executions by mistake.

> Source: Directives on Suppressing and Liquidating
> Counter-revolutionaries September 27 1950–2, April 1951.
> J. K. Leung and Y. M. Kau, *The Writings of Mao Zedong 1949–1976*, Vol. 2
> (Armonk, New York: M. E. Sharpe, 1992), pp. 180–1

7.6e 2 April 1951

The suppression of counter-revolutionaries must be strictly confined to such categories as bandit chiefs, incorrigible criminals, ruffians and petty tyrants, secret agents, and chiefs of reactionary secret organization sects. We cannot include petty thieves, drug addicts, common landlords, ordinary Kuomintang members and members of the [Kuomintang Youth] League, and common officers in the Kuomintang army. Death sentences must be for those who have committed serious crimes only. It is a mistake for a light sentence to be given out for a serious crime; it is equally a mistake for a heavy sentence to be given out for a small crime.

Source: **Directives on Suppressing and Liquidating**
Counter-revolutionaries September 27 1950–2 April 1951.
J. K. Leung and Y. M. Kau, *The Writings of Mao Zedong 1949–1976*, Vol. 2
(Armonk, New York: M.E. Sharpe, 1992), p. 183

7.7 Thought reform in Yenching University

Wu Ningkun, extracts from *A Single Tear*, 1993

Wu Ningkun had returned to China from the United States in 1951 and taught literature at Yenching University.

Thought reform, or brainwashing, became a new focal point of political and intellectual life among the faculty. After spending days in small groups studying Premier Zhou's report and subsequent reports by other Communist leaders, we began to apply the Communist method of 'criticism and self-criticism' to the dissection of our sinful past and bourgeois mentality. Before the fall semester was half over, the country was enveloped in a new political campaign against corruption, waste, and bureaucratism, known as the three antis, which were blamed on corrosion by capitalist ideas. Two veteran Communists in the central government were soon executed for embezzlement of state funds. For a regime that had been in power for only two years, the readiness to clean its own ranks certainly left a strong impression on me. Many innocent people, however, were suspected and accused on little evidence and then subjected to non-stop questioning and detention, setting a pattern for subsequent political campaigns. At first the university community thought such a campaign was none of their concern. They changed their minds when the Party, armed with Marxist dialectics, seized upon universities as hotbeds of capitalist ideas and the three antis took the form of thought reform on college campuses, with professors as the main targets of attack.

At Yenching University, 'US imperialist cultural aggression' was singled out as the root of all evil, and the three antis became a campaign to eliminate 'befriend the US, worship the US, and fear the US sentiments'. A special work group of Communists was sent by the Party Committee of Beijing to conduct the campaign and take over the administration of the University. Classes were suspended and students were mobilized into small groups to look into the history of the University and the past of its leaders and faculty members. Files were removed from the President's office and scattered all over the library's main reading room to be scrutinized by student activists for evidence of cultural aggression and possible espionage. In one letter, an American professor referred to Chinese students as 'guinea-pigs' used in an experiment with a new teaching method. This was pounced upon as evidence of US imperialists insulting and victimizing Chinese students as 'pigs' and became the subject of an indignant denunciation at a big rally. I did not know what to make of what was happening around me. As head of the Department, Lucy was constantly besieged by members of the work team and student activists ...

The President himself, the Dean of the Divinity School, and the Chairman of the Philosophy Department, all distinguished scholars, were made to confess their sins in serving the interests of US imperialism and subjected to a denunciation by students and faculty members alike. Though inured to it after a while, I was none the less shocked by the denunciations made at a schoolwide rally against the President by Wu Xinghua, known as the President's protege and bridge partner, and the President's only daughter, a senior at Yenching. The President's elderly maidservant, however, made news when she attempted to cut her own throat with a kitchen knife rather than denounce her master as a 'cruel exploiter' under the pressure of the work group. One of the serious charges against the Dean of the Divinity School, Dr T. C. Chao, was an honorary doctorate awarded him by Princeton University in 1946 in the company of General Eisenhower, among others. 'Is it not true that a man is known by the company he keeps? As we all know, Eisenhower is a bloody imperialist warmonger, then what does it make the divinity dean?' The accuser wallowed in his own rhetoric. The Chairman of the Philosophy Department, Professor Chang Tungsun, was accused of being a suspected spy serving US interests, although he had played a leading part in bringing about the 'peaceful liberation' of Beijing in 1949. All three, who had publicly supported the Communists before the success of the revolution, were denounced as 'US imperialist elements' and summarily stripped of their posts. The President's daughter, meanwhile, was rewarded with the honour of being appointed a People's Deputy to the municipal People's Congress of Beijing.

Source: Wu Ningkun, *A Single Tear* (London: Hodder and Stoughton, 1993), pp. 17–19

7.8 On the struggle against the 'three evils' and the 'five evils'

The campaigns against 'evils' are often referred to as the 'three antis' and the 'five antis'.

8 DECEMBER 1951

The struggle against corruption, waste, and bureaucracy should be stressed as much as the struggle to suppress counter-revolutionaries. As in the latter, the broad masses, including the democratic parties and also people in all walks of life, should be mobilized, the present struggle should be given wide publicity, the leading cadres should take personal charge and pitch in, and people should be called on to make a clean breast of their own wrongdoing and to report on the guilt of others. In minor cases the guilty should be criticized and educated; in major ones the guilty should be dismissed from office, punished, or sentenced to prison terms (to be reformed through labour), and the worst among them should be shot. The problem can only be solved in these ways.

26 JANUARY 1952

In all cities, and first of all in the big and medium-sized cities, we should rely on the working class and unite with the law-abiding capitalists and other sections of the urban population to wage a large-scale, resolute, and thoroughgoing struggle against those capitalists who are violating the law by bribery, tax evasion, theft of state property, cheating on government contracts, and stealing economic information; we should coordinate this struggle with that against corruption, waste, and bureaucracy, which is being waged inside the Party, government, army, and mass organizations. This is both imperative and very timely. In the struggle, Party organizations in all cities must carefully dispose the forces of the classes and masses and adopt the tactics of utilizing contradiction, effecting splits, uniting with the many, and isolating the few, so that, in the process, a united front against the 'five evils' will speedily take shape. In a big city, as the struggle against the 'five evils' gets into full swing, such a united front may well come into being within about three weeks. Once this united front is formed, those reactionary capitalists guilty of the worst crimes will be isolated, and the state will be in a strong position to mete out due punishment, such as fines, confiscation, arrest, imprisonment, or execution, without much opposition. All our big cities (including provincial capitals) should start the struggle against the 'five evils' in the first ten days of February. Please make prompt arrangements.

5 MARCH 1952

In the movement against the 'five evils', the basic principles in dealing with industrial and commercial units are: leniency for past offences and severity for new ones (for instance, payment of taxes that have been evaded is generally retroactive only to 1951); leniency towards the many and severity towards the few; leniency towards those owning up to their crimes and severity towards those refusing to do so; leniency for industry and severity for commerce; and leniency for commerce in general and severity for commercial speculation. The Party committees at all levels are asked to adhere to these principles in the movement against the 'five evils'.

> Source: 'On the Struggle Against the "Three Evils" and the "Five Evils"', Directives by
> CC of CCP December 1951 to March 1952, *Selected Works of Mao Tse-tung*, Vol. 5
> (Beijing: Foreign Languages Press, 1977), pp. 64, 65–6

7.9 Prisons in China

7.9a A British visitor's report

A British churchman, the Dean of Canterbury, the Rev. Hewlett Johnson (sometimes called the 'Red Dean'), visited China in 1932, 1952, 1956, and 1959. In a book on his 1956 journey he published reports on satisfactory prison conditions.

Dr Marcus Cheng told us that his social duties had taken him to inspect prisons – one at Lanchow and one at Sian. The latter contained 1,200 prisoners. But these prisons were not prisons in our sense of the word; they were factories: one for shoes and clothes, another to make matches, another for printing. Prisoners were not locked in cells, but slept in dormitories for 8 people, scrupulously clean. They could come and go inside as they pleased. The warden told Dr Cheng that the officers were not allowed to scold or be angry with the prisoners and never beat them. They looked happy, healthy, and strong. Sunday was a rest day. They had leisure time, and games and dramatics were organized. There was an excellent library. The prisoners had better food than most peasants could afford.

Among these 1,200 were very few ordinary criminals; they were mostly counter-revolutionaries. If ill, they were sent to hospital. 1,000 yuan was spent on one man who needed an operation; the other prisoners were much moved when he returned, well and strong.

Over 1,000 had been sentenced to death and reprieved for a year, during which time they began to work well and live a new kind of life. Not one death sentence had been carried out in the last four years.

In another prison, which Dr Marcus visited, two had been executed but all the others had radically changed their lives and were making good. Many of these men came to look upon this place as their home and did not want to leave it when their time was up. Compared with the terrible conditions of preliberation China, these conditions were, indeed, revolutionary.

In present-day China, we were assured, the number of ordinary criminals had greatly decreased. The number of thieves, bandits, opium smokers, gamblers, and prostitutes have phenomenally declined and, in many places, disappeared. This is largely because each one of the 650,000,000 people is organized in some kind of society or cooperative. They all know their neighbours and are known. They all join some kind of local organization. If anyone is in want, they will be helped.

Source: Hewlett Johnson, *The Upsurge of China* (Beijing: New World Press, 1969), pp. 228–9

7.9b Assessing prisons in post-liberation China

Frank Dikötter

As they marched into the city on 31 January 1949, the Communists found the prisons of Beijing almost entirely empty. Allegedly in order to save food and heat, the large-scale release of prisoners from gaol had been ordered by the municipal authorities a few months earlier. The penal institutions left behind by the Kuomintang were appropriated by the law-enforcement agencies of the Chinese Communist Party (CCP) in Beijing. As in the early years of the Soviet regime, when the notorious Cheka and revolutionary tribunals enforced a reign of terror to establish a new order, the Public Security forces started incarcerating enemies of the Party and common criminals on a large scale immediately after liberation. Political movements aimed at the elimination of 'counter-revolutionaries' and mass campaigns against 'bad elements' within the Party were soon launched throughout the country. As most provinces and municipalities had few gaols, the majority of prisoners were sent to labour camps (*laogai*). Even today, Beijing municipality has only five acknowledged prisons, namely prison number one, number two, number three, Qincheng prison, and Liuhai prison. Throughout the first decades of the new regime, a large number of inmates were sent to labour camps, which started to operate on a large scale during the mass campaigns in 1951 and 1952. Most labour camps were turned into self-sufficient units after September 1951, and by 1954 nearly 90 per cent of all prisoners were engaged in labour production.

Suspects accused of a political crime rarely went through any sort of legal procedure. People's courts (*renmin fayuan*) were established and made responsible for enforcing Party policies and regulations. More serious cases were often turned over to special revolutionary people's tribunals (*renmin fating*), ad hoc bodies established for the duration of mass campaigns. These tribunals were also under the tight control of the public security system and had the power to make arrests and pass sentences. According to one close observer, legal procedures were rarely followed, lawyers were not assigned for the accused, judges were insufficiently trained and inexperienced, records of trials were poorly kept, and sentences were generally dealt with too severely by judges who tried to adhere to government policies.

In principle, only criminals who had been arrested and sentenced were confined to prisons, as large numbers of people languished in detention camps for months before being sentenced. Political prisoners sometimes had no fixed sentence and were released only when they were sufficiently reformed. Regulations also existed concerning the separation of political prisoners from common criminals, although no strict segregation was actually enforced in prison or labour camps according to close observers. Following an internal CCP regulation, 'prisons will house criminals sentenced to death with a two year reprieve; counter-revolutionaries sentenced to life terms or terms of over five years; common criminals sentenced to terms of over 10 years; and special cases such as spies, foreign criminals, criminals with knowledge of classified material, and female criminals'. The profile of the prison register examined here corresponds to a great extent to that description, with the notable exception of a large presence of common criminals convicted of theft with sentences of less than 10 years. The incarceration of serious offenders was the result of the high security and tighter regime of prisoners in comparison with some labour camps. Political prisoners, on the other hand, were often sent to labour camps. As in the labour camps, however, penal institutions generally housed factories or workshops in which all prisoners were forced to work. The number of prisoners could range from 200 to 5000, while camps could harbour over 100,000 convicts.

Source: Frank Dikötter, 'Research Note: Crime and Punishment in Post-Liberation China', *China Quarterly*, No. 149, March 1997, pp. 148–9

7.10 The only road for the transformation of capitalist industry and commerce

Mao Zedong, 7 September 1953

Outline for a talk to representatives from the democratic parties and industrial and commercial circles.

The transformation from capitalism into socialism is to be accomplished through state capitalism:

1   In the last three years or so we have done some work on this, but as we were otherwise occupied, we didn't exert ourselves enough. From now on we should make a bigger effort.
2   With more than three years of experience behind us, we can say with certainty that accomplishing the socialist transformation of private industry and commerce by means of state capitalism is a relatively sound policy and method.
3   The policy laid down in Article 31 of the Common Programme should now be clearly understood and concretely applied step by step. 'Clearly understood' means that people in positions of leadership at the central and local levels should first of all have the firm conviction that state capitalism is the only road for the transformation of capitalist industry and commerce and for the gradual completion of the transition to socialism. So far this has not been the case either with members of the Communist Party or with democratic personages. The present meeting is being held to achieve that end.

4   Make steady progress and avoid being too hasty. It will take at least three to five years to lead the country's private industry and commerce basically onto the path of state capitalism, so there should be no cause for alarm or uneasiness.

5   Joint state–private management; orders placed by the state with private enterprises to process materials or manufacture goods, with the state providing all the raw materials and taking all the finished products; and similarly placed orders, with the state taking not all but most of the finished products – these are the three forms of state capitalism to be adopted in the case of private industry.

6   State capitalism can also be applied in the case of private commerce, which cannot possibly be dismissed by 'excluding it'. Here, our experience is limited and further study is needed.

7   With approximately 3,800,000 workers and shop assistants, private industry and commerce are a big asset to the state and play a large part in the nation's economy and the people's livelihood. Not only do they provide the state with goods, but they can also accumulate capital and train cadres for the state.

8   Some capitalists keep themselves at a great distance from the state and have not changed their profit-before-everything mentality. Some workers are advancing too fast and won't allow the capitalists to make any profit at all. We should try to educate these workers and capitalists and help them gradually (but the sooner the better) adapt themselves to our state policy, namely to make China's private industry and commerce mainly serve the nation's economy and the people's livelihood and partly earn profits for the capitalists and in this way embark on the path of state capitalism. The following table shows the distribution of profits in state-capitalist enterprises:

Income Tax	34.5%
Welfare fund	15.0%
Accumulation fund	30.0%
Capitalist dividends	20.5%
Total	100.0%

9   It is necessary to go on educating the capitalists in patriotism, and to this end we should systematically cultivate a number of them who have a broader vision and are ready to lean towards the Communist Party and the People's Government, so that most of the other capitalists may be convinced through them.

10 Not only must the implementation of state capitalism be based on what is necessary and feasible (see the Common Programme) but it must also be voluntary on the part of the capitalists, because it is a cooperative undertaking and cooperation admits of no coercion. This is different from the way we dealt with the landlords.

11 Considerable progress has been made in the last few years by the various nationalities, democratic classes, democratic parties, and people's organizations, and still greater progress will, in my opinion, be made in the next three to five years. So it is possible basically to accomplish the task of leading private industry and commerce onto the path of state capitalism in three to five years. The preponderance of state enterprises affords the material guarantee for the fulfilment of this task.

12 As for the completion of the task for the entire transition period, which consists of the basic accomplishment of the country's industrialization and the socialist transformation of agriculture, handicrafts, and capitalist industry and commerce, this cannot be done in

three to five years, but will instead take a period of several five-year plans. On this question it is necessary to oppose both the idea of leaving things to the indefinite future and
the idea of rushing things through.

**Source: Mao Tse-tung, 'The Only Road for the Transformation of
Capitalist Industry and Commerce',**
Selected Works of Mao Tse-tung, Vol 5, 1977, pp. 112–14

7.11   Agricultural cooperatives

7.11a Account of the cooperative movement in Houhua village

Wang Fucheng

In 1953 another work team from the government came to our village to mobilize us for a
different stage of development. Most members of the work team were from the township.
They were rural people, peasants, though some were office workers from Neihuang. The
only one I remember who came from a large city was a man named Ge, a bureau head who
came to inspect the work.

The work team held village meetings and told us that if we joined the land association and
formed cooperatives we would have a bright future. We would plow without oxen [i.e. with
tractors], light our houses without oil [electricity], and have machines for all work. I was an
activist promoting this movement, but many people didn't wish to join. Some said we would
have no freedom if we joined the association. One said, 'We are all so poor. How can we
have a happy future just by joining an association?' He and others didn't believe all of the
things the cadres were telling us.

There were about 300 households in the village then. About forty joined the land association and formed two cooperatives. Almost all who joined were poor. They had gotten land in
the land reform, but it was not enough. Some had already sold some land. Only those with
the least land joined the association. No one was forced to join. The cadres said to let them
wait; sooner or later all would join, all would follow the socialist road. The cooperatives
were first-level cooperatives: we pooled our animals and farmed the land together, but we
still owned our land and tools. What we received at harvest time was based on both the
amount of our property and the amount of work we did. This would change in the higher-
level cooperatives, when all land would be owned collectively and distribution would be
based on labor alone. These low-level cooperatives lasted two years.

The township government supported us by giving us advice and lending us money at low
rates of interest. We borrowed from a credit association of the township government. No
money was lent to individual farmers outside the cooperative. We bought donkeys, horses,
mules, and two horse carts.

In the early stage of the cooperative, some people wanted to drop out. The cadres talked
to them, and most were persuaded to stay in. Most of us who joined listened to Chairman
Mao's call and were fully dedicated in heart and mind. Men and women worked together in
the field. We didn't quarrel. After the first harvest we got more than those who worked
alone because they couldn't manage as well and also because the government gave us some
help. We paid back the loan after the harvest. The fence sitters became firm in the

cooperative, but it was impossible to attract new members to the two lower-level coopera-tives because the membership was already settled and there would have been accounting problems. No new lower-level cooperatives were formed in the village.

I was the manager of the land association. I was illiterate, but the villagers asked me to serve. I also became leader of the cooperative and then village leader at that time. There are two main leaders in the village. The top leader is the Party branch secretary, who is in charge of all village affairs and of Party work in the village. The village leader is second in importance. He is in charge of all farm work. I was not yet a Party member, though I had applied and been recommended many times …

Source: Peter J. Seybolt, *Throwing the Emperor from His Horse: Portrait of a Village Leader in China, 1923–1995* **(Boulder, Colorado: Westview Press, 1996), pp. 42–4**

7.11b Mao on cooperatives, 11 October 1955

Mao Zedong

We have not yet accomplished agricultural cooperation, the working class has not yet consolidated its alliance with the peasantry on a new basis, and the alliance remains unstable. The peasants are no longer satisfied with the alliance we formed with them in the past on the basis of the agrarian revolution. They are beginning to forget about the benefits they reaped from that alliance …

The old alliance to oppose the landlords, overthrow the local despots, and distribute land was a temporary one; it has become unstable after a period of stability. Since the agrarian reform, polarization has taken place among the peasants. If we have nothing new to offer them and cannot help them raise their productivity, increase their income, and attain collec-tive prosperity, the poor ones will no longer trust us and will feel that there is no point in following the Communist Party. Since they remain poor after land has been distributed to them, why do they still have to follow you? As for the well-to-do ones, namely those who have become rich peasants or grown quite well off, they won't trust us either and will invari-ably find the policies of the Communist Party not to their taste. As a result, neither the one nor the other, neither the poor nor the rich, will trust us, and the worker–peasant alliance will become quite shaky. To consolidate this alliance, we have to lead the peasants onto the road of socialism, enabling them to attain collective prosperity; not only the poor peasants but all of them must prosper and, what is more, they must become far better off than the present-day well-to-do peasants. Once the countryside goes cooperative, the life of the entire rural population will get better and better as the years go by and there will be more commodity grain and more industrial raw materials. By then the bourgeoisie will be silenced and find themselves completely isolated.

Source: Mao Tse-tung, on Agricultural Cooperativization and the Transformation of Capitalist Industry, *Selected Works of Mao Tse-tung,* **Vol. 5, 1977, pp. 212–1**

8

The Hundred Flowers

By the mid-1950s there were two fundamental problems – the strategy for economic development and the role of the intellectuals – which led to disagreement within the top leadership. These issues marked a watershed in the People's Republic.

The first Five-Year Plan had to be evaluated. Heavy industry as planned showed a higher growth rate than light industry. Agriculture was relatively disappointing. Mao envisaged that China's reforms should be less dependent on the Soviet model. He wanted an active intellectual force that would reduce reliance on Soviet experts and could also help to bypass bureaucratic channels.

In the early years, conformity had been enforced through the suppression of counter-revolutionaries together with the three-anti and five-anti campaigns and pressure for thought reform for intellectuals. In 1955, Mao started another round of suppressing dissent as highlighted by the case of Hu Feng. Hu, a literary critic who had been a close associate of Lu Xun and was a member of the National People's Congress, complained to the Central Committee that there were 'five daggers' directed at the heart of Chinese literature. Accusing the Party of dictating both the subjects and the forms of literature, Hu Feng questioned the need for writers to accept Communist ideology. At this point Mao himself intervened with an anonymous article in the *People's Daily*. By mid-1955, Hu Feng was in jail.

At this point, Mao and his colleagues believed that it was time to engage the intellectuals more enthusiastically in the life of the nation. To reassure them, in June 1955 Zhou Enlai convened a meeting of top scientists to discuss long-term research. In the following January, Zhou made a keynote speech. He reiterated that intellectuals would be well-treated and trusted. Meanwhile, more intellectuals would be allowed into the Party – a fifty per cent increase in the next year.

Then a bombshell was thrown into the ideological arena in February 1956, when the new Soviet leader Nikita Khrushchev denounced Stalin at the Twentieth Congress of the Communist Party of the Soviet Union. Mao resented the lack of prior consultation. Moreover, Khrushchev's reassessment was unacceptable. The Chinese Party issued its own statement on 5 April. It pointed out that the personality cult Stalin was supposed to have fostered was not relevant to China, where the order of the day was collective leadership and democratic centralism featuring the mass line.

In a speech on 'the 10 major relationships' on 25 April 1956, Mao said simplistically that Stalin's achievements outweighed his mistakes by seven to three. He went on to analyse the particular problems facing China, some of which had been exacerbated by slavishly following the Soviet Union. He suggested that more attention should be given to developing light industry and agriculture which would also provide funds for investment in heavy industry.

It was probably on the same day in a speech to the enlarged meeting of the Politburo of the Central Committee of the CPC, preceding the speech on 'the 10 major relationships', that Mao first used the phrases 'Let a hundred flowers bloom, let a hundred schools of thought contend'. The slogan not only had a long history dating from the Spring and Autumn period of more than 2000 years ago, but recently, on the 8 March, Liu Shaoqi had used a similar expression when speaking to the Party organization of the Ministry of Culture. Calling for a degree of tolerance in plays, films, and painting, he said, 'Our policy is to let a hundred flowers bloom, to develop something new from the old'. Then, on 26 May, Lu Dingyi, head of the Party propaganda department, spoke to writers, professionals, and academics, effectively launching the Hundred Flowers in words that most probably echoed the thoughts of Mao. However, although a die had been cast, any response was at first muted. Most writers, artists, and scientists were wary.

In September, the Party held its Eighth Party Congress, the first since it came to power (the last was in 1945). Membership had grown tenfold from 1.2 million to 10.7 million. Some rectification process was needed to test commitment and the ideological purity of Party members. Mao spoke of the importance of uniting the Party and the people, and Liu Shaoqi stressed that Party supervision was paramount. Deng Xiaoping spoke on the need for criticism within the Party. He also raised the question of personal versus collective leadership. But the two outstanding outcomes of the congress were that Mao Zedong Thought was no longer described in the new Party Constitution as the doctrine of the Chinese Communist movement, and the Congress maintained that the period of tempestuous class struggle was over.

In October and November 1956, the Poles and Hungarians, in response to de-Stalinization, began to challenge Soviet control. The Chinese had some sympathy with the rebels; until the point where the revolt in Hungary threatened the Communist system and the Warsaw Pact. Thereafter, Mao stood for the unity of the Bloc while diagnosing that opposition had been justified by excessive authoritarianism.

There were some, albeit much slighter, disturbances in China – strikes and withdrawals from the new agricultural collectives. At this point Mao might still have believed that frictions among the Chinese people could be settled in less confrontational ways. In February 1957, Mao spoke to a Supreme State Conference with an audience of 1800 people, which included writers, scientists, and leaders of the democratic parties. 'On the Correct Handling of Contradictions Between the People' lasted four hours, during which some high-ranking cadres walked out. Mao had set out the criteria for distinguishing between antagonistic contradictions, with the enemy, and non-antagonistic contradictions which could and should be resolved constructively. Some tape recordings circulated around China, and extracts were published in the *New York Times* but the original text has never been publicized.

The turn of events in the Socialist Bloc and in China itself had led Mao to believe that the Hundred Flowers could become a threat to the Party. Eventually, on 19 June an official version of the above speech was published in the *People's Daily*, but its tone had been changed from antileftist to antirightist as the antirightist campaign was launched early in June.

Some have supposed that the Hundred Flowers was simply a ploy – a plot to expose Mao's enemies. Mao had always distrusted intellectuals, those in humanities and social sciences in particular. Others have believed he was sincere in the early days of the policy. Controversy persists to this day.

With the crackdown, Deng, as the General Secretary of the Party, took charge of the antirightist campaign in which more than 700,000 Communist and non-Communist intellectuals and officials suffered remoulding. Many underwent labour reform and many were exiled to remote parts of the countryside. In some areas the local party designated a five per cent quota for the rightist label.

Mao spoke of lenient treatment. 'We are not going to handle them the way we did the landlords and counter-revolutionaries in the past'. But the bitter lesson had been learned. Intellectuals suffered and learned to keep their heads down.

8.1 The Eighth Party Congress

Deng Xiaoping, report on the revision of the CPC Constitution, 16 September 1956

The Eighth Party Congress was the first congress held since the Seventh Congress in 1945. Deng Xiaoping, as new General Secretary, argues tactfully here for collective leadership.

To completely remedy this defect [of not holding regular Party congresses] and raise democratic activities in the Party to a higher plane, the Central Committee has decided to introduce a fundamental reform in the draft Party Constitution. The National Party congress and the congresses at provincial and county levels are to have a fixed term respectively, somewhat similar to that of the people's congresses at the various levels. It is laid down in the draft Party Constitution that the National Party congress is to be elected for a term of five years, congresses at provincial level for three years, and congresses at county level for two years. Congresses at all three levels are to be called in session once a year; therefore, the original system of Party conferences at the various levels will no longer be necessary. A system of Party congresses with fixed terms will greatly reduce the burden of electing deputies, and the congresses may be convened at any time during the term of office. Since the congresses will be in session once a year, the occasion need not be an elaborate affair. The greatest merit of a system of fixed terms for the congresses is that it will make the congresses the Party's highest policy-making and supervisory organs operating with an effectiveness that is hardly possible under the present system whereby congresses are held once in a number of years, with deputies elected afresh each time. Under the new system the Party's most important decisions can all be brought before the congresses for discussion …

It must be emphasized that the Party is a militant organization. Without centralized and unified command it would be impossible to win any battles. The measures taken for the development of inner-Party democracy are not meant to weaken necessary centralization in the Party, but to supply it with a powerful and vigorous base. This is perfectly clear to every one of us. Our purpose in proposing to improve the system of congresses at all levels is to make it easier for the Party committees at all levels to solicit the opinions of the masses and to work more correctly and effectively. Our purpose in proposing to improve the working relationship between central and local and higher and lower bodies is to enable the central and higher bodies to exercise their leadership in closer conformity with actual conditions, to concentrate their attention on work that needs to be centralized, and to improve their inspection and guidance of the work of the local organizations and the lower bodies. We do not advocate strengthening collective leadership in order to reduce the role of the individual. On the contrary, the individual can play his role correctly only through the collective, while collective leadership must be combined with individual responsibility. Without division of labour and individual responsibility we would not be able to perform any complicated tasks and would find ourselves in the woeful predicament of no one being responsible for any particular job. Whatever the organization, we need not only division of labour and individual responsibility but also somebody assuming overall responsibility. Are we all not well aware that even a small group cannot function without a leader?

Here, I should like to say a few words about the role of the leaders in the Party. While recognizing that history is made by the people, Marxism never denies the historical role of outstanding individuals; Marxism simply points out that the individual role is, in the final analysis, dependent upon given social conditions. Likewise, Marxism never denies the role of leaders in political parties. In Lenin's famous words, the leaders are those who are 'the most authoritative, influential and experienced'. Undoubtedly, their authority, their influence, and their experience are valuable assets to the Party, the working-class, and the people ...

An important achievement of the Twentieth Congress of the Communist Party of the Soviet Union [which denounced Stalin] lies in the fact that it showed us what serious consequences can follow from deification of an individual. Our Party has always held that no political parties or individuals are free from flaws and mistakes in their activities, and this has now been written into the General Programme of the draft Party Constitution. For the same reason, our Party abhors the deification of an individual. At the Secondary Plenary Session of the Seventh Central Committee, held in March 1949 – that is, on the eve of the nationwide victory in the people's revolution – the Central Committee, at the suggestion of comrade Mao Zedong, decided to prohibit birthday celebrations for Party leaders and the use of Party leaders' names to designate places, streets, and enterprises. This has helped check the glorification and exaltation of individuals. The Central Committee has always been against sending the leaders messages of greetings or telegrams reporting successes. Likewise, it has been against exaggerating the role of leaders through works of art and literature. Of course, the cult of the individual is a social phenomenon with a long history, and it inevitably finds certain reflections in our Party and public life. It is our task to continue to observe fully the Central Committee's principle of opposition to the elevation and glorification of the individual and to achieve a real consolidation of the ties between the leaders and the masses so that the Party's democratic principle and its mass line will be carried out in every field of endeavour.

Source: 'Report on the Revision of the Constitution',
The Eighth Party Congress, Deng Xiaoping, *Selected Works of Deng Xiaoping (1938–1965)*
(Beijing: Foreign Languages Press, 1992), pp. 218–20

8.2 Mao Zedong introduces the hundred flowers

These notes of Mao's speech to the Politburo on 25 April 1956 are the first published reference attributed to Mao on the policy of 'letting a hundred flowers bloom'.

In their speeches [many comrades] displayed a lack of vigor. The relationship of the low-level [cadres] to the upper-level [cadres] is like that of a mouse when it sees a cat, as though its soul has been eaten away. There was so much [on their minds], they didn't dare speak out. This same problem of a lack of democracy also exists in the various provinces. However, there were some model workers who did speak out quite spiritedly. Our Financial and Economic [Work] Conference and the Fourth Plenum of the Central Committee had some side effects. Because of several stipulations, people did not venture to speak their minds. At the Economic and Financial [Work] Conference, certain comrades did not give appropriate speeches, and there were some who didn't dare speak up at all ...

We must delegate certain powers to the lower levels. Our [system of] discipline has come mostly from the Soviet Union. If the discipline is too strict, we will be fettering people. It is not possible to smash bureaucratism this way. The dictatorship of the proletariat requires an appropriate system. The Political Bureau and the State Council have not yet decided on either the problem of the division of power between the central government and the local areas, or how the one-person management system of the Soviet Union came about. The various provinces should share power, they should not be afraid of being called people who clamor for independence. As the Center has not yet arrived at a decision, we are free to speak up. Every locality can draw up its own regulations, bylaws, and methods as provided for by the Constitution. We must enable the various localities to be creative, spirited, and full of vigor. Beginning next year, we should convene a large conference annually ...

In art and literature, to 'let a hundred flowers bloom,' and in academic studies, to 'let a hundred schools of thought contend' (as a hundred schools contended during the Spring and Autumn period and Warring States period) should be taken as a guideline. This was the view of the people two thousand years ago.

Source: Notes on Mao's Speech of 25 April 1956 to the Politburo. Source Wansui 1969, pp. 35–40. J. K. Leung and Michael Y. M. Kau, *The Writings of Mao Zedong 1949–1976*, Vol. 2 (Armonk, New York: M. E. Sharpe, 1992), pp. 66, 70

8.3 Shanghai's strike wave of 1957

Elizabeth J. Perry

In the spring of 1957, a strike wave of monumental proportions rolled across the city in Shanghai. The strikes in Shanghai represented the climax of the national outpouring of labour protest that had been gaining momentum for more than a year. The magnitude of the 1957 strike wave is especially impressive when placed in historical perspective. Major labour disturbances erupted at 587 Shanghai enterprises in the spring of 1957, involving nearly 30,000 workers. More than 200 of these incidents included factory walkouts, while another hundred also involved organizing slowdowns of production. Moreover, more than 700 enterprises experienced less serious forms of labour unrest. These figures are extraordinary even by comparison with Republican-period Shanghai when the May 4th Movement of 1919, the May 30th Movement of 1925, the Shanghai workers three armed uprisings of 1926–7, and the protests of the civil war years gave rise to one of the most feisty labour movements in world history ...

The strikes of 1956 to 1957 ... were symptomatic of the severe social strains that predated and precipitated them and the antirightist crackdown. In demanding improved welfare and decrying the bureaucratism of local officials, strikers revealed the deep divisions within the Chinese working class itself. Partly a product of pre-1949 experiences and partly a result of the socialization of industry under communism, such fissures would shape the labour unrest in China for decades to come ...

SOURCES

Although there exists, so far as I'm aware, no English-language treatment of these events, we have for some time had access to fragmentary evidence about the labour unrest of the mid-1950s. First, hints about the magnitude of the protests appear in speeches by top leaders at the time. Mao Zedong in his famous address of February 1957, 'On the Correct Handling of Contradictions among the People,' notes that, 'In 1956, workers and students in certain places went on strike'. In the more candid collection of Mao's speeches published for internal circulation in 1969, *Mao Zedong sixiang wansui* (Long Live Mao Zedong Thought), there were more references. In a January 1957 speech, for example, Mao mentions widespread strikes and notes that a recent investigation found that only 25 per cent of the workers were reliable. And in the *Secret Speeches of Chairman Mao*, recently edited by Roderick MacFarquhar et *al.*, Mao cites a report by the All-China Federation of Trade Unions (ACFTU) in 1956 which noted, on the basis of only partial statistics, that some 50 strikes had recently taken place – the largest of which had more than 1000 participants.

Liu Shaoqi, speaking in December 1956, raised the question of how to deal with strikes and petitions, but did not answer it. The following spring, when the number of labour disputes had increased exponentially, Liu boldly proposed that union and Party officials should themselves participate in strikes in order to regain the workers' sympathy.

A second source for the strikes of the mid-1950s are central reports and directives, many of which were reprinted in the internal circulation journal *Zhongguo Gongyun* (the Chinese Labour Movement). In February 1957, the party group of the ACFTU issued a report noting that it had handled twenty-nine strikes and fifty-six petitions by disgruntled workers the previous year. The report pointed out that this was but a small percentage of the total number of disputes that had erupted across the country. In Shanghai, for example, six labour disturbances had broken out in the first three months of 1956; nineteen in the second trimester; twenty in the third trimester; and forty-one in the last trimester of that year. The following month, March 1957, Party Central issued a directive on the problem of handling strikes. Acknowledging that labour strikes, student boycotts, mass petitions, and demonstrations had increased dramatically in the previous past half-year, Party Central estimated (perhaps with some hyperbole) that more than ten thousand labour strikes had erupted across the country during this period.

A third and somewhat more accessible source is the official press. Newspapers from around the country carried stories about strikes, petitions, and other varieties of labour disputes in their locales. And on 13 May 1957, *Renmin Ribao* ran a lengthy editorial entitled 'On Labour Trouble,' which attributed the problem of strikes and petitions to a bureaucratism on the part of the leadership …

Fortunately, we are now able to go beyond speeches, central directives, and the official press in our investigation of this subject. The Shanghai Municipal Archives holds hundreds of detailed reports compiled in the spring of 1957 by the Shanghai Federation of Trade Unions and its district branches across the city on incidents that erupted in their areas of jurisdiction. These rich data offer a new perspective on the strike wave, allowing us to pose previously unanswerable questions about the origins and objectives of the protests.

CAUSES OF THE STRIKE WAVE

As studies of the Hundred Flowers movement have emphasized, Chairman Mao's role in encouraging the dissent of this period was of critical importance. Concerned about the unrest then sweeping Eastern Europe, Mao hoped that the release of the social tensions in China would avert a popular uprising at home. Whether the Chairman was setting a trap for his enemies (as most Chinese assume) or acting initially in good faith (as Western analysts generally believe), Mao clearly was anxious to defuse domestic contradictions. He referred repeatedly in both his published and unpublished speeches to the Hungarian revolt of 1956 and expressed the hope that strikes in China might help to forestall a larger and more serious insurgency.

The importance of state inspiration is undeniable. Without the Chairman's explicit encouragement, it seems inconceivable that the strike wave would have assumed such massive proportions. Moreover, previous mobilization of workers in state-sponsored campaigns to monitor capitalists had prepared the ground for the outburst of labour unrest at this time. Factionalism within the upper echelons of the Party leadership also fostered dissent among the populace at large. Even so, one is hard pressed to characterize the events of spring 1957 as a top-down affair. The archival materials give no hint of direct instigation by higher authorities, at either municipal or central levels. Although certainly stimulated by Mao's 'On the Correct Handling of Contradictions' speech, the protests evidenced considerable spontaneity and presented real problems for management, Party, and trade union officials alike.

Much of the explanation for the explosion of labour unrest lies with the economic restructuring of the day. The years 1956–7 were noteworthy not only for the Hungarian revolt abroad and Mao's Hundred Flowers initiative at home; they were also the period in which most of Chinese industry was socialized. Private firms were eliminated and replaced by so-called joint-ownership enterprises. Under this arrangement, the former owners became state employees, receiving interest on the value of their shares in the enterprise. The capitalists no longer enjoyed profits, nor did they exercise any real managerial initiative. Except for the fact that the former owners clipped coupons, the joint-owned companies were in effect wholly state-run entities.

The fundamental transformation of the Shanghai economy can be illustrated with a few figures. In the fall of 1950, a year after the establishment of the new socialist regime, more than 75 per cent of the city's industrial workforce was still employed at privately owned factories; state enterprises claimed a mere 21 per cent. In December 1957, by contrast, 72 per cent of Shanghai's labourers worked at joint ownership firms and another 27 per cent at state-owned enterprises. Private industry was a thing of the past.

The great majority of strikes in the spring of 1957 were concentrated in newly formed joint-ownership enterprises to protest the deterioration in economic security and political voice that accompanied the socialization of these firms. In most instances, the wage and welfare reforms that occurred with the formation of joint-ownership enterprises spelled a decrease in real income for workers.

STYLE OF PROTEST

Typically, a dispute could begin by raising repeated suggestions and demands to the factory leadership. When these were not dealt with, formal complaints were lodged with the higher authorities. The workers set deadlines by which they expected a satisfactory response and often staged rowdy meetings to publicize their grievances ...

Many of the protesters did demonstrate a desire to remain within the law. Pedicab drivers, before raising their demands, first sought legal counsel to ascertain that their three requests were legitimate ... Even so, over time many of the protests grew larger and more complicated, moving beyond simple requests about welfare provisions or leadership attitudes to involve bolder initiatives.

The protests evinced a remarkably wide repertoire of behaviour. Many workers put up big-character posters and wrote blackboard newspapers explaining their grievances; some workers went on hunger strike, some threatened suicide, some marched in large-scale demonstrations – holding high their workplace banners as they paraded vociferously down Nanjing Road; some workers staged sit-ins and presented petitions to government authorities, some organized action committees, pickets, and liaison officers to coordinate strikes in different factories and districts. In many cases, workers surrounded factory, Party, and union cadres, raising demands and imposing a deadline for a satisfactory response – refusing to disband until the request had been met.

Source: Elizabeth J. Perry, 'Shanghai's Strike Wave of 1957',
China Quarterly, **No. 137, March 1994, pp. 1–27 (extracts)**

8.4 Mao Zedong on contradictions among the people

Speech of 27 February 1957 to a meeting of the Supreme State Conference. This extract examines the Hundred Flowers movement. It was not published in the People's Daily, *until 19 June, after Mao had made some radical changes in the light of 'excessive blooming'. At the beginning of his speech, Mao distinguishes between antagonistic contradictions between ourselves and the enemy, and contradictions among the people themselves, which are non-antagonistic and should be resolved by discussion and education. The 'people' includes all who accept the revolution.*

'Let a hundred flowers blossom, let a hundred schools of thought contend' and 'long-term coexistence and mutual supervision' – how did these slogans come to be put forward? They were put forward in the light of China's specific conditions, on the basis of the recognition that various kinds of contradiction still exist in socialist society, and in response to the country's urgent need to speed up its economic and cultural development. Letting a hundred flowers blossom and a hundred schools of thought contend is the policy for promoting the progress of the arts and the sciences and a flourishing socialist culture in our land. Different forms and styles in art should develop freely and different schools in science should contend freely. We think that it is harmful to the growth of art and science if administrative measures are used to impose one particular style of art or school of thought and to ban another. Questions of right and wrong in the arts and sciences should be settled through free decision in artistic and scientific circles and through practical work in these fields. They should not be settled in summary fashion. A period of trial is often needed to determine whether something is right or wrong. Throughout history, new and correct things have often failed at the outset to win recognition from the majority of people and have had to develop by twists and turns in struggle. Often correct and good things have first been regarded not as fragrant flowers but as poisonous weeds. Copernicus' theory of the solar system and Darwin's theory of evolution were once dismissed as erroneous and had to win through over bitter opposition. Chinese history offers many similar examples. In a socialist society, conditions for the growth of the new are radically different from and far superior to those in the old society. Nevertheless, it still often happens that new, rising forces are held back and rational proposals constricted. Moreover, the growth of new things may be hindered in the absence of deliberate suppression simply through lack of discernment. It is therefore necessary to be careful about questions of right and wrong in the arts and sciences, to encourage free discussion and avoid hasty conclusions. We believe that such an attitude can help to enjoy a relatively smooth development of the arts and sciences.

Marxism, too, has developed through struggle. At the beginning, Marxism was subjected to all kinds of attack and regarded as a poisonous weed. It is still being attacked and is still regarded as poisonous weed in many parts of the world. In the socialist countries, it enjoys a different position. But non-Marxist and, moreover, anti-Marxist ideologies exist even in these countries. In China, although, in the main, socialist transformation has been completed with respect to the system of ownership, and although the large-scale and turbulent class struggles of the masses characteristic of the previous revolutionary periods have in the main come to an end, there are still remnants of the overthrown landlord and comprador classes, there is still a bourgeoisie, and the remoulding of the petite bourgeoisie has only just started. The class struggle is by no means over. The class struggle between the proletariat and the bourgeoisie, the class struggle between the different political forces, and the class struggle in the ideological field between the proletariat and the bourgeoisie will continue to be long and tortuous and at times even become very acute. The proletariat seeks to transform the world according to its own outlook, and so does the bourgeoisie. In this respect, the question of which will win out, socialism or capitalism, is still not really settled. Marxists are still in a minority amongst the entire population as well as among the intellectuals. Therefore, Marxism must still develop through struggle. Marxism can develop only through struggle, and not only is this true of the past and present, it is necessarily true of the future as well …

People may ask, since Marxism is accepted as the guiding ideology by the majority of the people in our country, can it be criticized? Certainly it can. Marxism is scientific truth and fears no criticism. If it did, and if it could be overthrown by criticism, it would be worthless. In fact, aren't the idealists criticizing Marxism every day and in every way? Aren't those who harbour bourgeois and petit-bourgeois ideas and do not wish to change, aren't they also criticizing Marxism in every way? Marxists should not be afraid of criticism from any quarter. Quite the contrary, they need to temper and develop themselves and win new positions in the teeth of criticism and in the storm and stress of struggle. Fighting against wrong ideas is like being vaccinated. A man develops immunity from disease as a result of vaccination. Plants raised in hothouses are unlikely to be sturdy. Carrying out the policy of letting a hundred flowers blossom and a hundred schools of thought contend will not weaken but strengthen the leading position of Marxism in the ideological field.

What should our policy be towards non-Marxist ideas? As far as unmistakable counter-revolutionaries and saboteurs of the socialist cause are concerned, the matter is easy: we simply deprive them of their freedom of speech. But incorrect ideas among the people are quite a different matter. Will it not do to ban such ideas and deny them any opportunity for expression? Certainly not. It is not only futile but very harmful to use summary methods in dealing with ideological questions among the people, with questions concerned with man's mental world. You may ban the expression of ideas, but the ideas will still be there. On the other hand, if correct ideas are pampered in hothouses without being exposed to the elements or immunized from disease, they will not win out against erroneous ones. Therefore, it is only by employing the method of discussion, criticism, and reasoning that we can really foster correct ideas and overcome wrong ones, and that we can really settle issues ...

At first glance, the two slogans let a hundred flowers blossom and let a hundred schools of thought contend have no class character; the proletariat can turn them to account, and so can the bourgeoisie or other people. The different classes, strata, and social groups each have their own views on what are fragrant flowers and what are poisonous weeds. What then, from the point of view of the broad masses of people, should be the criteria for distinguishing fragrant flowers from poisonous weeds? In the political life of our people, how should right be distinguished from wrong in one's words and actions? On the bases of the principles of our constitution, the will of the overwhelming majority of our people, and the common political positions that have been proclaimed on various occasions by political parties and groups, we consider that, broadly speaking, the criteria should be as follows:

1   Words and actions should help to unite, and not divide, the people of our various nationalities.
2   They should be beneficial, and not harmful, to socialist transformation and socialist construction.
3   They should help to consolidate, and not undermine or weaken, the people's democratic dictatorship.
4   They should help to consolidate, and not undermine or weaken, democratic centralism.
5   They should help to strengthen, and not discard or weaken, the leadership of the Communist Party.
6   They should be beneficial, and not harmful, to international socialist unity and unity of the peace-loving people of the world.

Source: Mao Tse-tung, 'On the Correct Handling of Contradictions Among the People' (Beijing: Foreign Languages Press, 1966). Reprinted by *China Pictorial*, 1967, pp. 20–4

8.5   Mao at odds with the Editorial Board of the *People's Daily*

8.5a   Continue to let go, implement the policy of letting a hundred flowers bloom and letting a hundred schools contend

Editorial in the *People's Daily*, 10 April 1957

This editorial led to Mao's meeting with the Editorial Board of the People's Daily *(see next item).*

It has been more than half a year since the Party Center proposed the policy of 'letting a hundred flowers bloom and letting a hundred schools contend.' How should we assess the early stages of the implementation of this policy?

We believe that, although it has only been implemented for a very short period of time, we are already able to perceive that the early results of the implementation of this policy are good ones. Some people have expressed doubts and a wavering attitude towards this policy, and believe that we should stop the 'blooming' and instead go into the 'retrenchment;' this opinion is entirely inaccurate.

'Letting a hundred flowers bloom, letting a hundred schools contend' is not a temporary, expedient measure; rather, it is a long-range policy necessary for cultural and scientific development. It will take a relatively long time before we can see this policy reach its tremendous results in cultural construction. Nevertheless, even in the last half-year or so, the various departments in scholarship and culture have already become more active and lively than before. Exciting free debates have already unfolded in the circles of philosophy, literature, economics, historical studies, legal studies, and biological studies. More critical research has appeared in the studies of the ancient and traditional cultural heritage of our country and in the study of the scholarship and ideas of capitalist countries. The universities have expanded their curricula. In the area of literary creation, of cinematic, dramatic, operatic, musical, and artistic activity, and in the areas of organizing the various nationalities' artistic and literary legacy and the promotion of the artistic and literary traditions, too, there has been an expression of flourishing liveliness. Many people have felt that their horizons have been expanded and their thought invigorated. All these are very good phenomena. The problem that faces us at the moment is not that the 'blooming' has been too free but that it has not been enough. The task for the Party is to continue to let go, and to insist on implementing the policy of 'letting a hundred flowers bloom, letting a hundred schools contend.'

Some people disagree with the Party Center over this policy. To them, if this were carried on, the intellectual circles would be thrown into chaos, the direction of cultural and scientific development would be blurred, there would be a deluge of bourgeois thought, and the theory of Marxism would be shaken – in short, the prospects are unthinkable.

The article 'Some of Our Opinions about the Literary and Artistic Work of the Moment,' published in this paper by comrades Chen Qitong, Chen Yading, Ma Hanbing, and Lu Le on 7 January, represents this tendency. In that essay, they painted a dismal and horrifying picture of the conditions of the literary and artistic circles at the present time. They said, 'In the last year, fewer and fewer people have promoted the literary and artistic orientation of serving the workers, peasants, and soldiers, or the creative methodology of socialist realism' ...

Quite obviously, such an assessment is an extreme distortion of reality. This has been pointed out in an article written by comrade Chairman Mao, printed here on 1 March, the article by a Mr Mao Dun of 18 March, and the responses of the majority of our readers collected and published here on page seven of the 4 April issue. The question is, how did such an extremely distorted assessment come about? It is because there are still quite a few comrades in the Party who do not in reality agree with the policy of 'letting a hundred flowers bloom and letting a hundred schools contend.' Therefore, they have one-sidedly collected information about some negative phenomena, or exaggerated them, and have attempted to use them to prove the 'damage' of this policy, and thus to 'counsel' the Party to change its own policy quickly. However, the Party cannot accept their 'counsel,' because their orientation is not Marxist, but rather anti-Marxist dogmatism and sectarianism. They do not understand that, at any time, incorrect ideas among the people cannot be dealt with by coercive methods and methods of prohibition. They can be dealt with only through rational discussion, criticism, persuasion, and education. Furthermore, at this time when a nation is just stepping into the transitional period of socialism, it is specifically significant that this policy can be upheld ...

Source: *People's Daily*, 10 April 1957, from J. K. Leung and Y. M. Kau,
The Writings of Mao Zedong 1949–1976,
Vol. 2 (Armonk, New York: M. E. Sharpe, 1992), pp. 479–81

8.5b Mao reprimands the Editorial Board of the *People's Daily*, 10 April 1957

From T. Cheek, *Propaganda and Culture in Mao's China*

Wang Ruoshui, the junior editor not formally on the paper's editorial board, had written the 10 April editorial under the usual guidance of Deng Tuo [Chief Editor] and the board. After lunch that day, Wang, Deng Tuo, and the entire board received an urgent summons: 'Chairman Mao has called you to go see him'. Naturally, Wang was concerned that Mao was unhappy with the editorial, but whatever it was, just to be able to see the Chairman was exciting. Deng Tuo gathered the editorial committee together, after mentioning to Wang: 'I think I'll take advantage of this opportunity to resign and have an end to it'. Indeed, Deng had already offered his resignation a number of times since the fall of 1956.

The full editorial board ... drove to Zhongnanhai in two cars ... The editors then filed into a smallish room that had originally been the Chairman's bedroom.

One need not be a psychologist to appreciate the shocking disrespect Mao showed his propagandists and his crude display of power. The editors ... were formally dressed and sat politely in a semicircle. A semicircle around the Chairman's bed. Although it was already afternoon, the Chairman was in his pyjamas. In fact, he had on only a pyjama top and a towel wrapped round his waist. He lounged on the bed (a large wooden affair piled with string-bound traditional Chinese books) and smoked continually ...

He began with menacing informality: 'I couldn't sleep. Decided to call you in for a chat. Looked at today's editorial. Even though it's a bit late, it finally shows your stand on the article by the four men including Chen Qitong. It's already been over a month since the SSC [the Supreme State Conference] and propaganda work conference, but there hasn't been a peep out of the Party papers. It's been left to the non-Party papers to raise that banner' ...

Deng Tuo tried to explain, offering a self criticism of his own actions, but he was repeatedly interrupted by Mao's petulant criticisms: 'I think you purposely sang a different tune, purposely praised Chen Qitong and the others'. 'You people are not the Party paper, you're a factional paper'. 'In the past I said you people were pedants running the paper. Wrong, I should say you are dead men running the paper' ...

Mao next went out of his way to praise the junior editor, Wang Ruoshui, in order to humiliate Deng Tuo. Mao praised Wang for writing the editorial (ignoring the obvious fact that he was assigned to do so by Deng) ...

Mao then turned to the assistant general editors: 'You people are really strange. Can it really be that you agree with him [pointing to Deng Tuo]? Is it that Deng Tuo is so good in uniting people that all your opinions are so uniform?' The editors were silent, unwilling to desert their chief editor. Mao continued: 'If you have an opinion, you can debate! If you want to raise criticisms with Deng Tuo, the most he can do is fire you. How come not even a breeze got through, how come that not one of you wrote a letter to the Party Centre reporting the situation? So long as you don't go making a ruckus in the street, then you can discuss any opinion. No doubt Deng Tuo has his virtues and you haven't the heart to oppose him. [To Deng Tuo] I think you very much resemble Emperor Yuandi of the Han, peaceable and easy-going but lacking the strength to make quick decisions (*yourou guaduan*). With you in the Emperor's seat, the nation would be lost!'

The menace of the last sentence shocked everyone. Wang Ruoshui couldn't help eyeing nervously the small mountain of history books on the Chairman's bed. Deng Tuo, too, had obviously also felt the force of the last sentence and probably felt the time had come for him to offer his resignation. He said, 'I myself do not know if I am Han Yuandi or not; none the less I feel my abilities are insufficient. It is hard to feel adequate for the job. I hope the Chairman will consider relieving me of my duties. Several times I have sincerely and in good faith raised this request' ...

Mao was incensed, finding Deng's explanation both patronizing and insubordinate: 'I don't believe that sincerity and good faith of yours! You only know the comings and goings of limousines, you live in luxury. Now, shit or get off the pot!' Every time the masses report new larger harvests, Mao went on, Deng Tuo insisted on lowering figures. Deng's attitude and his delay reflected just the sort of bureaucratic obstruction that Mao was trying to root out with his Hundred Flowers campaign. As for the resignation, Mao retorted: 'Are you a Party member or not?' Thus reminded of his duty, Deng Tuo continued on as editor for a few months, but Mao was through with him. He merely wanted to fire him, not receive his resignation.

The meeting, which lasted four hours, then degenerated into a long harangue by the Chairman and his views concerning the Hundred Flowers policy and the role of intellectuals. Ominously, he stressed that 'the hundred schools contending' was merely competition between the proletarian and the bourgeois classes for the services of wavering intellectuals. In short, he said, we buy them, just as we have bought the national capitalists. However, we mustn't be open about it.

In 1959 Deng Tuo was removed from the post of Chief Editor, and in 1966 he became one of the first victims of the Cultural Revolution.

**Source: T. Cheek, *Propaganda and Culture in Mao's China*
(Oxford: Clarendon Press, 1997), pp. 178–81**

8.6 Student protests

8.6a Lin Xiling's speech at a debate held on 23 May 1957 at Beijing University

This is a summary based on notes taken by Beijing University students. Lin begins by referring to the imprisonment in 1955 of the writer Hu Feng (a close friend of the famous writer Lu Xun). Hu had criticized the Party's tight control over literature.

I am very excited today to be able to breathe the fresh air of Peita [Beijing University]. The People's University is a great beehive of dogmatism with too heavy a bureaucratic atmosphere. Peita, after all, is Peita and inherits the traditions of the May 4th Movement.

Is Hu Feng a counter-revolutionary? This question still cannot be answered in the affirmative. It is too soon to draw conclusions, but the evidence submitted to prove that the Hu Feng clique is counter-revolutionary is very weak and absurd!

In the past, I, too, wrote articles criticizing Hu Feng. Now I believe that this was really very childish and shameful on my part.

If Hu Feng was a counter-revolutionary, why did he present his program to the Party Central Committee? Wasn't he making trouble for himself? Whether his program was correct or not, representative measures should not have been employed. Why is it counter-revolutionary to offer a few suggestions to the Party Central Committee? This is the method of Stalinism; this is sectarianism! Actually, Hu Feng's criticisms of sectarianism at that time didn't contain one per cent of what has now been exposed in real life! ...

If the Hu Feng case had taken place today, when the rectification campaign was proposed after the exposure of Stalin or the incidents in Poland and Hungary, it would not have been handled as it was. At that time [the handling of it] was too rude. If Hu Feng's program were proposed today, he would not be spoken of as a counter-revolutionary. If it had been proposed by Lu Hsün, it is even more unlikely that it would have been [considered] counter-revolutionary.

This past April, when Deputy Chief Procurator T'an of the Supreme Procuracy came to the People's University to make a report, someone asked him what had happened regarding the Hu Feng question. T'an said: 'The investigation has been completed, but Hu Feng is very lacking in humility! He refuses to accept the opinions of others!' Comrades, what does this explain? According to Deputy Chief Procurator T'an, can Hu Feng be considered a counter-revolutionary? It has been two years now, and the results of the Hu Feng case still haven't been published. I think that the Communist Party is in an embarrassing position and doesn't know how to get out of it. It knows it has made a mistake, but refuses to admit it. Chairman Mao, I think, may have [one of] two different things in mind: (1) he clearly knows that a mistake has been made, but refuses to admit it; or (2) he himself is aware of the error, but many high-ranking cadres still refuse to understand, and so [he finds it] difficult to conclude the Hu Feng case at the present time. It was said that, when Chairman Mao in his speech proposed the principle regarding the correct handling of contradictions among the people, eighty percent of the high-ranking cadres disapproved and some of them even got up and walked out of the meeting ...

Our country also expanded the scale of [the work of] suppressing counter-revolution, [but] our judicial system is unsound. I have already practiced in a District court, so I know that soon the People's Deputies will go out to inspect the work of suppressing counter-revolution. I saw that everywhere – from the Court and the Procuracy to the Public Security Bureau – everyone was busy correcting the records of cases and charge sheets that had [politically] wrong accusations. A reason was supplied wherever one was lacking. This certainly was arranged by the Party Central Committee, so what are the People's Deputies supposed to inspect?

I heartily agree with the Yugoslav opinion that the cult of personality is a product of the social system ...

Marxism tells us that all social phenomena have their social and historical origins. The problem of Stalin is not the problem of Stalin the individual; the problem of Stalin could only arise in a country like the Soviet Union, because in the past it had been a feudal, imperialistic nation. China is the same, for there has been no tradition of bourgeois democracy. This could not happen in France. I believe that public ownership is better than private ownership, but I hold that the socialism we now have is not genuine socialism; or that, if it is, our socialism is not typical. Genuine socialism should be very democratic, but ours is undemocratic. I venture to say our society is a socialist one erected on a feudal foundation; it is not typical socialism, and we must struggle for genuine socialism! ...

There has been a loosening up at Peita, but I am not optimistic about the [prospects for success of the] rectification [campaign], because there are still too many guardians of the rules. These guardians want to use the fruits of socialism, bought with the blood of the martyrs, as a ladder to climb to higher positions. It is said that there are signs of tightening up the contending movement in order to keep the people quiet ...

Peita has acted, and it is a good beginning. Now the students in the north-west, Wuhan, Nanking, and elsewhere are stirring. But we have no way to communicate with each other. No reports are available; there is a news blackout. If we utter one wrong word, [the guardians of the rules] can manufacture charges out of nothing and grab us by the queue. We should be vigilant! We are upright people! Upright people are found everywhere and we should unite! The blood of the Hungarian people was not shed in vain! Our success in winning this little bit of democracy today is inseparable from [the Hungarian people]. The masses of the people are not fools. A real solution to problems depends on the actions of the masses of the people, the creators of history!

I am not afraid to speak in this way. My friends constantly tell me: 'You little devil, all of us are going to find you in jail one day and we'll have to send your meals in to you.' Although this was said in jest, there is such a possibility. If you don't welcome me, I'll get out; but since I have come here, I accept the danger. It's not important if I'm thrown in jail.

Our struggle today is not merely personal grumbling. No reformist methods should be used to deal with shortcomings. Our objective is crystal clear: to establish genuine socialism – to lead the life of real people.

> **Source: Lin Hsi-ling, Speech at Beijing University, 23 May 1957. In Dennis Doolin,**
> *Communist China: The Politics of Student Opposition* **(Stanford, California: Hoover**
> **Institute, Stanford University, 1964), pp. 23–9**

8.6b I accuse, I protest, 2 June 1957

Anonymous wall poster at Qinghua University.

I was born and raised in the liberated area. For twenty years I've seen through the imperialists. Facing the enemy, my eyes are red with anger and I would risk losing my head and shedding my blood; but facing the dictatorship of the Communist Party I am cowardly and powerless. How small and pitiful is one individual! We have given our blood, sweat, toil, and precious lives to defend not the people but the bureaucratic organs and bureaucrats who oppress the people and live off the fat of the land. They are a group of fascists who employ foul means, twist the truth, band together in evil ventures, and ignore the people's wish for peace both at home and abroad ...

I protest against Chairman Mao's recent statement to the [Youth] League Central [Committee] that 'the Party is the leadership core in all work, and any deviation from socialism is erroneous.' This statement should be translated as follows: 'It is necessary to accept Party dictatorship; anyone who opposes the words of the super-emperor is wrong and should be killed forthwith.' They've prostituted the words 'people' and 'socialism' ...

The Chinese people have been deceived. When they courageously drove out the imperialists and the Chiang Kai-shek gang, they put their trust in the wrong man. We used a robber's knife to drive out another robber. When one robber had been killed, we gave the knife to the other one. This is the key problem. Oh, all you under the robber's knife – speak out! Oh, freedom! Oh, contending! Oh, blooming! This is so-called guided democracy and centralized democracy, Mao Tse-tung style.

There are only two ways out for our people: either obey the robber, become his disciples and grand-disciples, and maybe gain a position or a job; or snatch the knife from the robber and live like men. There is an old Chinese proverb that says 'Lay down thy butcher's knife and thou wilt at once become a Buddha.' As long as Mao Tse-tung has his Party guards and imperial army, he won't become a Buddha. He won't let others remold him; he only wants to remold others. ...

Your Majesty! Although you are contemptible and hateful, your common people are still willing to give you some advice. You're getting old. You can stop a man from using his pen, but you can never stop a man from using his memory. One of these days a genuine historian, perhaps an intimate of yours, will expose you for what you are ...

People will understand why I won't sign my name to this.

> Source: 'I Accuse', Anonymous wall poster of 2 June 1957. In Dennis Doolin,
> *Communist China: The Politics of Student Opposition* (Stanford, California: Hoover
> Institute, Stanford University, 1964), pp. 60–3, 64–6

8.7 I admit my guilt to the people, 13 July 1957

Fei Xiaotong

Fei Xiaotang, a prominent ethnologist and anthropologist, was a leading member of the Democratic League and had been urging greater intellectual freedom. Here he recants. The China Democratic League is one of the statutory political parties recognized in the constitution.

I admit my guilt to the people and continue to expose my crime. In doing so, I bear witness to the conspiracy of the Chang Lo alliance [Chang and Lo were leaders of the Democratic League].

I worked for the culture and education committee of the China Democratic League in the second half of 1955. For the purpose of uncovering questions concerning the intellectuals, I proposed organising small forums and inviting those Democratic League members who were dissatisfied with the Party and socialism, and the intellectuals connected with them, to air their views. Names of the persons attending the forums were off the record and no criticism was practised. This work, while reflecting the dark side of the problem concerning intellectuals and being of certain value for reference purposes, did extremely serious harm:

(i)   It encouraged uncritical growth and spread of backward reactionary thoughts.
(ii) It had its impact on the middle-of-the-road elements.
(iii) It shut off and isolated the progressive influence because few progressive elements were invited to the forums.
(iv) As the leading comrades made the namelists and held the forums freely and directly instead of through their regular organisational life, opportunity was given to the careerists to take advantage of the legal organisation and carry out conspiratorial activities in collaboration with the backward elements.
(v)   The backward and reactionary opinions were collected as the basis for evaluating the conditions of intellectuals. This created a wrong impression among the leading bodies of the League, provided the careerists with the propaganda material they needed, and encouraged their attempt to use these intellectuals as their political capital ...

I returned to Peking from the south-west region and in February this year I made an extremely absurd speech against the Party at a forum of the League Central Committee. At an NPC group meeting I have already made public the minutes of this speech. At that time, I held that the problem of intellectuals was mainly due to two lids not being lifted. Essentially these two lids were: idealism that was not released in learning, and bourgeois democracy that was not released in politics. This was completely an anti-Party and antisocialist demand pressed from the standpoint of the bourgeoisie. This also shows my erroneous view of the 'let all schools of thought contend' and 'mutual supervision' policies. The serious bourgeois thinking hidden in the depth of my heart was exposed. Bourgeois 'democracy' and 'freedom' not only stubbornly demonstrated themselves ideologically but also dominated my activities at the juncture of socialism. These absurd speeches were given importance by Chang and Lo and repeatedly propagated and enlarged upon.

I wrote 'Early Spring Weather for Intellectuals' based on that speech. Lo Lung-chi read my draft and egged me on to have it published. This article spread, in obscure, harsh, and concealed ways, the feelings of backward intellectuals, produced a stimulating effect, and aroused their anti-Party and antisocialist feelings. Linked up with the conspiracy of the Chang–Lo alliance, this article was indeed a signal for releasing anti-Communist and anti-socialist speeches in the attack on the Party. I accept and am thankful for the criticism and help by deputies Li Ta, Hsia Kang-nung and Yang Tung-chuan. I should go a step further to criticise myself ...

In the Shanghai *Wen Hui Pao*, at propaganda conferences called by the Chinese Communist Party, and in the *Cheng Ming* monthly, I time and again stood against the cancellation of bourgeois social science and demanded its restoration, and I also demanded early recall of those old social science workers who had changed trade. This was a reflection of the idea of bourgeois restoration. Moreover, I advanced from thought to action. For my part, the idea of restoring social science was inspired by the *Wen Hui Pao* ...

I hate my past and I must change my stand; I hate the Chang–Lo alliance and I must draw a boundary line against them and sever our connections. I'm grateful to the Party for keeping the door of reformation open to us guilty of mistakes and fallen into the quagmire of the rightists, and for doing its best to educate us. Permit me to enter this door courageously, embark upon the road to life, completely reform myself, and create an opportunity to atone for my crime to the people.

I have not awakened long and my understanding is still not deep. I will explain in detail and penetratingly examine my crime and my thoughts. The only thing I can do today is to continue to expose my crime at this congress, bear witness to the conspiracy of the Chang–Lo alliance, and own to my guilt to the people. I will continue to examine myself and take part in the antirightist struggle during which I will study and reform myself. I'm determined to accept Party education and follow the socialist road under Party leadership.

Source: Fei Hsiao-tung, 'I Admit My Guilt to the People', 13 July 1957,
Current Background, No. 470, pp. 10, 12–13

9

The Great Leap Forward

Eliminating the landlord class was only one step in the process of land reform. Socialism called for further egalitarianism and the cooperativization of resources. During the civil war the communist policy had wavered in regard to the respective treatment of the different classes of peasants. After 1949 it was time for unambiguous and uniform policies.

The process of the post land reform period went through defined stages. In its simplest manifestation, villagers used mutual aid teams, sharing production tasks and resources at planting and harvest time. The next stage was the creation of Agricultural Producers Cooperatives in which villagers benefited both from their labour and from the land and tools they contributed. Initially, this was described as a lower or semi-socialist APC, the forerunner of the 'higher' APC in which all resources were to be pooled and the income allocated solely on labour contributions, i.e. work points. The higher APC was synonymous with collectivization.

By December 1953 the results of land reform were perceived as unsatisfactory – in 1953–4 grain production had risen by less than two per cent; other crops such as cotton did even less well. This was incompatible with the need of China's growing population for food and clothes. What was wrong? Some, the gradualists, felt that China lacked the prerequisites for large-scale farming such as tractors and chemical fertilizers. An able official, Deng Zihui, was actually working to reduce the number of APCs in 1955. Then, on 31 July 1955, Mao delivered a speech castigating those who wanted to proceed slowly like tottering women with bound feet. The Central Committee decreed that the full cooperatives (higher APCs), the collectives, should be established by April 1958. Enthusiastic cadres in the countryside were anxious to prove their worth. By the end of 1957 the initial process of cooperativisation was virtually complete and the stage was set for the cooperatives to be collectives.

Since the villages were deemed to be too small as units of resource, it was decided that planning could best be done at the level of what had formerly been the *Xiang*. In Imperial China this comprised a number of villages with a population from 20,000 up to 50,000. It was now called a commune.

The new economic collectives at first organized at the village or team level were soon subsumed within the larger communes. The population was mobilized to develop not only agriculture and local industrial enterprises but also to take part (as appropriate) in large tasks such as water conservation and land reclamation. Living and working together, the peasants would be forged into a revolutionary corps. Cooking was to give way to mess halls, and children were to be looked after in crèches, thus liberating mothers to work in the fields and stoke the fires of improvised iron furnaces. By developing agriculture and industry side by side in the countryside, Mao was advocating an alternative to the Soviet model. It was expected that, within fifteen years, China would overtake Great Britain in industrial development.

It was the exaggerated reports of the cadres that undermined the success of the Great Leap Forward. Throughout the country, in both agriculture (grain and cotton) and industry (coal and steel), they issued wildly inflated production figures. Despite doubts raised at the Wuchang conference in November 1958, these figures were endorsed by the Central Committee in November–December 1958 and the planners were thus encouraged to set even higher targets for 1959. Benefiting from good weather conditions, the 1958 harvest had been good, with actual production of approximately 200–210 million tons of grain. Unfortunately, the figure claimed was 375 million tons, and with unbridled euphoria extra grain quotas went to the cities, while an extra fifty per cent went to the Soviet Union and free grain was sent to North Korea, North Vietnam, and Albania. By June 1959, with drought in the north-east and flooding in the south, it was clear that the 1959 harvest would be well down on expectations. One problem was shortage of manpower for harvesting since so many people were working in rural industries.

When both Peng Dehuai and Mao respectively visited their home villages in Hunan in April and June, it should have been clear that all was not well. The crisis was aired vigorously at the Central Committee meeting at Lushan in July 1959. Mao narrowed the debate into a choice between Peng and himself. The conference swung into line behind Mao. Peng was further tarnished by the fact that, on his visit to the USSR (24 April–13 June), Khrushchev had publicly condemned the communes. Moreover, Khrushchev had also in June formally reneged on the nuclear technology agreement – a sample atom bomb for China. Immediately after the Lushan conference, Mao convened a Politburo standing committee to deal with Peng. The Defence Minister was doomed. Within a month he had been replaced by Lin Biao and moved out of his office in Zhongnanhai – his career was over.

Although there was indeed a succession of bad harvests, Mao has a heavy responsibility for the course of events during the 'three bad years' 1959–61. The misreporting of grain production was one critical factor leading to starvation. The concept of diversifying industry in the countryside, most notably by setting up local blast furnaces, wasted resources and failed to produce usable steel. The commune structure on a large and impersonal scale diminished local initiatives, and the common mess halls proved to be seriously unpopular. The charade was not easily brought to an end. In August 1959 the Premier, Zhou Enlai, continued publicly to uphold mass participation in iron and steel production. In November, Mao addressed cadres at all levels, commenting on errors in agricultural policy and suggested solutions.

Mao's ultimate line was that he could not stomach any challenge to his fervent convictions. He maintained: 'The struggle at Lushan was a class struggle and a continuation of the life-and-death struggle between the two major antagonistic classes, the proletariat and the bourgeoisie. This kind of struggle will continue … in our Party for another twenty years and possibly for half a century'.

In an attempt to meet the problems of the Great Leap, individual farming on the lines later to be introduced as the family responsibility system appeared in parts of China in the early 1960s – only to be suppressed by the leftists.

The extreme socialist ambitions of the Great Leap Forward contributed to the widening rift between China and the Soviet Union. Soviet aid was suddenly withdrawn in 1960: the disagreements on a range of policies became increasingly public, although it was not until the 1990s that the Soviet archives became available.

9.1 China to overtake Great Britain in fifteen years, 4 April 1958

In an address of greetings to the Eighth All-China Congress of Trade Unions which was held last December in Peking, Liu Shao-chi, speaking on behalf of the Central Committee of the Chinese Communist Party, issued a call for China to strive to catch up or surpass Britain in output of iron and steel and other major industrial products within fifteen years. It should be remembered that China's first five-year plan began in 1953, nearly two hundred years after the industrial revolution of Britain. But the Chinese people have displayed amazing ability in building up their country.

Since the founding of new China, tremendous tasks have been accomplished by the Chinese working class and the Chinese people as a whole. The system of class exploitation that ruled for several thousand years has been in the main abolished; the basic victory of the socialist revolution and the great advance in socialist construction have laid the groundwork for a socialist industrialization.

In the first five-year plan period, the targets for total output value of industrial and agricultural production, and for many other tasks, were overfulfilled. From 1952 to 1957, the output of steel increased on average by 31.2 per cent a year, that of power by 21.4 per cent, and that of coal by 14 per cent. Compared with 1952, the total output value of modern industry in 1957 showed an increase of 132.5 per cent. On average, there was a new and large factory or mine coming into operation every two days. Now China can turn out jet planes, motor vehicles, sea vessels, locomotives, metallurgical equipment, and various new-type lathes.

Inspired by the success of the first five-year plan, the Chinese people are launching a new nationwide upsurge in industrial and agricultural production. China's second five-year plan is even more awe-inspiring than her first. In 1962, when the plan will be completed, the yearly output of steel will reach 12,000,000 tons, power 43,000,000,000 kilowatts, and coal 210,000,000 tons. It is therefore natural that the Chinese people are looking forward to their future with greater confidence than ever.

Source: 'China to Overtake Great Britain in Fifteen Years',
China Pictorial, **No. 4, April 1958**

9.2 Raise high the red flag of the people's commune and march forward

People's Daily, 3 September 1958

People's communes, which mark a new stage of the socialist development in China's rural areas, are now being set up and developed in many places at a rapid rate.

The movement has been started by the masses of the peasants spontaneously on the basis of their great socialist consciousness. When the small number of the earliest communes proved successful, many agricultural cooperatives immediately followed their example, so that the movement gradually developed. Now, with the encouragement and guidance given by the Central Committee of the Communist Party and Chairman Mao Tse-tung, it is making even bigger strides forward.

The masses of peasants in many areas have written large numbers of wall newspapers, applications, and resolutions, asking for the establishment of people's communes. Virtually all the peasants in Honan and Liaoning provinces are now in people's communes, while the movement is reaching its high tide in Hopei, Heilungkiang, and Anhwei provinces, and is spreading to other provinces in north-west China, along the Yangtze River, and to the south of it, with preparations for the establishment of people's communes in different stages and groups after the autumn harvest.

Where people's communes have already come into existence, the peasants, beating drums and cymbals, celebrated the occasion with revelry and their enthusiasm in production has reached a new peak. The poor and lower middle peasants, in particular, rejoice in it and regard it as 'the realisation of a long-cherished hope'.

Of the basic features of people's communes, the first is that they are big in scale and the second is that they are 'communal'.

The people's communes are big in scale, having a great number of members and vast land. They can develop agriculture, forestry, animal husbandry, fishery, and subsidiary production simultaneously and merge industry, agriculture, exchange, culture and education, and the militia into one.

The people's communes so far established generally embrace some 10,000 members or even 10,000 households and their area is equal to that of *hsiang* (where the original *hsiang* are too small, they can even be expanded and merged). With large numbers of people and greater strength, they can do many things that are impossible or not easy for the smaller farming cooperatives, such as bigger water conservancy projects, factories, and mines that require higher technique, larger projects of road and housing construction, establishment of secondary schools and higher educational institutions, and so on. The question of manpower shortage also becomes easier to tackle.

The people's communes are 'communal' in that they represent a higher level of socialist development and collectivisation than agricultural producer cooperatives. Their massive scale of production requires a higher efficiency and greater manoeuvrability of labour as well as the participation of women in production. Therefore, more and more common mess halls, nurseries, tailoring teams, and other similar establishments are being set up, and the last remnants of individual ownership of the means of production retained in farming coopera-tives are being eliminated. In many places, for example, the reserve plots, livestock, and orchards of individual peasants, and a portion of the larger production tools, and so on, have been transferred to the people's communes in the course of their establishment.

Ownership of the means of production by the whole people has been instituted by a few communes on the basis of self-consciousness and spontaneous agreement of the masses. In distribution they have carried out the wage system or supply wage system on an experi-mental basis. These experiments are useful because they point out the road to further devel-opment of productive relations in the countryside.

At the same time, because people's communes have gone beyond the limits of solely economic organisations, and have combined economic, cultural, political, and military affairs into one entity, there is now no longer any need for the separate governments of the *hsiang* level, and these must be integrated with the communes. The administrative committees of the communes are in fact the people's councils of the *hsiang*. There is also the tendency for a federation of people's communes in a *hsien* to become one with the people's council of that *hsien*. This facilitates unified leadership, closely combines the collective economy of farming cooperative with the state-owned economy of *hsiang* and *hsien*, and helps the transition from collective ownership to ownership by the people as a whole.

Therefore, people's communes are the most appropriate organisational forms in China for accelerating socialist construction and the transition to Communism. They will become the basic social units in the future Communist society, as Marx, Engels, and Lenin predicted on many occasions.

The transformation of agricultural producer cooperatives into people's communes is the inevitable trend in the development of Chinese history. China has now some 700,000 farming cooperatives, mostly set up in 1955 during the high tide of socialism, and gradually transformed into higher cooperatives thereafter. They are undoubtedly far superior to individual farming, mutual aid teams, and even the lower farming cooperatives, and have contributed enormously to the steady increase in China's farm output in the past few years. However, with the growth of agricultural production, especially the great leap forward in agriculture since last winter, these cooperatives have gradually become inadequate to meet the needs of development fully.

> Source: 'Raise High the Red Flag of the People's Commune and March Forward',
> 3 September 1958, *People's Daily, Current Background*, No. 517, pp. 5–6

9.3 Which kind of mess hall do the masses like?

People's Daily, 3 November 1958

The common mess halls, set up in Summer 1958, were promoted as a means of pooling resources, releasing women from household chores to work in the fields, and creating time for literacy campaigns and ideological education.

The first kind are organized with each original small production team as the unit. Thus, in one village there may be several mess halls …

The second kind are established with each village as the unit, ignoring both the former production units and the new form of production organization. No matter whether the village is large or small, and whether there are many or few households, one mess hall is set up for each village …

The third kind are organized with the newly formed production teams as the unit. One of the advantages of this kind of mess hall is that they can combine production, livelihood, and work in a unified manner.

WHICH TYPE IS THE BEST?

Mess halls of the first type sell only rice but not vegetables. After the setting up of mess halls of this type, actually each household still has to cook its own vegetables; the style of living with each individual household as the unit has not been completely changed, and women have still not been completely emancipated from household drudgery. The masses criticize this type of mess hall as having four outstanding defects: (1) the commune members doubt each other and have grudges against each other; (2) some members finish their meals quickly while others finish theirs slowly, and thus not all of them can go to work at the same time; (3) as every household has to cook its own dishes, people still argue about money for oil and salt; and (4) women are still not emancipated, and the tail of private ownership is still there. It seems, therefore, that the masses have many opinions about mess halls of this type. At the moment, some places are making changes.

The second type of mess hall sells both rice and vegetables but not water. Although mess halls of this type are better than those of the first type, the masses are still not accustomed to the fact that boiled water and hot water are not supplied. Some people said: 'After a whole day's work, there is not even hot water for us to soak our feet. How can we go on like this?' ...

Mess halls of the third type supply rice and vegetables as well as water. The mess hall in Liutsichieh is an example of this type which is comparatively higher in class. Commune members praised this type of mess hall as having five good points: good in water supply, good in taking care of the members' livelihood, good in economizing expenditure, good in bringing unity to families, and good in public health and sanitation.

In order gradually to develop themselves into this third type, some mess halls in the Hsinchow commune have adopted the following methods:

1   To dismantle all stoves in private households, and set up a small stove in each public mess hall, or leave one small stove for every five households. The masses do not like the practice of leaving one small stove for every five households, saying that it is a sign of private ownership; they quite agree on letting mess halls manage those small stoves. For instance, Hsia Hai-po, a 63 year old man in the Liutsichieh mess hall who has remained a bachelor for over 20 years, did not have anyone to take care of him when he was sick in the past; but when he was ill recently, the small stove in the mess hall cooked especially for him a bowl of noodles with sliced meat. Taking the bowl of noodles in his hand, he said smilingly: 'This is the best bowl of noodles I've ever eaten in my life. What more could I expect even if I had a son!'

2   With each mess hall as the unit, to concentrate all the vegetable gardens, plant vegetables collectively, and set up a special team to take charge, in order to be self-sufficient and even have a surplus in greens. At the very start, the Liutsichieh mess hall collectively planted 21 *mow* of vegetables and assigned six persons to take exclusive care of the job ...

3   With the problem of collective planting of vegetables solved, each mess hall as a unit should purchase the living pigs owned by its members or mobilize the members to invest their pigs in a mess hall at a certain cash value, so as to enable the mess hall to raise its own pigs for pork. Again, take the Liutsichieh mess hall as an example: within a single month, life has improved twofold and the masses have been served roast fish once and steamed meat once. Quite satisfied with their food, the masses are even higher in their labor enthusiasm.

Source: 'Which Kind of Mess Hall Do the Masses Like?' 3 November 1958,
People's Daily, Current Background, **No. 538, pp. 27–8**

9.4 No household drudgery

Verse about the communes, written by women in the Two Temples Subcommune in Hsiancheng County, Honan. Printed in China Pictorial, *1958*

On an economic and social par with men at last, the women are blossoming out in every way. They wear gay cotton prints to the fields and take more pains with their appearance. Some have developed an interest in poetry. A bit of verse one of the women has written sums up quite neatly how they feel about the communes:

> Nurseries, kindergartens, tailor shops,
> You don't do the cooking,
> Or feed pigs the slops.
> Machines make the clothing
> And grind the flour.
> When you give birth to a baby
> It's cared for every hour.
> Freed from household drudgery,
> Let's produce more by the day,
> And drive ahead to communism,
> It isn't far away!

**Source: Sidney Shapiro on Emancipation of Women,
including poem by Chinese women, *China Pictorial*, No. 101, 1958, p. 26**

9.5 Talks at the Wuchang Conference, 21–23 November 1958

This transcript of the discussion at the top-level conference includes a frank admission of mistakes by Mao and some critical interjections by Party officials present.

CHAIRMAN MAO: Should one pour cold water [on enthusiasm]? People must eat their fill, and sleep sufficiently, especially those who go all out and battle hard for days and nights. Once they come off work, they must – except under special circumstances – sleep for a while. At this point [we] should alleviate [people's] tasks. In the construction of irrigation works, between last winter and this spring we moved, nationwide, over 50 billion cubic meters of earth and stone, but from this winter to next spring we want to move 190 billion cubic meters nation-wide, an increase of well over threefold. Then we have to deal with all sorts of tasks: steel, copper, aluminum, coal, transport, the processing industries, the chemical industry – [they all] need hordes of people. In this kind of situation, I think if we do [all these things simultaneously] half of China's population unquestionably will die; and if it's not a half, it'll be a third or ten percent, a death toll of 50 million people. When people died in Guangxi, wasn't Chen Manyuan dismissed? If with a death toll of 50 million you didn't lose your jobs, I at least should lose mine; [whether I would lose my] head would also be open to question. Anhui wants to do so many things, it's quite all right to do a lot, but make it a principle to have no deaths. One hundred and ninety billion cubic meters of earth and stone is an awful lot; discuss it – if you insist on moving [that many], I can't do anything about it; but if people die [as a result], you cannot cut off my head. Last year must be surpassed by a bit, moving [say] 60 to 70 billion [cubic meters], but one doesn't want an excessive amount … As to 30 million tons of steel, do we really need that much? Are we able to produce [that much]? How many people do we have to mobilize? Could it lead to deaths? Even though you say that it is necessary to work on the basic points (steel, coal), how many months do you need to get that done? Hebei says half a year, which will have to include iron-smelting, coal, transport, steel rolling, and so forth; this has to be talked over.

XXX: The tasks for next year will be discussed severally by each province. Will they agree to 30 million tons or not? If not, [this target] will have to be changed and we'll have to consider whether it should be 30 million tons.

INTERRUPTION: Sixty million people turn out 10 million tons of iron. In fact, it is only 7 million tons, of which good iron amounts to only 40 percent; it is not as [claimed in] the high estimate. Once a base is established, bring back the [farm] laborers, or else there won't be anyone left even to harvest the seeds, and there won't be any exports [of agricultural products] either. Of 11 million tons of steel, good steel represents no more than 9 million tons or perhaps 8.5 tons. If we are aiming at 30 million tons, that is a two-and-a-half-fold increase.

CHAIRMAN MAO: This year there are two aspects [to be considered]. How many 60 millions can China's population be divided into? If, of the several million tons of local iron and local steel, only 40 percent are good, should we make an earnest effort to double that to get from 10.7 million tons this year to 21.4 million tons next year? If we produce yet another ten thousand tons, we should be able to manage 21.4 million tons next year. In my view, we should be a bit prudent. If water conservancy [construction] sticks at 50 billion cubic meters and doesn't multiply in any way, won't that still be 500 billion cubic meters after ten years? I say we should leave some things for our sons to do. Why should we finish everything?

Furthermore, as to the arrangements for different types of work – coal, electricity, oil, chemicals, afforestation, building materials, cloth and paper making – at this conference we should adopt a low-key approach and pipe down a bit. If, after having worked through the first half of next year, things go [well], there are reserve forces, and circumstances are favorable, then we might be a little more ambitious and ratchet up on the first of July. But one should not do it like the people who play the *huqin* at the opera, who risk breaking the strings when they tighten them too much. Perhaps this sounds a bit like pouring cold water, and the cadres at the lower levels who run the communes may have some objections and will not fail to curse us for rightist tendencies. [But] don't be afraid, toughen your scalps and let those below curse you. Doubling [output] has never happened in the world since Pan Gu separated heaven and earth – how is this a rightist tendency?

What are the targets for agriculture?

TAN ZHENLIN: Publicly we say we aim at about 10 billion catties which would give about two thousand catties per head.

CHAIRMAN MAO: These things from the Beidaihe conference have to be discussed again. You talk of right opportunism, [so] I proceed to double [targets]! [This year the target is] 80,000 machine tools, next year a fourfold increase, producing 320,000 – can that really be true? At the time of the Beidaihe conference we still had no experience in running industry; but when, after a bit more than two months, the transportation of iron and steel has clogged things up everywhere, we have become relatively experienced. Generally speaking, it's best if there's a practical possibility. There are two kinds of practical possibility: one is a real possibility, the other is an unreal possibility. For instance, it is unrealistic at present [for us] to make a satellite, but in the future this might be realized ...

The people's communes have to be overhauled for four months: in December, January, February, and March. An inspection force consisting of ten thousand people should be set up, mainly to see if people get eight hours of sleep a night. When they sleep only seven, that means they are not [able] to finish their tasks – I never finish my tasks; you can also investigate [me] and stick up a big character poster ... According to current reports from Hubei, at present 7 or 8 percent of the communes are running relatively well. I belong to the skeptical faction; I count it as a success if I see one out of ten people's communes is being run really well ... there is danger that the country will go under ... The mess halls may go under, and so may the nurseries; in Gucheng County in Hubei Province, there's a mess hall where things went like this. A number of the nurseries will most certainly be abolished .... In Henan there is a happiness home where, after 30 percent [of the residents] had died, all the rest ran away. I, too, would have run away: how could it not collapse? Given the fact that nurseries and happiness homes can collapse, why can't the people's communes? I think, as with everything, there are two possibilities: collapse and non-collapse ...

As to the question of falsification, the resolution on the communes has to be changed into a directive and has to have a special paragraph on the question of falsification. Originally, there were two sentences, but that's not enough- a special paragraph has to be written. If you lump it in with work methods, people won't pay attention. Now, no matter what, they want to launch 'Sputniks,' strive for fame, and don't care whether they fake it or not. When they don't really have all that many things, they fabricate them. There is a people's commune that itself had only a hundred pigs. To cope with a visit, they borrowed another two hundred fat pigs, and returned them after the inspection was over. If you have a hundred, you have a hundred; you don't have what you don't have – what is the purpose of making it up? ... I think there still is some falsification around. There are some people in this world who are not all that honest. I suggest you talk this over seriously with the secretaries of the county and require that they should be honest and not falsify ... The serious question at present is not only that the lower levels fabricate, but that we believe them; from the Center, the provinces, and the prefectures down to the counties, everybody believes them, primarily the first three levels – that's the danger. [But] if [you] don't believe anything, it becomes opportunism. The masses, in fact, do achieve successes. Why write off the successes of the masses? But by trusting fabrications, one will also commit mistakes. Take the 11 million tons of steel: to say that not even ten thousand tons exist is of course wrong. However, how much is there really? Or grain, how much is there in the last analysis?

**Source: Extracts from Talks at the Wuchang Conference, 21–23 November 1958,
R. MacFarquhar, T. Cheek, E. Wu, eds, *Secret Speeches of Chairman Mao*
(Cambridge, Massachusetts: Harvard University Press, 1989), pp. 490–2, 492–8, 507–8**

9.6 Mao's enthusiasm for the Great Leap is tempered by the visit to his home village in June 1959

Dr Zhisui Li, from *The Private Life of Chairman Mao*, 1994

Mao's earlier skepticism had vanished. Common sense escaped him. He acted as though he believed the outrageous figures for agricultural production. The excitement was contagious. I was infected, too. Naturally, I could not help but wonder how rural China could be so quickly transformed. But I was seeing that transformation with my own eyes. I allowed myself only occasional fleeting doubts.

One evening on the train, Lin Ke tried to set me straight. Chatting with Lin Ke and Wang Jingxian, looking out at the fires from the backyard furnaces that stretched all the way to the horizon, I shared the puzzlement I had been feeling, wondering out loud how the furnaces had appeared so suddenly and how the production figures could be so high.

What we were seeing from our windows, Lin Ke said, was staged, a huge multiact nation-wide Chinese opera performed especially for Mao. The Party secretaries had ordered furnaces constructed everywhere along the rail route, stretching out for ten li on either side, and the women were dressed so colorfully, in reds and greens, because they had been ordered to dress that way. In Hubei, Party Secretary Wang Renzhong had ordered the peasants to remove rice plants from far away fields and transplant them along Mao's route, to give the impression of a wildly abundant crop. The rice was planted so closely together that electric fans had to be set up around the fields to circulate air in order to prevent the plants from rotting. All of China was a stage, all the people performers in an extravaganza for Mao.

The production figures were false, Lin Ke said. No soil could produce twenty or thirty thousand pounds per mu. And what was coming out of the backyard steel furnaces was useless. The finished steel I had seen in Anhui that Zeng Xisheng claimed had been produced by the backyard steel furnace was fake, delivered there from a huge, modern factory ...

If Lin Ke was right, why was no one telling Chairman Mao? What about the Chairman's advisers – men like Tian Jiaying, Hu Qiaomu, Chen Boda, Wang Jingxian, Lin Ke, and leaders like Zhou Enlai? If they knew the reality, why did they not inform the Chairman? But no one, not even those closest to him, dared to speak out.

I wondered whether Mao, despite his outward enthusiasm, had his own private doubts.

From my conversations with Mao, I doubted that he really knew. In October 1958, Mao's doubts were not about the production figures or the miraculous increases in grain and steel production. There were exaggerations, perhaps, but he was worried most about the claims that communism was at hand. With the establishment of people's communes, the introduction of public dining halls, and the abundant harvest soon to come, word was spreading that communism was just around the corner. The creative enthusiasm of the Chinese peasantry had finally been unleashed. Mao's problem was how to maintain that mass enthusiasm while checking the belief that communism was upon us. 'No one can deny the high spirits and strong determination of the masses,' he said to me one night. 'Of course, the people's commune is a new thing. it will take lots of hard work to turn it into a healthy institution. Certain leaders, with good intentions, want to rush things. They want to jump into communism immediately. We have to deal with this kind of problem. But other people are still suspicious about the general line, the Great Leap Forward, and the people's communes. Some hopelessly stubborn people even secretly oppose them. When they go to see God, they'll probably take their marble heads with them' ...

In June 1959, Mao visited his home village in Shaoshan in Hunan Province for the first time in thirty-two years.

Mao stopped before a burial mound. It was only when he bowed from the waist in the traditional manner of respect that I realized we were standing before his parents' grave. Shen Tong, one of the security officers accompanying us, quickly gathered a bunch of wild flowers. Mao placed the flowers on the grave and bowed three times again. The rest of his entourage, standing behind him, bowed too. 'There used to be a tombstone around here,' Mao said. 'It has disappeared after all these years.' When Luo Ruiqing suggested that the site be repaired and restored, Mao demurred. 'It's good just to have found the place,' he said.

We continued walking down the hill, in the direction of the Mao clan ancestral hall. Again, Mao stopped, puzzled, looking for something. We were standing on the spot where the Buddhist shrine Mao had referred to so often in our conversations once stood – the shrine his mother used to visit when he was sick, where she burned incense and fed the ashes to her son, certain of their curative powers. The tiny shrine, like the tombstone, had disappeared, torn down only months before with the establishment of the commune. The bricks were needed to build the backyard steel furnaces, and the wood had been used as fuel.

Mao had fallen silent on our walk. The destruction of the shrine had saddened him. 'It's such a pity,' he said. 'It should have been left alone. Without money to see doctors, poor farmers could still come and pray to the gods and eat the incense ashes. The shrine could lift their spirits, give them hope. People need this kind of help and encouragement.' I smiled when he said this, but Mao was serious. 'Don't look down on incense ashes,' he said, repeating his admonition that medicine is good only for curable disease. 'Incense ashes give people the courage to fight disease, don't you think? You are a doctor. You should know how much psychology affects medical treatment.' People could not live without spiritual support, Mao believed.

My smile was not meant as disagreement. I have always believed that one's state of mind has a profound effect on health.

We went then to visit Mao's old family home. No one lived in it then. The personality cult surrounding Mao was still in its early stage, so the family house was still in its original state, old farming equipment neatly displayed on the porch. Only a wooden board above the entrance designated the place as Mao's childhood home. The style of the house was typical of that area – simple mud walls and a thatched roof. There was nothing modern about it. But with eight rooms built around a courtyard, the home was obviously that of a wealthy peasant.

The land Mao's father had once farmed, with help from temporary laborers, was now part of the people's commune. Just beyond the house was a pond lined with trees. 'That's where I used to go swimming and where the cattle drank water,' he said …

Mao began contacting his relatives to learn first hand how the Great Leap Forward had affected them. Only the women and children were at home. The men were away working on the backyard steel furnaces or water conservancy projects. Mao did not have to delve far to learn that life was hard for the families in Shaoshan. With the construction of the backyard steel furnaces, everyone's pots and pans had been confiscated and thrown into the furnace to make steel – and nothing had been returned. Everyone was eating in the public mess halls. The families had no cooking equipment. Even if they still had pots and pans, their earthen hearths had been destroyed so the mud could be used as fertilizer.

When Mao took a swim in the newly constructed Shaoshan reservoir that afternoon, he talked to the local folk about the project. Everyone criticized it. The reservoir had been poorly built, one old peasant pointed out. The commune secretary was in such a rush to finish that it leaked. The reservoir's capacity was too small, and when it rained, water had to be released to prevent flooding.

The commune directors called the menfolk back to meet with Mao in the evening, and Mao hosted a dinner party for them at his guesthouse – some fifty people in all. Everyone complained about the mess halls. The older people did not like them because the younger people always cut in and grabbed the food first. The younger people did not like the mess halls because there was never enough food. Fistfights often broke out, and much of the food was wasted when it ended up on the floor.

Mao asked about the backyard steel furnaces. Again, he heard nothing but complaints. Indigenous raw materials were scarce. They used locally mined low-quality coal to fuel the furnaces, but there was not enough coal and no iron ore at all. The only way to comply with the directive to build the furnaces was to confiscate the peasants' pots, pans, and shovels for iron ore and their doors and furniture for fuel. But the furnaces were producing iron nuggets that no one knew what to do with. Now, with no pots or pans, people couldn't even boil drinking water at home, let alone cook. The commune kitchens were no help with the water problem, because cooks had to devote all their energies to preparing the food.

When Mao's questions stopped, the room fell silent. An air of gloom descended. The Great Leap Forward was not going well in Shaoshan. 'If you can't fill your bellies at the public dining hall, then it's better just to disband it,' Mao said. 'It's a waste of food. As for the water conservancy project, I don't think every rural community has to build a reservoir. If the reservoirs are not built well, there will be big problems. And if you cannot produce good steel, you might as well quit.'

With these words, Shaoshan probably became the first village in the country to abolish the public dining halls, halt its water conservancy project, and begin dismantling the backyard steel furnaces. Mao's comments were never publicly released, but they spread quickly through word of mouth. Soon, many areas were dismantling their projects.

Source: Zhisui Li, *The Private Life of Chairman Mao*
(London: Chatto and Windus, 1994), pp. 278–9 and 302–4

9.7 Poem by Peng Dehuai

Peng visited his home village Niaoshi, also in Hunan, in 1959, and wrote this poem.

The millet is scattered all over the ground,
The leaves of the sweet potatoes are withered,
The young and the strong have gone to melt iron,
To harvest the grain there are children and old women.
How shall we get through next year?
I shall agitate and speak out on behalf of the People.

Source: Poem by Peng Dehuai, 1959. In R. MacFarquhar, *The Origins of the Cultural
Revolution*, Vol. 2 (Oxford: Oxford University Press, 1983), p. 177

9.8 Backyard steel production

9.8a Schoolchildren make steel

Sirin Phathanothai

A young girl, the ward of Zhou Enlai, proudly shows the Premier the product of the school blast furnace.

At school, suddenly, all the talk was about steel – about its key role in modernizing China, the need to produce more, the need for all of us to help set new production records. The 1958 target was set at 10.7 million tons – double the 1956 record. This goal could hardly be met by normal methods; creative new ones were called for. The older students worked day and night to build steel furnaces on the old sports ground. Students, once so attentive, came to class only to fall asleep. Awakened, they spoke excitedly of their great revolutionary production tasks.

My school alone had three furnaces. The students dug a big hole in the ground to the lowest level of the soil, the yellow earth. The displaced soil was then carefully sieved until it was very fine, and the hole was refilled with it. Layer by layer the earth was pressed down until it was solid and hard. Then spoons were used to hollow it out, leaving two holes to the surface. An electric blower was placed at one hole and wood fed into the furnace through the other. As soon as the wood was ablaze, the blower was turned on. When the fire began to roar, I would join the younger students in tossing on the scrap iron and broken pots and pans we had collected. The older students, sweating profusely from the intense heat, carefully stirred this bubbling mix with large pokers. All day and all night the fires roared, filling the night skies with their reddish glare and smoke. The results looked like a spongy mush to me, but everyone hailed them nonetheless. Tests were solemnly performed as we assembled to watch in the courtyard, and our product was duly declared to be crude steel. This was our contribution to the steel quota for 1958.

One day I spirited away a lump of our product and proudly carried it over for Zhou to see. His ready smile quickly disappeared when he saw what I'd brought.

'Is this what your school is working on day and night?' he said, his face taut.

'Of course', I replied. Something in his voice put me on guard.

Zhou took the mushy lump, turning it over and over in his hands. He was unusually preoccupied.

'Don't you like my joining in the steel campaign?' I asked.

At first he didn't answer. Then, looking at me but ignoring the question, he asked me to tell him exactly how this steel was made, how we had built the furnaces, and what else was happening at the school. He listened intently to my account, although my excitement was rapidly diminishing as I sensed his displeasure. I concluded by saying how much steel our school had produced.

'I don't believe it', he said. Zhou had never spoken quite like this.

'Now, I want you to remember to study your lessons. The children should get back to school. It is wrong for them to be pulled away from their classes like this'. Then he abruptly changed the subject.

**Source: Sirin Phathanothai, *The Dragon's Pearl*
(London: Simon and Schuster, 1994), pp. 155–7**

9.8b Report by Zhou Enlai, 26 August 1959

Some people hold that, during last year's mass campaign to make iron and steel, much manpower was used, much money was spent, and part of the total products was iron and steel made by indigenous methods, as a result, it was 'more loss than gain' or at most 'loss and gain was a 50–50 affair'. We consider this view utterly wrong.

In 1958, we produced 13.69 million tons of pig iron (excluding the 4–5 million tons of pig iron that were not suitable for steelmaking but good for the manufacture of simple farm implements and tools), which was 2.3 times as much as was produced in 1957, and 11.08 million tons of steel, which was more than double our production in 1957. In iron and steel production, the mass campaign to build small enterprises, use light equipment, and employ indigenous methods gave impetus to a further mass campaign in the big enterprises using heavy equipment and modern methods and to further mass campaigns covering the entire industrial front. With steel as the key lever, there was brought about the big leap forward in industry. The output of many important industrial products was doubled or went up several-fold, while the gross industrial output value in 1958 was 66 per cent higher than in 1957. Moreover, the mass campaign to make iron and steel paved the way for the future develop-ment of the iron and steel industry and industry as a whole. Many places that have suitable resources and where indigenous iron smelting furnaces and small blast furnaces were erected last year have developed groups of small blast furnaces and greatly raised the output and quality of pig iron produced after rationalizing the grouping of installations, adding equip-ment and improving technique during the last winter and spring. The aggregate volume of the small blast furnaces (between 6.5 and 100 cubic metres each) that are now in operation has mounted to 43,000 cubic metres, nearly twice as much as the total volume of the large blast furnaces in the country – 24,000 cubic metres. They are able to turn out about ten million tons of pig iron this year ...

Considerable progress has been made in the past few months in raising the quality of products from the small blast furnaces and in reducing their consumption of coal. By July, the proportion of pig iron produced up to standard by small blast furnaces had risen to about 75 per cent; the rate of coal consumption dropped to about four tons per ton of pig iron and the utilization coefficient of furnaces approached 0.7 tons of pig iron per cubic metre of furnace volume every 24 hours. This proves that the mass campaign in the iron and steel industry has tremendous vitality and has been raised to a new stage. It can be expected that even greater progress will be made in the near future in raising output and improving the quality of the products of the small blast furnaces and lowering their rate of coal consumption. The mass campaign to make iron and steel has also served to 'temper people': enable the masses to acquire technical skill and knowledge and large numbers of cadres to gain experience.

Source: Chou En-lai, Report on Steel Production,
Peking Review, 1 September 1959, pp. 12–13

9.9 *Beijing Review* continues to report overall progress in agriculture, November 1959

Recent estimates indicate that the output of food crops will be about 275 million tons, around 10 per cent heavier than in 1958; cotton output will probably be more than 10 per cent higher than it was last year. The outputs of tobacco, hemp and jute, tea, sugar, and oil-bearing crops are all bigger than in 1958. The expanding and diversified economies of the people's communes have insured an overall increase in the total value of agricultural and subsidiary rural production.

These excellent results were gained in the teeth of weather that was far from helpful. Drought, inclemently heavy rains resulting in waterlogging, wind storms, and insect pests, the worst natural calamities in post-liberation years, hit farmland in many parts of the country.

The drought which centred around Hupeh Province was the worst in the past 70 years. The heavy spring rain in Kwangtung Province was the heaviest in the last few decades and so were the floods north of Peking. Destructive typhoons ravaged the coastal areas, especially between Foochow and Amoy in Fukien. Insect pests, particularly locusts which usually come in the wake of droughts and floods, also made their own black records. Calamities of such an extent in old

China would have laid waste thousands of square kilometres of farmland. Millions would have died from hunger and disease. During the big 1942 drought in Honan Province in preliberation days, 3 million people starved to death. On this showing, if the 1959 drought had occurred before liberation, it would undoubtedly have caused many more deaths in Honan alone. But China today is a socialist country. Thanks to the all-out efforts of the people guided by the Communist Party, and the collective strength and concerted work of the people's communes, it was able to beat back all these natural calamities and keep up the leap forward in agriculture.

Some drought-stricken provinces actually reaped record harvests. The late rice harvest in the south is rated to be good; 30 million in the northern provinces gave a bigger output of rice than last year. Maize, millet, and sorghum show better results both for per mu yields and total output than in 1958 …

Source: Yang Min, Report on Agriculture, *Peking Review*, 17 November 1959, pp. 15–16

9.10 Six questions on agriculture, 29 November 1959

Mao Zedong

Comrades of the provincial, administrative district, *Hsien*, commune, brigade and team levels, I want to discuss with you comrades a few questions, all of which concern agriculture.

The first one is the question of fixing output quotas. Transplanting is being carried out in the south and spring farming is also underway in the north. The fixing of output quotas must be carried out to the letter. Basically, you should pay attention not to the instructions from a higher level but to the realistic possibilities. For example, the per mow yield amounted to only 300 catties last year, and it will be good if the yield could be increased by one or two hundred catties this year. It is no more than trumpet blowing to say that the yield will amount to 800 catties, 1,000 catties, 1,200 catties, and even more. This is actually unattainable, and what is the use of trumpet blowing in this way? …

The second one is the question of close planting. Crops should not be planted too wide apart nor too close. Because of their lack of experience, many young cadres and some organs at a higher level are bent on advocating close planting. Some people actually say the closer the better. This is undesirable, and the old peasants and middle-age people are also skeptical of the idea. It will be nice for these two kinds of people to hold a meeting to work out the proper density. Since production quotas have to be fixed, the question of close planting should be discussed and determined by the production brigades and teams. Any rigid order concerning close planting from a higher level is not only useless but also harmful …

The third one is the question of economy of grain. It is necessary to exercise a tighter grip and fix the quantity on a per capita basis. More grain should be consumed in the busy season and less grain should be consumed in the slack season. In the busy season, people should feed on solid rice and in the slack season they should feed alternately on solid rice and rice porridge mixed with sweet potatoes, vegetables, carrots, gourds, beans, taroes, etc. A tight grip should be exercised on this matter. Every year, the matter of harvesting, storage, and consumption must be firmly grasped. Furthermore, the matter must be grasped in the nick of time and no opportunity should be missed since time and tide wait for no man. There must be reserve grain and it is necessary to store away some grain every year. The quantity of grain stored should increase year by year. After eight or ten years of struggle, the grain problem can be solved. Within the next ten years we should never indulge ourselves in big and high-flown talk because this is very dangerous ...

The fourth one is the question of planting a greater acreage to crops. The plan of reaping a bigger harvest by planting a smaller number of high-yield crops is a long-term one that can be carried out, but it is not possible to carry out the whole or the greater part of it in the next ten years. Most of the plan cannot be carried out in the next three years. In the next three years, it is necessary to strive to plant more crops and simultaneously carry out the policies of the past few years – to plant a greater acreage to low-yield crops and to reap a bigger harvest through planting a small number of crops in bumper-harvest fields.

The fifth one is the question of mechanization. The fundamental way out for agriculture lies in mechanization. This requires ten years of time. It is necessary to solve the question on a small scale in four years, on an intermediate scale in seven years, and on a large scale in ten years ... Whenever mechanization is mentioned, it is necessary to take into consideration the mechanized production of chemical fertilizer. It is most important that the supply of chemical fertilizer should be increased year by year.

The sixth one is the question of telling the truth. When output quotas are fixed, we should make known the actual output quotas we can guarantee. We must not tell lies by fixing the output quotas at a level that is actually beyond our means to fulfill ... It should be said that many lies are told owing to the pressure of a higher level. When the higher level resorts to trumpet blowing, applying pressure, and making promises, it makes things difficult for the lower level. Therefore, while one must have drive, one must never tell lies.

You comrades are requested to study the six questions mentioned above. You may put forward different views with the object of getting at the truth. Our experience is still rather inadequate in agricultural work. By accumulating experience year after year, in another ten years the objective necessity can be gradually known to us, and there will be some degree of freedom for us. What is called freedom? Freedom is the knowledge of necessity.

Compared with the high-flown talk that is in vogue at present, what I have said here is low-key. My purpose is to arouse enthusiasm in the true sense and to attain the end of increasing production. If things are not as low as I talk about and a higher objective is achieved, thus turning me into a conservative, then I'll thank heaven and earth and feel greatly honored.

Source: 'A Letter to Production Team Leaders',
from 'Long Live Mao Tse-tung thought. Collection of Statements by Mao Tse-tung',
Current Background, No. 891, 8 October 1969

9.11 The people's communes

Joan Robinson, a Cambridge economist who visited China in the 1960s. Extract from
Notes From China, 1964

There is a curious line of argument, which seems to be shared by Mr Krushchev and the London Times correspondent in Hong Kong, according to which the formation of the agricultural communes in China was a wicked and stupid policy, aiming at destroying family life and reducing the helpless peasantry to a state of virtual serfdom, which has now proved a failure and cracked up. One would suppose that, if the policy was wrong, retreat from it must be regarded as an improvement. But the critics want to have it both ways. The pretended break-up of the communes is only evidence that the Chinese authorities have failed to fulfil the promises that they made to the people.

It is certainly true that in the exalted mood of the Great Leap in 1958 there was much Utopian talk and some schemes were started that proved impracticable. The commune system was thoroughly well put through the wringer during the three 'bitter years' of flood and drought that followed 1958 (when critics were shedding crocodile tears over the 'fam-ine') and has emerged in a sensible, flexible, and realistic form.

When I had the good fortune to visit China for two months in the summer of 1963, I decided to concentrate mainly on studying the commune system.

I had a very useful preliminary briefing in Peking. Although the achievements of the Great Leap in 1958 are a matter of pride and satisfaction to the Party and the people, it is admitted that serious mistakes were made and that overinvestment occurred which put the economy into an unbalanced position. In the normal way this would have been corrected over the course of a year or two without any great disturbance. But, as bad luck would have it, the three 'bitter years' of natural disasters followed, and the unbalanced state of the economy made them all the harder to meet.

In the course of struggling through the years of bad harvests, an important change in basic policy was made. The Soviet dogma of the permanent priority of heavy industry was aban-doned. It was realised that the limit to the development of industry is the agricultural surplus, and that to achieve a surplus it is necessary to offer to the peasants some goods that they want to buy. The new line is expressed in the slogan 'Agriculture the foundation, industry the leading factor'. Concretely, it is embodied in a redirection of the economic plan to promote a faster rise in agriculture output both by more direct investment (especially in fertilisers) and by increased production of goods to sell in the rural areas (bicycles, radio sets, and sewing machines are the favourites at present).

During the bitter years, the commune system was hammered into shape. The wild Utopian talk of jumping straight to communism was repudiated by the Party already before the end of 1958, but some unpractical notions were tried out. The most important was the system of so-called free food. Rations were calculated in terms of so much for a worker, so much for a school child, etc., and supplied to the families irrespective of their earnings. This proved both to be wasteful and to weaken the incentive to earn; it was generally abandoned in 1960. Village canteens went out of fashion at the same time. On a philosophical point, it is proclaimed that the communes are a *socialist* form of organisation (to each according to his work) not a *communist* one.

The three-tier system of teams, brigades, and communes has been grafted onto the ancient roots of rural life. On the one hand the staff of the commune has taken over the functions of the lowest rung in the old ladder of the administration – the *Hsiang*. It is the channel through which the villagers deal with high authorities for planning production, sales, purchases, taxation, and so forth. On the other hand, the individual household is fostered and encouraged as the basic unit of economic life. (The propagandist stories about the destruction of family life are very wide of the mark.) A team consists of the workers of twenty or thirty neighbour families. The land allotted to them is, in the main, the land that their forefathers worked, with some modifications for convenience in cultivation. Eight or ten teams are grouped in a brigade. In the plains, where villages are large, the brigade usually comprises a single village. There is emulation between brigades which enlists old village rivalries in a constructive cause. The commune comprises two or three dozen brigades and covers an area of anything from a thousand to fifty thousand acres, depending upon the nature of the terrain.

The change from the unitary cooperatives (generally set up in 1956) to the triple organisation of the communes corresponds to economic common sense. The cooperative, usually identical with the present-day brigade, was found generally to be too large a unit for the management of labour, and too small a unit for the management of land.

The problems of day-to-day direction of some thousand workers, in the cooperatives, of accounting for the labour time of each, and of reckoning the distribution of the product proved to be a strain on the managerial capacity available. Moreover, sharing in the product of such a large group weakened incentive. For these reasons it was found more practical to make the team the accounting unit. Each team has at its disposal a particular area of land, with implements and animals. It undertakes a particular part of the annual plan of production and of sales to the state procurement agency. From the year's gross proceeds in cash and kind are deducted costs, land tax, and contributions to the welfare fund and the accumulation fund of the team. The remainder (usually about 60 per cent of the gross proceeds) is distributed to the members of the team in proportion to the labour points that each has earned. Thus, what the workers bring to their household income depends on the work they each put in and upon the value of a work point in their own team. There is a wide variation in the value of a work point between one team and another. It is the business of the commune staff to find out the causes of low earning and to help the weaker teams to improve.

Source: Joan Robinson, *Notes from China* (Oxford: Blackwell, 1964), pp. 26–9

9.12 Famine in Anhui

J. Becker, extract from *Hungry Ghosts*, 1996

The Great Leap Forward began in Anhui, as everywhere else, with claims of extraordinary success. In Fengyang that year, one sputnik field supposedly grew a national record of 62.5 tonnes of tobacco in just 0.17 acres of land. Fantastic pressure was exerted at every level to meet quotas that Zeng set. Local Party secretaries were kept locked up in rooms for weeks until they agreed to meet their grain quotas and other targets. They in turn put their deputies through the same ordeal. So it went, from prefecture to county, from commune to brigade, from production team right down to the individual peasant. If a peasant didn't agree to double or treble or quadruple his harvest, the production team leader would beat him until he gave in. Nobody believed these targets could be reached but cadres reported that they had been. The lies went back up the pyramid from peasant to production chief, to brigade leader, to commune Party secretary, to county secretary, to prefectural leader and finally to Zeng Xisheng [First Secretary of Anhui] who reported to Mao. With each repetition, the lies became more and more fantastic, a ghastly parody of Chinese Whispers. All over the province, grain yields which were at best 726 lbs per 0.17 acres were inflated to an astonishing 33,000 lbs (14.7 tonnes).

Poor, impoverished Anhui now claimed to be flush with a fantastic bonanza, and Zeng began to deliver large amounts of grain to other parts of the country and even abroad – in 1959 alone Anhui exported 200,000 tonnes, although its grain harvest had shrunk to 4 million tonnes from the record 10 million tonnes harvested in 1958. In 1959, the state demanded that the peasants of Anhui hand over 2.5 million tonnes, that is 40 per cent of the harvest.

In Fengyang, the year before had been bad enough. In 1958, the county had harvested 89,000 tonnes but reported 178,500 tonnes to cover up a sharp decline in output. Some of this grain was not even gathered in, but rotted in the fields because too many peasants were out making steel or building dams. After the peasants deducted what they needed to eat and to keep for seed, a surplus of only 5,800 tonnes was left to deliver to the state, but the grain levy was fixed at 35,000 tonnes on the basis of the false harvest reported. The missing 29,200 tonnes had to be extracted by force. In 1959, the county authorities lost all touch with reality. The county reported that 199,000 tonnes were harvested, a little higher than the reported figure for 1958, but in fact the harvest had further declined from 89,000 to 54,000 tonnes. Of this, the state demanded 29,464 tonnes ...

As the communes in the county trumpeted their new riches, the cadres were busy seizing whatever the peasants owned. All private property had to be handed over, including private land, draught animals, carts, and even milling stones and houses. In Fengyang, the cadres commandeered over 11,000 houses, and, to feed the backyard furnaces, they took bicycles, scissors, knives, cooking utensils, and even iron fences. When the Party needed more carts for its schemes, the cadres simply knocked down houses to take the necessary wood. Some peasants were left entirely homeless, others forced to live ten to a room. Even the huts that remained were stripped of their wooden doors and furniture to fuel the backyard furnaces. In the most fanatical villages, men were not even allowed to keep their wives who were forced to live separately.

In the run-up to the creation of the communes in 1958, the peasants went into a frenzy, eating as much of their food as they could and selling their livestock. People chopped down trees, dug up their vegetables, and did everything to ensure that as little as possible was handed over. When the communes were established, the entire administration of daily life changed. Every minor decision or arrangement previously decided by the villagers now had to be passed to the commune headquarters which looked after around 5,000 households. By the end of September 1958, the communes were in full operation, and eating at the collective kitchens was compulsory. By the Spring Festival of 1959, peasants in Fengyang and everywhere else in Anhui were starving. As food supplies dwindled, fights broke out at the collective kitchens. The only food that was served was a watery soup. Those who were unfortunate received the thin gruel at the top of the pot, those who were lucky got the richer liquid at the bottom. Amidst this desperate struggle for food in early 1959, the Party launched the first anti-hiding-grain campaign in Anhui which, in its brutality, rivalled that in Henan. After the harvest of 1959 was taken away in the autumn, people began to starve to death in large numbers. A sense of what life was like in the winter of 1959–60 is evoked by one survivor, now a grandmother, who then lived in another county near Fengyang on the Huai River plain:

> In the first year [1958–9], we earned work points and the communes distributed grain to each family. This we kept at home. But in the second year [1959–60], there was nothing left at home, it had all been taken away. Nevertheless, the village cadres came to every household to search for food. They took away everything they could find, including our cotton eiderdowns, several bags of carrots, and the cotton we had saved to make new clothes.
>
> The communal canteen did not serve any proper food, just wild grasses, peanut shells, and sweet potato skins. Because of this diet we had terrible problems. Some were constipated but others had constant diarrhoea and could not get beyond the front door ...

My legs and hands were swollen and I felt that at any moment I would die. Instead of walking to the field to look for wild grass I crawled and rolled to save energy. Several old women tried to get grass from ponds or rivers, but because they had to stand in water their legs became infected.

All the trees in the village had been cut down. Any nearby were all stripped of bark. I peeled off the bark of a locust tree and cooked it as if it were rice soup. It tasted like wood and was sticky ...

More than half of the villagers died, mostly between New Year [1960] and April or May. In one of our neighbour's houses, three boys and a girl starved. In one brother's family two children died. Another family of sixteen died. Many families disappeared completely with no survivors at all. The production team chief's daughter-in-law and his grandson starved to death. He then boiled and ate the corpse of the child, but he also died. When the village teacher was on the verge of death, he said to his wife, 'Why should we keep our child? If we eat him then I can survive and later we can produce another child'. His wife refused to do this and her husband died ...

Later, when the wheat was harvested, the situation improved, but we had to carry on eating at the canteen all through 1960. It was a good harvest and there were far fewer mouths to feed. The autumn harvest was also good and later we were allowed to eat at home. We had nothing to cook with and went to our neighbours to borrow pots. Some of the houses I went to were empty because everyone had fled.

Source: Jasper Becker, *Hungry Ghosts, China's Secret Famine*
(London: John Murray, 1996), pp. 132–7

9.13 The Great Leap and the responsibility system

Deng Hansheng, from *Research in Party History*, No. 6, December 1981

The responsibility system that was set up in the collective agricultural economy, in fact, was not first created in the 1960s. It had appeared earlier, soon after the National Cooperative Movement in Agriculture. This system was at first created by the peasants for the management of agricultural cooperatives, so that the cooperative members could be paid according to their work. During Spring 1957, there were already various forms of responsibility system in production management tried out in some areas such as 'Division of land according to labour, household contracts for production', 'Household contracts for the entire or part of the agricultural tasks', and the 'Area responsibility system'.

In September 1957, the Rural Work Department of the Central Committee considered these new forms of management to be favourable to the consolidation of the fruits of the Cooperative Movement, and suitable for the collective economy for truly implementing the principle of distribution according to work. Therefore, according to the demands of the people, they made regulations that 'The production brigades ... with regard to the specific conditions of the various areas can carry out "contracting work to the teams", "contracting miscellaneous field work to the households"'. This policy was designed to adapt to the characteristics of 'the disparities in agricultural production, and in the geographic, seasonal and natural limitations'. They advocated 'collectively undertaking large-scale work, separately undertaking small-scale work, one should not go swarming in to work completely disorganized, without clear definition of responsibilities, and going roughshod over agricultural tasks'. This regulation of agricultural policy has been written into the directive rectified by the Party Central Committee called 'Directive of the Central Committee Concerning Making Good the Work in Production Management in the Agricultural Cooperatives'.

Regrettably, owing to mistakes committed under the 'leftist' influences within the Party, the fresh experiences coming from the base level and from the valuable creative spirit of the cadres and of the masses were ignored and had not been implemented. After the Nanning conference in January 1958, the leadership of Comrades Zhou Enlai and Chen Yun was being condemned for its policies 'against rash advances in economic construction'. After the upsurge of the 'Great Leap Forward', both the Rural Work Department of the Central Committee and many of their policies were being called factions for 'deceleration'. And the system of responsibility was called 'individual farming'. After the upsurge of the People's Commune Movement, many regulations on management and administration including the responsibility system were scattered to the winds. As a result of the violation of the economic law that the productive relationship must adapt to the level of productive development, from 1959 onwards the volume of national production of the major agricultural crops such as grain, cotton, and oil continuously plummeted downwards. The agricultural productive forces suffered a severe setback. Just taking large livestock, for example, in 1961 the national figure of agricultural beasts of burden had decreased from the 57,240,000 heads of 1954 to 38,180,000 heads. The figure was even lower than the 40,400,000 heads of 1949. The total population of China from 1959 to 1960 decreased by 13,000,000. Food was in short supply. Disasters were still spreading. The circular of the Party Central Committee of March 1962 pointed out that, because of the new spring famine, there were shortages of food and fuel and refugees were running away from many disaster areas. And those areas were spreading and shortages increasing in intensity. The medium and large cities all over China depended on importation of grain and food supply. According to the forecast of the Central Committee, the shortage in food supplies would not only affect the spring cultivation and summer harvest of the current year, it would affect the recovery of agriculture and the readjustment of the entire national economy. In addition, it might also cause riots in some disaster areas and towns. Inevitably, the whole nation and Party had to face the task of carrying out readjustments in the rural collective economy by taking all measures, including 'emergency measures' as some leading comrades of the Central Committee put it, to restore agricultural production.

The so-called 'emergency measures' indicated that the responsibility system in production management had to be different from the usual collective 'mass mobilization' inside the brigades. These measures had to be bold enough to break with old traditions, and to adapt themselves to the existing agricultural production levels but at the same time mobilize the enthusiasm of the peasants.

In 1960, in Su County of Anhui Province, there was such an incident. An old peasant over seventy years old was unable to take part in collective production because he had to look after his son who was suffering from tuberculosis. In order not to overburden the collective, he suggested taking his son into the mountains in order that his son could recuperate. They would try to fend for themselves. They would hand over any excess production to the nation. Or else, they would not ask the nation to provide any relief. Consequently, at the end of the year, by using a hoe and a rake, he opened up sixteen mu (1.07 hectares) of virgin land. He harvested 1,500 catties (750 kg) of grain, seeds, and fodder to feed his family. He also handed over to the commune 1,800 catties (900 kg) of grain and sixty yuan in cash obtained from raising pigs and chicken. This incident was a great revelation for the local cadres. The productivity of this type of contracting land to labour force could obtain much greater results

than 'mass mobilization'. The discrepancy was so enormous! As a consequence, some peasants of Su County asked if land could be contracted to the commune members to cultivate,
while the distribution could be unified. In Spring 1961, the peasants of the county of Quanjiao
also asked for 'Contracting production targets to the area of land to be cultivated and
contracting personal responsibility to cultivate the land'.

The Communist Party Committee of Anhui Province, under the vociferous demands of
the peasants of the counties of Su and Quanjiao to alter the management and administration
of labour, realized that, under the severely damaged conditions of the rural economy, they
were obliged to fulfil the wishes of these peasants. Beginning from March 1961, the Communist Party Committee of Anhui Province tentatively and experimentally applied the system of
management and administration of 'Contracting production targets to the area of land to be
cultivated and contracting personal responsibility to cultivate the land' inside Anhui Province.
In concrete terms, large agricultural tasks were contracted to the work teams under the
production brigades, while smaller jobs such as field management were contracted to households. That is to say, the field management on a certain piece of agricultural land was entirely
contracted to a household. The bonus was calculated according to the proportion of work
needed for major or minor tasks. Later on, this method was renamed 'Field Responsibility
System plus Bonus', or 'Responsibility Field'. During the trial period, this system spread like
wild fire, and within a month 39.2 per cent of the production brigades began to carry out this
system. By the end of the year of 1961 the number increased to 85.4 per cent.

**Source: The Great Leap and the 'Responsibility System' by Deng Hansheng, *Research in
Party History* (Beijing), No. 6, December 1981, pp. 23–7. Translated by M. F. Chen**

9.14 The Chinese view of the Sino-Soviet rift: extract of meeting of the CPSU and CCP delegations, 8 July 1963

*Between 5 and 20 July, Party delegations met in Moscow in what was to be a last attempt to solve the
disputes. The final meeting broke up on 20 July with no agreements and no plans for further meetings.
From then on the rift became public. This is a speech by the head of the CCP delegation, Deng Xiaoping.*

It can be said with all candor that a whole series of disagreements of a fundamental character
that exist today in the International Communist movement started at the Twentieth
Congress of the CPSU [Communist Party of the Soviet Union].

In the past, we never spoke about this openly, because we were taking into account the
situation you were in. We only mentioned that the disagreements that have arisen in the past
few years in the international Communist movement were provoked by the violation of the
Declaration of 1957 by comrades from several fraternal parties ... We have always considered and still consider that the Twentieth Congress of the CPSU put forward positions on
the issues of war and peace, peaceful coexistence, and peaceful transition that went against
Marxism–Leninism. Especially serious are two issues: the issue of the so-called peaceful transition and the issue of the full, groundless denunciation of Stalin under the pretext of the so-
called struggle with the cult of personality ...

Here, I want just briefly to say the following: a criticism of some errors by Stalin is necessary;
taking off the lid, so to speak, and ending superstition is a good thing. However, this criticism must
be correct both from the point of view of principles and from the point of view of methods.

Since the Twentieth Congress of the CPSU, the facts demonstrate that the full, groundless denunciation of Stalin is a serious step undertaken by the leading comrades from the CPSU with the aim of laying out the path to the revision of Marxism–Leninism on a whole series of issues ... After the Twentieth Congress of the CPSU, as a consequence of the so-called struggle against the cult of personality and the full, groundless denunciation of Stalin, a wave of anti-Soviet and anti-Communist campaigns was provoked around the whole world ... The most prominent events that took place in this period were the events in Poland and Hungary.

We have always considered and still consider that, in resolving the issues connected with the events in Poland, the CPSU took a position of great-power chauvinism, trying to exert pressure on the Polish comrades and to subordinate them to itself by means of coercion, and even tried to resort to military force. We consider that such a method is not only evidence of great-power chauvinism in relation to fraternal countries and to fraternal parties, but also evidence of adventurism.

Following this, the counter-revolutionary rebellion in Hungary took place. The Hungarian events by their character differ from the events in Poland ... And what position did the CPSU take in regard to the counter-revolutionary revolt in Hungary? The leadership of the CPSU at one time tried to leave socialist Hungary to the mercy of fate. You know that at that time we spoke out against your position on the matter. Such a position was practically tantamount to capitulation. The course and details of these two events are well known to you and to us. I do not want to dwell on them ... Back in April 1956, Comrade Mao Zedong stated our opinion on the issue of Stalin in a discussion with Comrade Mikoyan and also, after that, in a discussion with Ambassador Comrade Iudin.

Comrade Mao Zedong emphasized that it is incorrect to think that 'Stalin's errors and contributions are divided into equal halves;' 'whatever happened, all the same, Stalin's contributions are greater than his errors. One must evaluate it as follows, that his contributions make up 70 percent, and his mistakes 30 percent. It is necessary to make a concrete analysis and to give an all-around assessment' ...

On 18 January 1957, in Moscow, at the fifth discussion with the government delegation of the Soviet Union, Comrade Zhou Enlai touched on the events in Hungary, noting that the counter-revolutionary revolt in Hungary was connected, on the one hand, with some mistakes made by Stalin when resolving issues of mutual relations between fraternal parties and fraternal countries, and, on the other hand, with mistakes committed by the leadership of the CPSU in its criticism of Stalin. In discussion, Comrade Zhou Enlai again set out the aforementioned three points on this issue to the leadership of the CPSU; the lack of an all-round analysis, the lack of self-criticism, and the lack of consultation with the fraternal countries ...

From that very time, you, considering that your internal problems had already been resolved, started to direct the cutting edge of your action against Marxism–Leninism, against fraternal parties defending the principles of Marxism–Leninism, and began to engage in activities directed against the CCP, against the PRC, and these activities are of a serious character.

What has been done by you over this period? Let us cite some of the facts, so as to make things clear.

From April to July 1958 the CPSU put to China the issue of the creation of a long-wave radar station and a joint fleet, trying thereby to bring China under its military control. But we guessed your intentions and you were not able to attain your goals.

Following that, you started both in statements and in actions to carry out anti-Chinese activities in an intensified manner. You continually spoke out attacking the internal policies of the CCP, in particular on the people's communes. By way of example one can refer to the conversation by Comrade Khrushchev with the American Congressman [Hubert] Humphrey in December 1958 and to the speech by Comrade Khrushchev in a Polish agricultural cooperative in July 1959.

In June 1959 you unilaterally annulled the agreement on rendering help to China in developing a nuclear industry and in producing atom bombs.

Following this, on 9 September 1959, TASS made an announcement about the incident on the Chinese–Indian border and displayed bias in favor of the Indian reaction, making the disagreements between China and the Soviet Union clear to the whole world for the first time.

In November of that year, Comrade Khrushchev openly accused China of having acted 'stupidly' and 'regrettably' in a conversation with a correspondent of the Indian daily *New Age* ...

In February 1960, during the meeting of the Political Consultative Council of the participating countries of the Warsaw Pact, Comrade Khrushchev spoke rudely using an expression like 'old galoshes.' Meanwhile, the CC CPSU, in its oral presentation to the CC CCP, accused China of committing such mistakes as a 'narrowly nationalist approach' and of acting on 'narrowly nationalist interest,' in relation to the issues of the Indian–Chinese border.

The meaning of all these statements and speeches is understood by you and by us, and also by our enemies ... In such circumstances we could not remain silent any longer. We published three articles 'Long Live Leninism!' and others, in which we defended Marxism–Leninism and the Moscow Declaration, and exposed some revisionist and opportunist views to criticism. But in these articles, we as before directed the brunt of our struggle for the most part against imperialism and Yugoslav revisionism without open criticism of comrades from the CPSU. Following this, such events occurred as the intrusion of the American U–2 plane into USSR air space, the collapse of the meeting of the heads of government of the four powers in Paris, and the collapse of the entirely nonexistent so-called 'spirit of Camp David.' All of this proved the error of the views of our comrades from the CPSU and the correctness of our views ...

In June 1960 in Bucharest, the leadership of the CPSU mounted a sudden attack on the CCP, disseminated an informational note of the CC CPSU that contained an all-round attack on the CCP, and organized a campaign by a whole group of fraternal parties against us ...

On 16 July 1960, the Soviet side unilaterally decided to withdraw between 28 July and 1 September over 1,300 Soviet specialists working in China. Over 900 specialists were recalled from [extended] business trips, and contracts and agreements were broken ...

On 25 August 1962, the Soviet government informed China that it was ready to conclude an agreement with the United States on the prevention of the proliferation of nuclear weapons. In our view, you were pursuing an unseemly goal in coming to such an agreement, namely: to bind China by the hands and feet through an agreement with the United States.

After India started a major attack on the border regions of China in October 1962, the Soviet Union began to supply India with even larger quantities of military matériel, to do its utmost to give [India] an economic blood transfusion, to support [Jawaharlal] Nehru by political means, and to spur him on in the struggle against China ...

At the congresses of these [Communist] parties, another strange phenomenon was observed. On the one hand, at these congresses they attacked the CCP and completely removed the Albanian Workers' Party, and, on the other hand, they forcibly dragged the Titoist clique in Yugoslavia into the ranks of the international Communist movement and tried to rehabilitate that clique. In addition, at the Congress of the Socialist Unity Party of Germany, there was noise, whistling, and stamping right at the time when our representative subjected Yugoslav revisionism to criticism on the basis of the Moscow Declaration by citing the Moscow Declaration verbatim.

What do the facts we have cited above, which took place after the Twenty-second Congress of the CPSU [in October 1961], testify to? These facts testify to the fact that comrades from the CPSU have taken further steps to create a split in the ranks of the international Communist movement and, moreover, have done so in an increasingly sharp, increasingly extreme form, in an increasingly organized [way], on an increasingly large scale, trying, come what may, to crush others.

I would like to note that using such methods is a habitual affair for you. You began using such methods as far back as the Bucharest conference. During the bilateral meeting between the representatives of our two parties in 1960, I said that it was fortunate that Comrade Peng Zhen went to the Bucharest meeting; he weighs approximately 80 kilograms, and for that reason he endured; if I had gone, and I weigh only a bit over 50 kilograms, I could not have endured. After that it was just as well that Comrade Wu Xiuquan, who weighs more than 70 kilograms, went to the GDR, and was able to endure. Frankly speaking, such methods do not help matters. You cannot prove by such methods that you are in the right; you cannot prove that the truth is on your side. Quite the opposite; the use of such methods is an insult to the glorious Marxist-Leninist Party.

The Chinese leaders had complained that they were not given enough food to eat during the meetings in Bucharest and Berlin.

Source: Extract of meeting of CPSU and CCP Delegations, July 1963, *Cold War International History Project Bulletin*, No. 10, March 1998, pp. 376–8, 379, 380–1, 382

10

The Cultural Revolution

The Cultural Revolution arose out of the disagreements that Mao was having with his colleagues in the aftermath of the Great Leap Forward. As policies in the rural sector veered to the right with restoration of incentives and private plots, Mao saw his vision of revolution in the countryside fading – worse, there was evidence of corruption among rural cadres.

During the Socialist Education Campaigns (Siqing) in 1962–5, Mao Zedong, Deng Xiaoping, and Liu Shaoqi respectively issued the Early Ten Points, the Later Ten Points, and the Revised Later Ten Points. Believing that his two colleagues had not got to the heart of the matter, Mao produced the Twenty-three Articles in January 1965. This was not only an attack on individual enterprise (in rural activities) and on corruption; Mao insisted that reform was needed at all levels – up to the Central Committee itself.

Meanwhile, Lin Biao, who had replaced Peng Dehuai as Minister of Defence in 1959, was emerging as a loyal acolyte of Mao. He compiled (May 1964) a breviary of Mao's writing as a pocket book for the troops, later dubbed the Little Red Book. In September 1965, Lin published a long article 'Long Live the Victory of People's War'. On the one hand it was a statement of foreign policy – no compromise with the Soviet Union, no direct involvement in Vietnam – but it was also timed as a declaration of on-going revolution in China.

Liu Shaoqi, Mao's likely successor, had failed to respond to the Twenty-three Articles, and Mao was getting ready to take the offensive. Well known as a supporter of Liu was Beijing Vice-Mayor Wu Han, an historian of the Ming Dynasty. His play 'Hai Rui Dismissed from Office' was seen to imply that Mao's mistreatment of Peng Dehuai was comparable to a Ming emperor's treatment of an honest official. In the Politburo, Mao urged that Wu Han be criticized, while, in Shanghai, under the guidance of Mao's wife Jiang Qing, the radical writer Yao Wenyuan published an article criticizing Wu Han. Cited as 'the first bugle call of the Great Proletarian Cultural Revolution', this was the cultural origin of what was to be fundamentally a political upheaval.

Peng Zhen, the Mayor of Beijing, was made chairman of a five-person group to deal with Wu Han. They recommended that Wu Han be reasoned with rather than politically suppressed. But Mao was obdurate; he refused to read or comment on the proposal. Meanwhile, Lin Biao was setting up a forum for literature and art for the armed forces. The *Liberation Army Journal* published a key article showing that the struggle between the two roads in literature and art had to be reflected in the army which must continue to maintain vigilance against an insidious 'antisocialist black line'. In a letter of 7 May 1966 to Lin Biao, Mao envisaged a broad role for the PLA and for workers, students, and peasants who would also study military affairs as well as politics and culture.

Having summoned the Standing Committee of the Politburo (17–20 March), followed by a Central Committee work conference, Mao set up a new body – the Cultural Revolution group. Its members included not only Jiang Qing, Yao Wenyuan, and Chen Boda, senior Party member, but also key figures who apparently knew better than to stand up to Mao – Liu Shaoqi, Deng Xiaoping, and Zhou Enlai. Peng Zhen was dismissed.

Important decisions were made at an enlarged meeting of the Politburo between 4 and 18 May, notably the 16 May circular which emphasized the threat from counter-revolutionaries 'who had sneaked into the Party and the Government, the army and various cultural circles'. Moreover, there were 'top Party people in authority who were taking the capitalist road'.

Meanwhile, the universities became involved with some lecturers and students responding dramatically to the 16 May circular. Hoping to uphold the role of the Party, maintain his own position, and control the burgeoning unrest, Liu Shaoqi sent work teams into universities and colleges. The work teams laid down rules of behaviour, putting pressure on the Youth League and demanding self-criticism from Party cadres – some of whom were sent to labour camps. But Mao was not impressed by Liu's zealous activity. He saw it as window dressing intended to keep the Party in control and its leaders above criticism.

Hearing that a female lecturer at Beijing University, Nie Yuanzi, had put up a big-character poster that had been suppressed, Mao ordered it to be published in the *People's Daily*. He subsequently produced his own poster 'Bombard the Headquarters', which explicitly criticized the activities of the work-teams and the head of state, Liu Shaoqi himself. When the work teams were withdrawn and the Youth League, which had been monopolized by cadres' children and those of 'good' (i.e. worker/peasant) background, suspended its activities, it was a victory for the more radical students.

At the Eleventh Plenum, Mao's triumph over Liu Shaoqi was complete. The Central Committee set out guidelines ostensibly to keep the revolution under control. Meanwhile, young people, with schools and colleges closed during the summer, were encouraged to travel freely on the trains. In the months to come, millions made the pilgrimage to successive rallies in Beijing or travelled to other provinces to exchange experiences. With wild enthusiasm these 'Red Guards' set out to destroy the 'four olds': old thought, old culture, old customs, old habits, to which was added anything considered decadent, e.g. Beethoven's music. They turned their attention on 'capitalist roaders' and those stigmatized as bourgeois intellectuals, including their teachers. Anyone unfortunate enough to be denounced was liable to be physically abused and even driven to suicide. While groups of Red Guards fought one another, the PLA received secret instructions not to intervene. Mao was tolerant of the youngsters' excesses. At a work conference in October 1966, Liu Shaoqi and Deng Xiaoping confessed their errors, and a few days later Mao took the podium at a mass rally exhorting the students to 'Let politics take command … conduct the Great Proletarian Cultural Revolution even better'.

Chaos was rife during the winter of 1966–7. In Shanghai and some other cities the workers became involved. A so-called Shanghai Paris Commune, although it was in line with the mass political involvement envisaged in the 16 points directive, proved a step too far. Mao noted that the demand to do away with the leaders of society was unrealistic and anarchic. 'In reality there will always be "Heads"'.

In due course the device of the three-in-one revolutionary committee was used to restore order in all institutions throughout China. It comprised radical leaders of the masses, Party cadres, and the army. Thus, the cultural revolution became institutionalized. With the clampdown maintained by the military presence in the three-in-one committees, the visible manifestations of Maoism continued to prevail. The new look in the arts under Mao's wife Jiang Qing was dedicated to 'serving the people'. Big statues of Mao appeared in public halls and parks. When the schools and universities were reopened, the curriculum was heavily indoctrinated with the sayings of Mao. Entrance exams were in abeyance. The criteria for success were the class consciousness of the candidate and the recommendation of his unit.

The Cultural Revolution had deepened the divide between China and the Soviet Union. Confrontational border incidents had been increasing annually until, in March 1969, fighting broke out over a disputed island, Zhenbao, in the Ussuri River. The Chinese propaganda reflected the extreme language of the Cultural Revolution.

10.1 Hold high the great red banner of the Thought of Chairman Mao Tse-tung and take an active part in the Great Socialist Cultural Revolution, 18 April 1966

From the *Liberation Army Journal*

Chairman Mao has taught us that in the socialist society there still exist classes and class struggle. He said: In our country 'the class struggle between the proletariat and the bourgeoisie, the class struggle between the political forces of various factions, and the class struggle between the proletariat and the bourgeoisie in the ideological sphere will still be prolonged, devious, and sometimes even very violent.'

The struggle on the cultural front to build up proletarian ideology and get rid of the bourgeois ideology is an important aspect of the class struggle – the struggle between proletariat and bourgeoisie, between the socialist and the capitalist roads and their ideologies. While the proletariat wishes to transform the world according to it own world outlook, the bourgeoisie wishes to do the same. Socialist culture has the purpose of serving the workers, peasants, and soldiers, of serving proletarian politics, the consolidation and development of the socialist system, and the gradual transition to communism. Bourgeois and revisionist culture serves the bourgeoisie and paves the way for the restoration of capitalism. Any position on the cultural front that is not occupied by the proletariat will necessarily be occupied by the bourgeoisie. This represents sharp class struggle.

The remnant forces of the bourgeoisie in our country are still relatively great, there are still many bourgeois intellectuals, the influence of bourgeois ideology is still quite serious, and the tactics of their struggle against us are becoming more and more cunning and camouflaged. If we slightly relax our attention, we shall not easily discern all this, shall be hit by bourgeois sugar-coated cannon balls, and shall even lose our positions. In this respect, the question of which shall win – socialism or capitalism – has not yet been settled. Struggle is inevitable, and revisionism will appear if we lose.

The People's Liberation Army is a people's army created and led by the Chinese Communist Party and Chairman Mao, a most subservient tool of the Party and the people, an important pillar of proletarian dictatorship. It has consistently played a vital role in the proletarian revolutionary cause and will also play an important part in the great socialist cultural revolution ...

SHARP CLASS STRUGGLE EXISTS ON THE CULTURAL FRONT

For the last 16 years a sharp class struggle has existed on the cultural front.

In both the new democratic and socialist stages of China's revolution, the struggle on the cultural front has gone on between the two classes and the two roads, the struggle between proletariat and bourgeoisie for leadership on the cultural front.

In the history of our Party, too, the struggle against the 'left' and 'right' opportunism also included the struggle between the two lines on the cultural front ...

Ever since the founding of new China more than ten years ago, an anti-Party line has existed in literary and art circles, a black antisocialist thread that runs counter to Mao Tse-tung's thinking. It is a conglomeration of bourgeois and modern revisionist conceptions of literature and art, and of what is presumed to have been the literature and art of the 1930s. Representing this point of view are concepts about 'writing the truth,' about 'the broad road of realism,' about the 'deepening of realism,' about opposing the 'content as the decisive factor,' about 'the portrayal of middle characters,' about opposing 'the smell of gunpowder,' about 'compounding the spirit of the times,' and so on and so forth.

In general, all this was criticized and rejected by Chairman Mao in his 'Talks at the Yenan Forum on Literature and Art.'

In film circles, some people also advanced the so-called theory of 'departing from the classics and the road,' that is, the classical works of Marxism–Leninism and the Thought of Mao Tse-tung and the road of the people's revolutionary war. Despite the influence or control by these bourgeois and modern revisionist ideas of literature and art, we also produced during the past decade more good or basically good works depicting the people's wars, the people's army, and other military subjects – works that really praise revolutionary heroes and serve the workers, peasants, and soldiers and socialism. But such works are not many.

Not a few are works in an intermediate state. Also, some are anti-Party and antisocialist poisonous weeds. Some distort historical facts, and, instead of presenting the correct lines, portray the erroneous ones.

Some works depict heroes who nevertheless violated discipline, or mold a hero but finally let him die, thus creating a tragic ending. Some works, instead of writing on heroic characters, concentrate on 'middle' characters who are actually backward, thereby tarnishing the images of the workers, peasants, and soldiers, while, in describing the enemies, they do not expose their class nature of exploiting and oppressing people or even prettify their character.

In addition, there are works that deal exclusively with nothing but love and vulgar tastes, saying 'love' and 'death' are eternal themes. All these are bourgeois and revisionist things which must be resolutely opposed.

The struggle between the two roads on the literary and art front in society in general is inevitably reflected within the army. For the army does not exist in a vacuum and is certainly no exception. Our army is one of the chief instruments of the dictatorship of the proletariat. Without a people's army led by the Communist Party, there would be no victorious revolution, no proletarian dictatorship, no socialism, and the people would have nothing. Therefore, by hook or by crook the enemy must try to undermine our army in all respects and will certainly use the weapon of literature and art to corrupt it. We must maintain keen vigilance in this connection ...

This is a formidable, complicated, and prolonged struggle calling for the efforts of several decades or even several centuries. We must unswervingly carry the great socialist revolution through to the end. This is a big matter bearing on the revolutionary construction of our army, on the future of our revolution, and also on the future of the world revolution.

Source: 'Hold High the Great Red Banner of the Thought of Mao Tse-tung', Editorial, *Liberation Army Journal*, *Survey of the China Mainland Press*, No. 3687, pp. 4–7

10.2 The educational role of the People's Liberation Army, 7 May 1966

Mao Zedong in a letter to Lin Biao

In this letter, Mao describes the role that the army can play in educating the people.

So long as there is no world war, the armed forces should be a great school. Even under the conditions of a third world war, it is also quite possible to form such a great school, and, apart from fighting, the armed forces can also perform various kinds of work. Wasn't this what we did in the various anti-Japanese bases during the eight years of the Second World War?

In this great school, our armymen should learn politics, military affairs, and agriculture. They can also engage in agricultural production and side occupations, run some medium and small factories, and manufacture a number of products to meet their own needs or exchange with the state at equal values. They can also do mass work and take part in the socialist education movement in the factories and villages. After the socialist education movement, they can always find mass work to do, in order to ensure that the army is always as one with the masses. They should also participate in each struggle of the cultural revolution as it occurs to criticize the bourgeoisie. In this way, the army can concurrently study, engage in agriculture, run factories, and do mass work. Of course, these tasks should be properly coordinated, and a difference should be made between the primary and secondary tasks. Each army unit should engage in one or two of the three tasks of agriculture, industry, and mass work, but not in all three at the same time. In this way, our army of several million will be able to play a very great role indeed.

While the main task of the workers is in industry, they should also study military affairs, politics, and culture. They, too, should take part in the socialist education movement and in the criticizing of the bourgeoisie. Where conditions permit, they should also engage in agricultural production and side occupations, as is done at the Tach'ing oilfield.

While the main task of the peasants in the communes is agriculture (including forestry, animal husbandry, side occupations, and fishery), they should at the same time study military affairs, politics, and culture. Where conditions permit, they should collectively run small plants. They should also criticize the bourgeoisie.

Source: 'Letter to Comrade Lin Biao', 7 May 1966, from 'Long Live Mao-Tse-tung Thought', *Current Background*, No. 891, 8 October 1969

10.3   Igniting the Cultural Revolution

10.3a   A big-character poster at Beijing University, 25 May 1966

Nie Yuanzi

Nie Yuanzi, a woman philosophy lecturer, put up a poster accusing the University President of wrongly interpreting Mao's calls for a Cultural Revolution. When the Party attempted to suppress the text of this poster, Mao had it published in the People's Daily *and broadcast throughout China. In support, Mao wrote his own poster entitled 'Bombard the Headquarters' (see document 10.3c)*

At present, the people of the whole nation, in a soaring revolutionary spirit that manifests their boundless love for the Party and Chairman Mao and their inveterate hatred for the sinister anti-Party, antisocialist gang, are making a vigorous and great cultural revolution; they are struggling thoroughly to smash the attacks of the reactionary sinister gang, in defence of the Party's Central Committee and Chairman Mao. But here in Beida [Beijing University] the masses are being kept immobilized, the atmosphere is one of indifference and deadness, whereas the strong revolutionary desire of the vast number of the faculty members and students has been suppressed. What is the matter? What is the reason? Something fishy is going on. Let's take a look at what has happened very recently! …

On 14 May, Lu Ping (President of Peking University and Secretary of its Party Committee) hastily transmitted the 'directive' issued by Sung Shih (deputy head of the department in charge of university affairs under the Peking Municipal Party Committee) at an emergency meeting of the department. Sung Shih said that at present the movement 'badly needs a strengthened leadership and the Party organizations in the colleges are required to strengthen the leadership and stand fast at the posts.' 'When the masses arise they need to be led onto the correct path' … 'In case the angry masses demand that a big meeting be held, do not suppress them but guide them to hold small group meetings, study documents, and write small-character posters' …

'It is not suitable for Beida to stick up big-character posters,' we 'must guide them to hold small group meetings and write small-character posters.' Why are you so afraid of big-character posters and the holding of big denunciation meetings? To counterattack the sinister gang which has frantically attacked the Party, socialism, and Mao Tse-tung's Thought is a life-and-death class struggle. The revolutionary people must be fully aroused to vigorously and angrily denounce them, and to hold big meetings and put up big-character posters is one of the best ways for the masses to do battle. By 'guiding' the masses not to hold big meetings, not to put up big-character posters, and by creating all kinds of taboos, aren't you suppressing the masses' revolution, not allowing them to make revolution and opposing their revolution? We will never permit you to do this!

You shout about having to 'strengthen the leadership and stand fast at the posts.' This only exposes who you really are. At a time when the revolutionary masses are vigorously rising up, in response to the call of the Party's Central Committee and Chairman Mao, firmly to counterattack the anti-Party, antisocialist sinister gang, you shout: 'Strengthen the leadership and stand fast at the posts.' Isn't it clear what 'posts' you want to hold fast, and for whom, and what kind of people you are, and what despicable tricks you are up to? Right up to today you are still desperately resisting. You still want to 'stand fast' at your 'posts' so as to sabotage the cultural revolution. We must tell you, a mantis cannot stop the wheel of a cart and mayflies cannot topple a giant tree. You are simply daydreaming!

All revolutionary intellectuals, now is the time to go into battle! Let us unite, holding high the great red banner of Mao Tse-tung's Thought, unite round the Party's Central Committee and Chairman Mao, and break down all the various controls and plots of the revisionists; resolutely, thoroughly, totally, and completely wipe out all ghosts and monsters and all Khrushchovian-type counter-revolutionary revisionists, and carry the socialist revolution through to the end.

Defend the Party's Central Committee!
Defend Mao Tse-tung's Thought!
Defend the dictatorship of the proletariat!

Source: 'Ignite the Cultural Revolution in the Universities', a big-character poster, 25 May 1966, *Peking Review*, No. 37, 9 September 1966, pp. 19–20

10.3b All conventions must be smashed

Mao Zedong talking to Central Committee leaders, 21 July 1966.

Nieh Yuan-tzu's big-character poster of 25 May is a declaration of the Chinese Paris Commune of the 1960s. Its significance surpasses the Paris Commune. It is beyond us to write this kind of big-character poster ...

Under the pretext of 'drawing a dividing line between insiders and outsiders,' some fear the revolution, and they cover up the posters that have been put up. This situation cannot be tolerated. It is an error in direction and must be changed at once. All conventions must be smashed.

We should trust the masses and be their pupils before we can be their teachers. The current great cultural revolution is an earth-shaking event. Can we or do we dare undergo the test of socialism? The aims in the final analysis are to wipe out classes and reduce the three great differences.

Opposition – particularly to the 'authoritarian' ideology of the bourgeoisie – is destruction. Without such destruction, socialism cannot be established. We must carry out struggle, criticism, and transformation.

It won't do just to sit in an office and listen to reports. We should rely on and have faith in the masses, and make trouble to the end. Be prepared for the revolution coming over your own head. Leaders of the Party and the government and responsible comrades of the Party must be so prepared. Presently, we must carry the revolution through to the end. By tempering and remolding ourselves in this field, we can catch up with others. Otherwise, we can only stay outside ...

It won't do to lay down conventions for the masses. Seeing that the students were on their feet, Peking University laid down conventions and glorified this as 'putting things on the correct track.' Actually, things were led astray ...

(Someone asked: What should we do if our archives are thrown into disorder in a confusion?) Chairman Mao said: Who are you afraid of? Those who are bad will prove they are bad. Why should you be afraid of the good people? Replace the word 'fear' with the word 'dare;' it is necessary to prove whether you will ultimately be able to pass the test of socialism.

No person who suppresses the student movement will come to a good end.

Source: 'Talks to Central Committee Leaders', 1966 (21 July handwritten in margin of original document), from 'Long Live Mao-Tse-tung Thought', Current Background, No. 891, 8 October 1969, pp. 58–9

10.3c Bombard the headquarters – Mao's big-character poster, 5 August 1966

Mao Zedong

Mao issued this poster in the middle of the ten day Central Committee Eleventh Plenum where there was a struggle between Mao's group and Liu Shaoqi and his supporters. Beijing Review *commented: 'This big-character poster is a most brilliant revolutionary document. It provided the guiding thought for the session and laid down the general principles for the great proletarian cultural revolution'.*

China's first Marxist-Leninist big-character poster and the commentator's article on it in *Renmin Ribao* (*People's Daily*) are indeed superbly written! Comrades, please read them again. But in the last fifty days or so some leading comrades from the central down to the local levels have acted in a diametrically opposite way. Adopting the reactionary stand of the bourgeoisie, they have enforced a bourgeois dictatorship and struck down the surging movement of the Great Cultural Revolution of the proletariat. They have stood facts on their head and juggled black and white, encircled and suppressed revolutionaries, stifled opinions differing from their own, imposed a white terror, and felt very pleased with themselves. They have puffed up the arrogance of the bourgeoisie and deflated the morale of the proletariat. How poisonous! Viewed in connection with the Right deviation in 1962 and the wrong tendency of 1964, which was Left in form but Right in essence, shouldn't this make one wide awake?

Source: Mao Zedong, 'Bombard the Headquarters', 5 August 1966.
Peking Review, No. 33, 11 August 1967, p. 9

10.4 Decision of the Central Committee of the Chinese Communist Party concerning the Great Proletarian Cultural Revolution, adopted 8 August 1966

This '16-point decision' laid down the main guidelines for the Cultural Revolution.

I A NEW STAGE IN THE SOCIALIST REVOLUTION

The Great Proletarian Cultural Revolution now unfolding is a great revolution that touches people to their very souls and constitutes a new stage in the development of the socialist revolution in our country, a deeper and more extensive stage ...

2 THE MAIN CURRENT AND THE TWISTS AND TURNS

The masses of the workers, peasants, soldiers, revolutionary intellectuals and revolutionary cadres form the main force in this Great Cultural Revolution. Large numbers of revolutionary young people, previously unknown, have become courageous and daring pathbreakers. They are vigorous in action and intelligent. Through the media of big-character posters and great debates, they argue things out, expose and criticise thoroughly, and launch resolute attacks on the open and hidden representatives of the bourgeoisie. In such a great revolutionary movement, it is hardly avoidable that they should show shortcomings of one kind or another; however, their general revolutionary orientation has been correct from the beginning. This is the main current in the Great Proletarian Cultural Revolution. It is the general direction along which this revolution continues to advance ...

3 PUT DARING ABOVE EVERYTHING ELSE AND BOLDLY AROUSE THE MASSES

(i)   There is the situation in which the persons in charge of Party organizations stand in the van of the movement and dare to arouse the masses boldly ...
(ii)   In many units, the persons in charge have a very poor understanding of the task of leadership in this great struggle, their leadership is far from being conscientious and effective, and they accordingly find themselves incompetent and in a weak position ...
(iii) In some units, the persons in charge, who have made mistakes of one kind or another in the past, are even more prone to put fear above everything else, being afraid that the masses will catch them out. Actually, if they make serious self-criticism and accept the criticism of the masses, the Party and the masses will make allowances for their mistakes ...
(iv)   Some units are controlled by those who have wormed their way into the Party and are taking the capitalist road. Such persons in authority are extremely afraid of being exposed by the masses and therefore seek every possible pretext to suppress the mass movement ...

4 LET THE MASSES EDUCATE THEMSELVES IN THE MOVEMENT

Trust the masses, rely on them, and respect their initiative. Cast out fear. Don't be afraid of disturbances. Chairman Mao has often told us that revolution cannot be so refined, so gentle, so temperate, kind, courteous, restrained, and magnanimous. Let the masses educate themselves in this great revolutionary movement and learn to distinguish between right and wrong and between correct and incorrect ways of doing things ...

5 FIRMLY APPLY THE CLASS LINE OF THE PARTY

Who are our enemies? Who are our friends? This is a question of the first importance for the revolution and it is likewise a question of the first importance for the great Cultural Revolution ...

6 CORRECTLY HANDLE CONTRADICTIONS AMONG THE PEOPLE

A strict distinction must be made between the two different types of contradiction: those among the people and those between ourselves and the enemy. Contradictions among people must not be made into contradictions between ourselves and the enemy; nor must contradictions between ourselves and the enemy be regarded as contradictions among the people ...

7 BE ON GUARD AGAINST THOSE WHO BRAND THE REVOLUTIONARY MASSES AS COUNTER-REVOLUTIONARIES

In certain schools, units, and work teams of the Cultural Revolution, some of the persons in charge have organised counterattacks against the masses who put up big-character posters criticising them. These people have even advanced such slogans as: Opposition to the leaders of the unit or a work team means opposition to the Central Committee of the Party, means opposition to the Party and socialism, means counter-revolution. In this way it is inevitable that their blows will fall on some really revolutionary activists. This is an error in matters of orientation, an error of line, and is absolutely impermissible ...

8 THE QUESTION OF CADRES

The cadres fall roughly into the following four categories:

(i)   good;
(ii) comparatively good;
(iii) those who have made serious mistakes but have not become anti-Party, antisocialist Rightists:
(iv) the small number of anti-Party, anti-socialist Rightists;

The anti-Party, anti-socialist Rightists must be fully exposed, refuted, overthrown, and completely discredited, and their influence eliminated. At the same time, they should be given a chance to turn over a new leaf.

9 CULTURAL REVOLUTIONARY GROUPS, COMMITTEES, AND CONGRESSES

Many new things have begun to emerge in the Great Proletarian Cultural Revolution. The cultural revolutionary groups, committees, and other organisational forms created by the masses in many schools and units are something new and of great historic importance ...

The struggle of the proletariat against the old ideas, culture, customs, and habits left over by all the exploiting classes over thousands of years will necessarily take a very, very long time. Therefore, the Cultural revolutionary groups, committees, and congresses should not be temporary organisations but permanent, standing, mass organisations. They are suitable not only for colleges, schools, and government and other organisations, but generally also for factories, mines, other enterprises, urban districts, and villages.

It is necessary to institute a system of general elections, like that of the Paris Commune, for electing members to the cultural revolutionary congresses. The list of candidates should be put forward by the revolutionary masses after discussion, and the elections should be held after the masses have discussed the lists over and over again ...

10 EDUCATIONAL REFORM

In this great Cultural Revolution, this phenomenon of our schools being dominated by bourgeois intellectuals must be completely changed.

In every kind of school we must apply thoroughly the policy advanced by Comrade Mao Tse-tung of education serving proletarian politics and education being combined with productive labour, so as to enable those receiving an education to develop morally, intellectually, and physically and to become labourers with socialist consciousness and culture ...

11 THE QUESTION OF CRITICISING BY NAME IN THE PRESS

Criticism of anyone by name in the Press should be decided after discussion by the Party committee at the same level, and in some cases submitted to the Party committee at a higher level for approval.

12 POLICY TOWARDS SCIENTISTS, TECHNICIANS, AND ORDINARY MEMBERS OF WORKING STAFF

As regards scientists, technicians and ordinary members of working staff, as long as they are patriotic, work energetically, are not against the Party and socialism, and maintain no illicit relations with any foreign country, we should in the present movement continue to apply the policy of 'unity, criticism, unity' ...

13 THE QUESTION OF ARRANGEMENTS FOR INTEGRATION WITH THE SOCIALIST EDUCATION MOVEMENT IN CITY AND THE COUNTRYSIDE

The Socialist Education Movement now going on in the countryside and in enterprises in the cities should not be upset where the original arrangements are appropriate and the movement is going well, but should continue in accordance with the original arrangements. However, the questions that are arising in the present Great Proletarian Cultural Revolution should be put to the masses for discussion at the proper time, so as further to foster vigorously proletarian ideology and eradicate bourgeois ideology ...

14 TAKE FIRM HOLD OF THE REVOLUTION AND STIMULATE PRODUCTION

The aim of the Great Proletarian Cultural Revolution is to revolutionise people's ideology and as a consequence achieve greater, faster, better, and more economical results in all fields of work. If the masses are fully aroused and proper arrangements are made, it is possible to carry on both the Cultural Revolution and production without one hampering the other, while guaranteeing high-quality in all our work ...

15 THE ARMED FORCES

In the armed forces, the Cultural Revolution and the Socialist Education Movement should be carried out in accordance with the instructions of the Military Commission of the Central Committee of the Party and the General Political Department of the People's Liberation Army.

16 MAO TSE-TUNG'S THOUGHT IS THE GUIDE TO ACTION IN THE GREAT PROLETARIAN CULTURAL REVOLUTION

In the Great Proletarian Cultural Revolution, it is imperative to hold aloft the great red banner of Mao Tse-tung's Thought and put proletarian politics in command. The movement for the creative study and application of Chairman Mao Tse-tung's works should be carried forward among the masses of the workers, peasants and soldiers, the cadres and the intellectuals, and Mao Tse-tung's Thought should be taken as the guide to action in the Cultural Revolution.

Source: 'Decision of the CCP Central Committee Concerning the Great Proletarian Cultural Revolution', *Peking Review*, **No. 33, 12 August 1966**

10.5 Top-secret instructions forbidding the use of military force, 21 August 1966

When students recently took to the streets to demonstrate in Guilin, Xi'an, Lanzhou, Baotou, and other places, local Party and government organs asked for contingents of armed soldiers to be mobilized to protect their premises. In Guilin, an entire armed battalion has apparently been mobilized for contingency use. In other places, demands have been made for carloads of soldiers to be sent to factories and schools to talk to and dissuade the students from demonstrating. As a result, the relationship between the army and the students has become quite tense, and some students and masses have engaged the soldiers in arguments and put up big-character posters. Teachers and students in some schools have sent a stream of telegrams to the Central Military Commission claiming that revolutionary teachers and students are being surrounded by the army. The situation has already pitted the army against the revolutionary students, and we must regard it with the utmost seriousness. Consequently, we have drawn up the following regulations:

1   No part of the armed forces may under any circumstance suppress the revolutionary student movement by force, much less open fire at the students. Even to fire blanks at the students is a serious political error against which serious disciplinary action will be taken.

2   If the local Party and government authorities invite the army to join the National Day celebrations, the army may with permission from the Party Committee of the Military

Region allow a limited number of men to take part, but they must not under any circumstances bear arms.

3   Regardless of the circumstances, the local Party and government authorities may mobilize the army only with the permission of the Central Military Commission.

4   The army should not become involved when students clash with other students or with the masses. Definite cases of active counter-revolution such as manslaughter, arson, poisoning, destruction of property, and theft of state secrets should be handled according to law by local public security organs. In such cases, if the power of the public security organs is insufficient and if requests for help are made, the army may provide assistance.

5   The army should not send soldiers to factories and schools to engage in propaganda and discussion.

6   The army should not put up big-character posters criticizing the local schools, factories, or government organs. The army should warmly welcome the [critical] big-character posters directed at it appearing in local schools, factories, and government organs.

7   Any person who attempts to avoid the struggle by escaping to and hiding on military premises should be asked to go back to where he came from and not be given a hiding place.

All units must earnestly respect and implement the above regulations.

> Source: 'The People's Liberation Army is Ordered not to Curtail the Cultural
> Revolution', 21 August 1966, Michael Schoenhals, ed., *China's Cultural Revolution
> 1966–1969: Not a Dinner Party* (Armonk, New York: M. E. Sharpe, 1996), pp. 48–9

10.6 Vigorously and speedily eradicate bizarre bourgeois hairstyles

Revolutionary workers of the hairdressing trade in Guangzhou, 27 August 1966

Holding high the great red banner of Mao Zedong Thought and displaying vigorous revolutionary spirit, young revolutionary fighters in Guangzhou have been busy putting up revolutionary big-character posters in the streets to attack the old ideas, culture, customs, and habits of all exploiting classes, in a determined effort to build Guangzhou into a city extraordinarily proletarian and extraordinarily revolutionary in character …

All revolutionary workers of the hairdressing trade should take prompt action by smashing all shop signs tinged with feudal, capitalist, and revisionist ideas. They should replace old signs with new ones fraught with revolutionary significance so our shops will forever shine with revolutionary brilliance!

All revolutionary workers in hairdressing salons should first and foremost make self-revolution in a determined manner, whether concerning what they have in mind, what they wear, or their own hairstyles. They should vigorously rebel against all those bizarre and fantastic things that do not conform to Mao Zedong Thought. They should forgo the 'cowboy' hairstyle and shed their 'cowboy' outfits. They should uphold revolutionary ideas, go in for revolutionary hairstyles, and put on revolutionary clothes.

We refuse to serve those customers who insist on 'cowboy' or 'bun-like' hairstyles! We boycott all customers who are dressed like 'cowboys' or 'cowgirls'.

We welcome customers who want to change their bizarre hairdos. We may even attend to them on a priority basis so that their bizarre hairstyles and new fangled ideas may be changed as soon as possible.

Source: 'Eradicate Bizarre Bourgeois Hairstyles', 27 August 1966, *Survey of China Mainland Press*, No. 3776, 8 September 1966

10.7 Go on red! Stop on green!

Yu Xiaoming

Many absurd dramas in history have been acted out in an atmosphere of extreme seriousness. As a result, absurdities have sometimes acquired an aura of mystique. To prevent absurdities from turning into disasters is a serious task. At the same time, absurdity is sometimes the only form in which the serious can act itself out.

The latter half of 1966 was truly a time of madness. Red Guards were running about 'smashing the four olds,' swearing completely to upset the status quo. At the time, some Red Guards discovered that there was a problem with the traffic lights: red, the color of revolution meant stop and hence served to 'obstruct the progress of revolution'! They pointed out that this was nothing less than blasphemy. It was an error that had to be corrected: red should mean 'go'! The red light ought to illuminate the progress of revolution.

If a demand like this one were to have been accepted, it would have created chaos in our country's traffic control system and caused any number of accidents. At that time, who dared to go against the trend and turn down this absurd and ignorant demand raised by the Red Guards in the name of revolution? Fortunately, Premier Zhou was able to prevent a disaster by engaging the Red Guards in a rather humorous discussion!

One day in September, I and many other self-appointed 'most revolutionary' Red Guards presented Premier Zhou with many 'most utmost revolutionary proposals' at a meeting in a small hall in the Working People's Palace. We all sat on the floor. When someone brought up the matter of the traffic lights, Premier Zhou said: 'I already heard about this suggestion a few days ago, and I really envy your excellent revolutionary spirit. I went to ask my driver and some other comrades, and they told me that the distinguishing feature of the red light is that, no matter if it is day or night, clear or foggy, it can be seen from afar. The green and yellow lights are not like that, and under certain conditions they are not very visible. It is precisely for this reason that, all over the world, the red light is used as a stop sign: to ensure the safety of drivers by reducing the risk of a collision.' Having said this, the Premier paused briefly. He went on: 'Can we agree on the following, that the red light is the light of revolution that guarantees the safety of all revolutionary activities?' We answered in unison: 'Agreed!' Premier Zhou went on: 'So it is OK for me to say that continued use of red as a stop sign is meant to guarantee the safety of revolutionary activities?' We Red Guards shouted back: 'OK!' With an understanding laugh, Premier Zhou waved his hand and said: 'We are in agreement.' The Red Guards raised their arms high in the air, as if they had just passed a resolution affecting the world revolution. They laughed and expressed their approval.

I was sitting only a few meters from Premier Zhou when all of this happened, and I can still recall his relaxed posture and smiling face. Twenty years later, the memory has not yet faded.

However, with the passage of time I have gradually come to realize that it takes true wisdom to tell the sound of a wise laugh from that of an ignorant laugh.

Source: 'Go on Red! Stop on Green!', Michael Schoenhals, ed.,
China's Cultural Revolution 1966–1969: **Not a Dinner Party**
(Armonk, New York: M.E. Sharpe, 1996),, pp. 331–3

10.8 Students attack teachers, July 1966

Rae Yang

In the beginning, the Cultural Revolution exhilarated me because suddenly I felt that I was allowed to think with my own head and say what was on my mind. In the past, the teachers at 101 had worked hard to make us intelligent, using the most difficult questions in mathematics, geometry, chemistry, and physics to challenge us. But the mental abilities we gained, we were not supposed to apply elsewhere. For instance, we were not allowed to question the teachers' conclusions. Students who did so would be criticized as 'disrespectful and conceited,' even if their opinions made perfect sense. Worse still was to disagree with the leaders. Leaders at various levels represented the Communist Party. Disagreeing with them could be interpreted as being against the Party, a crime punishable by labor reform, imprisonment, even death.

Thus, the teachers created a contradiction. On the one hand, they wanted us to be smart, rational, and analytical. On the other hand, they forced us to be stupid, to be 'the teachers' little lambs' and 'the Party's obedient tools.' By doing so, I think, they planted a sick tree; the bitter fruit would soon fall into their own mouths …

Looking back on it, I should say that I felt good about the Cultural Revolution when it started. It gave me a feeling of superiority and confidence that I had never experienced before. Yet amidst the new freedom and excitement, I ran into things that made me very uncomfortable.

I remember one day in July, I went to have lunch at the student dining hall. On the way I saw a crowd gathering around the fountain. I went over to take a look …

On this day I saw a teacher in the fountain, a middle-aged man. His clothes were muddy. Blood was streaming down his head, as a number of students were throwing bricks at him. He tried to dodge the bricks. While he did so, without noticing it, he crawled in the fountain, round and round, like an animal in the zoo. Witnessing such a scene, I suddenly felt sick to my stomach.

Sitting in an empty classroom, I wondered why this incident upset me so much …

Then it dawned on me that I was shocked by the ugliness of the scene.

This teacher survived; another was not so fortunate. Teacher Chen, our art teacher, was said to resemble a spy in the movies. He was a tall, thin man with sallow skin and long hair, which was a sign of decadence. Moreover, he seemed gloomy and he smoked a lot. 'If a person weren't scheming or if he didn't feel very unhappy in the new society, why would he smoke like that?' a classmate asked me, expecting nothing but heartfelt consent from me. 'Not to say that in the past he has asked students to draw naked female bodies in front of plaster statues to corrupt them!' For these 'crimes,' he was beaten to death by a group of senior students.

When I heard this, I felt very uncomfortable again. The whole thing seemed like a bad joke to me. Yet it was real! Teacher Chen had taught us the year before and, unlike Teacher Lin and Teacher Qian, he had never treated students as his enemies. He was polite and tolerant. If a student showed talent in painting, he would be delighted. On the other hand, he would not embarrass a student who 'had no art cells.' I had never heard complaints about him before. Yet somehow he became the first person I knew who was killed in the Cultural Revolution.

Source: Rae Yang, *Spider Eaters: A Memoir*
(Berkeley, California: University of California Press, 1977), pp. 115, 118

10.9   Examples of attacks on Liu Shaoqi and his wife

10.9a Interrogation of Wang Guangmei at Qinhua University, 10 April 1967

Wang Guangmei was the wife of Liu Shaoqi, a central target for criticism during the Cultural Revolution, and referred to here as a 'Three-Anti Element' (i.e. anti-Party, anti-Mao Zedong Thought, and antisocialist). Wang was paraded before 300,000 at the university wearing a necklace of ping pong balls.

INTERROGATOR: You must put on that dress! …
WANG: I am not going to put on that dress. It is not presentable.
INTERROGATOR: Why then did you wear it in Indonesia?
WANG: It was summer at that time, and I wore it in Djakarta …
INTERROGATOR: Let me tell you: you are being struggled against today. You'd better be careful if you are not honest with us! …
WANG (angrily): On no account can you encroach upon my personal freedom.
INTERROGATOR (amid the sound of laughter): You are the wife of a Three-Anti Element, a reactionary bourgeois element, and a class-alien element. You will not be given an iota of small democracy, let alone extensive democracy! Dictatorship is exercised over you today, and you are not free.
WANG (interrupting): Who says I am the wife of a Three Anti-Element?
INTERROGATOR: We do.
WANG: I will not put on that dress, come what may. If I have committed mistakes, I am open to criticism and struggle.
INTERROGATOR: You are guilty of crimes! You are being struggled against today, and you will also be struggled against hereafter. Put it on! …
WANG: No.
INTERROGATOR: All right! We'll give you ten minutes. Watch what happens at a quarter to seven. Try to defy us by not wearing that dress. We mean what we say. (Wang remains silent.)
INTERROGATOR: Wang Guangmei, what's your opinion of Liu Shaoqi's fall from grace?
WANG: It is an excellent thing. In this way, China will be prevented from going revisionist.
INTERROGATOR: One day we are also going to drag out Liu Shaoqi and struggle against him. Do you believe us?
WANG: You just go on with your struggle; just carry on … (silent)
WANG: You members of the Jinggangshan Regiment are thoroughly revolutionary. Except, the form of struggle that you employ is no good. Could you not find a more sophisticated form of denunciation?
INTERROGATOR: Pay no attention to what she says! We shall see what you look like when your ten minutes are over …

WANG: You don't have the right.

INTERROGATOR: We have this right! You are being struggled against today. We are at liberty to wage struggle in whatever form we may want to, and you have no freedom.. You might as well forget about your vile theory of 'everybody being equal before truth.' We are the revolutionary masses, and you are a notorious counter-revolutionary old hag. Don't try to confuse the class demarcation line!

(At the time limit set, the [Jinggangshan] 'Ghostbusters' (Zhouguidui) begin to force Wang to put on the outlandish dress.)

WANG: Wait a moment. (They ignore her. Wang Guangmei sits on the floor and refuses to allow them to slip the dress on her. Eventually she is pulled to her feet and the dress is slipped on her.)

INTERROGATOR: Have you got it on now? (Wang Guangmei had said that the dress was too small for her.)

WANG: You have violated Chairman Mao's instruction about not struggling against the people by force.

([RED GUARDS] Reading in unison [from Mao's 'Little Red Book']: 'A revolution is not a dinner party, or writing an essay, or painting a picture, or doing embroidery; it cannot be so refined, so leisurely and gentle, so temperate, kind, courteous, restrained, and magnanimous. A revolution is an insurrection, an act of violence by which one class overthrows another.')

WANG: You violate Chairman Mao's instructions by saying ... (Wang Guangmei is interrupted and forced to wear silk stockings and high-heeled shoes and a specially made necklace. She is photographed.)

WANG: My point is that you are using coercion. Chairman Mao says that nobody is allowed to strike, abuse, or insult another person.

INTERROGATOR: Nonsense! It is you who have insulted us. By wearing this dress to flirt with Sukarno in Indonesia, you have put the Chinese people to shame and insulted the Chinese people as a whole. Coercion is called for when dealing with such reactionary bourgeois elements as you – the biggest pickpocket on the Qinghua campus!

([RED GUARDS] Reading in unison [from Mao's 'Little Red Book']: 'Everything reactionary is the same; if you don't hit, it won't fall.')

WANG: One day we shall see if I am indeed 'reactionary' or not!

INTERROGATOR: What! Are you trying to reverse the verdict? (Everybody begins listing her crimes.)

WANG (denies the accusations): I wish you would make a proper investigation ...

INTERROGATOR: How many revolutionary masses have been branded as counter-revolutionaries by you alone? How many persons have you victimized?

WANG: We have not branded a single person as counter-revolutionary.

INTERROGATOR: There is no way for you to deny the fact that you 'hit at a great many in order to protect a handful!'

WANG: Facts are facts, and conclusions should be drawn according to facts. That is Mao Zedong Thought.

INTERROGATOR: Wrong! The standpoint is the most important thing. Taking the reactionary stand, you see only the dark side of the revolutionary masses and are opposed to the Great Cultural Revolution. The facts we have studied and collected are different from yours.

WANG: Now some people want to shift the responsibility to others ... A person should dare to acknowledge facts, if he is a genuine revolutionary leftist. It is wrong to 'doubt everything.' Who was it that advocated 'doubting everything?'

INTERROGATOR: You have doubted all revolutionary things and attacked all of the revolutionary masses and cadres …

WANG: I am a Communist and fear nothing. I am not afraid of death by a thousand cuts …

INTERROGATOR (shouting a slogan): Down with the Three-Anti Element Wang Guangmei! …

INTERROGATOR: So tell us, how many students did you brand as counter-revolutionaries?
There are quite a few of us here.

WANG: In any case, we only criticized people and did not brand them as counter-
revolutionaries.

INTERROGATOR: Who told you to oppose what you called 'sham leftists?'

WANG: Not Liu Shaoqi. It was the work team, Ye Lin and Yang Tianfang, who asked me …

INTERROGATOR: Did Liu Shaoqi issue any instructions?

WANG: Liu Shaoqi issued very few instructions concerning Qinghua University …

INTERROGATOR: Wang Guangmei, tell us how you feel about Liu Shaoqi being the biggest
Party-person in power taking the capitalist road?

WANG: Subjectively, my understanding is not yet up to that level. In any case, before the
Eleventh Plenum of the Eighth Central Committee, the Chairman entrusted Liu Shaoqi and
the Central Secretariat with many tasks, and, if anything happened, [Liu] would of course
have been responsible. But now he has had to step aside and is no longer responsible and no
longer in power! At that time of the 'reactionary line' [the initial period of the Cultural Revolution when Liu was in charge], he traversed a stretch of the capitalist road.

INTERROGATOR: Only at the time of the reactionary line! That's all?

WANG: Of course not. Anyone who makes an error in line will have traversed a stretch of
the capitalist road …

INTERROGATOR: We intend to struggle against you reactionary bourgeois element and big
pickpocket on the Qinghua campus.

WANG: I am not what you say I am; I am a Communist Party member.

INTERROGATOR: Don't try to denigrate our Party. Haven't you done enough filthy things
already? …

INTERROGATOR: Wang Guangmei! Are you afraid?

WANG: Why should I be? I am not afraid. A Communist has nothing to fear. (As she is about
to go downstairs, her shaking hands are unable to put things in the proper place.)

WANG: I want a glass of water.

WANG: Where is that PLA comrade? Old Ma, I want a tranquilizer.

INTERROGATOR: Are you afraid?

WANG: My mind is calm. I have to take medicine because I am sick. My nerves are no good.
(She gasps for breath.)

INTERROGATOR: Wang Guangmei's hands are trembling.

WANG: There is some trouble with my hands. I am not afraid, and I am very calm in mind.
(Wang Guangmei asks for two tranquilizer tablets, but the PLA comrade gives her only one.)
All right. I'll take one as you say. (As she is dragged out, she becomes downcast and turns
pale. She drags her feet step by step and again asks for a tranquilizer.) Where is the PLA
comrade? I want some more medicine.

INTERROGATOR: Didn't you say you were not afraid? Paper tiger!

WANG: I am not afraid, and I am willing to go through with the meeting, but I have been
running a fever these past few days. Liu Shaoqi is also sick, and I have nursed him a number of
days. (She then purses her lips, and the veins stand out on her hands.)

INTERROGATOR: What have you in mind now?

WANG (in a low voice):   I am now ready to face the criticism, repudiation, and struggle of the masses.

Source: 'Interrogation of Wang Guangmei at Qinghua University',
10 April 1967, from *Three Trials of Pickpocket Wang Kuang-mei*,
a Red Guard pamphlet, *Current Background*, No. 848

10.9b Big scab Liu Shao-chi is the mortal foe of the working class, 10 January 1969

From the *Beijing Review*

Liu Shaoqi was removed from his post as Head of State in October 1968 and died from illness and neglect in 1969.

During the last few decades, masquerading as the 'leader of the workers' movement,' the big scab Liu Shao-chi engaged in deception and blackmail everywhere and committed innumerable crimes. He did his best to sell out the power of leadership of the working class, vigorously spread the theories of 'class collaboration' and 'the dying out of class struggle,' and tried to emasculate the revolutionary soul of the workers' movement and corrupt and disintegrate the working-class ranks through economism. In the crucial moments of the revolution, he brutally suppressed the workers' movement in a vain attempt to liquidate the proletarian revolution and subvert the proletarian dictatorship. He is a jackal from the same lair as the world's scabs old and new – Bernstein, Kautsky, Khrushchov, Thorez, Togliatti, and their like. He is the mortal foe of the working class ...

After the liberation of the country, the big scab Liu Shao-chi made use of the Party and government power he had usurped and stood completely on the side of the bourgeoisie to urge 'the capitalists to struggle against the workers.' He always opposed Chairman Mao's great teachings on carrying out large-scale mass movements in the factories and mines, slandered the mass movements as 'something that was started haphazardly,' and stifled them in every way. Under the signboard of 'scientific management,' he controlled and punished the workers and advocated the enforcement of capitalist discipline. When the storm of the great proletarian cultural revolution approached, Liu Shao-chi hastily dished out the bourgeois reactionary line to suppress the revolutionary masses and launched a converging attack against the revolutionaries in a vain attempt to put down the great proletarian cultural revolution movement personally initiated by Chairman Mao.

The arch scab Liu Shao-chi's numerous crimes of suppressing the workers' movement before and after liberation fully prove him to be the top spy sent by the Chiang Kai-shek regime into the ranks of the working class ...

Over the past decades, Liu Shao-chi has always taken the reactionary stand of the landlord class and the bourgeoisie. Catering to the needs of imperialism, modern revisionism, and the Kuomintang reactionaries, he has betrayed the fundamental interests of the working class and committed towering crimes ... The great proletarian cultural revolution personally initiated and led by Chairman Mao has proclaimed the death sentence on the big scab Liu Shaochi politically and the total bankruptcy of the counter-revolutionary revisionist line in the workers' movement. We must carry on and deepen the revolutionary mass criticism and repudiation and thoroughly wipe out the pernicious influence of the big scab Liu Shao-chi's counter-revolutionary revisionist line in the workers' movement.

Source: 'Big Scab Liu Shao-chi Is the Mortal Foe of the Working Class',
Peking Review, **No. 2, 10 January 1969, pp. 12–14**

10.10 Revolutionary committees are fine

From *Peking Review*, 5 April 1968

The spring breeze of Mao Tse-tung's Thought has reached every corner of our motherland. The revolutionary committees which have come into being one after another stand like red flags flying in the wind. To date, revolutionary committees have been established in 17 provinces and municipalities and in one autonomous region. Vast numbers of units at the grassroot level have set up their own revolutionary committees ...

When the new-born revolutionary committees appeared on the eastern horizon a year ago, our revered and beloved leader Chairman Mao, with his great proletarian revolutionary genius, pointed out with foresight: 'In every place or unit where power must be seized, it is necessary to carry out the policy of the revolutionary 'three-in-one' combination in establishing a provisional organ of power that is revolutionary and representative and enjoys proletarian authority. This organ of power should preferably be called the Revolutionary Committee'.

Our great leader Chairman Mao again recently pointed out: 'The basic experience of revolutionary committees is this – they are threefold: they have representatives of revolutionary cadres, representatives of the armed forces, and representatives of the revolutionary masses. This forms a revolutionary 'three-in-one' combination. The revolutionary committee should exercise unified leadership, do away with redundant or overlapping administrative structures, have 'better troops and simpler administration', and organize a revolutionized leading group that is linked with the masses'.

The 'three-in-one' organ of power enables our proletarian political power to strike deep roots among the masses. Chairman Mao points out: 'The most fundamental principle in the reform of state organs is that they must keep in contact with the masses'. The representatives of the revolutionary masses, particularly the representatives of the working people – the workers and peasants – who have come forward en masse in the course of the great proletarian cultural revolution are revolutionary fighters with practical experience. Representing the interests of the revolutionary masses, they participate in the leading groups at various levels. This provides the revolutionary committees at these levels with a broad mass foundation ...

This 'three-in-one' organ of power strengthens the dictatorship of the proletariat. 'If the army and the people are united as one, who in the world can match them?' The great Chinese People's Liberation Army is the main pillar of the dictatorship of the proletariat and a great wall of steel defending the socialist motherland. The revolutionary 'three-in-one' combination carries our army–civilian unity to a completely new stage. In its work of helping the Left, helping industry and agriculture, exercising military control, and giving military and political training, the People's Liberation Army has made big contributions over the past year and more and has been well steeled in the process ...

Revolutionary leading cadres are the backbone of the 'three-in-one' organs of power. They have rich experience in class struggle and are a valuable asset to the Party and people. By going through the severe test of the great proletarian cultural revolution and receiving education and help from the masses, they were touched to the soul and remoulded their world outlook further ...

This 'three-in-one' organ of power has absolutely nothing in common with the overstaffed bureaucratic apparatus of the exploiting classes in the old days. It has an entirely new and revolutionary style of work of its own and it functions in a way that is beneficial to the people ... 'Remain one of the common people while serving as an official'. Maintain 'better troops and simpler administration', and drastically reform old methods of office and administrative work. Have a small leading body and a small staff, as certain revolutionary committees have begun doing, so that there is no overlapping or redundancy in the organization and no over-staffing, so that bureaucracy can be prevented. In this way, the style of hard work, plain living, and economy is fostered; corrosion by bourgeois ideology is precluded; and the revolutionary committee becomes a compact and powerful fighting headquarters that puts proletarian politics to the fore and is full of revolutionary enthusiasm and capable of taking prompt and resolute action.

Source: 'Revolutionary Committees Are Fine'.
Editorial in *Peking Review*, No. 14, 5 April 1968, pp. 6–7

10.11 Soviet intrusion into Chenpao Island

10.11a Grassland herdsmen show wolves no mercy

Poroldai, *Peking Review*, 21 March 1969

The author was Chairman of the Revolutionary Committee of the Wushenchao People's Commune, Wushen Banner, Inner Mongolian Autonomous Region, and a poor herdsman.

The Soviet revisionist renegade clique's crimes of armed intrusion into China's territory Chenpao Island fully reveal it as a gang of wolves in sheep's clothing and its true social-imperialist and social-fascist nature. We herdsmen on the grassland who never show wolves any mercy are good at wiping them out. We are well prepared. When Chairman Mao, the greatest leader of the people of all nationalities in China, gives the order, we will wipe out the intruding Soviet revisionist aggressors, like we do to the wolves.

Tempered in the battles of the tremendous, great proletarian cultural revolution, the people of all nationalities in China unite still more closely around the proletarian headquarters with our great leader Chairman Mao as its leader and Vice-Chairman Lin as its deputy leader and, by attaining unity in thinking, policy, plan, command, and action under the command of Mao Tse-tung's Thought, have grown into an invincible force. Unity among the people of all our nationalities has never been as close as it is today. The Chinese people's level of consciousness of Mao Tse-tung's Thought has reached a new high. Whoever dares invade our great socialist motherland will be crushed!

Profound revolutionary friendship exists traditionally between the Soviet working people and the people of all nationalities in China. The Chinese and Soviet peoples have always been comrades-in-arms, supporting each other and fighting shoulder to shoulder. We firmly believe that the great and glorious Soviet people will not tolerate the Soviet revisionist renegade clique's rule for long. We stand foursquare behind them in their heroic struggles against the Soviet revisionist renegade clique.

On the Inner Mongolian grassland lit by the red sun, every household of the broad masses of poor herdsmen is a sentry post against revisionism and every poor herdsman an antirevisionist fighter. We poor herdsmen of the Inner Mongolian Autonomous Region are determined to unite still more closely with the people of all nationalities in our country, vigorously grasp revolution and promote production, and repel the Soviet revisionist armed provocations with concrete actions. We will increase our vigilance a hundredfold and we stand ready at all times to fight in defence of our socialist motherland!

Source: Poroldai, 'Grassland Herdsmen Show Wolves No Mercy',
Peking Review, No. 12, 21 March 1969, pp. 19–20

10.11b Sketch map showing the Sino-Soviet Boundary at the disputed area of Chenpao Island, March 1969

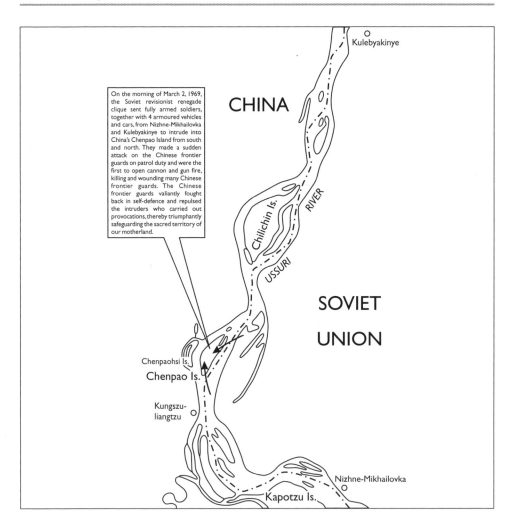

11

Years of transition

The Ninth Party Congress, April 1969, coming at the end of the furious years of the Cultural Revolution, with Lin Biao formally installed as Party Chairman in waiting, might have presaged a period of retrenchment and stability. But within less than three years there were dramatically changed circumstances. Diplomatically, China leapt from being ostracized as America's worst enemy, to taking its rightful seat among the five permanent members of the Security Council of the United Nations Organization.

China's political leadership at the beginning of 1970 can be defined in three main groups: the radicals with Jiang Qing and other enthusiasts of the Cultural Revolution; the moderates headed by Premier Zhou Enlai; and the military under Lin Biao. Mao harboured suspicions about Lin Biao, doubting his loyalty, and began systematically to undermine Lin's supporters in the military. Did Lin or his associates in desperation plan to assassinate Mao? Lin certainly panicked. It was alleged that, after a failed plot, he attempted to flee to the Soviet Union and was killed in a plane crash in September 1971.

After the military confrontation on the Ussuri River, Moscow pressed for talks which were eventually conceded in September 1969. Kosygin and Premier Zhou Enlai met at Beijing airport and it was agreed on 7 October that the status quo should be maintained and there should be no use of force. However, the Chinese had reason to fear the threat posed by Soviet forces, both conventional and nuclear. The course of American politics made a diplomatic revolution possible. Rapprochment with China was seen as a plausible step to getting out of Vietnam, firstly by President Johnson. Subsequently it became the keystone of incoming President Nixon's policy. After two years of secret diplomacy – so secret that the US Secretary of State was kept in the dark until after Dr Kissinger's visit to Beijing in July 1971 – the Shanghai communiqué of 27 February agreed to the peaceful settlement of differences and to extend diplomatic and cultural contacts leading to 'normalization'.

Even before Nixon arrived in China, the majority of the United Nations General Assembly swung in favour of Beijing's admission, and voted for an Albanian motion to seat the Communists. A US-sponsored motion that would have permitted the Republic of China (Taiwan) to keep its seat was defeated.

Subsequently, Nixon won re-election, but the new relationship made little progress between 1973 and 1976. It was not helped by the leadership crises that affected both China and the United States.

Meanwhile, the radicals led by Jiang Qing continued to emphasize moral incentives and decentralization in contrast to the new five-year plan 1971–75 which gave scope to material incentives and central planning. Associated with these reforms under Premier Zhou Enlai was Deng Xiaoping, now rehabilitated after the Cultural Revolution. He was appointed Vice

Premier and had a seat on the standing committee of the Politburo. In January 1975 the fourth National People's Congress formally approved a policy of four modernizations – for agriculture, industry, national defence, and science and technology. However, Zhou Enlai, stricken with cancer, died in January 1976 and Mao, although seriously ageing, was ambivalent about his support for Deng. On the one hand he stigmatized Jiang Qing radicals as a 'gang of four', yet he encouraged two of them, Zhang Chunquiao and Yao Wenyuan, to publish their views on the importance of class struggle. To succeed Zhou as acting Premier, Mao appointed a relatively obscure official, the Minister of Public Security Hua Guofeng.

Although the radicals had tried to play down the mourning for Zhou Enlai by not announcing where the cremation ceremony would take place, they failed to suppress the crowds who flocked to Tiananmen Square on the occasion of Qingming (4 April 1976), bearing wreaths in honour of Zhou Enlai. This led to disturbances in which the police and militia intervened. The blame for the incident was put on Deng Xiaoping who was removed from all his posts.

Meanwhile, Mao Zedong was fading fast. He died on 9 September. Hua's claim to succeed him was based on some remarks Mao was alleged to have made at a meeting with Hua at the end of April. '1. Carry out the work slowly, not in haste; 2. Act according to the past principles; 3. With you in charge I am at ease'.

Since 8 April, Hua had been Premier in his own right. On Mao's death, Jiang Qing and her associates attempted to extend their power. They were forestalled by a countercoup involving the military leader Ye Jianying and the head of the Communist Party guard unit Wang Dongxing. On 6 October, Hua ordered the arrest of the Gang of Four and more than twenty of their supporters, and the arrests were made public on 21 October with organized demonstrations across China. Hua's image was promoted in giant posters side by side with Mao. In February 1977, The *People's Daily* declared: 'We resolutely defend whatever policies Chairman Mao has formulated and unswervingly adhere to whatever instructions Chairman Mao has issued'.

Already there was a formidable change in the wind. In July 1977, Deng Xiaoping, who had been lying low in Guangzhou since spring 1976, was reinstated in the positions he held before the Tiananmen incident. A deal had been struck in which Deng was to support Hua. In fact, a slow process of rivalry had been commenced in which Deng distanced himself from Mao's policies in the Cultural Revolution and by the end of the decade was recognized as 'paramount leader'.

On 22 December 1978, a communiqué of the Central Committee announced an important 'shift to socialist modernization'. This reassessed the Cultural Revolution, rehabilitated certain political leaders, and condemned the overconcentration of authority, stressing the need to give responsibility at lower levels.

As the Cultural Revolution was winding down and Maoist policies were replaced, it was time for a historical reassessment for the Communist Party. Consideration of 'certain questions in the history of our Party' began in spring 1980 and was completed by June 1981. The resolution, which became required reading for the 39 million members of the CCP, recognized that, notwithstanding Mao's mistakes, he was a 'great proletarian revolutionary', that the Cultural Revolution was a grave blunder, and that the way was now clear for turning China into a modern socialist country.

In the meantime the chief 'culprits' for the 'lost years' were put on trial (20 November 1980 to 25 January 1981). The ten accused were the Gang of Four, Jiang Qing, Zhang Chunqiao, Yao Wenyuan, Wang Hongwen, five of Lin Biao's generals, and Chen Boda. All the accused confessed except Zhang Chunqiao, who refused to acknowledge the tribunal, and Jiang Qing who made a spirited defence.

11.1 Reviewing China's relations with Moscow and Washington

11.1a Report on the struggle between China, the United States, and the Soviet Union

Four Chinese Marshals – Chen Yi, Ye Jianying, Nie Rongshen, and Xu Xiangqian – to the CCP Central Committee, 17 September 1969

1   The Soviet revisionists indeed intend to wage a war of aggression against China. Their strategic goal is to redivide the world with the US imperialists. They vainly hope to bring China into the orbit of social imperialism. Recently, the Soviet revisionists have intensified whipping up public opinion for a war against China, openly threatening us with a nuclear strike, and conspiring to launch a surprise attack on our nuclear facilities. The Cultural Revolution in our country is still under way, our nuclear weapons are still under development, and the Vietnam War has not ended. A group of adventurers in the Soviet revisionist leadership want to seize this opportunity to use missiles and tanks to launch a quick war against China and thoroughly destroy China, so that a 'mortal danger' for them will be removed ...

2   To a large extent, the Soviet revisionists' decision to launch a war of aggression against China depends on the attitude of the US imperialists, which is far from satisfactory to them so far, and is their utmost worry in a strategic sense. The last thing the US imperialists are willing to see is a victory by Soviet revisionists in a Sino-Soviet war, as this would [allow the Soviets] to build up a big empire more powerful than the American empire in resources and manpower. Several times the US imperialists have expressed a willingness to improve relations with China, which reached a peak during Nixon's recent trip to Asia. The Soviet revisionists are scared by the prospect that we might ally ourselves with the US imperialists to confront them. On 26 July, the first day of Nixon's trip to Asia, the Soviet revisionists hurriedly handed to our side the statement issued by the Soviet Council of Ministers to our government. This move fully revealed the anxiousness on the part of the Soviet revisionists. The Soviet revisionists' fears about possible Sino-American unity makes it more difficult for them to launch an all-out attack on China. Considering several other factors, it can be concluded that the Soviet revisionists dare not start a major war against China.

3   Kosygin's trip to Beijing reflected [the Soviet revisionists'] reactionary pragmatism. The Soviet revisionists want to get out of difficulties at home and abroad by attempting to modify a brink-of-war policy toward China ...

4   In the struggle between China, the United States, and the Soviet Union, the United States hopes to utilize China and the Soviet Union, and the Soviet Union hopes to exploit China and the United States, so that one of them will gain the utmost strategic advantages. We must wage a tit-for-tat struggle against both the United States and the Soviet Union, including using negotiation as a means of fighting against them. We should be firm on principles and flexible on tactics. The Soviet revisionists have requested holding negotiations on the border issue, to which we have agreed. The US imperialists have suggested resuming the Sino-American ambassadorial talks, to which we should

respond positively when the timing is proper. Such tactical actions may bring about results of strategic significance.

Source: Report by Four Chinese Marshals to the CCP Central Committee: 'On the struggle between China, the United States and the Soviet Union', 17 September 1969, *Cold War International History Project Bulletin*, No. 11, Winter 1998, p. 170

11.1b Further thoughts by Marshal Chen Yi on Sino-American relations, 17 September 1969

This report [the report by the four marshals] mainly deals with Kosygin's trip to China and the possibility for Soviet revisionists to launch a large-scale attack on China, and it thus fails to provide a detailed analysis of whether or not the Sino-American ambassadorial talks in Warsaw should be resumed. I have considered for a long time on how to achieve a breakthrough in Sino-American relations. The talks in Warsaw have been conducted for more than ten years without producing anything. Even if the talks are resumed now, they will not bring about breakthrough in Sino-American relations. I have read relevant reference materials. On 27 October 1955, we suggested that China and the United States hold talks at foreign minister level to relax and eliminate tension in the Taiwan region. On 18 and 24 January 1956, our Foreign Ministry spokesman issued two statements, pointing out that the Taiwan problem had proven too serious to be solved by the Sino-American ambassadorial talks, and that only talks at foreign minister level could relax and eliminate tension in the Taiwan region. This suggestion, though with great significance, was rejected by the United States. The situation has changed today. Because of the strategic need for dealing with the Soviet revisionists, Nixon hopes to win over China. It is necessary for us to utilize the contradiction between the United States and the Soviet Union in a strategic sense, and pursue a breakthrough in Sino-American relations. Thus, we must adopt due measures, about which I have some 'wild' ideas. First, when the meetings in Warsaw are resumed, we may take the initiative in proposing to hold Sino-American talks at the ministerial or even higher levels, so that basic and related problems in Sino-American relations can be solved. We should only make suggestions about at which level and on which topics talks should be held. In my judgement, the Americans may accept the suggestion. It is possible that, if we do not take the initiative, the Americans may make such a suggestion. If that is the case, we should accept it. Second, a Sino-American meeting at higher levels holds strategic significance. We should not raise any prerequisite, which does not mean that we have departed from our previous stand on the Taiwan question. The Taiwan question can be gradually solved by talks at higher levels. Furthermore, we may discuss with the Americans other questions of strategic significance. These tasks cannot be fulfilled with talks at the ambassadorial level. Third, when the talks in Warsaw are resumed, we do not need to use the meeting place provided by the Polish government. To keep the meetings secret, the talks should be held at the Chinese embassy.

Source: Further Thoughts by Marshal Chen Yi on Sino-American Relations, 17 September 1969, *Cold War International History Project Bulletin*, No. 11, Winter 1998, pp. 170–1

11.2 President Nixon meets Chairman Mao in Beijing, 21 February 1972

Extracts from *The Kissinger Transcripts*

[Memorandum of Conversation] Top-secret/Sensitive/Exclusive Eyes Only. Participants: Chairman Mao Zedong; Prime Minister Zhou Enlai; Wang Hairong, Deputy Chief of Protocol of the Foreign Ministry; Tang Wensheng, Interpreter; President Nixon; Henry A. Kissinger, Assistant to the President for National Security Affairs; Winston Lord, National Security Council Staff (Notetaker)

Date and time: Monday, February 21, 1972 – 2.50–3.55 p.m.

Place: Chairman Mao's Residence, Beijing

(There were opening greetings during which the Chairman welcomed President Nixon, and the President expressed his great pleasure at meeting the Chairman.)

PRESIDENT NIXON: You read a great deal. The Prime Minister said that you read more than he does.

CHAIRMAN MAO: Yesterday in the airplane you put forward a very difficult problem for us. You said that what it is required to talk about are philosophic problems.

PRESIDENT NIXON: I said that because I have read the Chairman's poems and speeches, and I knew he was a professional philosopher. (Chinese laugh) …

CHAIRMAN MAO: We two must not monopolize the whole show. It won't do if we don't let Dr Kissinger have a say. You have been famous about your trips to China …

DR KISSINGER: It was the President who set the direction and worked out the plan …

PRESIDENT NIXON: He is the only man … who could go to Paris 12 times and Peking once and no one knew it, except possibly a couple of pretty girls (Zhou laughs).

DR KISSINGER: They didn't know it; I used it as a cover …

PRESIDENT NIXON: Anyone who uses pretty girls as a cover must be the greatest diplomat of all time.

CHAIRMAN MAO: So your girls are very often made use of?

PRESIDENT NIXON: His girls, not mine. It would get me into great trouble if I used girls as a cover.

PRIME MINISTER ZHOU: (Laughs) Especially during elections (Kissinger laughs). Dr Kissinger doesn't run for President because he wasn't born a citizen of the United States.

DR KISSINGER: Miss Tang is eligible to be President of the United States.

PRESIDENT NIXON: She would be the first woman President. There's our candidate.

CHAIRMAN MAO: It would be very dangerous if you have such a candidate. But let us speak the truth. As for the Democratic Party, if they come into office again, we cannot avoid contacting them.

PRESIDENT NIXON: We understand. We will hope that we don't give you that problem.

CHAIRMAN MAO: Those questions are not questions to be discussed in my place. They should be discussed with the Premier. I discuss philosophical questions. That is to say, I voted for you during your election …

PRESIDENT NIXON: When the Chairman says he voted for me, he voted for the lesser of two evils.

CHAIRMAN MAO: I like rightists. People say you are rightists, that the Republican Party is to the right, that Prime Minister [Edward] Heath is also to the right …

PRESIDENT NIXON: I think the important thing to note is that in America, at least this time, those on the right can do what those on the left talk about.

DR KISSINGER: There is another point, Mr President. Those on the left are pro-Soviet and would not encourage a move toward the People's Republic, and in fact criticize you on those grounds.

CHAIRMAN MAO: Exactly that. Some are opposing you. In our country also there is a reactionary group which is opposed to our contact with you. The result was that they [the Lin Biao group] got on an airplane and fled abroad.

PRIME MINISTER ZHOU: Maybe you know this …

CHAIRMAN MAO: As a suggestion, may I suggest that you do a little less briefing? (The President points at Dr Kissinger and Zhou laughs.) Do you think it is good if you brief others on what we talk about, our philosophic discussions here?

PRESIDENT NIXON: The Chairman can be sure that whatever we discuss, or whatever I and the Prime Minister discuss, nothing goes beyond the room. That is the only way to have conversations at the highest level.

CHAIRMAN MAO: That's good.

PRESIDENT NIXON: For example, I hope to talk with the Prime Minister and later with the Chairman about issues like Taiwan, Vietnam, and Korea. I also want to talk about – and this is very sensitive – the future of Japan, the future of the subcontinent, and what India's role will be; and on the broader world scene, the future of US–Soviet relations. Because only if we see the whole picture of the world and the great forces that move the world will we be able to make the right decisions about the immediate and urgent problems that always completely dominate our vision.

CHAIRMAN MAO: All those troublesome problems I don't want to get into very much. I think your topic is better – philosophic questions.

PRESIDENT NIXON: For example, Mr Chairman, it is interesting to note that most nations would approve of this meeting, but the Soviets disapprove, the Japanese have doubts which they express, and the Indians disapprove. So we must examine why, and determine how our policies should develop to deal with the whole world, as well as the immediate problems such as Korea, Vietnam, and, of course, Taiwan.

CHAIRMAN MAO: Yes, I agree.

PRESIDENT NIXON: We, for example, must ask ourselves – again in the confines of this room – why the Soviets have more forces on the border facing you than on the border facing Western Europe. We must ask ourselves, what is the future of Japan? Is it better – here I know we have disagreements – is it better for Japan to be neutral, totally defenseless, or is it better for a time for Japan to have some relations with the United States? The point being – I am talking now in the realm of philosophy – in international relations there are no good choices. One thing is sure – we can leave no vacuums, because they can be filled. The Prime Minister, for example, has pointed out that the United States reaches out its hands and that the Soviet Union reaches out its hands. The question is which danger the People's Republic faces, whether it is the danger of American aggression or Soviet aggression. These are hard questions, but we have to discuss them.

CHAIRMAN MAO: At the present time, the question of aggression from the United States or aggression from China is relatively small; that is, it could be said that this is not a major issue, because the present situation is one in which a state of war does not exist between our two countries. You want to withdraw some of your troops back on your soil; ours do not go abroad. Therefore, the situation between our two countries is strange because during the past 22 years our ideas have never met in talks. Now the time is less than 10 months since we began playing table tennis [as a means of contact]; if one counts the time since you put forward your suggestion at Warsaw, it is less than two years. Our side also is bureaucratic in dealing with matters. For example, you wanted some exchange of persons on a personal level, things like that; also trade. But rather than deciding that, we stuck with our stand that without settling major issues there is nothing to do with smaller issues. I myself persisted in that position. Later on I saw you were right, and we played table tennis. The Prime Minister said this was also after President Nixon came to office.

The former President of Pakistan introduced President Nixon to us. At that time, our Ambassador in Pakistan refused to agree on our having a contact with you. He said it should be compared whether President Johnson or President Nixon would be better. But President Yahya said the two men cannot be compared, that these two men are incomparable. He said that one was like a gangster – he meant President Johnson. I don't know how he got that impression. We on our side were not very happy with that President either. We were not very happy with your former Presidents, beginning from Truman through Johnson. We were not very happy with these Presidents, Truman and Johnson. In between there were eight years of a Republican President. During that period probably you hadn't thought things out either …

DR KISSINGER: Mr Chairman, the world situation has also changed dramatically during that period. We've had to learn a great deal. We thought all socialist/communist states were the same phenomenon. We didn't understand until the President came into office the different nature of revolution in China and the way revolution had developed in other socialist states.

PRESIDENT NIXON: Mr Chairman, I am aware of the fact that over a period of years my position with regard to the People's Republic was one that the Chairman and Prime Minister totally disagreed with. What brings us together is a recognition of a new situation in the world and a recognition on our part that what is important is not a nation's internal political philosophy. What is important is its policy toward the rest of the world and toward us. That is why – this point I think can be said to be honest – we have differences. The Prime Minister and Dr Kissinger discussed these differences.

It also should be said – looking at the two great powers, the United States and China – we know China doesn't threaten the territory of the United States; I think you know the United States has no territorial designs on China. We know China doesn't want to dominate the United States. We believe you too realize the United States doesn't want to dominate the world. Also – maybe you don't believe this, but I do – neither China nor the United States, both great nations, wants to dominate the world. Because our attitudes are the same on these two issues, we don't threaten each others' territories.

Therefore, we can find common ground, despite our differences, to build a world structure in which both can be safe to develop in our own ways on our own roads. That cannot be said about some other nations in the world.

CHAIRMAN MAO: Neither do we threaten Japan or South Korea.

PRESIDENT NIXON: Nor any country. Nor do we.

CHAIRMAN MAO: (Checking the time with Zhou) Do you think we have covered enough today?

PRESIDENT NIXON: Yes. I would like to say as we finish, Mr Chairman, we know you and the Prime Minister have taken great risks in inviting us here. For us also it was a difficult decision. But, having read some of the Chairman's statements, I know he is one who sees when an opportunity comes that you must seize the hour and seize the day. I would also like to say in a personal sense – and this to you Mr Prime Minister – you do not know me. Since you do not know me, you shouldn't trust me. You will find I never say something I cannot do. And I always will do more than I can say. On this basis I want to have frank talks with the Chairman and, of course, with the Prime Minister …

(There were some closing pleasantries. The Chairman said he was not well. President Nixon responded that he looked good. The Chairman said that appearances were deceiving. After handshakes and more pictures, Prime Minister Zhou then escorted the President out of the residence.)

Source: Conversation between President Nixon, Chairman Mao and others in Beijing, 21 February 1972, *The Kissinger Transcripts* (New York: New Press, W.W. Norton, 1999), pp. 59–65

11.3   Lin Biao's downfall

11.3a   Official communiqué on the death of Lin Biao

Communiqué of the Central Committee of the Chinese Communist Party concerning Lin Biao's '12 September' anti-Party incident, 18 September 1971. Top-secret document

On 12 September, when Chairman Mao was making an inspection tour in the south, Lin Biao took advantage of the opportunity and attempted to blow up the train in which Chairman Mao was riding near Shanghai in order to accomplish his objective of assassinating Chairman Mao. When the plot failed and was exposed, Lin Biao hurriedly left Peking on the afternoon of 12 September and boarded a British-made Trident jet military transport, with the intention of surrendering to the enemy and betraying his own country. After crossing the national border, his plane crashed near Undur Khan in Mongolia. Lin Biao, Ye Qun [his wife], Lin Liguo [his son], and the pilot were all burned to death.

Lin Biao, by his act of surrendering to the enemy and betraying his own country, invited his own destruction. Yet his death could not redeem his crime, and his notoriety will last for ten thousand years to come. What has been most intolerable is that Lin Biao stole a huge quantity of secret documents and foreign currencies and shot and wounded one of his long-time bodyguards. Lin Biao's sworn followers, Yu Xinye, Zhou Yuzhi, and Chen Liyun, took off separately in two military helicopters in an attempt to escape from the country. They were intercepted by the Air Force units of the Peking Region. Yu Xinye and Zhou Yuzhi shot the pilots to death and then committed suicide. Chen Liyun put up a fight and was seriously wounded. All the documents they had attempted to take with them aboard the two aircraft were recovered.

Lin (Toutou), daughter of Lin Biao, placed national interest above filial piety by refusing to escape with Lin Biao, and she reported the situation to the Premier in time, which led to the foiling of her father's monstrous conspiracy. Lin (Toutou) has thus performed a great service to the Party and the state and helped the Party Central Committee smash a serious counter-revolutionary coup d'etat.

Source: Official Communiqué on the Death of Lin Biao, 18 September 1971, *Issues and Studies*, No. 6, March 1974

11.3b What happened to Lin Biao

Jin Qui, *The Culture of Power,* 1999

Two final questions about the Lin Biao incident remain unanswered: Why did the plane eventually turn north toward the Soviet Union? And how did the plane crash? Before Lin's family left Building No. 96 for the airport, Ye Qun and Lin Liguo had mentioned going to Dalian, Guangzhou, and even Hong Kong, but no one had heard them say a word about going to the Soviet Union. People sympathetic to Lin Biao have indulged in much speculation. Some believe that the reason Lin's plane turned northward had much to do with Zhou's order to ground all planes, for the order effectively closed all airports. It was thus impossible for the plane to land in China, even if the pilot had intended to return to Shanhaiguan airport. According to two Air Force officers I interviewed, however, Captain Pan made no attempt to contact an airport. The pilot shut off the communication system after the plane took off.

As to the second question, we can rule out the possibility that the plane was shot down by Chinese missiles. No proof has ever been found that Zhou or anyone else issued an order to shoot it down. In his speech to the leading officials of the Guangzhou Military Region, Zhou Enlai himself made the following explanation:

> I will say, once again, that I gave no order to shoot down Lin Biao's plane. It exploded during its forced landing. It was a self-destruction. Consider that Lin was Vice-Chairman of the CCP Central Committee, but I am only a member of the Executive Committee. In the armed forces, he was Vice-Commander, but I have no official position. How could I order the troops to shoot down [the plane of] the Vice-Chairman of the CCP Central Committee and the Vice-Commander of the Armed Forces? And he was the designated successor, which had been made clear by the Party regulation adopted by the Ninth Party Congress! What could I have said to the whole Party, the whole country, and the whole population if I had ordered the troops to shoot him down?! ...
>
> Of course, I reported to the Chairman when Lin Biao's plane was on its way abroad. This is the basic principle that a Party member should observe! But the Chairman said that rain would fall and widows would remarry. Let him go if he wanted to go. If the Chairman could be tolerant to Lin Biao, why should I, Zhou Enlai, stop him? The Chairman also said during his inspection tour to the south that [he would] still protect Lin Biao. If he could admit his mistakes, [the Chairman] would still keep him in the Politburo. If the Chairman could forgive Lin Biao, why should I put him to death?

Zhou's account is reasonable. The actual causes of the plane crash thus remain unknown. It is not clear whether the plane ran out of fuel, as the official documents claim, or the crash resulted from a mechanical problem or a fight inside the plane. Interestingly, the Chinese government awarded the title 'Revolutionary Martyr' to Pan Jingyin, the captain of the plane, several years after the crash. The award rehabilitated Pan and the other crew members, absolving them of any involvement in the 'plot'. But what about Lin Biao? Is it possible that someday he will be so honoured and absolved?

**Source: Jin Qui, *The Culture of Power*
(Stanford, California: Stanford University Press, 1999), pp. 194–5**

11.4 Official broadcast in Tiananmen Square, 5 April 1976

The government spokesman, Wu De, Party Secretary of Beijing, criticizes the demonstrators who are in mourning for Zhou Enlai. Deng Xiaoping is the target of this attack on rightists.

In the past few days, while we were studying our great leader Chairman Mao's important instructions, counterattacking the right deviationist attempt to reverse correct verdicts, and grasping revolution and promoting production, a handful of bad elements out of ulterior motives made use of the ching ming festival deliberately to create a political incident, directing their spearhead at Chairman Mao and the Party Central Committee in a vain attempt to change the general orientation of the struggle to criticize the unrepentant capitalist-roader Teng Hsiao-ping's revisionist line and beat back the right deviationist attempt. We must see clearly the reactionary nature of this political incident, expose the schemes and intrigues of the bad elements, heighten our revolutionary vigilance, and avoid being taken in.

Revolutionary masses and cadres of the Municipality must take class struggle as the key link, act immediately, and by concrete action defend Chairman Mao, defend the Party Central Committee, Chairman Mao's proletarian revolutionary line, and the great capital of our socialist motherland, deal resolute blows at counter-revolutionary sabotage, and further strengthen and consolidate the dictatorship of the proletariat and develop the excellent situation. Let us rally round the Party Central Committee headed by Chairman Mao and win still greater victories!

Today, there are bad elements carrying out disruption and disturbances and engaging in counter-revolutionary sabotage at Tienanmen Square. Revolutionary masses must leave the square at once and not be duped by them.

Source: Official Broadcast in Tiananmen Square, Mayor of Beijing, 5 April 1976,
***Survey of the China Mainland Press*, May 1976, p. 10**

11.5 What is wrong with being Red and expert? 7 November 1977

From *Red Flag*

During the Cultural Revolution it was asserted that revolutionary zeal transcended technical expertise. This article attempts to resolve the dichotomy of 'Red versus expert.' It also blames the Gang of Four for maligning Deng Xiaoping, who was accused of denigrating the Maoist-inspired 'barefoot doctors' who offered simple health care to the peasants.

In the sinister article by 'Miao Yu,' the Gang of Four, self-styled 'protectors' of new socialist things, raised the issue 'the role of barefoot doctors and the cooperative medical service cannot be negated,' vigorously criticizing the 'idea of shoes' for barefoot doctors they themselves had put forward, and accusing those advocating the need for barefoot doctors continuously to raise their level of 'creating public opinion for suppressing this new thing.'

Barefoot doctors, like the cooperative medical service, are a new socialist thing that has gradually developed under the guidance of Chairman Mao's revolutionary line. This is an unprecedented act of drawing on collective strength of the poor and lower-middle peasants to fight disease. In supporting this new thing, we must first adhere to the direction pointed out by Chairman Mao, seek its continuous consolidation and improvement, and stimulate its growth ...

In order to frame Comrade Teng Hsiao-ping, the Gang of Four and their flunkeys in the Ministry of Public Health openly spread through the sinister article by 'Miao Yu' the rumor about Comrade Teng Hsiao-ping's advocating barefoot doctors' 'wearing leather shoes' ...

In the name of criticizing 'viewing technical knowledge as one's private property', the Gang of Four in the sinister article by 'Miao Yu' vociferously cried: Advocating that medical and health workers and leading cadres of public health departments should 'bone up on professional matters' and 'study technical things' to become 'Red and expert' means 'negating the Party's basic line and peddling the idea of the dying out of class struggle' and 'launching a rabid attack against the proletariat on behalf of the bourgeoisie' ...

According to the logic of the Gang of Four and their flunkeys in the Ministry of Public Health, advocating medical and health workers' studying technique for the revolution to become Red and expert seems diametrically opposed to the matter of adhering to the Party's basic line and solving the principal contradictions in socialist society. This seemingly revolutionary but actually counter-revolutionary viewpoint is absurd theoretically and reactionary in practice ...

Redness and expertise, politics, and professional matters form a unity of opposites. We oppose those armchair politicians seeking to be 'Red but not expert' and also oppose those stray pragmatists seeking to be 'expert but not Red.' We emphasize the need to study and master technique for the revolution in order to become both Red and expert. Chairman Mao taught us: 'INTELLECTUALS MUST BE RED AND EXPERT AT THE SAME TIME.' In his brilliant work 'In Memory of Norman Bethune,' Chairman Mao called on us to acquire comrade Bethune's spirit of 'UTTER DEVOTION TO OTHERS WITHOUT ANY THOUGHT OF SELF' and 'CONSTANTLY IMPROVING HIS SKILL.' Comrade Bethune set us a good example in being Red and expert. Medical and health workers use medical and scientific skills to serve the people. It naturally follows that they should study technique, just as armed fighters must know how to handle their weapons ... Politics guides technique but is no substitute for technique. Medical skill is a science. With proletarian politics in command, so long as we study and train hard, we can master a skill and can go on making discoveries ...

**Source: 'Who is the One Suppressing the Growth of New Socialist Thinking?',
7 November 1977, *Red Flag*, No. 11, 1977, Foreign Broadcast Information Service,
Vol. 1, No. 231, 1 December 1977, PRC National Affairs, extracts from E. 16, 17, 18**

11.6 The 'Two Whatevers' do not accord with Marxism, 24 May 1977

Deng Xiaoping

The People's Daily had declared in February 1977: 'We resolutely defend whatever policies Chairman Mao formulated and unswervingly adhere to whatever instructions Chairman Mao has issued'. Those in the Party anxious to remain faithful to Mao's Cultural Revolution policies were dubbed the 'whateverists', as symbolized by Hua Guofeng.

A few days ago, when two leading comrades of the General Office of the Central Committee of the Party came to see me, I told them that the 'two whatevers' are unacceptable. If this principle were correct, there could be no justification for my rehabilitation, nor could there be any for the statement that the activities of the masses at Tiananmen Square in 1976 were

reasonable. We cannot mechanically apply what Comrade Mao Zedong said about a particular question to another question, what he said in a particular place to another place, what he
said at a particular time to another time, or what he said under particular circumstances to
other circumstances. Comrade Mao Zedong himself said repeatedly that some of his own
statements were wrong. He said that no one can avoid making mistakes in his work unless he
does none at all. He also said that Marx, Engels, Lenin and Stalin had all made mistakes –
otherwise why did they correct their own manuscripts time and time again? The reason they
made these revisions was that some of the views they originally expressed were not entirely
correct, perfect, or accurate. Comrade Mao Zedong said that he too had made mistakes and
that there had never been a person whose statements were all correct or who was always
absolutely right. He said that if one's work was rated as consisting 70 per cent of achievements and 30 per cent of mistakes, that would be quite all right, and that he himself would be
very happy and satisfied if future generations could give him this '70–30' rating after his death.
This is an important theoretical question, a question of whether or not we are adhering to
historical materialism. A thoroughgoing materialist should approach this question in the way
advocated by Comrade Mao Zedong. Neither Marx nor Engels put forward any 'whatever'
doctrine, nor did Lenin or Stalin, nor did Comrade Mao Zedong himself. I told the two
leading comrades of the Central Committee's General Office that, in my letter of April to the
Central Committee, I had proposed that 'from generation to generation, we should use
genuine Mao Zedong Thought taken as an integral whole in guiding our Party, our army, and
our people, so as to advance the cause of the Party and socialism in China and the cause of
the international Communist movement'.

> **Source: Deng Xiaoping, 'The "Two Whatevers" Do Not Accord with Marxism',**
> **24 May 1977, Deng Xiaoping, *Selected Works of Deng Xiaoping (1975–1982)*, Vol. 2**
> **(Beijing: Foreign Languages Press, 1984), pp. 51–2**

11.7 Deng Xiaoping on the four modernizations, 18 March 1978

Deng Xiaoping

We have waged a bitter struggle against the Gang of Four over the question of whether the
four modernizations are needed or not. The Gang made the senseless statement that 'the
day the four modernizations programme is realized will mark the day of capitalist restoration'. Their sabotage brought China's economy to the brink of collapse and led to a constant
widening of the gap between us and the countries with the most advanced science and technology. Did the Gang really want to build socialism and oppose the restoration of capitalism?
Not in the least. On the contrary, socialism sustained grave damage wherever their influence
was strongest. Their misdeeds, serving as a negative example, make us realize all the more
clearly that, even though we have a dictatorship of the proletariat, unless we modernize our
country, raise our scientific and technological level, develop our productive forces, and thus
strengthen our country and improve the material and cultural life of our people – unless we
do all this, our socialist political and economic system cannot be fully consolidated, and there
can be no sure guarantee for the country's security. The more our agriculture, industry,
national defence, and science and technology are modernized, the stronger we will be in the
struggle against forces that sabotage socialism, and the more our people will support the

socialist system. Only if we make our country a modern, powerful socialist state can we more effectively consolidate the socialist system and cope with foreign aggression and subversion; only then can we be reasonably certain of gradually creating the material conditions for the advance to our great goal of communism.

The key to the four modernizations is the modernization of science and technology. Without modern science and technology, it is impossible to build modern agriculture, modern industry, or modern national defence. Without the rapid development of science and technology, there can be no rapid development of the economy ...

Everyone who works, whether with his hands or with his brain, is part of the working people in a socialist society. With the advance of modern science and technology and with progress in the four modernizations, a great deal of heavy manual work will gradually be taken over by machines. Among workers directly engaged in production, manual labour will steadily decrease while mental labour will constantly increase. Moreover, there will be a growing demand for researchers and for scientists and technicians. The Gang of Four distorted the division of labour between mental and manual work in our society today, misrepresenting it as a class antagonism. Their aim was to attack and persecute intellectuals, undermine the alliance between the workers and peasants and the intellectuals, damage the productive forces, and sabotage our socialist revolution and construction.

Science and technology are part of the productive forces. Mental workers who serve socialism are part of the working people. A correct understanding of these two facts is essential to the rapid development of our scientific enterprises ... For this is essential if we are to accomplish the four modernizations in the short space of 20-odd years and bring about a gigantic growth in our productive forces.

> Source: Deng Xiaoping, 'On the Four Modernizations', 18 March 1978,
> Selected Works of Deng Xiaoping (1975–1982), Vol. 2
> (Beijing: Foreign Languages Press, 1984), pp. 102–5

11.8 Shift to socialist modernization. Communiqué of the third plenary session of the 11th Central Committee of the Communist Party of China, 22 December 1978

The plenary session decided that, since the work of the Central Committee following its second plenary session had proceeded smoothly and the large-scale nationwide mass movement to expose and criticize Lin Piao and the Gang of Four had in the main been completed victoriously, the stress of the Party's work should shift to socialist modernization as of 1979. The plenary session discussed the international situation and the handling of foreign affairs, reaching the view that the foreign policy of the Party and the government was correct and successful. The plenary session also discussed the question of how to speed the growth of agricultural production and arrangements for the national economic plans for 1979 and 1980 and adopted relevant documents in principle. The plenary session examined and solved a number of important questions left over from history and the question of the contribution and faults, the correctness and incorrectness of some important leaders. In order to meet the needs of socialist modernization, the plenary session decided to strengthen democracy in Party life and in the political life of the state, put forward in explicit terms the Party's ideological line, strengthen the Party's leading organs, and set up a Central Commission for Inspecting Discipline ...

There is still in our country today a small handful of counter-revolutionary elements and criminals who hate our socialist modernization and try to undermine it. We must not relax our class struggle against them, nor can we weaken the dictatorship of the proletariat. But as Comrade Mao Tse-tung pointed out, the large-scale turbulent class struggles of a mass character have in the main come to an end. Class struggle in socialist society should be carried out on the principle of strictly differentiating the two different types of contradiction and correctly handling them in accordance with the procedures prescribed by the Constitution and the law. It is impermissible to confuse the two different types of contradiction and damage the political stability and unity required for socialist modernization ...

The session points out that one of the serious shortcomings in the structure of economic management in our country is the overconcentration of authority, and it is necessary boldly to shift it under guidance from the leadership to lower levels so that the local authorities and industrial and agricultural enterprises will have greater power of decision in management under the guidance of unified state planning; big efforts should be made to simplify bodies at various levels charged with economic administration and transfer most of their functions to such enterprises as specialized companies or complexes ...

The plenary session holds that the whole Party should concentrate its main energy and efforts on advancing agriculture as fast as possible because agriculture, the foundation of the national economy, has been seriously damaged in recent years and remains very weak on the whole. The rapid development of the national economy as a whole and the steady improvement in the living standards of the people of the whole country depend on the vigorous restoration and speeding up of farm production, on resolutely and fully implementing the policy of simultaneous development of farming, forestry, animal husbandry, side-occupations, and fisheries ... Taking this as the guideline, the plenary session set forth a series of policies and economic measures aimed at raising present agricultural production. The most important are as follows: the right of ownership by the people's communes, production brigades, and production teams and their power of decision must be protected effectively by the laws of the state; it is not permitted to commandeer the manpower, funds, products, and material of any production team; the economic organizations at various levels of the people's commune must conscientiously implement the socialist principle of 'to each according to his work', work out payment in accordance with the amount and quality of work done, and overcome equalitarianism; small plots of land for private use by commune members, their domestic side-occupations, and village fairs are necessary adjuncts of the socialist economy, and must not be interfered with; the people's communes must resolutely implement the system of three levels of ownership with the production team as the basic accounting unit, and this should remain unchanged ...

The session held a serious discussion on the question of democracy and the legal system. It holds that socialist modernization requires centralized leadership and strict implementation of various rules and regulations and observance of labour discipline. Bourgeois factionalism and anarchism must be firmly opposed. But the correct concentration of ideas is possible only when there is full democracy. Since for a period in the past democratic centralism was not carried out in the true sense, centralism being divorced from democracy and there being too little democracy, it is necessary to lay particular emphasis on democracy at present, and on the dialectical relationship between democracy and centralism, so as to make the mass line the foundation of the Party's centralized leadership and the effective direction of the organizations of production. In ideological and political life among the ranks of the people only democracy is permissible and not suppression or persecution ... The constitutional rights of citizens must be resolutely protected and no one has the right to infringe upon them.

In order to safeguard people's democracy, it is imperative to strengthen the socialist legal system so that democracy is systematized and written into law in such a way as to ensure the stability, continuity, and full authority of this democratic system and these laws ...

The session highly evaluated the discussion of whether practice is the sole criterion for testing truth, noting that this is of far-reaching historic significance in encouraging comrades of the whole Party and the people of the whole country to emancipate their thinking and follow the correct ideological line. For a party, a country, or a nation, if everything had to be done according to books and thinking became ossified, progress would become impossible, life itself would stop and the Party and country would perish.

> **Source: Extract from Communiqué of the Third Plenary Session of 11th Central Committee of the CCP, 22 December 1978,** *Peking Review*, **No. 52, 29 December 1978, pp. 6–7, 11, 15**

11.9 Chairman Hua gives an interview to Felix Greene, author and filmmaker, October 1979

Q: Many people in the West think that many of Chairman Mao's ideas are being quite discarded. What would you say about this?

A: Some people in the West say that we are 'discarding' many of Chairman Mao's ideas. And I know that some even say we are engaged in 'de-Maoification'. This is not at all the case. Even a cursory review of how things stand in China will show exactly the opposite. Lin Biao and the Gang of Four wilfully distorted and tampered with Marxism–Leninism and Mao Zedong Thought. They alleged that Chairman Mao had developed Marxism–Leninism to the highest peak and that one sentence of his had the strength of ten thousand sentences. They claimed that there was a bourgeois class within the Communist Party, that veteran cadres were bourgeois revolutionaries and had or would inevitably become capitalist-roaders. We launched a nationwide campaign to criticize and repudiate these utterly idealistic fallacies of theirs and called on the people to learn and master Marxism–Leninism and Mao Zedong Thought in a comprehensive and faithful way. We did this to clarify the issues and thus defend and develop this system of thought. Our current national discussion on the question of the sole criterion of truth is exactly what Comrade Mao Zedong advocated all along, namely to proceed in all cases from reality, to seek truth from facts, and to integrate theory with practice. These are all basic tenets of our ideology.

Q: People in the West have noticed that great emphasis is now being placed on examinations for the young people, and they think that, by pushing the brighter pupils ahead, a new kind of – let's call it – intellectual elite may develop. Do you think this is a danger?

A: Some people had the misunderstanding that an important element of the revolution in education was opposition to examinations. Examinations are an acceptable means to help students and stimulate them in their studies. Comrade Mao Zedong was never against examination as such. He was only against such uncalled-for methods of examination as deliberately trying to baffle students or take them by surprise. The Gang of Four, however, considered it a 'heroic act' to turn in a blank paper at examinations and made much publicity about it. They urged young people against reading books or pursuing their studies. Students didn't learn much at school, their quality dropped drastically, and there is consequently a lack of trained young people for work in various fields. In the last two years, we have reinstituted correct educational methods, including that of examinations … It will have a significant bearing on our effort to raise the level of general knowledge and scientific knowhow of all our people in the drive for achieving the four modernizations.

As to the emergence of an intellectual elite, this is something to watch out for. I don't think that letting diligent and brilliant students pursue their studies will result in the emergence of an intellectual elite. An elite only emerges in certain social systems with their corresponding educational systems. Our drive for socialist modernization requires that we do our best to ensure that talented people get training and put their talents to the best use, to the benefit of our country and our society …

We operate a wide variety of spare-time education, including workers' universities, spare-time universities, spare-time schools, etc., all of which are providing the children of working people and the industrial and agricultural workers themselves with ever greater educational opportunities. I believe that this is a practicable way to prevent the monopoly of knowledge by the few. A more important factor, of course, is the fact that our socialist system itself and the policies and corresponding measures that we formulate in conformity with socialist principles will enable us to avoid the emergence of an intellectual elite …

Q: Don't you think that 'modernization' might lead to a kind of 'Westernization' of China, with all the problems involved? For example, machines replace workers – so won't this only increase your problem of unemployment?

A: I think you may have noticed that China's modernization programme rests on two premises. The first is to achieve modernization on the foundation of a socialist system. The second is that it must be carried out in the light of conditions in China and done in a Chinese way.

Socialism and modernization are closely linked and not at all contradictory. There are no grounds whatever for thinking that it will inevitably lead to 'Westernization' or bring us back to capitalism. Our accepting foreign investments and increasing economic and cultural exchanges with other countries may, of course, be accompanied by the spread of some Western influences. This is something to watch out for. We believe that our people can tell the good from the bad and will resist and overcome bad influences.

Source: Chairman Hua interviewed by Felix Greene, October 1979,
Beijing Review, **No. 42, 19 October 1979, pp. 10–12**

11.10 Resolution on certain questions in the history of our Party since the founding of the People's Republic of China, 27 June 1981

CCP Central Committee

This resolution was required reading for 39 million Party members.

The Cultural Revolution which lasted from May 1966 to October 1976 was responsible for the most severe setback and the heaviest losses suffered by the Party, the state, and the people since the founding of the People's Republic. It was initiated and led by Comrade Mao Zedong. His principal theses were that many representatives of the bourgeoisie and counter-revolutionary revisionists had sneaked into the Party, the government, the army, and cultural circles, and leadership in a fairly large majority of organizations and departments was no longer in the hands of Marxists and the people …

[These theses] were incorporated into a general theory – the 'theory of continued revolution under the dictatorship of the proletariat' – which then took on a specific meaning. These erroneous 'Left' theses, upon which Comrade Mao Zedong based himself in initiating the Cultural Revolution, were obviously inconsistent with the system of Mao Zedong Thought, which is the integration of the universal principles of Marxism–Leninism with the concrete practice of the Chinese revolution ...

The history of the Cultural Revolution has proved that Comrade Mao Zedong's principal theses for initiating this revolution conformed neither to Marxism–Leninism nor to Chinese reality ... The Cultural Revolution was defined as a struggle against the revisionist line or the capitalist road. There were no grounds at all for this definition. It led to the confusing of right and wrong on a series of important theories and policies. Many things denounced as revisionist or capitalist during the Cultural Revolution were actually Marxist and socialist principles, many of which had been set forth or supported by Comrade Mao Zedong himself ...

The confusing of right and wrong inevitably led to confusing the people with the enemy. The 'capitalist-roaders' overthrown in the Cultural Revolution were leading cadres of Party and government organizations at all levels, who formed the core force of the socialist cause. The so-called bourgeois headquarters inside the Party headed by Liu Shaoqi and Deng Xiaoping simply did not exist. Irrefutable facts have proved that labeling Comrade Liu Shaoqi a 'renegade, hidden traitor, and scab' was nothing but a frame-up by Lin Biao, Jiang Qing, and their followers ...

Chief responsibility for the grave 'Left' error of the Cultural Revolution, an error comprehensive in magnitude and protracted in duration, does indeed lie with Comrade Mao Zedong. But after all it was the error of a great proletarian revolutionary. Comrade Mao Zedong paid constant attention to overcoming shortcomings in the life of the Party and state. In his later years, however, far from making a correct analysis of many problems, he confused right and wrong and the people with the enemy during the Cultural Revolution. While making serious mistakes, he repeatedly urged the whole Party to study the works of Marx, Engels, and Lenin conscientiously and imagined that his theory and practice were Marxist and that they were essential for the consolidation of the dictatorship of the proletariat. Herein lies his tragedy. While persisting in the comprehensive error of the Cultural Revolution, he checked and rectified some of its specific mistakes, protected some leading Party cadres and non-Party public figures, and enabled some leading Party cadres to return to important leading posts. He led the struggle to smash the counter-revolutionary Lin Biao clique. He made major criticisms and exposures of Jiang Qing, Zhang Chunqiao, and others, frustrating their sinister ambition to seize supreme leadership. All this was crucial to the subsequent and relatively painless overthrow of the Gang of Four by our Party ...

Most of our Party cadres, whether they were wrongly dismissed or remained at their posts, whether they were rehabilitated early or late, are loyal to the Party and people and steadfast in their belief in the cause of socialism and communism. Most of the intellectuals, model workers, patriotic democrats, patriotic overseas Chinese and cadres, and masses of all strata and all nationalities who had been wronged and persecuted did not waver in their love for the motherland and in their support for the Party and socialism. Party and state leaders such as Comrades Liu Shaoqi, Peng Dehuai, He Long, and Tao Zhu and all other Party and non-Party comrades who were persecuted to death in the Cultural Revolution will live forever in the memories of the Chinese people. It was through the joint struggles waged by the entire Party and the masses of workers, peasants, PLA officers and men, intellectuals, educated youth, and cadres that the havoc wrought by the Cultural Revolution was somewhat mitigated. Some progress was made in our economy despite tremendous losses. Grain output increased relatively steadily. Significant achievements were scored in industry, communications, and capital construction and in science and technology. New railways were built, and the Changjiang River Bridge at Nanjing was completed; a number of large enterprises using advanced technology went into operation; hydrogen bomb tests were successfully undertaken and man-made satellites successfully launched and retrieved; and new hybrid strains of long-grained rice were developed and popularized. Despite the domestic turmoil, the People's Liberation Army bravely defended the security of the motherland. And new prospects were opened up in the sphere of foreign affairs. Needless to say, none of these successes can be attributed in any way to the Cultural Revolution, without which we would have scored far greater achievements for our cause.

> Source: 'Resolutions on Certain Questions in the History of Our Party Since the
> Foundation of the People's Republic of China', 27 June 1981,
> *Beijing Review*, No. 27, 4 July 1981, pp. 20–6

11.11 The verdict of the trial of the Gang of Four, 25 January 1981

PREFACE BY FEI XIAOTONG, DIRECTOR OF THE INSTITUTE OF SOCIOLOGY, CHINESE ACADEMY OF SOCIAL SCIENCES

Let me say first that the trial introduced several new features to Chinese law. The legal procedures established will be of long-term significance. One salient feature of this major trial was the clear separation of what was legally criminal from what was political.

The case before us was closely tied to a major political issue, the Cultural Revolution ...

... Beginning in 1966, during the Cultural Revolution, when nothing was allowed to remain intact, the rule of law was also demolished and lawlessness prevailed. For example, Chairman of the People's Republic Liu Shaoqi, elected by the whole people, was publicly humiliated and persecuted, and ruthlessly 'struggled against' with the active connivance of Jiang Qing and her cohorts. His home was violated and sacked and he was physically manhandled and violently abused and reviled. This, one must remember, took place despite the Constitution of 1954 specifically guaranteeing that the freedom of the person was inviolable and the homes of the citizens of the People's Republic of China were also inviolable. His was not the only case. During those ten years of the Cultural Revolution the Constitution was ignored and the country's laws and decrees were blithely discarded and people were detained and tortured and their homes sacked.

The years of lawlessness ended with the arrest of the Gang of Four in 1976, and the whole nation began, sore at heart, quietly to review the past, firmly determined never to let such a tragedy happen again. It was recognized that socialist legality must prevail. In 1979 the National People's Congress enacted a series of important laws, including the Criminal Law of the People's Republic of China and the Law of Criminal Procedure. These came into force in 1980. Prior to this there was a nationwide movement to familiarize the people with the rule of law and impress on all that everyone is equal before the law.

This being so, the Lin Biao and Jiang Qing cliques were also charged for crimes according to the law, although everyone in China already knew that they were guilty of many heinous crimes. As a member of the panel of judges I know that, from the very start of the proceedings, it was particularly stressed that facts were the basis and the law was the sole criterion. This is a set principle not to be affected by feelings or other factors.

The court investigated and determined according to the law the criminal liability of the principal members of the two cliques and duly meted out punishment. At the same time the trial provided the people of the country with a lesson, vivid and profound, on the rule of law.

Because of the limited number of seats in the public gallery, only some 1,200 people could attend the two tribunals at a time. These representatives of the public came from all over the country and from every circle and every stratum, and new groups came on different days. The newspapers gave the trial extensive coverage. Some articles were quite long. The television coverage was quite extensive too. Sometimes it ran over an hour. Radio coverage was the widest, reaching a much greater public everywhere. Even those living in the most remote hamlet could follow the trial closely. The trial was followed with great interest by the public and no doubt has had a tremendous impact in a country lacking in a tradition of rule by law. More often than not, people's knowledge of trials in history was confined to what they had seen in old operas or had read in stories handed down the centuries, where the plaintiff had to kneel before the magistrates, and criminals were cangued [pilloried] and chained and so on. To the younger generation brought up during the Cultural Revolution on a diet of kangaroo courts, the trial had added significance. It showed that ransacking homes, beating up people, publicly humiliating people, making unfounded accusations, and persecuting people were not 'normal' nor 'revolutionary action' as they had once been taught.

The recent trial allowed the masses of people to see for themselves what was meant by the rule of law and how trials are conducted. In China there is an old saying that 'regardless of his social status, whether a prince or a commoner, a criminal is a criminal'. This, in feudal society, was more a pious wish than a fact. But today people have seen this take place. No matter who he is or what high position he holds, he must be subjected to the rule of law once he violates it. Jiang Qing and other high and mighty were charged and tried according to law for crimes they had committed …

From a historic point of view, I see the trial as marking the formal ending to a very unfortunate period in the history of socialist China. When the Gang of Four was demolished in October 1976, the decade of chaos was swiftly terminated too. But the trial and sentencing of the accused must be seen as the formal finale to that period. In its wake, a new period has appeared, a period marked by stability and unity, by democracy and the rule of law, a period in which the nation works together heart and soul for the realization of socialist modernization. We are moving forward, we are seeking a way, to building up our country of one billion people into a beautiful society. In a sense, the trial was a milestone and I am honoured to have had the opportunity to serve in this historic trial.

SUMMARY OF THE STATEMENT BY THE CHIEF DEFENDANT, JIANG QING

Jiang Qing chose to defend herself instead of entrusting lawyers with her defence and spoke for nearly two hours on her own behalf. Unable to rebut the overwhelming evidence adduced by the prosecution, she shrugged off the charges against her as 'negligible issues aimed at defaming me', an attempt 'to pick a bone out of an egg'.

She argued that she had done everything during the Cultural Revolution 'on behalf of Chairman Mao Zedong' or 'according to his instructions'. Again and again she repeated these assertions of hers: 'Arresting me and bringing me to trial is a defamation of Chairman Mao

Zedong', 'Defaming Chairman Mao Zedong through defaming me', 'I have implemented and defended Chairman Mao's proletarian revolutionary line'. She shrilled: 'During the war I was the only woman comrade who stayed beside Chairman Mao at the front; where were you *hiding yourselves* then?' – a statement that made it difficult for those in the public gallery to suppress their laughter – generals who fought hundreds of battles, pioneers in establishing revolutionary bases, underground workers operating at all hazards in the KMT-controlled or Japanese-occupied areas.

Jian Qing declared: 'Trying me amounts to smearing hundreds of millions of people'. It 'amounts to denigrating the proletarian cultural revolution in which hundreds of millions took part'. It amounts to 'preventing the red guards and little red guards in the Cultural Revolution from holding up their heads'. She shrieked: 'Now I'm doing my best for the defence of the proletarian cultural revolution'. She attacked the redressing of wrongs done to innocent people after the fall of the Gang of Four as 'actually a reversal of the correct verdict passed on them'.

She shouted at the bench: 'Like a monk under an umbrella, I am without law and without heaven'. [*he shang da san, wu fa wu tian*; since the Buddhist monk is bald and, being under an umbrella, can't see the sky, he is 'hairless and skyless', a pun meaning 'without law and without heaven' – Ed.])

COURT JUDGEMENT

After lasting a total of 67 days, the trial of the Lin Biao and Jiang Qing counter-revolutionary cliques concluded on 25 January 1981. The judgement on Jiang Qing and nine other defendants was announced at the Special Court:

*   Jiang Qing was sentenced to death with a two-year reprieve and permanent deprivation of political rights;
*   Zhang Chunqiao was sentenced to death with a two-year reprieve and permanent deprivation of political rights;
*   Yao Wenyuan: 20 years imprisonment and deprivation of political rights for five years;
*   Wang Hongwen: life imprisonment and permanent deprivation of political rights;
*   Chen Boda: 18 years imprisonment and deprivation of political rights for five years;

[The five defendants of the Lin Biao clique were sentenced to between eighteen and sixteen years imprisonment and deprivation of political rights for five years.]

Source: *A Great Trial in Chinese History*
(Beijing: New World Press, 1981), pp. 1, 9–10, 102

12

Modernization in the 1980s

From about 1980 until his death in 1997, Deng Xiaoping was recognized as China's 'paramount leader'. Taking up Zhou Enlai's 'four modernizations', he masterminded China's remarkable economic growth with a series of revolutionary processes that have transformed agriculture and industry. He was challenged as early as 1978 to recognize a 'fifth modernization' (democracy). However, the Communist Party has firmly refused to consider the introduction of Western concepts of a constitution with a genuine multiparty system. While it is questionable whether the population at large is seriously worried about such matters, the concerns of some intellectuals and students have engaged the world's attention.

The household responsibility system by which the peasants, now known as farmers, took charge of food production as well as diverse activities in the countryside led to a remarkable increase in productivity. Parallel reforms in industry involved a measure of decentralization. There was some overall increase in production: smaller enterprises requiring less capital were relatively more profitable. 100,000 private businesses were registered in 1978, 6 million in 1983 and 17 million in 1985. Determined to attract foreign capital and new technology, the government set up 'special economic zones' beginning in 1979 which have transformed the coastal cities and their environments.

As some individuals and regions benefited more than others, there were questions about the social and political implications of the reformed system – hence the mantra of building socialism with Chinese characteristics. Aware that 'opening the windows would let in the flies', the government sought to repel 'spiritual pollution' (which included pornography and individualistic literary values) and to combat flagrant corruption.

With more and more students travelling and with access to worldwide information technology there was a growing challenge to the conservatives in the Communist Party. This was manifested during the 1980s in a recurring pattern of relaxation and control when the toleration of intellectual freedom was perceived to overstep the mark and resulted in a conservative backlash. Among the most outspoken critics of the regime was well-known astrophysicist Fang Lizhi. In November 1986 he argued that China was backward in all respects and needed complete modernization. When enthusiastic students responded with demonstrations and were inspired to burn the *Beijing Daily* on 5 January 1987, they were strongly rebuked by Deng Xiaoping. Bourgeois democracy was a gimmick. China had no use for constitutional separation of powers as in the West. Thus, the government adopted sternly avuncular measures. Not until 1989 did a new cycle of protest break out with cataclysmic effect in Tiananmen Square.

With the resignation of Hua Guofeng in June 1981, Hu Yaobang had succeeded to the head of the Party (as Party Secretary since the chairmanship ceased with Hua). Together with Premier Zhao Ziyang, Hu was to preside effectively during a time of great change. As a proponent of reforms he was an enthusiast for Westernization and even went so far as to suggest that chopsticks should be replaced by knives and forks. It was his misfortune, being held responsible for the 1986 student demonstrations, to be dismissed as General Secretary in January 1987 (while retaining a place on the Politburo). Zhao Ziyang became (Acting) General Secretary, Li Peng became Premier.

The year 1989 was not only the fortieth anniversary of Communist China, it was also the seventieth anniversary of 4 May 1919. To mark the occasion, Fang Lizhi sent an open letter to Deng Xiaoping proposing an amnesty for political prisoners including dissident Wei Jingsheng be declared. Then, on 8 April, Hu Yaobang, having made a speech to an enlarged meeting of the Politburo, calling for the Party to increase its support for education, had a heart attack and died a week later. His death provided the occasion for a popular display of political grief akin to the 1976 incident in memory of Zhou Enlai. At first hundreds, then, within a few days, tens of thousands of students marched to Tiananmen Square. The student protest movement at Beijing University set out its demands which it addressed to the NPC Standing Committee. On 22 April, the day of official mourning for Hu Yaobang, the Politburo decided not to give way to student demands. The following day, Zhao Ziyang left on a planned visit to North Korea while Premier Li Peng convened the Standing Committee in order to take strong action against a 'planned conspiracy, a riot, whose real nature was fundamentally to negate the leadership of the Communist Party'.

Mounting protest across the country, and a student hunger strike, coincided with the visit of Mikhail Gorbachev, General Secretary of the Soviet Union, whose planned visit to the Great Hall of the People was barred by protesters. On 18 May the Politburo met with Deng and the 'Elders' to impose martial law.

12.1a Wei Jingsheng on the fifth modernization

Wei Jingsheng, a 'big-character' poster that was put up on Beijing's Democracy Wall,
5 December 1978

After the arrest of the Gang of Four, the people eagerly hoped that Vice Chairman Deng Xiaoping, who might possibly 'restore capitalism,' would rise up again like a magnificent banner. Finally, he did regain his position in the central leadership. How excited the people felt! How inspired they were! But alas, the old political system so despised by the people remains unchanged, and the democracy and freedom they longed for has not even been mentioned ...

Why democracy?

People have discussed this question for centuries. And now those who voice their opinions at Democracy Wall have carried out a thorough analysis and shown just how much better democracy is than autocracy.

'People are the masters of history.' Is this fact or merely empty talk? It is both fact and empty talk. It is fact that without the effort and participation of the people there can be no history.

The people should have democracy. When they call for democracy they are demanding nothing more than that which is inherently theirs. Whoever refuses to return democracy to them is a shameless thief more despicable than any capitalist who robs the workers of the wealth earned with their own sweat and blood.

Do the people have democracy now? No! Don't the people want to be the masters of their own destiny? Of course they do! That is precisely why the Communist Party defeated the Nationalists. But what became of all their promises once victory was achieved? Once they began championing a dictatorship, even the 'democracy' still enjoyed by a tenth of a millionth of the population was displaced by the individual dictatorship of the 'great leader' ...

I would like to ask everyone: What do we want modernization for? ... Ordinary people ... want simply to have the chance to enjoy a happy life, or at least one that is no less than what people enjoy in other countries. A prosperity that all members of society can enjoy equally will only be achieved by raising the level of social productivity. This is quite obvious, but some people have completely overlooked one important point: when social productivity increases, will the people be able to enjoy prosperous lives? The problems of allocation, distribution, and exploitation still remain ...

What is democracy? True democracy means placing all power in the hands of the working people. Are working people unable to manage state power? Yugoslavia has taken this route and proven to us that people have no need for dictators, whether big or small; they can take care of things much better themselves.

What is true democracy? It is when the people, acting on their own will, have the right to choose representatives to manage affairs on the people's behalf and in accordance with the will and interests of the people. This alone can be called democracy. Furthermore, the people must have the power to replace these representatives at any time in order to keep them from abusing their powers to oppress the people. Is this actually possible? The citizens of Europe and the United States enjoy precisely this kind of democracy and can run people like Nixon, de Gaulle, and Tanaka out of office when they wish and can even reinstate them if they so desire. No one can interfere with their democratic rights. In China, however, if a person even comments on the 'great helmsman' or the 'Great Man peerless in history,' Mao Zedong, who is already dead, the mighty prison gates and all kinds of unimaginable misfortunes await him. If we compare the socialist system of 'centralized democracy' with the 'exploiting class democracy' of capitalism, the difference is as clear as night and day.

Will the country sink into chaos and anarchy if the people achieve democracy? On the contrary, have not the scandals exposed in the newspapers recently shown that it is precisely on account of an absence of democracy that the dictators, large and small, have caused chaos and anarchy ...

Those who worry that democracy will lead to anarchy and chaos are just like those who, following the overthrow of the Qing dynasty, worried that, without an emperor, the country would fall into chaos. Their recommendation was: Patiently suffer oppression! For without the weight of oppression, the roofs of your homes might fly off!

To such people, I would like to say, with all due respect: We want to be the masters of our own destiny. We need no gods or emperors and we don't believe in saviors of any kind. We want to be masters of our universe; we do not want to serve as mere tools of dictators with personal ambitions for carrying out modernization. We want to modernize the lives of the people. Democracy, freedom, and happiness for all are our sole objectives in carrying out modernization. Without this 'Fifth Modernization,' all other modernizations are nothing but a new promise.

**Source: Wei Jingsheng, *The Courage to Stand Alone*
(Harmondsworth: Penguin, 1998), pp. 201–9**

12.1b Wei Jingsheng sentenced

From *Beijing Review*, 26 October 1979

The Intermediate People's Court of Beijing sentenced Wei Jingsheng to 15 years imprisonment at a public trial on 16 October [for passing] on military intelligence to a foreigner and carrying out counter-revolutionary agitation. The court also ruled that Wei would be deprived of political rights for another three years after serving his sentence.

Wei Jingsheng, 29, was a worker at the Beijing Public Parks Service Department before he was arrested last March. He joined the army in 1969 and was demobilized in 1973.

Shortly after China launched the self-defensive counterattack last February to defend its frontier regions against Vietnamese aggression, Wei supplied a foreigner with military intelligence, including the names of the commanders, the number of Chinese troops, the developments of the fighting at the front, and the number of casualties. During the period between December 1978 and March 1979, Wei wrote and distributed articles slandering Marxism–Leninism–Mao Zedong Thought and agitated for the overthrow of the dictatorship of the proletariat and the socialist system and the seizure of state power. Some of these articles were posted up on the walls in downtown Beijing and some were published in the journal *Explorations*, of which he was the chief editor. The journal was posted, distributed, and sold in Beijing and Tianjin.

The trial was attended by 400 people from various walks of life …

While making investigations, the court produced part of the evidence that proved him guilty of the crime. Two witnesses, Liu Jingsheng (a worker at the Beijing No. 4 People's Bus Depot) and Yang Guang (a second-year student of the Beijing University of Engineering, now in custody) gave testimony. Both had helped the accused edit, sell, and distribute *Explorations*. In the face of irrefutable evidence, Wei Jingsheng admitted the facts concerning the commission of the crimes as stated in the indictment.

Before the trial, Wei was told that he could have a lawyer to defend his case. But Wei refused to have a lawyer and conducted his own defence at the trial. Citing conclusive evidence and relevant laws, the prosecutor refuted all of Wei's arguments.

The Constitution guarantees the people democratic rights. The people have the right to criticize the government's work and the government welcomes such criticism and is ready to make self-criticisms. But it will not tolerate anyone carrying out activities, under the cloak of 'democracy' and 'human rights,' aiming at overthrowing the dictatorship of the proletariat and the socialist system.

Source: Wei Jingsheng Sentenced, *Beijing Review*, No. 43, 26 October 1979, pp. 6–7

12.2a The household responsibility system and market reforms

E. J. Perry and Mark Selden, 2000

The centrepiece of post-Mao reform nevertheless was agricultural decollectivization and market opening, which proceeded by fits and starts between 1978 and 1982. Although land ownership has remained in collective hands to this day, individual households were permitted to sign contracts that afforded them effective control over the management, output, and marketing of agricultural production in exchange for payments in the form of crops and labor to the village, and taxes in kind to the state. China's 30 year experiment in collective farming was in essence repudiated in favor of a return to family farming, officially styled the Household Responsibility System (HRS). With pressures from below from villagers and some cadres to expand the scope of market, mobility, and household activity, and with increasing doubts at the center concerning the viability of collective agriculture, in just a few years virtually the entire countryside had dismantled collective agriculture in favor of some form of household contracting that restored the primacy of the family farm. In 1984, these contracts were deemed valid for 15 years; in 1993, they were extended to 30 years; and in 1998, President Jiang Zemin announced that contracts would remain in effect for at least an additional 30 years.

Alongside the HRS, the state-sanctioned free markets encouraged diversification of rural enterprises in the form of small-scale industry and handicrafts, relaxed restrictions on rural–urban migration, and substantially boosted state procurement prices for agricultural prod-ucts in an effort to jump-start the rural economy. In each of these instances, the state now responded positively to pressures from below for the expanded scope of household and market that had built throughout the era of antimarket collective agriculture. The immediate result of this policy package, which included far more than decollectivization, was a huge spurt in agricultural output and the first major gains in rural income since the start of the collective era a quarter-century earlier. As farmers regained control of their labor power and the state relaxed prohibitions on markets and sideline production, rural labor and capital swiftly flowed in new channels and villagers experienced new earning opportunities.

This did not constitute a complete break with the revolutionary era. Not only did land ownership continue to reside in collective hands, but there was also continuity in the mana-gerial role of collectives, notably in directing rural industry and sideline production. The household economy had in fact never completely disappeared in Mao's China as most fami-lies continued to cultivate individual plots of land. Hence, foundations for reform existed in embryonic form throughout the countryside.

Perhaps the most dynamic response to the new opportunities presented by reform was the growth of township and village enterprises (TVEs) which mushroomed across the countryside. Many of the TVEs had their roots in earlier commune and brigade industries, but in the reform era under relatively open market conditions – including access to interna-tional markets and capital and with the infusion of migrant labor – they injected unprece-dented dynamism into rural industry, notably in coastal and suburban regions. Over time, many of these collectively owned and operated enterprises have converted into share-holding companies (*gufen gongsi*) or private firms or joint ventures, including some with foreign investment.

Demand for labor mobility went hand in hand with pressures to relax the household registration (*hukou*) system that had segregated citizens by rigid categories designed to forestall rural-to-urban migration as well as to deter movement up the hierarchy of urban centers. Reform generally has allowed people the freedom to change their place of work and residence. But as 'outsiders' in the city or in richer agricultural areas, migrants face formidable official and unofficial restrictions in their new domicile and remain ineligible for many benefits enjoyed by those with legal urban registration. Despite the important contri-butions that migrant workers have made to China's economic growth, the state continues to view them as second-class citizens, a 'floating population,' and a potential source of unrest, and therefore denies them most of the benefits of urban registration. As their numbers soared into the range of fifty to one hundred million people, permanent urban residents also came to see the floaters as a source of crime and, increasingly, as a threat to their own jobs.

While economic and social transformations in much of the countryside were remarkably swift and far-reaching, urban industry proved more resistant to change. Because the state, rather than lower-level collectives, owned and operated the major urban factories, and depended heavily upon them as its primary source of revenue, it was wary of changes that might undermine its power economically and politically or call into question its important social base among the urban workers who had been among the major beneficiaries of the revolution. In particular, state leaders feared that moves that jeopardized the security and welfare benefits of workers at state-owned enterprises (SOEs) could precipitate widespread labor unrest. By contrast, villagers had enjoyed comparatively few state or other welfare benefits and were tightly controlled under the collective. From the late 1970s, as pressures mounted across the countryside to expand the scope of market and mobility and to curb the collective, workers in the city frequently resisted tendencies associated with reform as a direct threat to their income, security, and prestige …

The initial suspicions of Chinese labor proved prescient. Not only did reform bring few gains to SOE workers, it also meant that industrial laborers lost status to rising entrepreneurs and eventually millions lost lifetime employment and even such welfare benefits as pensions that they had worked a lifetime to secure. Many who retained their jobs were required to sign contracts with their employers, frequently for 5 years, thereby severing the promise of lifetime employment. Neither the long-promised conversion of SOEs to shareholding corporations nor the forced bankruptcies of inefficient enterprises have yet to materialize fully, but, with economic growth slowing in the late 1990s, massive lay-offs have ensued nonetheless. Older and women workers have borne the brunt of dislocation and unemployment among SOE workers. Competition with joint ventures and private companies has further threatened the once hegemonic status of state industry.

The gap separating rich and poor, both between and within regions, has grown apace under the reforms. In contrast to industrial relocation to poorer and peripheral regions during the Mao era, Deng Xiaoping's reform heavily favored coastal over inland areas with state investment and privileged access to international capital and markets. And in contrast to earlier class leveling, reformers promoted and exalted the new rich. Indeed, by the 1990s some analysts concluded that China in the course of a few decades had moved from the ranks of the world's most egalitarian societies to one of the most unequal in its distribution of income, wealth, and opportunity. Deng Xiapoing's famous adage that 'to get rich first is glorious' has left many of the less fortunate distraught, angry, and wondering if their time will ever come. Such economic and social inequalities may be multiplied by distinctions of gender and ethnicity. In a context where increased mobility and greater media access have heightened awareness of income differentials and lavish conspicuous consumption, these disparities may prove explosive.

Source: E. J. Perry and Mark Selden, *Chinese Society* (London: Routledge, 2000), pp. 2–5

12.2b Grain output and gross agricultural production values, 1981–90

By 1984 there was too much grain to be stored properly. When the government reduced the rate paid for the grain quota, the peasants reacted by producing other products for market.

	Grain output		Gross agricultural production value*	
	Volume (million tons)	Annual growth rate (%)	Value (million yuan)	Annual growth rate (%)
1981	325.02	1.4	218.1	5.8
1982	354.50	9.1	248.3	11.3
1983	387.28	9.2	275.0	7.7
1984	407.31	5.2	321.0	12.3
1985	379.11	−6.9	361.9	3.4
1986	391.51	3.3	401.3	3.4
1987	402.98	2.9	467.6	5.8
1988	394.08	−2.2	586.5	4.0
1989	407.55	3.4	653.5	3.1
1990	435.00	6.7	738.2	6.9

* At current price.

Source: 'Grain Output and Gross Agricultural Production Values Since 1981', Table, *People's Daily*, 23 February 1991, p. 3, from *Zhongguo tongji nianjian (Statistical Year Book of China)*, 1990, pp. 335, 336

12.3 Building socialism with a specifically Chinese character

Deng Xiaoping, 30 June 1984

At the founding of the People's Republic, we inherited from old China a ruined economy with virtually no industry. There was a shortage of grain, inflation was acute, and the economy was in chaos. But we solved the problems of feeding and employing the population, stabilized commodity prices, and unified financial and economic work, and the economy rapidly recovered. On this foundation we started large-scale reconstruction. What did we rely on? We relied on Marxism and socialism. Some people ask why we chose socialism. We answer that we had to, because capitalism would get China nowhere. If we had taken the capitalist road, we could not have put an end to the chaos in the country or done away with poverty and backwardness. That is why we have repeatedly declared that we shall adhere to Marxism and keep to the socialist road. But by Marxism we mean Marxism that is integrated with Chinese conditions, and by socialism we mean a socialism that is tailored to Chinese conditions and has a specifically Chinese character ...

The superiority of the socialist system is demonstrated, in the final analysis, by faster and greater development of those [productive] forces than under the capitalist system ... Pauperism is not socialism. Still less communism.

Given that China is still backward, what road can we take to develop the productive forces and raise the people's standard of living? This brings us back to the question of whether to continue on the socialist road or to stop and turn onto the capitalist road. Capitalism can only enrich less than 10 per cent of the Chinese population; it can never enrich the remaining more than 90 per cent. But if we adhere to socialism and apply the principle of distribution to each according to his work, there will not be excessive disparities in wealth. Consequently, no polarization will occur as our productive forces become developed over the next 20–30 years.

The minimum target of our modernization programme is to achieve a comparatively comfortable standard of living by the end of the century. By a comparatively comfortable standard we mean a per capita GNP of US$800.

The present world is open. One important reason for China's backwardness after the industrial revolution in Western countries was its closed-door policy. After the founding of the People's Republic, we were blockaded by others, so the country remained virtually closed, which created difficulties for us. The experience of the past thirty or so years had demonstrated that a closed-door policy would hinder construction and inhibit development. There could be two kinds of exclusion: one would be directed against other countries; the other would be directed against China itself, with one region or department closing its doors to the others. Both kinds of exclusion would be harmful. We are suggesting that we should develop rapidly, but not too rapidly because that would be unrealistic. To do this, we have to invigorate the domestic economy and open to the outside world.

Proceeding from the realities in China, we must first of all solve the problem of the countryside. Eighty per cent of the population lives in rural areas, and China's stability depends on the stability of those areas. No matter how successful our work is in the cities, it won't mean much without a stable base in the countryside. We therefore began by invigorating the economy and adopting an open policy there, so as to bring the initiative of 80 per cent of the population into full play. We adopted this policy at the end of 1978, and after a few years it has produced the desired results. Now the recent Second Session of the Sixth National People's Congress has decided to shift the focus of reform from the countryside to the cities. The urban reform will include not only industry and commerce but science and technology, education, and all other fields of endeavour as well. In short, we shall continue the reform at home and open still wider to the outside world.

We have opened 14 large and medium-sized coastal cities. We welcome foreign investment and advanced techniques. Management is also a technique. Will they undermine our socialism? Not likely, because the socialist sector is the mainstay of our economy. Our socialist economic base is so huge it can absorb tens and hundreds of billions of dollars worth of foreign funds without being shaken. Foreign investment will doubtless serve as a major supplement in the building of socialism in our country ...

Well, those are our plans. We shall accumulate new experience and try new solutions as new problems arise. In general, we believe that the course we have chosen, which we will call building socialism with Chinese characteristics, is the right one. We have followed this road for five and a half years and have achieved satisfactory results; indeed, the pace of development has so far exceeded our projections. If we go on this way, we shall be able to reach the goal of quadrupling China's GNP by the end of the century. And so I can tell our friends that we are even more confident now.

**Source: Deng Xiaoping, 'Building Socialism with a Specifically Chinese Character',
30 June 1984 (interview with Japanese delegation), *Selected Works of Deng Xiaoping
(1982–1992)*, Vol. 3 (Beijing: Foreign Languages Press, 1994), pp. 72–5**

12.4 Reform corruption: a discussion on China's current development

Stephen K. Ma, Spring 1989

Concomitant with China's rapid and radical reform there has been rampant corruption among its bureaucrats. Chinese authorities have exhorted cadres to get rich last in the wake of the coming Communist prosperity. Deng Xiaoping favours a pattern in which 'some people will become prosperous first and others later'. But many government officials, [who] wanted to be first and not last on the road towards common prosperity, have turned a deaf ear to the Party's advice, and so the nation's leaders have resorted to various means of intimidation – 'executing one as a warning to a hundred'. Yet just as a Chinese saying proclaims that 'not even a prairie fire can destroy the grass, it grows again when the spring breeze blows,' corruption remains chronic and contagious and does not seem to be tapering off. Addressing this perennial problem, this paper argues that reform corruption in China has much to do with ideological confusion, lack of incentive, lack of deterrence, and deficiencies in management, all of which have been either created or exacerbated in the course of reform. The paper suggests that ideological indoctrination alone does not tackle the issue adequately and that structural changes may assist in reducing corruption.

As early as December 1951, when the 'Three-Anti' campaign was launched against corruption, waste, and bureaucratism, bourgeois ideas were already selected as a favourite scapegoat, as a major cause of corruption. This approach is adopted by some foreign observers as well. John Gardner, for example, writes that corruption of veteran and new Party cadres resulted from 'an environment in which the bourgeoisie retained a dominant position'. The authorities have repeatedly employed this kind of attack in political movements since 1950, but seeing the bourgeoisie as an easy target has blinded Chinese leaders to other causes of bureaucratic corruption ...

Even after more and more cases of corruption are disclosed in the news media, the nation's leaders still talk of corruption caused by the bourgeoisie. Deng warns the Chinese people not 'to be corrupted by capitalist thinking', and Hu Qili, a new political star in China, alerts the Party cadres 'against ushering in corrosive ideologies of capitalism and its values suggesting that money talks', while Chen Yun, First Secretary of the Party's Central Commission for Discipline Inspection, blames 'a bourgeois decadent ideology' for 'seriously corrupting Party conduct and social conduct'. Not surprisingly, therefore, few efforts have been made to find structural defects that make corruption possible. Deng's acknowledgment that problems do exist in 'organizational and work systems' was not made public until Autumn 1983, but no serious investigation followed his statement. Avid and well-publicized academic discussions on political reform in the middle of 1986 seemed to signal a new dawn for administrative restructuring, yet this did not happen in a new round of the fight against 'bourgeois liberalization', which culminated in the Party General Secretary's resignation in January 1987. ...

REFORM CORRUPTION

Deng's bold economic reforms have a bearing on the widespread corruption in post-Mao China, and yet the corruption that occurs during such reforms is a different kind. While political corruption is a common phenomenon in all cultures ... the conception of 'reform corruption' involves much more. This is not to suggest that reform *necessarily* provokes reform corruption but that corruption can be easily triggered by reform policy.

Profiting from reformist policies, some members of the non-elite earn ten times as much as an average bureaucrat, and Deng's reform has given birth to quite a few 'ten thousand yuan households'. Reports on the new rich began to surface in the news media. In some cases, their wealth was compared directly with the income of government officials, eclipsing the latter's considerably. Peasants in northern China's Taihang Mountains could now afford tractors which cost 5,000 yuan each in China, and a 'poor villager' bought a colour TV set for 1,500 yuan, an ordinary cadre's annual salary. The average annual per capita income in Luizhuang village in central China's Henan Province in 1983 exceeded the county head's earnings, with the annual family incomes in this village ranging between around 10,000 and 4,000 yuan. A woman worker in north-eastern China's Heilongjiang Province set up the area's first household-run chicken farm in 1981, making a profit of 50,000 yuan in 1984.

On the other hand, the bureaucrats' incomes climb at a snail's pace; pay rises received by the Party and government cadres hardly satisfy their expectations and fail to rescue them from losing superiority over the non-elite groups in society. On 1 July 1985 a new wage system was placed in effect. The new scheme, termed 'structural wage system' (*jiegou gongzizhi*), is composed of 'basic wage' (*jichu gongzi*), 'duty wage' (*zhiwugongzi*), 'service length allowance' (*gongling jintie*), and 'bonus' (*jiang-li gongzi*). It was reported that Chinese bureaucrats would receive 'the largest pay increase since the founding of the PRC in 1949'. Actually, the average real monthly increase for a cadre amounts to only 18 yuan. This paltry rise for bureaucrats lags far behind the doubled and redoubled income of an increasing number of businessmen who have fully benefited from market-oriented reform. A county head's monthly salary of 122 yuan, as suggested in the new wage system, may be attractive to many ordinary cadres with a university education, whose salary starts at 57 yuan per month. However, this pales in comparison with the dazzling income of those who have been allowed to get rich 'first'.

Reform, then, has clearly disfavoured bureaucrats, financially elevating members of non-elite groups in society to an unprecedented height in the history of the PRC. In such circumstances corruption seems to be the only option available for bureaucrats who are reluctant to witness their cherished status passing away and who are itching to regain it. Moreover, corruption in certain forms such as gift-taking may not jeopardize their position … Thus, corruption can reinstate a bureaucrat's status without costing him his job.

Source: Stephen K. Ma, 'Reform Corruption: A Discussion',
Pacific Affairs, Vol. 62, No. 1, Spring 1989, pp. 40, 44–5

12.5 Fang Lizhi calls for 'complete Westernization'. Speech at Tongji University, Shanghai, 18 November 1986

Our goal at present is the thorough modernization of China. We all have a compelling sense of the need for modernization. There is a widespread demand for change among people in all walks of life; and very few find any reason for complacency. None feel this more strongly than those of us in science and academia. Modernization has been our national theme since the Gang of Four were overthrown ten years ago, but we are just beginning to understand what it really means. In the beginning we were mainly aware of the grave shortcomings in our production of goods, our economy, and our science and technology, and that modernization was required in these areas. But now we understand our situation much better. We realize that grave shortcomings exist not only in our 'material civilization' but also in our 'spiritual civilization' – our culture, our ethical standards, our political institutions – and that these also require modernization.

The question we must now ask is, what kind of modernization is required? I think it's obvious to all of us that we need complete modernization, not just modernization in a few chosen aspects. People are now busy comparing Chinese and Western culture – including political, economics, science technology, education, the whole gamut – and there is much debate over the subject. The question is, do we want 'complete Westernization' or 'partial Westernization'? Should we continue to uphold the century-old banner of 'using Western methods but maintaining the Chinese essence,' or any other 'cardinal principle'? Of course this is not a new discussion. A century ago, insightful people realized that China had no choice but to modernize. Some wanted partial modernization, others wanted complete modernization, and thus they initiated a debate that continues down to the present day.

I personally agree with the 'complete Westernizers.' What their so-called complete Westernization means to me is complete openness, the removal of restrictions in every sphere. We need to acknowledge that, when looked at in its entirety, our culture lags far behind that of the world's most advanced societies, not in any one specific aspect but across the board. Responding to this situation calls not for the establishment of a priori barriers but for complete openness to the outside world. Attempting to set our inviolable 'essence' off limits before it is even challenged makes no sense to me. Again, I am scarcely inventing these ideas. A century ago people said essentially the same thing: Open China up and face the challenge of more advanced societies head on, in every aspect from technology to politics. What is good will stand up, and what is not good will be swept away. This prognosis remains unchanged.

Why is China so backward? To answer this question, we need to take a clear look at history. China has been undergoing revolutions for a century, but we are still very backward. This is all the more true since liberation, these decades of the socialist revolution that we all know first hand as students and workers. Speaking quite dispassionately, I have to judge this era a failure. This is not my opinion only, by any means; many of our leaders are also admitting as much, saying that socialism is in trouble everywhere. Since the end of World War II, socialist countries have by and large not been successful. There is no getting around this. As far as I'm concerned, the last thirty-odd years in China have been a failure in virtually every aspect of economic and political life.

We need to take a careful look at why socialism has failed. Socialist ideals are admirable. But we have to ask two questions about the way they have been put into practice: Are the things done in the name of socialism actually socialist? And, do they make any sense? We have to take a fresh look at these questions, and the first step in that process is to free our minds from the narrow confines of orthodox Marxism ...

We've talked about the need for modernization and reform, so now let's consider democracy. Our understanding of the concept of democracy is so inadequate that we can barely even discuss it. With our thinking so hobbled by old dogmas, it is no wonder we don't achieve democracy in practice. Not long ago it was constantly being said that calling for democracy was equivalent to requesting that things be 'loosened up.' In fact the word 'democracy' is quite clear, and it is poles apart in meaning from 'loosening up.' If you want to understand democracy, look at how people understand it in the developed countries, and compare that to how people understand it here, and then decide for yourself what's right and what's wrong.

I think that the key to understanding democracy lies first of all in recognizing the rights of each individual. Democracy is built from the bottom up. Every individual possesses certain rights, or to use what is a very sensitive expression indeed in China, everyone has 'human rights.' We seldom dare to utter the words 'human rights', but actually human rights are very basic …

Democracy is based on recognizing the rights of every single individual. Naturally, not everyone wants the same thing, and therefore the desires of different individuals have to be mediated through a democratic process, to form a society, a nation, a collectivity. But it is only on the foundation of recognizing the humanity and the rights of each person that we can build democracy. However, when we talk about 'extending democracy' here, it refers to your superiors 'extending democracy' for you. This is a mistaken concept. This is not democracy.

'Loosening up' is even worse. If you think about it, what it implies is that everyone is tied up very tightly right now, but if you stay put, we'll loosen the rope a little bit and let you run around. The rope used to be one foot long, now we'll make it five feet. This is a top-down approach …

Now what about our 'true democracy?' I have never received any document telling me what issues my representative talked about, or how he or she voted at the NPC. I have never known what my representative supported or opposed, or what his or her accomplishments in office were. And the next time I have to go to cast my vote for this person, I will still be totally in the dark. Our 'true democracy' had better get on the ball until it can do better than their [Western] 'false democracy!' I lived in China a long time without being aware of these problems. But when I went abroad and was finally able to see for myself, the contrast was glaringly obvious …

In democratic societies, democracy and science – and most of us here are scientists – run parallel. Democracy is concerned with ideas about humanity, and science is concerned with nature. One of the distinguishing features of universities is the role of knowledge; we do research, we create new knowledge, we apply this knowledge to developing new products, and so forth. In this domain, within the sphere of science and the intellect, we make our own judgments based on our own independent criteria.

This is the distinguishing characteristic of a university. In Western society, universities are independent from the government, in the sense that even if the money to run the school is provided by the government, the basic decisions – regarding the content of courses, the standards for academic performance, the selections of research topics, the evaluation of results, and so on – are made by the schools themselves on the basis of values endemic to the academic community, and not by the government. At the same time, good universities in the West are also independent of big business. This is how universities must be. The intellectual realm must be independent and have its own values.

This is an essential guarantee of democracy. It is only when you know something independently that you are free from relying on authorities outside the intellectual domain, such as the government. Unfortunately, things are not this way in China.

Source: Fang Lizhi, *Bringing Down the Great Wall: Writings on Science, Culture and Democracy*, edited by Jim Williams (New York: Alfred A. Knopf, 1990), pp. 157–161, 166–9, 171

12.6 Statement by student hunger strikers, 13 May 1989

The students' original demands in April included more funds for education, rehabilitation of those victimized, and freedom of the press. By mid-May some were calling for more far-reaching democratic reform. A few hundred students began a hunger strike in the Square on 13 May – the numbers soon rose to over 2,000.

We commence our hunger strike in the lovely May sunshine. In the full bloom of youth, however, we leave beautiful things behind, but with great reluctance.

Yet the condition of our country is one of rampant inflation, economic speculation by officials, extreme authoritarian rule, serious bureaucratic corruption, a drain of products and people to other countries, social confusion, and an increase in the number of criminal acts. It is a crucial moment for the country and its people. All compatriots with a conscience, please heed our call:

> The country is our country.
> The people are our people.
> The government is our government.
> If we do not cry out, who will?
> If we do not take action, who will? ...

REASONS FOR THE HUNGER STRIKE

First, to protest against the casual attitude of the government towards the demonstration of the Beijing students. Second, to protest against the government's continued refusal to engage in dialogue with the representatives of Beijing's institutions of higher education. Third, to protest against the government's condemnation of the patriotic movement as 'turmoil', and the distortions of the media.

DEMANDS OF THE HUNGER STRIKERS

First, that the government quickly enters into equal, concrete discussion with the Dialogue Group of the Beijing institutions of higher education. Second, that the government retract its statements concerning the nature of the Student Movement, and evaluate it fairly and honestly as a patriotic and democratic movement.

Source: 'Statement by Student Hunger Strikers, 13 May 1989'.
In Mok Chiu Yu and J. Frank Harrison, eds,
Voices from Tiananmen Square: Beijing Spring and the Democracy Movement
(Montreal: Black Rose Books, 1990), pp. 95–7. Document XXI

12.7 A million Beijing residents demonstrate in support of the students and demand that Deng Xiaoping step down

Editorial Board of *Xinwen Daobao*, 17 May 1989

On 17 May, hundreds of thousands of the capital's residents demonstrated in support of the students. They used various expressions to demand that Deng Xiaoping step down. Although as early as 15 April, big and small posters at several universities had already directly criticized Deng Xiaoping, this was the first time city residents widely expressed their forceful aversion to Deng.

People uninhibitedly shouted this head of state's name. One fat woman led workers in shouting 'Xiaoping, Xiaoping, is over eighty. His body's OK, but not his mind' ...

In the evening, as groups of workers from the Railway Ministry and construction workers passed through Tiananmen Square, a worker carried aloft a certificate of 'glorious retire-ment' which caught the attention of everyone in the square. On the certificate in ink were the names of Deng Xiaoping, Zhao Ziyang , and Li Peng ...

One worker told a reporter, 'He is too old.' This probably refers not just to Deng's age, but Deng's age is clearly an issue of interest for many people. One banner humorously reads: 'Friendly competition between China and the Soviet Union – score 85 to 58. China holds a temporary lead.' This scroll tells people the exact age of [Deng Xiaoping and China's] visitor, Gorbachev ...

Residents also insisted that Li Peng resign, with many yelling: 'Li Peng, step down.' This reporter found many similar banners in different groups with the words: 'Wanted – Prime Minister.' 'Prime Minister – where are you?' 'Prime Minister Zhou Enlai, where are you?' In front of one group was a big portrait of Zhou Enlai. People expressed their anger over Li Peng's reluctance to come out and talk with the students. They expressed dissatisfaction with Li Peng by mourning Prime Minister Zhou Enlai. The relationship between Li Peng and Zhou Enlai is not just that they were both prime ministers at different times, but that Li Peng is Zhou's adopted son. In contrast, attitudes toward Zhao Ziyang were more moderate ...

In addition to demonstrators from colleges and universities in the capital and other prov-inces, people from the media, hospitals and medical institutions, democratic parties, religious circles, scientific research institutes, and law firms, there are also many groups of workers, high school students, private businessmen, and people from financial circles. Most noticeable are the groups of people from the Capital Iron and Steel Plant, Central Radio and China Central TV, the Party School of the Beijing Party Committee, the Ministry of Public Security, the United Front Department of the Central Committee, workers from Kunming Munici-pality, unemployed youths with criminal records, peasants, noncommissioned PLA officers, China's National Men's Volleyball Team, deaf workers of Shanlu Factory, Christians, and about one hundred Buddhist monks wearing patchwork outer garments.

Source: 'A Million Beijing Residents Demonstrate in Support of Students and Demand that Deng Xiaoping Step Down', 17 May 1989, *Xinwen Daobao*, 18 May 1989. In Suzanne Ogden et al., eds, *China's Search for Democracy: The Student and Mao Movement of 1989* (Armonk, New York: M. E. Sharpe, 1992), pp. 228–30

12.8   Dissent over the imposition of martial law

12.8a Two Politburo members oppose martial law, 17 May 1989

Extracts from minutes of Politburo Standing Committee Meeting in The Tiananmen Papers *compiled by Zhang Liang. Zhao Ziyang was General Secretary of the Party. Hu Qili was a secretary of the Central Secretariat in charge of ideology and propaganda, who was removed from all his offices after 4 June. The authenticity of these secret papers cannot be guaranteed, but Orville Schell comments in the Afterword that confidence in the Chinese compiler 'was one of the most important factors leading us to believe in this material' (p. 473).*

ZHAO ZIYANG: The question for this evening's meeting is martial law. First we need to consider whether the situation has reached a point where martial law is our only option. Will martial law help solve the problem or only enlarge it? Is it in fact necessary to impose martial law? I hope we can discuss these questions calmly.

LI PENG: The decision on martial law, Comrade Ziyang, was made by Comrade Xiaoping at this morning's meeting. I support Comrade Xiaoping's views on martial law. I believe that the topic for the present meeting is not whether martial law should or should not be imposed but, rather, what steps to use in carrying it out.

YAO YILIN: I strongly support Comrade Xiaoping's proposal to impose martial law in Beijing's urban districts. Taking this powerful measure will help restore the city to normalcy, end the state of anarchy, and quickly and effectively stop the turmoil.

ZHAO ZIYANG: I'm against imposing martial law in Beijing. My reason is that, given the extreme feelings of the students at this juncture, to impose martial law will not help calm things down or solve problems. It will only make things more complicated and more sharply confrontational. And after all, things are still under our control. Even among the demonstrators the vast majority are patriotic and support the Communist Party. Martial law could give us total control of the situation, yes: but think of the terror it will strike in the minds of Beijing's citizens and students. Where will that lead? ... In the forty years of the People's Republic, our Party has learned many lessons from its political and economic mistakes. Given the crisis we now face at home and abroad, I think that one more big political mistake might well cost us all our remaining legitimacy. So I see martial law as extremely dangerous. The Chinese people cannot take any more huge policy blunders.

HU QILI: After much careful thought, I too have decided that I am against martial law in Beijing. In the complicated political situation we now face, we have to be wary of high-pressure tactics that could aggravate the confrontation. To be quite frank, I worry that martial law could lead to an even more serious social crisis: it could ignite new mass resistance, and it could make even more people join this student movement which should have been brought to an end long ago. It could leave us with a situation even harder to handle, and it could lead to extremes. In short, I don't see how martial law is going to help us toward peaceful resolution of the situation.

QIAO SHI: I've wanted to express my view all along. We can't afford any more concessions to the student movement, but on the other hand we still haven't found a suitable means for resolving the situation. So on the question of martial law, I find it hard to express either support or opposition.

BO YIBO: This is a Standing Committee meeting in which Comrade Shangkun and I are only observers. We don't have voting rights, but we both support Comrade Xiaoping's proposal to impose martial law. Just now everyone on the committee had a chance to express his opinion. I think we should make the opinions even by taking a vote, by saying 'yes,' 'no,' or 'abstain.' This has been our Party tradition when we face important questions of principle.

Following Bo Yibo's suggestion, the five workers of the Standing Committee took a formal vote: Li Peng and Yao Yilin voted for martial law; Zhao Ziyang and Hu Qili voted against it; Qiao Shi abstained.

YANG SHANGKUN: The Party permits differing opinions. We can refer this evening's vote to Comrade Xiaoping and the other Party Elders and get a resolution as soon as possible.

ZHAO ZIYANG: My duties must end here today; I cannot continue to serve. My view of the nature of the student movement differs from those of Comrade Xiaoping and from those of most of you here. With my different thinking, how can I carry on as General Secretary? And if I can't carry on, it will make things difficult for the rest of you on the Standing Committee. So I'm asking to resign.

BO YIBO: Don't bring up this question, Comrade Ziyang. Didn't you agree at the morning meeting with Comrade Xiaoping that the minority should yield to the majority? Didn't you also say that it's better to have a decision than not to have one? You mustn't drop the ball now.

YANG SHANGKUN: Your attitude is incorrect, Comrade Ziyang. How can you bail out right now, when we most need unity? Whatever you do, you mustn't make things hard for the Party right at this moment.

ZHAO ZIYANG: My health hasn't been good. I've had dizziness constantly for the last few days. I have low blood pressure.

BO YIBO: Since the Standing Committee can't reach a consensus, we'll have to bring the question back to Comrade Xiaoping for a solution in any case.

On 18 May at 8.30 a.m. the 'Eight Elders', veteran Party Leaders, headed by Deng Xiaoping, met with Politburo Standing Committee members, Li Peng, Qiao Shi, Hu Qili, and Yao Yiling, plus three members of the Military Affairs Commission. Zhao Ziyang failed to attend this meeting, but (see next item) had found time to meet student hunger strikers.

Source: 'May 16–19 The Fall of Zhao Ziyang: The Standing Committee Resumes its Meeting', *The Tiananmen Papers*, compiled by Zhang Liang, edited by Andrew J. Nathan and Perry Link (New York: Public Affairs, 2001), pp. 192–3

12.8b Zhao Ziyang decides to resign, 18 May 1989

On 18 May at 5 a.m. Zhao Ziyang and Li Peng, with others, visited fasting students in hospital, urging them to discontinue fasting. Subsequently, his decision to resign is explained by Yang Shangkun. After he visited the students, Zhao went straight to his office and drafted a letter of resignation.

To the Standing Committee of the Politburo and to Comrade Xiaoping. After much thought I have concluded that, given my current level of awareness and my state of mind, I simply cannot carry out the decision on implementing martial law in Beijing that you have decided on. I still maintain my original opinion. Accordingly, I request to resign as General Secretary of the Communist Party of China and as First Vice Chair of the Military Affairs Commission.

Zhao Ziyang, May 18

After finishing the letter, Zhao first sent it to Yang Shangkun, marked 'extra urgent'. He wanted Yang to see it before he sent it to the others because Yang was his closest confidant among the Party Elders and could help him check the letter for political soundness. Yang telephoned Zhao as soon as he had read the letter.

YANG SHANGKUN: You can't do this, Ziyang. Why send a letter like this? Can you imagine the consequences?

ZHAO ZIYANG: I can't work with them anymore.

YANG SHANGKUN: But whatever you do, you can't do something that puts the Party in the lurch. If you resign you'll have a polarizing effect on society. And anyway, you can still get along with the others on the Standing Committee ... Have you thought about how you're going to explain this to the nation? To the Party? To the Politburo and the Standing Committee? And most important, to Comrade Xiaoping? Aren't you always saying how important it is that we guard Comrade Xiaoping's prestige? On this one, Comrade Xiaoping spoke out – and you said you agreed. So what are you, anyway – for him or against him?

After listening to Yang's advice and getting control of his agitation, Zhao said:

'I'll think it all over once more, Comrade Shangkun. But right now my chest feels stuffy and my head a bit dizzy. I won't be going to the meeting this morning. Please tell the others I'm ill.'

Shortly afterwards he sent Yang Shangkun another letter:

Comrade Shangkun:
Thank you for your criticism.
In respect for your opinion I will not send my letter. But I still maintain my views, and hence my work will be very difficult. I cannot carry out this policy.

Zhao Ziyang, May 18

But Zhao's decision to skip the meeting that was to make arrangements for martial law hardly reduced the intensity of his worry. That afternoon he wrote again to Deng Xiaoping, urging Deng to reconsider his views, to change the official judgment of the student movement as presented in the 26 April People's Daily *editorial, and to come out against martial law in Beijing. As a precaution, he again telephoned Yang Shangkun:*

ZHAO ZIYANG: Comrade Shangkun, I just wrote another letter to Comrade Xiaoping asking him to change the official view of the student movement from what's in the 26 April editorial. No matter what, I believe I have the right to express my disagreements inside the Party. I hope you can explain my views to comrade Xiaoping one more time, and I hope he'll change his judgment on the student movement.

YANG SHANGKUN: I cannot say that to him. That question is huge, you know. Changing the judgement would be a slap in the face to all the university presidents, faculty, and student activists. [Here 'activists' refers to pro-government activism.] It would leave them no leg to stand on, and we'd all come crashing down. Trust me, you're better off not sending that letter.

Source: 'May 16–19 The Fall of Zhao Ziyang: May 18 An Unsent Letter of Resignation',
The Tiananmen Papers, **compiled by Zhang Liang, edited by Andrew J. Nathan**
and Perry Link (New York: Public Affairs, 2001), pp. 200–1

12.9 What do you lack? On martial law in Beijing

A commoner, published in *Xiwen Daobao*, 22 May

Newspapers are in your hands
Radio stations are in your hands
Guns are in your hands
Prisons are in your hands
Everything is in your hands
What do you lack, Emperor?
Only the popular will!
Only the truth!

Source: 'What Do You Lack?' On Martial Law in Beijing. Poem from *Xinwen Daobao*.
In Suzanne Ogden et al., eds, *China's Search for Democracy:*
The Student and Mao Movement of 1989
(Armonk, New York: M. E. Sharpe, 1992), p. 253

12.10 A statement to all soldiers, 21 May 1989

This document was distributed by students at the Six Mile Bridge military camp on the western outskirts of Beijing. It refers to the refusal by Commander Xu Qinxian, of the 38th Army, to lead his troops against the demonstrators. Commander Xu, after receiving and passing on his orders, checked into hospital (he had in fact earlier broken his leg), and was court martialled and sentenced to 18 years for his action.

Dear Soldiers of the Liberation Army,

The PLA is made up of the sons and brothers of the people. You guard and protect the republic, not just a small minority. In a life or death situation you should look closely at the wishes of the people, and not become the tool of their repression at the orders of one or a few.

In the development of the patriotic Democracy Movement you have supported the people in your own way. The soldiers of the 38th Army have refused to obey the illegal order to suppress the people, and are thereby the brilliant representatives of the people, who welcome them.

Stand with the people! Protect the Constitution! Maintain democracy and reform!

Source: 'A Statement to All Soldiers, 21 May 1989'.
In Mok Chiu Yu and J. Frank Harrison, eds,
Voices from Tiananmen Square Beijing Spring and the Democracy Movement
(Montreal: Black Rose Books, 1990), p. 103. Document XXVIII

12.11 Declaration of Guandong Independent Workers' Union, 4 June 1989

This was one of several statements issued by ad hoc unions formed at this time.

The GWAU, a local patriotic organization developed within the framework of the nation-wide patriotic Democratic Movement, declares itself established. It is an organization initiated by the Guandong workers, and supervised by the citizens, with the purpose of uniting as many elements as possible for the pursuit of freedom, democracy, and the well-being of a long-suffering China.

Now that the soldiers have opened fire in Beijing, and the people lie bleeding, the nation has reached a critical juncture. A historical burden falls on the shoulders of every worker. We have no other choice than to oppose the violence, support the students, and promote both democracy and knowledge.

The nation is confused and disrupted, flooded with bureaucracy, with a corrupt political and economic system. The future of the nation has become a personal concern of each individual worker. The Guandong workers cannot stand by, and the GWAU urgently appeals to people from every walk of life to support and participate in the nationwide, patriotic Democratic Movement.

Source: 'Declaration of Guandong Independent Workers' Union, 4 June 1989'.
In Mok Chiu Yu and J. Frank Harrison, eds,
Voices from Tiananmen Square Beijing Spring and the Democracy Movement
(Montreal: Black Rose Books, 1990), pp. 119–20. Document XLVI

12.12 Deng Xiaoping's speech to officers in command of enforcing martial law in Beijing, 9 June 1989

You comrades have been working hard.

First of all, I'd like to express my heartfelt condolences to the comrades in the People's Liberation Army, the armed police, and police who died in the struggle – and my sincere sympathy and solicitude to the comrades in the army, the armed police, and police who were wounded in the struggle, and I want to extend my sincere regards to all the army, armed police, and police personnel who participated in the struggle.

I suggest that all of us stand and pay a silent tribute to the martyrs.

I'd like to take this opportunity to say a few words. This storm was bound to happen sooner or later. As determined by the international and domestic climate, it was bound to happen and was independent of man's will. It was just a matter of time and scale. It has turned out in our favor, for we still have a large group of veterans who have experienced many storms and have a thorough understanding of things. They were on the side of taking resolute action to counter the turmoil. Although some comrades may not understand this now, they will understand eventually and will support the decision of the Central Committee.

The 26 April editorial of the *Renmin Ribao* classified the problem as turmoil. The word was appropriate, but some people objected to the word and tried to amend it. But what has happened shows that this verdict was right. It was also inevitable that the turmoil would develop into a counter-revolutionary rebellion.

We still have a group of senior comrades who are alive, we still have the army, and we also have a group of core cadres who took part in the revolution at various times. That is why it was relatively easy for us to handle the present matter. The main difficulty in handling this matter lay in that we never experienced such a situation before, in which a small minority of bad people mixed with so many young students and onlookers. We did not have a clear picture of the situation, and this prevented us from taking some actions that we should have taken earlier. It would have been difficult for us to understand the nature of the matter had we not had the support of so many senior comrades. Some comrades didn't understand this point. They thought it was simply a matter of how to treat the masses. Actually, what we faced was not just some ordinary people who were misguided, but also a rebellious clique and a large quantity of the dregs of society. The key point is that they wanted to overthrow our state and the Party. Failing to understand this means failing to understand the nature of the matter. I believe that after serious work we can win the support of the great majority of comrades within the Party.

The nature of the matter became clear soon after it erupted. They had two main slogans: to overthrow the Communist Party and topple the socialist system. Their goal was to establish a bourgeois republic entirely dependent on the West. Of course we accept people's demands for combating corruption. We are even ready to listen to some persons with ulterior motives when they raise the slogan about fighting corruption. However, such slogans were just a front. Their real aim was to overthrow the Communist Party and topple the socialist system ...

The outbreak of the rebellion is worth thinking about. It prompts us to calmly think about the past and consider the future. Perhaps this bad thing will enable us to go ahead with reform and the open-door policy at a more steady, better, even a faster pace. Also, it will enable us more speedily to correct our mistakes and better develop our strong points.

Source: Deng Xiaoping's Address to Officers in Command of Enforcing Martial Law in Beijing, 9 June 1989, *Selected Works of Deng Xiaoping (1982–1992),* **Vol. 3, (Beijing: Foreign Languages Press, 1994) pp. 294–9**

13

Defining the Chinese nation
Hong Kong, Tibet, and the minorities

By 1984 the British Crown colony in Hong Kong was not only a relic of 152 years of imperialism; it had grown to be a formidable economic power, of immense significance to Chinese trade. Under a benevolent British despotism it had prospered particularly since World War II, its population swollen with émigrés from the mainland. The Chinese Communists were adamant on the question of sovereignty; on the other hand it was very unlikely, least of all under the pragmatic leader Deng Xiaoping, that they would wantonly diminish Hong Kong's assets. A deadline was looming. Whereas Hong Kong island and the mainland tip of Kowloon had been handed over permanently in 1832 and 1860 respectively, the more extensive hinterland, the 'new territories', had been acquired in June 1898 on a hundred year lease. Therefore it would have been legally possible for Britain to argue for the continued possession of Hong Kong island and Kowloon. At one time Mrs Thatcher considered this option which would have been very difficult, if not impossible, to sustain: a wiser course prevailed and the complete handover was agreed. The Chinese were ready to grant a formula of 'one country, two systems'. To allay business fears, the PRC agreed that Hong Kong's system would be unchanged for fifty years. The Joint Agreement signed in 1984 was subsequently ruffled by the Chinese perception that Chris Patten, the last Governor, was unnecessarily introducing new democratic processes in the last years. However, the handover has gone forward with general acceptance. It provides a model for a similar constitutional arrangement for Taiwan.

Both Communists and Nationalists have consistently maintained that the island of Taiwan is an integral part of China. The Japanese had taken over the island in 1895 in the Treaty of Shimonoseki, as a consequence of the Sino-Japanese war, and ruled there until the end of World War II. In the Cairo Declaration of 1 December 1943 it was announced that Taiwan, along with Manchuria and the Pescadores, should be restored to the Republic of China. The prospects of an early Communist invasion were forestalled by the Korean War. The two regimes were locked in cold war confrontation while the Nationalists held the five-member permanent seat in the UN Security Council. The United States signed a Mutual Defence Treaty with the Republic of China (Taiwan) on 2 December 1954. Thereafter, American pressure at the United Nations continued to prevent the admission of Communist China. Not until 25 October 1971, and as a premature consequence of the news of Nixon's visit to China, did the UN General Assembly vote by a large majority for the admission of the People's Republic and the expulsion of the Nationalists.

Since then the Americans have indicated that they will accept peaceful unification if the two parties agree. Meanwhile, Taiwan is now loathe to sacrifice its new version of Western-style democracy in a merger with the democratic centralist polity maintained in the People's Republic. However, trade and cultural relations are developing, and the two-system status of Hong Kong may offer a way forward.

The People's Republic was established in 1949 as a unified nation that was approximately 93 per cent Han – ethnic Chinese – and the rest was divided into fifty-six national minorities. These included the Hui, Chinese-speaking Muslims, and the Miao, scattered over several provinces, as well as the culturally and linguistically distinct provinces of Xinjiang and Tibet where Chinese were in a minority. Five autonomous provinces were created: Tibet, Xinjiang, Ningxia, Guangxi, and Inner Mongolia. Other areas were made autonomous districts and counties.

Deng's regime sought to placate the nationalities by encouraging cultural autonomy while keeping religion under political control. State funds were available to repair temples, mosques, and monasteries. Religious schools re-emerged, where, for example, children learnt the Koran. Native languages were tolerated in the media; by 1994 it was claimed that every nationality population of 100,000 or more in Xinjiang had its own radio and television stations.

Deng was hoping that development strategies leading to a higher standard of living would keep the minorities happy. This may well succeed with scattered ethnic groups in the south-western provinces, but it is less likely to placate those peoples with a strong desire for separation – the Uighurs, Mongolians, and Tibetans. They are unlikely to be satisfied with anything less than a political solution.

Cadres during the Cultural Revolution were particularly harsh on Tibetan Buddhism. In 1980, when touring Tibet, Party Secretary Hu Yaobang said: 'We feel very bad. We have worked for thirty years, but the life of the Tibetan people has not notably improved. Are we not to blame?' A more tolerant policy was promoted, notably after the arrival of Wu Jinghua as Regional Party Secretary of the Tibet Autonomous Region in 1985. In December 1988, Wu was demoted by the central authorities in Beijing who feared that liberalization policies in Tibet (which had inspired complaints and demonstrations) were going too far. From Autumn 1987 to March 1989 there were twenty-one incidents of violent dissent. On 8 March 1989 martial law was declared in Tibet, two months earlier than in Beijing.

13.1 One country, two systems, 22–23 June 1984

Deng Xiaoping

Statement on policy for resolving problems of Hong Kong and Taiwan. On 26 September 1984 the joint agreement on Hong Kong was signed by Britain and China, guaranteeing the existing rights in Hong Kong for fifty years.

The Chinese Government is firm in its position, principles, and policies on Hong Kong. We have stated on many occasions that, after China resumes the exercise of its sovereignty over Hong Kong in 1997, Hong Kong's current social and economic systems will remain unchanged, its legal system will remain basically unchanged, its way of life and its status as a free port and an international trade and financial centre will remain unchanged, and it can continue to maintain or establish economic relations with other countries and regions. We have also stated repeatedly that, apart from stationing troops there, Beijing will not assign officials to the government of the Hong Kong Special Administrative Region. This policy too will remain unchanged. We shall station troops there to safeguard our national security, not to interfere in Hong Kong's internal affairs. Our policies with regard to Hong Kong will remain unchanged for 50 years, and we mean this.

We are pursuing a policy of 'one country, two systems'. More specifically, this means that, within the People's Republic of China, the mainland with its one billion people will maintain the socialist system, while Hong Kong and Taiwan continue under the capitalist system. In recent years, China has worked hard to overcome 'Left' mistakes and has formulated its policies concerning all fields of endeavour in line with the principle of proceeding from reality and seeking truth from facts. After five and a half years, things are beginning to pick up. It is against this background that we have proposed to solve the Hong Kong and Taiwan problems by allowing two systems to coexist in one country.

We have discussed the policy of 'one country, two systems' more than once. It has been adopted by the National People's Congress. Some people are worried that it might change. I say it will not. The crux of the matter, the decisive factor, is whether the policy is correct. If it is not, it will change; otherwise it won't. Besides, is there anyone who can change China's current policy of opening to the outside world and invigorating the domestic economy? If it were changed, the living standard of 80 per cent of the Chinese population would decline, and we would lose the people's support. If we are on the right track and enjoy the people's support, the policy will not change.

Our policy towards Hong Kong will remain the same for a long time to come, but this will not affect socialism on the mainland. The main part of China must continue under socialism, but a capitalist system will be allowed to exist in certain areas, such as Hong Kong and Taiwan. Opening a number of cities on the mainland will let in some foreign capital, which will serve as a supplement to the socialist economy and help promote the growth of the socialist productive forces. For example, when foreign capital is invested in Shanghai, it certainly does not mean that the entire city has gone capitalist. The same is true of Shenzhen, where socialism still prevails. The main part of China remains socialist.

The concept of 'one country, two systems' has been formulated according to China's realities, and it has attracted international attention. China has not only the Hong Kong problem to tackle but also the Taiwan problem. What is the solution to these problems? As for the second, is it for socialism to swallow up Taiwan, or for the 'Three People's Principles' preached by Taiwan to swallow up the mainland? The answer is neither. If the problem cannot be solved by peaceful means, then it must be solved by force. Neither side would benefit from that. Reunification of the motherland is the aspiration of the whole nation. If it cannot be accomplished in 100 years, it will be in 1,000 years. As I see it, the only solution lies in practising two systems in one country. The world faces the choice between peaceful and non-peaceful means of solving disputes. One way or the other, they must be solved. New problems must be solved by new means. The successful settlement of the Hong Kong question may provide useful elements for the solution of international questions. Has any government in the history of the world ever pursued a policy as generous as China's? Is there anything recorded in the history of capitalism about any Western country doing something similar? When we adopt the policy of 'one country, two systems' to resolve the Hong Kong question, we are not acting on impulse or playing tricks but are proceeding from reality and taking into full account the past and present circumstances of Hong Kong.

We should have faith in the Chinese of Hong Kong, who are quite capable of administering their own affairs. The notion that Chinese cannot manage Hong Kong affairs satisfactorily is a leftover from the old colonial mentality. For more than a century after the Opium War, the Chinese people were looked down upon and humiliated by foreigners. But China's image has changed since the founding of the People's Republic. The modern image of China was not created by the government of the late Qing Dynasty, nor by the northern warlords, nor by

Chiang Kai-shek and his son. It is the People's Republic of China that has changed China's image. All Chinese have at the very least a sense of pride in the Chinese nation, no matter what clothes they wear or what political stand they take. The Chinese in Hong Kong share this sense of national pride. They have the ability to run the affairs of Hong Kong well and they should be confident of that. The prosperity of Hong Kong has been achieved mainly by Hong Kong residents, most of whom are Chinese. Chinese are no less intelligent than foreigners and are by no means less talented. It is not true that only foreigners can be good administrators. We Chinese are just as capable. The view that the people of Hong Kong lack self-confidence is not really shared by the people of Hong Kong themselves.

Source: Deng Xiaoping, 'One Country, Two Systems', 22–23 June 1984,
Selected Works of Deng Xiaoping (1982–1992), Vol. 3,
(Beijing: Foreign Languages Press, 1994), pp. 68–71

13.2 The Tibetan people agree to return to the big family

The agreement of the Central People's Government and the Local Government of Tibet on measures for the peaceful liberation of Tibet, 23 May 1951.

The Tibetan nationality is one of the nationalities with a long history within the boundaries of China and, like many other nationalities, it has done its glorious duty in the course of the creation and development of the great motherland. But over the last hundred years and more, imperialist forces penetrated into China, and in consequence, also penetrated into the Tibetan region and carried out all kinds of deception and provocation. Like previous reactionary governments, the KMT [Guomindang] reactionary government continued to carry out a policy of oppression and sowing dissension among the nationalities, causing division and disunity among the Tibetan people. The Local Government of Tibet did not oppose imperialist deception and provocations, but adopted an unpatriotic attitude towards the great motherland. Under such conditions, the Tibetan nationality and people were plunged into the depths of enslavement and suffering. In 1949, basic victory was achieved on a nationwide scale in the Chinese people's war of liberation; the common domestic enemy of all nationalities – the KMT reactionary government – was overthrown; and the common foreign enemy of all nationalities – the aggressive imperialist forces – was driven out. On this basis, the founding of the People's Republic of China and of the Central People's Government was announced. In accordance with the Common Programme passed by the Chinese People's Political Consultative Conference, the Central People's Government declared that all nationalities within the boundaries of the People's Republic of China are equal, and that they shall establish unity and mutual aid and oppose imperialism and their own public enemies, so that the People's Republic of China may become one big family of fraternity and cooperation, composed of all its nationalities. Within this big family of nationalities of the People's Republic of China, national regional autonomy is to be exercised in areas where national minorities are concentrated, and all national minorities are to have freedom to develop their spoken and written languages and to preserve or reform their customs, habits, and religious beliefs, and the Central People's Government will assist all national minorities to develop their political, economic, cultural, and educational construction work. Since then, all nationalities within the country, with the exception of those in the areas of Tibet and Taiwan, have gained liberation. Under the unified leadership of the Central People's Government and the direct leadership of the higher levels of people's governments, all national minorities have fully enjoyed the right of national equality and have exercised, or are exercising, national regional autonomy. In order that the influences of aggressive imperialist forces in Tibet may be successfully eliminated, the unification of the territory and sovereignty of the People's Republic of China accomplished, and national defence safeguarded; in order that the Tibetan nationality and people may be freed and return to the big family of the People's Republic of China to enjoy the same rights of national equality as all other nationalities in the country and develop their political, economic, cultural, and educational work, the Central People's Government, when it ordered the People's Liberation Army to march into Tibet, notified the Local Government of Tibet to send delegates to the Central Authorities to hold talks for the conclusion of an agreement on measures for the peaceful liberation of Tibet. In the latter part of April 1951, the delegates with full powers from the Local Government of Tibet arrived in Peking. The Central People's Government appointed representatives with full powers to conduct talks on a friendly basis with the delegates of the Local Government of Tibet. The result of the talks is that both parties have agreed to establish this agreement and ensure that it be carried into effect.

Source: 'The Seventeen Point Agreement. Agreement of the Central People's Government and the Local Government of Tibet on Measures for the Peaceful Liberation of Tibet', 23 May 1951. In Pierre-Antoine Donnet, *Tibet: Survival in Question* (Delhi: Oxford University Press, 1994), pp. 221–3

13.3 Cultural clash in the land on the roof of the world

John Gittings. 8 February 2002

It is early morning outside the Potala Palace, the former home of the Dalai Lama, pilgrims from all over Tibet have begun the sacred circuit – and the Chinese flag is flying in the breeze. Nomads with sunburnt faces as dark as their cloaks, Khampa ex-warriors with red tassels in their hair, farmers with leggings, their wives with striped aprons, plus ordinary folk from the city, old and young, walk briskly in the grey dawn. Many twirl their prayer wheels, some prostrate themselves on mats, and one or two even drive a sheep before them around the circuit. The lucky animal is then allowed to live to the end of its natural days. It is an advertisement of sorts for the religious freedom that China says is fully allowed in Tibet. 'How can the foreign press accuse us of suppressing religion', asks an official, 'when you can see it in the streets?'

The Potala receives an average of 800 pilgrims a day. It works out at about a tenth of the entire Tibetan population every year. However, the Chinese flag flying boldly – provocatively, even – in front of the Potala is a reminder that this is freedom within limits. The vast stretch of paved space behind it has been built since I was last in Lhasa. With its flagpole and ornamental lights, it is a miniature Tiananmen Square exported to Tibet.

A Chinese official confirms for the first time unofficial reports that in August 1999 the flag was targeted by a pro-independence Tibetan activist. 'Of course the Dalai [Lama] clique is trying to obstruct the modernisation of Tibet', exclaims the region's planning director, Wang Dianyuan. 'Didn't they try to blow up the flagpole two years ago?' The 'clique' is also blamed for earlier explosions at the gate of a government headquarters in Lhasa, and outside the home of a senior pro-Beijing official.

Virtually all Tibetans in the region or abroad who call for independence accept the supreme authority of the Dalai Lama who has condemned any violence. However, there is a radical minority in favour of stronger action.

Another official admits that large numbers of Tibetans still support the Dalai Lama. 'That many people believe in the Dalai Lama is well known', says Tu Deng, the Tibetan head of the religious affairs committee that enforces government policy. 'Our main task is to help people understand his real character'. Mr Tu describes the Dalai Lama as 'a splittist and an enemy of China' whose picture is therefore banned in public places. This has created a bizarre situation in which the Chinese admit that the Dalai Lama is still the spiritual leader of Tibetan Buddhism but have airbrushed him out of the picture …

In front of the most holy chapel in the Potala, a nomad from the plateau hands her tiny baby wrapped in a sheepskin to an older child, and prostrates herself on the floor. A smartly dressed young lady from Lhasa lies down alongside. Both then climb a wooden ladder to touch their foreheads against the statue of Arya Lokeshvara dating from the seventh century. A party of Chinese tourists clamber up noisily behind; one of them leans against the shrine and takes a call on his mobile.

MONASTERIES DESTROYED

'Some monks in the monasteries tell us this is just a performance for the tourists', says another foreigner who travelled widely without an official guide. It is generally assumed that some monks are spying for the authorities.

It is not as simple as that. On the roof of the Lhasa's Jokhang temple, Tibet's most sacred site, groups of monks are disputing theology with an enthusiasm that can hardly be feigned. Two seated monks question a third who stands before them, clapping his hands in triumphant emphasis when he concludes a point.

Nowhere else in the People's Republic of China does Beijing have to cope with a population so overwhelmingly attached to a non-communist ideology, and the monasteries are the focus for this central contradiction in Chinese rule.

Tibet's religious character has survived a decade of persecution during the Cultural Revolution (1966–76) when almost every monastery was destroyed by Red Guard factions among the Chinese and a much smaller number of radical Tibetans.

I am given official figures claiming that before the 1959 rebellion, when the Dalai Lama fled Tibet, there were 110,000 monks and nuns living in some 2,000 monasteries across the region. Now there are said to be 47,500 monks and nuns in 1,700 religious establishments which have been rebuilt with Chinese state funds and offerings by local communities. The figures are unreliable. An earlier Chinese version puts the original figure of monasteries at 2,700. Exiles claim there were thousands more before the mass destruction which began after the 1959 rebellion and culminated in the Cultural Revolution (1966–8) when Chinese Red Guards and Tibetan radicals joined forces.

Religion was completely banned during the Cultural Revolution, when monks were sent to prison or to work in the fields. Prayer flags and other displays of faith were also prohibited. The 'excesses' of that period were denounced in the early 1980s when religion was allowed a reprieve, but the Chinese attitude remains equivocal. Last December the official *Tibet Daily* said that it is necessary to 'wipe out the negative influence of religion'.

The number of monks is lower now because in the past, officials explain, under the Dalai Lama's 'feudal rule', families were forced to send sons to the monasteries. There is also a ban on admitting people of 15 or under to become acolytes because they should be 'receiving normal education'.

Despite official tolerance for everyday worship, senior officials have described Buddhism as a long-term obstacle to the transformation of Tibet.

'The centre [in Beijing] demands that we should maintain stability in Tibet and weaken the influence of religion', said Dan Zeng, the Tibetan Communist Party leader, at an education conference three years ago. He added that the Chinese president, Jiang Zemin, had endorsed the campaign launched in 1996 to conduct 'patriotic education in the monasteries'.

Mr Tu claims that the campaign has been successful, although 'we cannot change people's minds in a short space of time'. Like all officials interviewed, Mr Tu often speaks in set formulas as if from a manual. 'Through "patriotic education" the monks have learned "what is not allowed' and "what is illegal"', he tells me. Asked for clarification, he explains that monks teaching children is 'not allowed'. Monks demonstrating with pro-independence slogans is 'illegal'. Mr Tu dismisses stories of brutality and torture. 'A person is responsible for his own law-breaking', he says calmly. 'Our responsibility is to look after the great majority of [law-abiding] lamas'.

The London-based Tibet Information Network says it knows of at least 210 monks and nuns still in jail for taking part in peaceful demonstrations over the past decade. Merely to shout a pro-independence slogan may earn a sentence of eight years. There are frequent stories – routinely denied by Beijing – of inmates being beaten with iron rods and electric batons. Several allegedly died during a protest at Drapchi prison in 1998.

Life seems more relaxed in Lhasa than during my last visit in 1994 when memories were fresh of pro-independence marches and the 1989 imposition of martial law. The Chinese military maintains a low profile, although Lhasa houses the massive headquarters of half a dozen different commands – from border guards to riot troops.

In the square before the Jokhang temple, where monks and nuns once marched, two bored policemen sit on chairs barking through a loudspeaker at anyone who pauses for too long.

DALAI LAMA'S ILLNESS

No one now expects the intermittent dialogue between the Dalai Lama and Beijing since the early 1980s to produce results. A Beijing magazine this month has repeated the standard line that he can 'return to the embrace of the motherland if he gives up his independence demand'. But asked if the Dalai will ever return, Mr Tu replies contemptuously that 'he has now sunk in the mud too deep to renounce all he has done in the past'.

The Dalai Lama's nuanced proposals, made over the past 15 years, for Tibet to enjoy something short of independence are dismissed as insincere. His recent illness has also raised questions about the future in the event of his death. China would undoubtedly seek to control the choice of his next 'reincarnation', as they did in 1995 after the death of the Panchen Lama, Tibet's second spiritual leader.

The new boy Panchen is now being educated in Beijing 'in religious studies and science', it is said in Lhasa. He is being groomed to play a political role that could one day supplant the paramount status of the Dalai Lama.

Yet official statements have made it clear that the dominance of Buddhism in Tibet, however tightly controlled, is seen as a continuing threat to Chinese-led 'stability'. And that threat will only diminish if the economy of Tibet – still the poorest region of China- can finally be transformed.

Source: John Gittings, 'Cultural Clash in Land on the Roof of the World',
***The Guardian*, 8 February 2002, p. 17**

13.4 Race and history in China

W. J. F. Jenner, *New Left Review*, September 2001

One of the many ways in which China's policies have changed in the 25 years since Mao's death has been the subtle downgrading of one of its key terms, 'the Chinese people' – *Zhongguo renmin*, and the rise of an expression not much heard in that distant age: 'Zhonghua nation' – *Zhonghua minzu*. The difference matters. For most of the Mao era, the expression 'the Chinese people' was used so frequently that one hardly noticed it – except when the meaning was changed. In the first years of the People's Republic, 'the people' of China consisted principally of four officially designated but ill-defined classes: workers, peasants, national bourgeoisie (i.e capitalists deemed to be neither part of the Guomindang ruling group nor working for foreign businesses), and petty bourgeoisie. Each of these classes was represented on the new state's flag with a little yellow star, doing homage to the Communist Party's big yellow star. 'The people' excluded Chinese nationals who belonged to enemy classes, such as rural landlords and bureaucratic capitalists. The term said nothing about ethnicity: it referred only to those who belonged to the country, and the state, of China. As with the notion of 'the Soviet people', it suggested both vertical divisions – between the subjects of one state and those of others – and horizontal ones, between classes, which could potentially override national frontiers.

But the term's meaning was not fixed. By the 1960s, Mao found his earlier definition of 'the people' too inclusive. Reconceptualizing the nature of Chinese society after the imposition of socialism, he now saw its essential contradiction as the hostile divide between bourgeoisie and proletariat. Both these groupings were imaginary rather than socioeconomic: they existed in the Chairman's mind, distinguished by their supposed attitudes to his kind of chiliastic socialism. Two of the classes on which the regime had purported to base itself in 1949 – the national and the petty bourgeoisie – now no longer had a good claim to belong to 'the people'. At the height of Maoist fervour in the late 1960s, the very term 'people' seemed too conciliatory and inclusive, and was generally replaced by more militant formulations such as 'revolutionary people', 'labouring people', 'revolutionary masses', 'workers, peasants, and soldiers' and so on. The state was no longer a 'people's democratic dictatorship' but a 'proletarian dictatorship'. The most important divisions were the horizontal ones.

One of the clearest signs that late Maoism was finished, after Deng Xiaoping's takeover in December 1978, was the reversion to the formulation 'people's democratic dictatorship' and a broadening of the category 'people', as the Communist Party dropped large-scale class struggle from its self-given mission. This process has now gone a great deal further. Especially since the crisis of 1989, the Communist Party has been redefining itself as what is in effect (though not yet in name) a national socialist party, with growing emphasis on the first adjective and ever less on the second. While the militantly nationalist words and actions of the Chinese state have received a lot of attention around the world over the last decade, the redefining of this nationalism and its curious intellectual foundations have not. It is an awkward topic, and it is understandable that most Western observers should show a certain reluctance to draw attention to a rather embarrassing tendency in some intellectual circles in China towards nationalism with racial overtones.

Consider the statement of one of the country's most distinguished archaeologists, writing in 1991, that 'China's culture is an indigenous one with a tradition of nearly two million years'. These words express an attitude to the past of what is now China that goes far beyond the conventional clichés about four, five, or six thousand years of Chinese civiliza-tion. They indicate a new task being undertaken by certain palaeontologists and archaeolo-gists: that of creating a 'scientific' Chinese national identity of immense chronological depth, distinct from that of the rest of humanity. Attitudes such as these have political implications – whether or not the people of China and East Asia really did develop from *Homo erectus* to *Homo sapiens* independently of human evolution elsewhere. Relatedly, there is the interesting implication of suggestions made in recent years that China is only superficially a polyethnic country, in which up to fifty-six politically recognized nationalities share a common citizen-ship — the official position for the last forty years or so. A new argument, or rather a newly revived one, has it that China is actually inhabited by a single ethnic group. In other words, all the nationalities are, beneath their apparent diversity, one …

The Communist Party stopped making offers of secession after the Long March, when it was in regular contact with Mongols, Huis, and other non-Hans who might have been tempted to go their own way. By the time it seized nationwide power it was committed to the idea of a multinational China, with compulsory membership for all within its claimed fron-tiers. Two days before the proclamation of the People's Republic, Article 50 of the Common Programme of the Chinese People's Political Consultative Conference banned 'actions to split the solidarity of the various nationalities'. It also laid down the principles of nominal autonomy for ethnics. With variations of phrasing, similar provisions have been made in all later constitutions of the People's Republic. For the rest of Mao's reign the doctrine of many nationalities was taken seriously, and racial thinking was treated as an evil characteristic of the West …

The difficulties of holding together a group as large, diverse, and multilingual as the Hans may also underlie the profound unease in China about the process of self-conscious ethnogenesis going on in Taiwan. For the first time ever, a significant number of an originally Han-Chinese population living within the former boundaries of the Qing empire have begun to define themselves politically as other than Chinese, and to see their Chineseness as a back-ground identity to their primary one.

RESURRECTING PEKING MAN

It may well be that worries about holding China together lie behind a strange reversion, in the 1980s, to a notion of Chinese ethnicity curiously similar to that held by Chiang Kai-shek. When lecturing at the Chinese University of Hong Kong in 1985, Fei Xiaotong, the doyen of Chinese sociologists who had been much involved in the process of ethnic classification in the early 1950s, advanced – as if for the first time – the concept of a single Zhonghua nation-ality for all Chinese citizens that embraced all other ethnic identities – Hans, Uygurs, Yaos, and everyone else. For Fei, Zhonghua nationality has a 'pluralistic unitary structure': the distinct identities of the various nationalities, though still recognized, are secondary to their identity as Zhonghua; the whole course of Chinese history has led to the fusion of what have been distinct ethnic groups into one. A similar process has been happening in the writing of history. In the first of the projected forty-two parts of the *General History of China* under the editorship of Bai Shouyi, the very first chapter has the revealing title, 'A Unitary Polyethnic History' – a form of words that projects into remote antiquity the statement in the preamble to the 1982 Constitution that the People's Republic of China is a 'unitary polyethnic state'.

The point of emphasizing unity over multiplicity may well be an attempt to discredit claims by any nationality to self-determination or independence. How could any part of the Zhonghua nation legitimately secede from itself? One can see an example of this kind of thinking in the *faux-naif* comments of a 1993 volume, a sustained attack on the legitimacy of Mongolian independence:

> Right up to today the broad people (*guangda renmin*) of the PRC feel confused about the independence of Outer Mongolia. In their deep-seated traditional thinking it seems wrong that the vast Outer Mongolian grasslands should have been separated from the map of China. People still see the Mongolian *zu* [a term that could mean nationality or could mean rather less] as an organic part of the Hua-Xia [broadly synonymous with Zhonghua] nation. People often think of the outstanding Mongol hero Chinggis Khan as a hero of the whole of China …

The newly reinvented, unitary Chinese national identity raises many questions – including the problem of whether it has been racialized.

There are some worrying trends. One is the notion discussed above that human evolution from *Homo erectus* to *Homo sapiens* took place separately in different parts of the world and that today's Chinese have been biologically distinct from 'whites' and 'blacks', through tens of thousands of generations. This runs counter to the more widely accepted view that all members of the human race alive today spring from the same early *Homo sapiens* stock, which replaced more primitive hominids around a hundred thousand years ago … The point to consider here is not whether the Chinese palaeontologists who argue for separate development are correct; that issue will probably be resolved within a few years … We are here concerned rather with the use to which such theories are put …

The appropriation of early hominid remains as ancestors can be seen very clearly in the treatment of the Peking Man site at Zhoukoudian, now a shrine; a head has been reconstructed to make him look as Chinese as possible as he gazes purposefully into the brilliant future of his descendants. Another sign of the return to respectability of racial concepts is the 1984 *Dictionary of Nationalities*, which – in contrast to the *Great Chinese Encyclopaedia* referred to earlier – carries careful articles on racial characteristics, racial discrimination, and the disappearance of races. A textbook on ethnology published by the Central Nationalities Institute in 1990 has a whole chapter on 'The Races of Humanity' which affirms the biological reality of supposedly racial differences even while playing down their cultural significance.

While archaeologists and ethnologists have been moving rather carefully into racial questions, others have shown fewer inhibitions. A handbook on *guoqing* – loosely translatable as Chineseness – produced in 1990 and evidently aimed at a mass market, includes the following entry:

> *The Zhonghua race.* A race formed over the last four million years on the Great Zhonghua Land ... Its main characteristics include shovel shaped incisors ...

The entry goes on to list other physical characteristics, notably features of the skull ... The article also asserts that 'China's Yunnan may be one of the birthplaces of the world's human race. China is the original home (*guxiang*) of the modern Yellow Race'. This brings us back to the concerns about the potential political implications of such thinking, referred to at the beginning of this essay. Though there have been disquieting signs in recent years, racism is not yet part of the official ideology of the state. Previously, such tendencies had been associated with the crumbling rule of the Guomindang. The danger is that a moribund Communist Party dictatorship may now be turning to a racially tinged nationalism for its own support.

If we look back over the Jiang Zemin era, from its ill-defined opening when Deng Xiaoping lost the ability to control policy, around 1995, there has been a growing tendency to talk of the *minzu*, or nation: of its greatness, its destiny, the wrongs it has suffered. The *minzu* seems by now to be coming close to replacing the *renmin*, the people, in much official discourse. In October 2000, for example, in a speech on the fiftieth anniversary of China's entry into the Korean war, Jiang made much of the achievements of the Chinese 'people's volunteers' in defending the 'dignity of the nation'. The previous year, he marked the eightieth anniversary of the wave of demonstrations that began on 4 May 1919, against China's shameful treatment at the Paris Peace Conference, by identifying with the protesters' nationalism – and playing down the May 4th Movement's demands for a cultural revolution to replace many of China's dominant traditions with Western values of science and democracy.

In the long and almost astonishingly boring speech attributed to Jiang to mark the eighty-first anniversary of the Communist Party of China on 1 July 2001, the speech-writing team tried to play a complicated game. They deliberately evoked memories of 'On the People's Democratic Dictatorship', the pithier piece that Mao's scribes had produced for the twenty-eighth anniversary in 1949 – maintaining a rhetorical continuity with that era by making much use of the propaganda term 'Chinese people'. At the same time, they worked in a number of references to the 'Zhonghua nation'. The resulting document – setting out as it did the Jiang case for a Communist Party that did not merely accept a need to encourage capitalism but welcomed capitalists into its ranks and opposed class conflict – signally failed to resolve its own contradictions. But it left no doubt about one thing. For a regime that has given up on socialism and the rhetoric of class struggle, the appeal to nationalist sentiment is now all important.

Source: W. J. F. Jenner, 'Race and History in China',
New Left Review, No. 11, September/October 2001, pp. 55–7, 71, 73–7

14

China enters the twenty-first century

As China entered the twenty-first century it demonstrated unprecedented economic growth. In the coastal cities, skyscrapers mushroomed. New and improved railways appreciably shortened journey times between Beijing and Guangzhou and Beijing and Xian. Most farmers have continued to prosper, while many workers as well as the self-employed are better off and can set their sights on a greater variety of personal possessions. Private car ownership is now possible for many.

In such times of change, however, new problems have arisen from, for example, the migration from countryside to cities, the chronic water shortage, industrial pollution, and social inequalities arising from the end of the 'iron rice bowl' (jobs for life). There remains the problem of the growing population and the side effects of the single child policy, compounded with longevity. In 1949 the average life span was thirty-five, by 1993 it was seventy.

Economic reform and closer links with the West have also, however, promoted greater individual and intellectual freedom, and emerging non-governmental organizations are making use of the internet. At the lowest levels of government there is also limited scope for individuals not backed by the Party to intervene in politics, and some public protest is tolerated. But the Communist Party still imposes censorship – including of the web – and punishes some forms of dissent very severely.

Economic reform has encouraged corruption – not only the bribery often associated with pioneering entrepreneurial expansion but also extortion by Party officials. The power of these men has enabled them to make and break contracts, practise nepotism, and get rich ingloriously!

The Communist Party is still seated firmly in power, its leadership significantly younger than it was at the time of Deng's death in 1997. At the Sixteenth Party Congress held in November 2002, the 76 year old Jiang Zemin stepped down as Party General Secretary in favour of his deputy Hu Jintao, who is 59 years old. But Jiang seems to retain significant control as head of the Party's military commission.

On 1 July 2001 at the meeting celebrating the eightieth anniversary of the Communist Party, Jiang Zemin delivered a cornerstone speech 'intended to push Party building in an all-round way in the new century'. 'The Three Represents' is an up-to-date statement on 'building socialism with Chinese characteristics'. Since it rejects a class-based approach to politics, it appears to favour the private businesses of 'the advanced productive forces' and has met criticism from the left. In the end, the Sixteenth Party Conference decided that 'The Three Represents' was to be the new 'guiding ideology' for the foreseeable future rather than the doctrines of Marx and Lenin.

On the international stage, China is a world trader of consequence – a regional power capable of hosting the Asia Pacific Economic Cooperation group with aplomb. In 2001, after fifteen years of negotiations, China was accepted into the World Trade Organization. Even more spectacularly in the eyes of ordinary Chinese, China for the first time qualified for the World Football Cup finals in 2002 and 'best of all' is set to host the Olympic Games in 2008.

14.1 Changes in Chinese women's social status

From *Beijing Review*, 30 December 1991

In September 1990, the All-China Women's Federation and the State Statistical Bureau jointly conducted a major survey of the social status of Chinese women, the first survey of its kind since the founding of New China. The result of the survey shows that in the past four decades the social status of Chinese women, 50 percent of China's population, has changed tremendously ...

Recently, the All-China Women's Federation and the State Statistical Bureau published a compilation of these data and the computer analysis of the material:

1 **Employment** This is the most important condition for an improvement in the social status of women and the material basis for achieving equality with men. The result of the survey indicates that the proportion of employed women is 9.8 percentage points lower that that of men. However, the figure is 20.7 percentage points higher than that of the previous generation. Of those women under the age of 40 surveyed, 5.18 percent were engaged in household chores; the figure was 27.54 percent for the previous generation. The data also indicate that, of women workers, the proportion engaged in mental and more complex jobs is on the increase.

2 **Educational level** A solid education is the foundation upon which women's development potential for productive employment is based. It is not only an important gauge of women's social status but a factor that can affect their upward mobility. Statistics show that the educational level of women is higher as age decreases. Of those women below 40 years of age, 61.25 percent have an education level above junior middle school, some 32.2 percentage points higher than those above the age of 40, and 49.9 percentage points higher than that of the previous generation. In accordance with the standards for eliminating illiteracy that were formulated by the State Council, 78.22 percent of urban and 48.4 percent of rural women are now literate and able to read and write. A survey of adult education shows that 31.74 percent of women receive adult education.

3 **Marital status** The option of marrying someone of their own choice has basically replaced mercenary marriages. This conclusion was confirmed in the survey. Of married women, those who 'decided to marry' or 'jointly decided to marry' accounted for 73.89 percent. With regard to decision making in household affairs, 53.47 percent of the women surveyed confirmed that their family economy is jointly decided upon with their husbands. The women surveyed were fairly sanguine about their status, and 51.96 percent of them considered their status 'high' or 'very high' in their family life. Only 2.04 percent considered their status 'fairly low' or 'very low.'

4 **Self-image** Women's self image and their knowledge of external affairs play an important role in the formation and development of their social status. The survey shows that Chinese women are enterprising and that most have full confidence in their ability, demanding of themselves that they accomplish something in their life ...

5   **Women's status** The highest appraisal of whether the status of men and women is equal is in terms of the law. Some 81.07 percent of women surveyed are of the opinion that men and women are equal before the law. Next in importance behind their legal status is their status in the family, politics, and the economy. The lowest criterion by which women judge their status is based on social opinion; only 40.39 percent believe that men and women are equal in this regard.

Initial analysis of the survey shows that, in the past four decades, the social status of Chinese women has undergone historical changes. The socialist society has not only legally established equality between men and women but also offered the economic means to realize that equality in real life so that the social gap between them has narrowed. Generally speaking, the social status of Chinese women has made rapid progress over the past four decades. However, the development is uneven and dependent on the region and particular social and economic situations. Inequality still exists between men and women in some areas. For instance, the opportunity for employment is not equal, as is the opportunity to enrol in schools. In some rural areas, if women give birth to a female child, they will be discriminated against.

> Source: 'Changes in Chinese Women's Status',
> *Beijing Review*, Vol. 34, No. 52, 30 December 1991, pp. 22–3

14.2 The water crisis

Felicity Thomas, *China In Focus*, 1998

China, with a quarter of the world's population, is facing a water crisis in terms of both water pollution and depletion of potable water. Should the government fail to find adequate solutions to this crisis, water issues could become a major obstacle to future development and could even threaten social stability.

WATER POLLUTION

Water in the Huaihe River which traverses Anhui and Jiangsu provinces in the north of China is seriously polluted. A Chinese reporter writing a story about the pollution asked a seven-year-old Chinese child: 'What is the colour of water'. Without hesitation, the child replied, 'Black'. Public attention to the Huaihe River problem has encouraged central government support of a clean-up of China's major water bodies as part of the ninth five-year plan (1996–2000). An estimated 182 billion yuan (23 billion US dollars) is required for water pollution control projects in China.

The Huaihe River valley is one of China's largest paper-producing regions. Henan's 600 mills, almost all town and village enterprises, account for one-seventh of the country's total paper production and are located in this valley. More than 2.6 billion tons of primarily untreated waste water is discharged into the river each year. The Ministry of Agriculture has declared the river unfit for irrigation owing to its high levels of pollution, but it is the only source of water for some 10 million residents. The State Environmental Protection Agency (SEPA) has made efforts to reduce pollution, but many factories it closed down on pollution grounds have been reopened. Others have ceased using environmental technologies they were forced to purchase.

Pollution of other major water arteries in China has resulted in damage to human health, fisheries, and agriculture, and has undermined ecosystems through eutrophication and the loss of plant and animal species. (Owing to ever-increasing demand and resources depleted by pollution, the cost of clean water has been steadily increasing. Although the quality of China's surface water and ground water has been significantly impaired since the 1980s, the good news is that, overall, industrial waste water emissions appear to have remained relatively stable during the 1990s.)

One major cause of water pollution is municipal sewage discharges, which nearly tripled between 1981 and 1995 and are increasing at about 7% a year. According to a World Bank report, the Yellow, Huai, Hai, Luan, and Daliao rivers are all unusable for potable water systems, and Guangdong environmental officials have estimated that, although 80% of industrial waste water discharges are treated, only 10% of sewage waste receives treatment.

LACK OF GRASS-ROOTS SUPPORT

Unfortunately, the central government's attempts to reduce pollution have been thwarted by a lack of local government support for policies that appear likely to limit economic development. For example, even though the clean-up of the 425 square km Taihu lake, a major source of drinking water for Shanghai, has been targeted as a top environmental priority, SEPA says that little progress had been made in meeting environmental goals and that local authorities 'do not realise the importance of this task'.

One of the obstacles in enforcing new stringent environmental policies is a lack of environmental awareness and the desperate desire of individuals to improve their living conditions at any cost. Before rash judgements are passed, it should be understood that approximately 72% of the Chinese population are peasants living on an income equivalent to less than 130 US dollars per year ...

PRIVATISATION?

As of October 1997 there were only 150 sewage treatment plants in China, most of which were constructed after 1988. Investment in treatment plants only covers facility construction and equipment, so the costs of operation and sewer network construction fall to local governments which often lack adequate financial means ...

Leading the way in new reform initiatives, Shanghai has been discussing a management system reform that would result in the establishment of private waste water treatment companies. Such companies would be authorised to collect waste water tariffs in return for full responsibility over ensuring treatment plant operation, maintenance, and loan repayment.

WATER SHORTAGES

Northern China faces a 'serious water shortage' due to inadequate reserves and rapid urban growth. Nationwide, water shortages are expected to reach one billion cubic metres a year by the year 2010. The Ministry of Water Resources has calculated that urban Chinese 'will be unable to drink clean water' within 30 years unless new conservation measures are implemented. The SEPA has indicated that 'about 60 million people still find it difficult to get enough water for their daily needs' ...

Of 640 cities in China, more than half have inadequate local water supplies, and 108 cities face chronic shortages that resulted in 27.7 billion US dollars worth of lost industrial output last year; the equivalent of 3% of the country's gross domestic product.

THE PRICE OF WATER

Recently, an official from the Ministry of Construction observed that: 'In most parts of the country the existing water management system, formed under a planned economy, is not suitable for a socialist market economy. The unreasonably low price of water means losses for water supply and sewage treatment companies and contributes to the public's low awareness level of the need to save water'.

According to the ministry, leaky plumbing fixtures result in the loss of approximately 440 million tons of water each year. Authorities have also calculated that an additional 25% of urban water supplies are lost to leakage in underground utility lines at a cost of 360 million US dollars each year.

Water is routinely rationed in cities owing to periodic droughts and inadequate reserves. State planners have, however, not gone so far as to raise water rates, and urban householders typically pay a subsidised rate equivalent to approximately one US dollar a month for water.

GOVERNMENT CONCERN

The rapid degradation of China's water resources has not gone unnoticed by the government. In 1996, officials from SEPA stated: 'We are clearly aware that the situation of the environment in our country is still quite severe. Environmental pollution in centre cities is worsening and is extending into rural areas, and the scope of ecological damage is increasing'.

In order to tackle the current water crisis, the Chinese government must increase investment; however, they cannot shoulder the full burden alone. Financing for treatment may have to be obtained by issuing bonds or by attracting private or public investments. The Ministries of Water Resources and Construction are discussing plans to refer the real cost of water treatment to consumers and of developing schemes to entice foreign investment into the water treatment infrastructure.

What is encouraging is that the Chinese government appears to be fully aware of the extremity of the current water crisis and is making concentrated efforts to move policies forward to resolve the problem. Only the future will reveal whether these policies can attract enough private and public sector investment to avoid a situation where many Chinese citizens do not have access to potable water.

Source: Felicity Thomas, 'Perilous Waters', *China in Focus*, No. 4, 1998, pp. 12–13

14.3 The election campaign, October 1998

Yang Yonghe

In 1988 the Chinese Government set up direct elections for village committees. During the 1990s, elections were held in over half of China's 930,000 villages. Peasant Yang Yonghe seized the opportunity to stand when an election was announced in his village in Henan Province in October 1998.

If you trace back eight generations of my ancestors, you won't find any in a position of authority. But so what?! As a carpenter, a 'commoner', I too now have the right to be elected village leader. The idea to contest for the leadership got into my head in spring 1998, watching the *In Focus* programme after the national news ...

I didn't have to wait long. In early October, we were told that on the twenty-eighth there would be an election for the new village-committee chairman and two committee members. For the first time, it would be a direct election by secret ballot, open to all voters. I was very excited; it meant a more democratic election, and more opportunity for a commoner like me. I must admit I have never served as a cadre in the village. There were supposedly two elections before, but I only remember one half a dozen years ago. Even though I was over 18, I had nothing to do with that election, and only a few representatives cast votes. To be honest, most people didn't even care at that time, as they assumed, 'The candidates were nominated by the authorities, so that's it!' Some hold such views even today.

All villagers here in Shangzhuang are divided into twelve groups. The head of ours was Mr Yang, a relative of mine – up to 90 per cent of the villagers share the family name Yang and many are related. One day, he showed me a piece of paper with three names on it. 'Do you agree that these three will be our representatives?' I asked what for and he couldn't even give me a clear answer. Most people just agreed without asking. I then found out these representatives were the important people who would decide the candidates for the election. The old village committee nominated three representatives from each group, supposedly with the consent of villagers.

I immediately threw myself into the election campaign. I told my fellow villagers, and particularly the representatives, that I wished to run for village-committee chairman. On the twenty-second, the day before voting for preliminary candidates, I put up three big-character posters in which I declared my administrative programmes if elected. I concentrated on three issues: firstly, I want to solve the old problem of village chiefs spending public funds on lavish banquets; secondly, I want to deal with the distribution of land for housing in a just and fair way; finally, I plan to set up a service company to engage in various businesses. My poster roused a big stir. Such behaviour was unheard of! Some appreciated my efforts, some said I just wanted to satisfy my thirst for power, and others thought I was crazy. Anyway, probably with the help of my posters, I got myself elected as one of six preliminary candidates. I was the odd one out: the other five previously held positions in the production team and all are Party members.

On 25 October, three days before the real election, the names for the final candidates were decided according to election procedure. As expected, I failed ... Disappointed, I did not want to give up yet. The day before polling, I put up another poster, signed by five respected old Party members, in which I urged people to cherish their sacred ballots and elect someone they really trust. This caused more gossip, and some criticized my 'Cultural Revolution style'. I argued that I didn't ask people to vote for me, only to vote carefully.

That same night, our Party secretary called on me. By the way, the Party secretary is appointed, not democratically elected, yet he is just as powerful as the village-committee chairman, if not more so. He asked me what all the fuss was about. I explained I did not mean to make trouble, but to take part in the election sincerely. I asked if he could talk to the election work team and let me give a speech, even a very short one, as I knew candidates may make campaign speeches if they wish. He refused at first but I begged him, and he eventually agreed to speak to them, but made no promises.

On 28 October, election day, I got up early, anxious and excited. That morning, my younger brother, the village electrician, set up a loudspeaker at the primary school where polling would take place. How I wished I could use that loudspeaker! When he returned, he brought me back a message, saying the election work team wanted to see me. I found the team in a classroom. Made up of rank-and-file villagers, they were very polite but soon came to the point: did I have any intention of making a speech. I replied, 'Yes'. They first praised my enthusiasm but suggested I forget the idea, as they were under pressure to ensure the election was carried out smoothly. 'You have no chance anyway', they pointed out, 'Why make things difficult for everyone?' That was my weak point: I knew I had little chance, and, after hesitation, I agreed.

I felt so depressed at that moment, but I remained civil. I heard in other villages, when people were unhappy with elections for some reason, they burnt the ballot boxes and boycotted elections. Walking out of the classroom, I met some friends and confessed my agreement not to speak. 'Silly man!' they replied, 'Why don't you try?! You have lots of good ideas'. I began to regret I had given up so readily.

At 10 a.m., the election began, accompanied by the national anthem. The chairperson announced the election procedures and rules. Just as people were about to cast their ballots, on impulse I threw myself to the ground. Kneeling in front of the podium, I pleaded, 'Please give me a chance! I want to say a few words'. Kneeling down is a traditional way to beg from the authorities ...

The civil affairs officer who came to supervise the election explained that only formal candidates have the right to deliver campaign speeches. Others added that, if everyone wanted to give a speech, there would be chaos. It was indeed getting chaotic, as more and more people entered the room to have a look or shout 'give him a chance to speak!' I was too excited for words and hot tears rolled down my face. 'A real man does not shed tears easily'. I didn't know why I cried. As the situation was getting out of control, the election team decided to let me speak. There was no other way for the election to continue.

Overjoyed, I went to the podium and made a passionate speech, the only one of my life, in front of my fellow villagers. I basically summarized my administrative programme. When I finished twenty minutes later, I was greeted with loud applause. I thought people would like my points. We all hate to see village leaders entertain their bosses from the township or higher authority with expensive banquets, or find all kinds of excuse to treat themselves. True, this is a common problem in China's countryside, but our place is poor: average annual income was RMB 1,600 in 1998.

Another major complaint concerned land for housing, as the government in recent years has restricted non-farming land usage, to protect shrinking arable land. As it grew more and more difficult to get permission to build new houses, the village committee took advantage by letting people bid for plots of land. Prices soared, from RBM 2,000 to a record RMB 36,500, and that doesn't include the actual construction cost. I believe such practice is illegal.

Finally, I don't think the village committee tried hard at all in leading the villagers to get rich. I frequently go out as a temporary migrant worker and see changes happening every-where. How about us? There are a couple of iron mines which started back in Chairman Mao's time, plus profit from house-bidding, and limited farming income. That's all we have. There are no rural enterprises or any other kind of business. The idea of my service company is to provide farmers with more business opportunities, such as raising animals, or some kind of processing industry, to help people get rich.

The results came out in the afternoon: there were 1,230 villagers qualified to vote, but I am not sure how many votes were valid. The two official candidates Yang Yanqing and Yang Shukuan won 337 and 150 respectively, and I myself 197. If it had been explained properly how to vote for unlisted candidates, I believe I might have won 100 more. Voters needed to cross out the listed candidates and add my name, but many did not cross them out, or circled them and added my name. Since none of us received more than half of all votes, the election was declared a failure. Another one will have to be held.

My life changed completely after the election. I was shunned by village leaders as well as their families. On the other hand, I won sympathy from people who felt that I had said what they wanted to say …

I don't know when the new election will be. Of course, I will contest it again, but I'm not going to waste my time waiting. I've just invested in a new type of sweet potato which is said to give higher yields and has better resistance to pests. If it's successful, I will introduce it to my fellow villagers, as I want to have more to offer them when I am village leader. I don't mean to promise miracles – I am no miracle worker with three heads and six arms. What I can promise is a clean chief keen to work for their interests.

I don't know much about Western democracy, but I'm confident about China's grass-roots version. I heard about President Clinton's sex scandal from the television. In their system, there are incredible events like putting the president on trial. I'm not sure we want that kind of democracy. But as China develops, maybe one day we will have a democratically elected president too.

Source: Yang Yonghe, 'The Election Campaign: October 1998'. In Zhang Lijia and Calum Macleod, *China Remembers* (Hong Kong: Oxford University Press, 1999), pp. 279–83

14.4 China loses battles in its 'war' on births

John Pomfret, *Washington Post*, May 2000

Uneven enforcement undermines one-child policy, and sets the scene for severe social problems.

No one can accuse Huo Suifa of not knowing what he wanted. The 47 year old farmer dreamed of having a son. After seven daughters, he finally got a male heir in 1989.

Although eight children make a big brood anywhere – and although China is notorious for what on paper is a draconian one-child policy – Huo's family is not that unusual in China. Almost 20 years after the government began to try limiting the population, the controversial initiative appears seriously undermined by the widely disparate way it is administered from town to town, province to province, and year to year.

The policy is still on the books, particularly in cities. But its reach in many places has been limited by corruption, economic development, erosion of central control over local governments, grave demographic problems, and the growing unwillingness of the Chinese people to tolerate controls on their personal lives.

The policy's slow dissipation is not being pushed from above. Only recently, for instance, President Jiang Zemin called on Party members to treat population control and family planning as a 'protracted war'. But uneven pursuit of the war around the country and relaxed enforcement of penalties – combined with the failure to find new ways to limit a population already estimated at 1.3 billion – risk magnifying already serious demographic challenges.

China's family planning effort remains perhaps the most misunderstood, complex, and varied of all the policies the country has embraced in its race to become a modern nation. On the one hand, the campaign has prompted intense criticism from the West. Human rights advocates have denounced forced abortions, destruction of homes, coerced sterilizations, and the killing of female babies that were triggered in part by strict population controls.

On the other, little mention has been made of the fact that the policy has been neglected more than it has been carried out, that many exceptions have been allowed, and that, according to Chen Shengli, a senior official at the State Family Planning Commission, only 60 million of the 300 million children under 14 today are from single-child families. That means 80 percent of China's children have brothers or sisters, and many have both.

'It wasn't easy to have all those children, but it wasn't hard either,' said farmer Huo, as he squatted near his one-third acre field of winter wheat in this district 420 miles south-west of Beijing. 'If things became tough in our village, my wife went to another township to have the child.'

And so, as census takers fan out across China this year for the fifth national census, they will find a country that has implemented the one-child policy in enormously varied ways. No cities so far have loosened the reins on 200 million urban dwellers, still limited to one child and held back by a system of fines and the reality of crowded city living. But some townships in the central province of Ningxia, China's poorest region, openly tolerate families with five or six children. Others, such as villages in mountainous Anhui province, have been mandating sterilizations after just one child.

Thus administered, the one-child policy has created enormous demographic stresses and set the scene for severe social problems. In some areas, there are two boys for every girl, a product of the Chinese preference for male heirs combined with the restrictions on births. That in turn has spawned a growing industry in the trafficking of women.

In other areas, however, corruption has weakened population controls. Interviews throughout the country indicate that, in general, as long as a rural family has enough money, the couple can have as many children as they want. In some places, family planning workers encourage more births, because more births mean fines, and fines mean more pocket money for government officials.

While the population in the countryside is rising, the population in cities is tumbling, increasing the gap between China's haves, most often small families, and its have-nots, particularly the rural poor with large families …

Corruption also has played a role in weakening the one-child policy. Underreporting of births could mean that China's population is already as high as 1.4 billion or even 1.5 billion, some experts say.

In the Miaoxia township here in northern Henan province, family planning bureaucrats were ordered for years to bring in $1,250 a month in fines as a way to enrich government officials. They also could sell birth permits. The township's population boomed, but the area never reported a high birth rate to Beijing. ...

One of this country's looming social problems is a shortage of women. In 1995, the results of a population survey showed 36.8 million more men than women in China and that single men aged 25 to 49 outnumber single women by 15 times. Today, the divergence is even greater. Experts estimate that there are 66 million more men than women ...

Source: John Pomfret, 'China Loses the Battle in its "War" on Births',
***Washington Post,* reprinted in *Guardian Weekly,* 18–24 May 2000, p. 29**

14.5 China faces the challenge of an aging society

Zhang Zhiping, *Beijing Review,* 19 July 2001

The fifth national census reveals significant changes in the structure of the Chinese population. Accounting for 22.89 percent of the total population are newborns to teenagers of 14 years of age, a decrease of 4.8 percentage points compared with the 1990 census, while people over 65 years of age account for 6.96 percent of the total, an increase of 1.39 percentage points. With the elderly making up 6.96 percent of the total population, China faces challenges associated with the problems of aging.

ACCELERATED AGING

Generally speaking, the criterion for an elderly society is when people over the age of 60 make up more than 10 percent of the total population and people over 65 make up 7 percent.

According to data from the fifth national census, people over 60 in China number 132 million, or 10 percent of the total population. It is predicted that, in the next 50 years, China's elderly population will grow by an average annual rate of 3.2 percent. By 2040, the number of elderly people over the age of 60 will reach 400 million, or 26 percent of the total population. That means on average there will be one elderly person among nearly every four Chinese. In big cities, there will be one senior citizen among every two to three people ...

INCOMPLETE SOCIAL SECURITY MEASURES

An 'empty nest' family is one with an elderly person living alone or with his or her spouse. The children have left home like birds flying away from the nest, and the elderly are left behind lonely and without the care of their children ...

Yet, corresponding social security measures lag far behind. According to statistics from relevant departments, fewer than 1 million elderly people live in homes for the aged with relatively complete facilities, which comprise a tiny portion of the total number of senior citizens. In some homes for the aged with comparatively fine conditions and facilities, the occupancy rate is only 30 percent. Influenced by Chinese tradition, most elderly people, especially those with children, are unwilling to spend their later years in a home for the aged. They believe that living there is disgraceful because it indicates that their children have no filial piety …

STARLIGHT PROGRAM

In early June this year, the Ministry of Civil Affairs announced that China would launch a nationwide campaign of community service for the elderly called the 'Starlight Program' as a measure to cope with the aging population.

Under the program, departments of civil affairs from the central to local levels will use the majority of funds raised through welfare lotteries over the next three years to aid in the construction of community facilities and exercise sites for the elderly in urban areas and homes for the aged in rural areas.

The Starlight Program is a major move by the Chinese government to cope with the challenge of an aging population. It means that, in a short period, a community service system covering residential quarters with relatively complete facilities in large and medium-sized cities will take form, which will be of far-reaching significance in the country.

Source: Zhang Zhiping, 'China Faces the Challenge of an Aging Society',
Beijing Review, Vol. 44, No. 29, 19 July 2001, pp. 12–15

14.6 Worker protest from 'Fighting to Organize'

Jiang Xueqin, from *Far Eastern Economic Review*, 6 September 2001

On a hot, still summer's afternoon in Zhengzhou, the industrial wasteland capital of China's Henan province, a convoy of vans arrives at the gates of a factory. The doors of the vans burst open, revealing an army of about 300 men. Jumping down into the dust of the road, the men rush the gates of the factory. Inside, a small group of workers springs into action. They ring the factory bell, and within minutes almost a thousand workers materialize. Overwhelmed, and beaten back with kicks and punches, the invaders struggle back to the vans and speed off.

For the workers at Zhengzhou Power Generation Apparatus Works, the battle on 24 July this year was a small victory in a long and difficult war. Back in 1996, the 1,800 employees at this state-owned factory were told that it was to be closed and liquidated. Shocked at the prospect of losing their jobs, they could at least comfort themselves with the knowledge that they would receive – as set down in the law – a substantial share of the proceeds from the sale of the factory's assets.

But when trucks arrived one night and started moving out equipment, the workers realized what was going on: factory managers were attempting to sell the equipment and land for fire-sale prices to their friends, and pocketing the proceeds.

The workers were furious. A small group of them sought the advice of outside labour activists and began organizing their fellow workers to resist the asset-stripping. Today, after almost five years of confrontations and several arrests, the former employees remain defiant. 'The workers are united, and we're confident we'll win', says Zhou Jinduo, one of the worker leaders.

In recent years, scenes like these at state-owned enterprises have been repeated across China as the country moves to a market economy. Few groups have been hit harder by the end of the iron rice bowl than the 80 million or so people who once worked at state-owned factories. Since the early 1990s, more than half are estimated to have lost their jobs.

Few outsiders would argue that many of these factories were living on borrowed time, but what has shocked almost everyone is the way that the state-owned assets of these enterprises have been systematically looted by their former managers. In 1998, the liberal economist He Qinglian wrote a best-selling book, *China's Pitfalls*, about the phenomenon. Dai Jianzhong, a sociologist at the Chinese Academy of Social Sciences who specializes in labour relations, believes the culture of corruption is in itself an active factor in the collapse of many state-owned factories: 'The most important reason for failures is lack of accountability in management, who use power to transfer wealth from workers to themselves'.

Anger over such acts is one factor in the huge rise in spontaneous worker protests. On 9 July this year, for instance, about 10,000 workers of the state-owned railway blocked a major railway line in Jilin province, demanding unpaid wages. According to the Hong Kong-based Information Centre for Human Rights and Democracy, China witnessed a total of 60,000 labour protests in 1998, most involving former state employees; the following year there were 100,000.

For the ruling Communist Party, such incidents represent one of its biggest headaches: in its eyes, independent organized labour can represent only one thing – a threat to its monopoly on power. Unlike the Falun Gong, though, the workers can't be dismissed as an evil cult. These, after all, are the proletariat – the backbone of Mao's People's Republic.

For remnants of the Left, many still wedded to Mao's vision for China, the rising anger of workers represents an opportunity once again to wield influence in China. 'Most state enterprises are finished', says one Beijing-based activist. 'But they have equipment and land that could be sold off, so workers have something to fight for. Workers only ask for what is theirs, and to work to make a living'.

Wu Qiang (not his real name) is typical of the far-Left labour organizers active in China. On a humid afternoon, he arrives at a watch factory in Chongqing to discuss with workers an offer aimed at settling a four year stand-off. Back in 1997, a local entrepreneur attempted to merge his company with the watch factory. The 'merger' was soon exposed for what it was: asset-stripping. The workers managed to hold their ground, and today, after four years without a salary, they want advice from Wu on whether they should accept an offer from the businessman to split the proceeds of the asset sale.

'You must refuse to compromise', shouts Wu, banging his fist on the table. 'You should use the law, sue him, and get the factory back'. After convincing the workers, Wu races out and spends the rest of the afternoon trying to find a lawyer to represent the workers.

For Wu, a strong-looking man in his mid-50s, such battles are about more than just workers' rights. Just graduating when Mao Zedong declared his back-to-basics Cultural Revolution, few can have heeded Mao's call with greater passion than Wu, and his devotion turned him into a powerful figure in Chongqing. But after Mao's death and the fall of the Gang of Four, the glory days ended, and Wu was imprisoned for 15 years.

Released in the early 1990s, Wu found himself in an unfamiliar country. Industry was booming, and Deng Xiaoping's economic reforms had raised standards of living, lifting 200 million out of poverty. But amid the progress, all Wu could see was corruption, an ever-growing wealth gap – and disgruntled workers. Unable to find work and driven by nostalgia for the past, he returned to organizing workers, supported mainly by the generosity of his friends. Today, Wu admits the going is tough: his once-proud Left is powerless, its ranks filled mainly with relics of the past.

Beijing, though, is taking few chances that it might revive. Just weeks ago, it ordered the effective closure of the Left's two main mouthpieces, *The Pursuit of Truth* and *Indomitable* – both vital to the labour activists' propaganda efforts – after criticisms by leading leftists of President Jiang Zemin's decision to welcome capitalists into the Communist Party.

The secret police, too, have long been wary of labour activists, fearing that as they travel across China they are building the foundations of a future nationwide labour movement. That's why most of the activists interviewed for this article asked not to be named. It's also why they refrain from forming an active network, and try to keep a low profile. 'We only work as consultants, because organizing is too sensitive', says the Beijing-based activist. 'We research the workers' situation, find out what ways work best. We only help workers who request help. If they don't request help its best to keep a distance from them'.

The wariness of workers is evident during a visit by labour activist Li Liqun (not his real name) to staff laid off from a ceramics factory in Zhengzhou. University-educated, Li is a rare young face among the ranks of China's labour activists. While most of his peers headed off into good jobs after leaving college, Li took the activist's path, becoming part of what's often called the 'New Left' – Marxists who spurn both the excesses of Mao and the reforms of Deng, and seek instead an egalitarian society through continued heavy state involvement in the economy, but with greater democratic representation.

Today, in Zhengzhou, Li is on his third visit, but only slowly gaining the trust of the suspicious workers, who are idly playing cards opposite the site of their old factory.

'They're selling off the inventory for 10% of value – the police, government, and factory managers are all in the scheme', complains one old woman. 'They've sold off the equipment already'. Turning to a group of workers, Li asks, 'Why don't you stop them from taking the property?'

'Don't dare', comes the reply.

'Workers don't recognize they have the power to protest', says a frustrated Li, a tall young man with crewcut hair and deep-set eyes. 'As long as they can eat they'll remain obedient. If they can't eat then they'll sell off their belongings. Workers believe it is right that managers have all the power and workers have none'.

Adds Wu in Chongqing: 'Workers who are employed are afraid if they organize they'll lose their job. Workers who are unemployed cannot organize because they are dispersed'.

Many observers believe that independent organized labour poses no real threat to Western multinationals operating in China. 'Most of the instances of worker unrest that are reported occur where local management, due to corruption, has caused the collapse of an enterprise', says Lawrence Brahm, a Beijing-based consultant to multinationals. 'This situation does not generally apply to multinationals, which offer higher wages, incentive programmes, and have the financial sustainability to provide long-term employment'.

According to sociologist Dai, it is the Communist Party that has most to fear. 'The government will not permit workers to organize because they're afraid of the Solidarity example in Poland', he says. In addition, the lack of an independent voice for workers allows officials to sweep injustices under the mat. 'Beijing thinks that, without an organization, workers are not a real threat, so they can just brush aside the problem', says Dai. The government, for instance, is able to shortchange workers of statutory payments, as it is doing in Zhengzhou, according to Zhang Yuzhu, head of the city government's statistics department. 'In Zhengzhou every person is supposed to get 170 renminbi a month as social security. Since 1998, most workers have each collected only about 1,000 renminbi altogether'.

According to Marc Blecher, a political scientist at Oberlin College in the United States who has studied China's labour problems, Beijing's approach to labour unrest mixes the occasional carrot with plenty of stick. The government 'puts fingers in dykes, paying off protesters where possible, and arresting some of the ringleaders where necessary'. The New York-based China Labour Watch, an international human rights organization, has records of a number of labour activists who are spending time in prison. These include Hu Shigen, a professor at the Beijing Languages Institute, who was jailed in 1993 for 20 years for attempting to organize the Free Labour Union of China – an independent rival to the official All-China Worker's Federation, which Dai describes as a 'Party tool'.

More broadly, says Blecher, Beijing hopes to see the tensions resolve themselves 'by relying on workers to seek new employment in the labour market; by continuing to adopt policies that fragment the working class; by relying on workers' propensity to blame themselves'.

Still, if all else fails, there's always brute force: 'The police are the most basic instrument of social security, and right now we are good at keeping a lid on things', says Huang Jian, head of the Chongqing police department's public relations operation. At a time of rising unemployment, the police are recruiting: 'We have close to 30,000 officers – we estimate we need 60,000. We're offering higher pay and benefits to attract new officers'.

According to the labour activist Wu, the police are now experienced in breaking up demonstrations: 'Police shove workers off the street, and if workers are stubborn then police will throw them into vans and drive them to the countryside. By the time the scattered workers walk back, everything is over'.

Will these strategies work forever? Police spokesman Huang admits they may not: 'Worker protests are a national phenomenon', he says, 'and there's no way to address this problem'. Labour activists, meanwhile, believe time is on their side: China's membership of the World Trade Organization will force markets to open further, placing further pressure on inefficient state-owned enterprises. 'We're optimistic', says the Beijing-based activist. 'Life will become more difficult so workers will have to organize. We're waiting for China's WTO entry'.

Back in Zhengzhou, the workers are beginning to hope that their five-year battle may not have been in vain. Following the violent clash in July, workers say the municipal government now seems ready to talk to them about turning the factory over to its former employees.

'We can manage the factory ourselves', says Zhou, the workers' leader, whose role in leading the fight landed him in jail for two months last year. 'Back in 1996 we let factory managers just tell us what to do – now we want control of our fate'.

Source: Jiang Xueqin, 'Fighting to Organize',
Far Eastern Economic Review, 6 September 2001, pp. 72–5

14.7 Should students be praised for playing the stock market?

From *Beijing Review*, 5 July 2001

In March, a newspaper based in Nanjing covered the story of Zhao Fan, a successful stock dealer who gained 500,000 yuan by trading on the stock market. Most noteworthy is that Zhao is a second-grade student at a senior middle school. Zhao told the reporter that his next objective was to become a millionaire. At the conclusion of the report, the reporter could not help but raise these questions: 'Is Zhao Fan's behavior praiseworthy or not? In today's China, should Zhao Fan be considered an outstanding student or a boy with a problem?'

A debate on whether middle school students should be allowed to play the stock market is sweeping the country.

Gao Youhe (a Harvard lecturer): Middle school students should be encouraged to invest in stocks, but not to speculate on the stock market.

First, I unconditionally agree with the idea that 'investment is a kind of expertise.' Appropriate investment will not only benefit the investor, but will also boost the national economy. In addition to savings deposits, investment also involves the purchase of stocks and bonds.

Second, middle school students should foster a reasonable concept of consumption at an early stage in their growth ...

Third, I'd say: Investment, yes; purchase of stocks, yes; but speculation on the stock market, no! Investment indicates payment based on the correct judgment and forecast of a business's performance and prospects ... As for speculation, I define it as a way to make money by taking advantage of the differences between the prices of purchase and sale. Without any analysis of the fundamentals of a business, speculation ... is equivalent to a gamble indeed, which is valueless to society and is especially harmful to the growth of middle school students.

Fourth, how can we ensure the investment is immune from speculation? I propose classes be launched to guide middle school students correctly to analyze the performance of listed companies, their accounting indices, and business features. In addition, the schools should organize their students to visit listed companies and invite staff workers of listed companies to give lectures on their respective commercial plans and implementation as well as their expected prospects and accounting situations. Education programs of this kind are expected to achieve satisfying results in the cultivation of entrepreneurs, which China very much lacks nowadays.

Source: 'Should Students be Praised for Playing the Stock Market?',
Beijing Review, Vol. 44, No. 27, 5 July 2001, pp. 26–7

14.8 The Three Represents, 1 July 2001

From Jiang Zemin's speech at the meeting celebrating the 80th Anniversary of the
Communist Party

'The Three Represents' are the foundation for building the Party, the cornerstone for its exercise of state power, and a source of its strength. They are also the fundamental requirements for us to push Party building in an all-round way in the new century, constantly bring forth new ideas in theories, institutions, and science and technology, and win fresh victories in building socialism with Chinese characteristics.

1   In order always to represent the requirements of the development of China's advanced productive forces, it is necessary to bring the Party's theory, line, program, principles, policies, and all endeavors of work into line with the law governing the development of the productive forces, especially in the development of advanced productive forces so that the living standards of the people improve steadily through the development of the productive forces ...

    After the founding of New China, we carried out the socialist transformation of agriculture, handicraft industry, and commerce in order to establish the socialist relations of production, and, on that economic base, bring the socialist superstructure to perfection so as to further release and expand the productive forces. It is for the same purpose that we have since the Third Plenary Session of the 11th Party Central Committee [see document 11.8] implemented the reform and opening-up policies to adjust and reform the part of the socialist relations of production that is incompatible with the demand of the development of the productive forces, and that of the socialist superstructure that is incompatible with the economic base. Over the past twenty-plus years, we have, through bold explorations and practice, pushed forward the reforms in the economic and political structures and other areas, which has greatly released and developed the country's social productive forces, bringing about tremendous changes in the national economic development and social progress. ...

2   To ensure that our Party forever represents the orientation of the development of China's advanced culture, it is imperative that the Party's theories, line, program, principles, policies, and all its work should orient toward modernization, the world, and the future, reflect the requirements of developing a national, scientific, and popular socialist culture, serve to upgrade the ideological and ethical standards and scientific and cultural levels of the whole nation, and provide spiritual and intellectual support for the economic development and social progress ...

    A vital principle we must follow in developing China's advanced culture is to emphasize the central theme of the socialist culture, persevere in serving the people and socialism, and let a hundred flowers blossom and a hundred schools of thought contend. We should master and develop all kinds of modern means of communication and promote the spreading of the advanced culture.

    To promote the socialist ideological and ethical standards constitutes an essential component of and a key link in developing China's advanced culture. We must realize that we would lose the common objective of struggle and reject the accepted code of conduct if we only valued material gains and money without thinking of ideals and moral standards. We should combine the rule of law with the rule of virtue in order to lay a lofty ideological and ethical foundation for a good public order and a healthy environment. We should advocate patriotism, collectivism, and socialism among all people, combat and resist money worship, hedonism, ultra-egoism, and other decadent ideas, enhance the Chinese people's national self-esteem, self-confidence, and the sense of pride, and inspire them to work unremittingly for the rejuvenation of the Chinese nation ...

3   To ensure that our Party always represents the fundamental interests of the overwhelming majority of the Chinese people, our Party must, in all its work, theories, line,

program, principles, and policies, always take the fundamental interests of the people as the starting point and purpose, bring into full play the people's enthusiasm, initiative, and creativity, and ensure the people continued tangible economic, political, and cultural benefits on the basis of steady social development and progress …

We should adhere to the mass line of the Party by going down to the people at the grass-roots level to hear their views, reflect their will, and pool their wisdom, so that all our policy decisions thus made and our work may conform to the reality and the demands of the masses. All cadres who are Party members must properly assume and exercise the power truly on behalf of the people, and in no way should they be allowed to abuse power for personal gains or form any vested interest groups. In the process of attaining the common prosperity of the people across the country, cadres who are Party members must correctly handle the relationships between becoming well-off early and late, and between personal prosperity and common prosperity. All leading Party cadres should be concerned about the country and the people before anything else; should be the first to bear hardships and the last to enjoy themselves; should support and help others first instead of only thinking about how to get rich themselves. The last thing they should do is to abuse power for unlawful interests …

Representing the requirements of the development of China's advanced productive forces, representing the orientation of the development of China's advanced culture, and representing the fundamental interests of the overwhelming majority of the Chinese people are interrelated and mutually supportive. They thus constitute an integral whole. To develop the advanced productive forces is a basic condition for developing an advanced culture and ensuring the people their own fundamental interests. Ceaselessly to develop the advanced productive forces and culture is, in the final analysis, aimed at meeting the growing material and cultural needs of the people and continously realizing the fundamental interests of the people.

Source: Jiang Zemin, 'The Three Represents', Speech celebrating 80th Anniversary of CCP, I July 2001. *People's Daily* version of speech available in two parts on the Internet: http://english.peopledaily.com.cn/200/107/01/eng20010701_73919.html; http://english.peopledaily.com.cn/200/107/01/eng20010701_73927.html

14.9 Call to put the market into Marxism splits China's Communist Party

John Gittings, *The Guardian*, 21 August 2001

OLD-GUARD REBELS AGAINST PRESIDENT JIANG'S REFORM PLANS IN RUN-UP TO CRUCIAL CONGRESS

China's official media has rallied to the defence of President Jiang Zemin against critics who say his new reforms are 'threatening the future of the Communist Party'. Every night, national television shows scenes of government and military officials studying a controversial speech Mr Jiang made last month in which he proposed that private businessmen should be allowed to join the Party.

A dissenting manifesto from old-guard Party socialists has objected that the proposal 'will split the Party' and, if successful, will destroy the organisation's support base in the working class. Most ordinary Chinese pay no attention to the new ideological debate, but there is widespread scepticism about closer links between the ruling party and private business. In the words of one cynical intellectual: 'Party members all want to get rich anyway. If they become capitalists, that will speed things up and save a lot of argument'.

Mr Jiang has prepared the way over the past year by propounding a new theory to 'develop' the ideas of Marx, Lenin, and Mao Zedong. Known as the theory of 'three representations', it says that the Party should represent the majority interests of society. It rejects by implication a class-based approach to politics and legitimises the approach to private business which represents society's 'advanced productive forces'.

The idea has been taken up enthusiastically in the go-ahead southern province of Guangdong. Party commentators there say that Mr Jiang's theory will allow more flexible industrial policies as China prepares to enter the World Trade Organisation. This month the Chinese Communist Youth League sent a group of graduates to Gaozhou, the rural area in Guangdong where Mr Jiang first announced his new ideas last year. The tour was the subject of a popular TV magazine programme, showing students and peasants pooling ideas on how to develop the local economy, and declaring that they had been inspired by Mr Jiang's theories. The Youth League plans to send hundreds more groups of graduates and students to the countryside in coming months.

Left-wing critics have compared Mr Jiang's ideas with those put forward in the Soviet Union before its collapse 10 years ago. Their manifesto argues that, far from the class struggle becoming less important, it has become 'increasingly vigorous'. As the gap widens between rich and poor, 'the bourgeoisie now appears as a class of its own'. The apparently authentic text of the manifesto, which is circulating on the internet, is signed by a group of former officials who describe themselves as 'veteran Party members of decades' standing'. Led by the former propaganda boss Deng Liqun, the group includes Yuan Mu, the chief government apologist in 1989 for the suppression of the student movement in Tiananmen Square. But despite the group's dogmatic tone, their criticism of the unhealthy relationship between the Party and private enterprise echoes concerns that are shared widely ...

The left-wing manifesto is said to have been high on the agenda of the annual meeting of senior leaders. Hong Kong newspapers say Mr Jiang was enraged by the attack, which compared him with Mikhail Gorbachev and said he was promoting his own personality cult. Beijing has now closed down a theoretical journal called *Pursuit of Truth* which was the left-wingers' house magazine. Tighter controls are expected on all forms of deviant thought in the run-up to next year's crucial congress when Mr Jiang has to step down as the Party's General Secretary.

The State Press Administration has published a list of topics that the media are forbidden from covering. Internet comment is likely to remain more varied because it has less impact – although Mr Jiang is rumoured to follow the proceedings of the Strong Nation discussion group run by the *People's Daily*. Items posted on the site this weekend included the suggestion that the Party and private business are merely 'rival interest groups struggling for power'. There was criticism of Mr Deng, who was described as 'an ideologue who has brought disaster on the nation'. A new proposed reform to abolish the household registration system – which prevents people from moving freely to other parts of the country – is generally supported. However, the hyping of Mr Jiang's new theories attracts unfavourable comment. 'It's not for the government to say whether or not it is great', said one contributor. 'It is for the people to decide'.

Source: John Gittings, 'Jiang Zemin's Proposal that Businessmen Should be Allowed to Join the Party is Criticised', *The Guardian,* **21 August 2001, p. 10**

14.10 China looks forward to entering the World Trade Organization

Wu Ming, *Beijing Review,* 18 October 2001

China was formally admitted to the WTO in November 2001.

After 15 years of effort, China finally sees the light at the end of the tunnel in its endeavor to join the World Trade Organization (WTO) …

Chinese Minister of Foreign Trade and Economic Cooperation, Shi Guangsheng, said WTO entry is an event of great historical significance in China's opening up to the outside world and modernization drive. The event itself fully reflects the determination of the Chinese Government for deepening reform and furthering the opening up, as well as the proactive pose, of China, participating in economic globalization and integration into the world economic mainstream …

China joins the WTO as a developing country, and it will make unremitting efforts to safe-guard the interests of developing countries, as it has always done. In this way, it will make due contributions to the establishment of a truly just new international economic order.

CHINA TO FULFILL ITS PLEDGES

When China's WTO entry has become a foregone conclusion, will the country's rise threaten other countries? Chinese leaders have solemnly expressed on a number of occa-sions that China will strictly abide by WTO rules and earnestly fulfill its pledges.

In accordance with its own level of economic development, China will make active contri-butions to strengthening the multilateral trade systems …

China has approved a series of obligations to open its social system. Only by doing so can it contribute to global economic growth and provide a predictable environment for trade and foreign investment. The six major obligations China is to bear following its WTO entry are:

1   China is to treat each WTO member equally. All individuals and organizations involved in foreign investment, including individuals and organizations that have not invested or registered in China, will enjoy at least the same treatment as Chinese enterprises regarding rights of trade.
2   China is to abolish the practice of double-tracking pricing as well as different treatments for domestically sold goods and export goods.
3   Price control will not aim to provide protection to domestic manufacturers and service companies.

4   China is to modify existing domestic legislation and draft new laws in a unified and effective manner strictly in line with the WTO Agreement, so as to meet requirements of the WTO Agreement.
5   Three years after its WTO entry, except for a handful of cases, all enterprises will have the right to import and export goods and conduct trade within the customs territory.
6   Farm products will have no export subsidies in any form.

After China fulfills all its pledges, its average tariff of farm products will drop to 15 percent, while tariffs of industrial goods will drop to 8.9 percent.

Subsequent to China's WTO accession, foreign companies involved in services will be allowed to establish equity joint ventures in China, which, no longer limited in number, can provide services in some cities. Five years after WTO accession, foreign financial institutions will be allowed to provide Renminbi services to all Chinese customers. Foreign insurance companies can set up non-life insurance subsidiaries or joint ventures in China, and foreign businesses will be allowed to establish solely foreign-owned subsidiaries.

Source: Wu Ming, 'China to Enter the World Trade Organization',
Beijing Review, **18 October 2001, pp. 12–15**

14.11 China's class structure in the year 2000

He Qinglian

This article was first published in March 2000 in the journal House of Books *in Changsha, and was denounced by the Party. But her article has been widely discussed in intellectual circles. The author was reported to have left China for the United States in July 2001 to avoid possible detention.*

The class structure of Chinese society has undergone a profound transformation since the beginnings of the reform-policy period in 1978. The elite, previously selected on a political basis, is now also being recruited on the basis of 'wealth' and 'merit' – profoundly affecting the underlying social structure. These new sections of the elite are now beginning to form their own interest groups, social organizations, and lobbying channels, beyond the already established political ones. The working class, hitherto the constitutionally decreed 'leading class', and the peasantry, the 'semi-leading' class, have both been marginalized; intermediate social organizations are developing apace. All these processes have led to thoroughgoing changes in the relations between the state, society, and the individual ...

Before the Reform Era, China was a highly unified, centralized society, in which political, economic, and ideological centres largely overlapped. The whole society obeyed a paramount interest – that of the Party – and the value system appeared to be equally unified. This situation reflected the distribution of essential resources. At that time, the government monopolized not only the basic material resources of society – land, property, income, and so forth – but also the political resources of power and prestige, and the cultural resources of education and information. There were no independent, non-governmental resources, and no intermediate organizations; an essentially binary structure, 'state versus people', prevailed. Chinese people at that time had no material goods beyond some furniture, clothing, cooking-ware, bedding, and so on. Their incomes, too, were woven into the governmental distribution system. Peasants lived under the rural institutions of the people's communes, mainly dependent on the labour-point system for their earnings, while urban dwellers relied on the wage scale fixed by the Personnel and Labour Ministries. Under this highly unified, monolithic state, it was impossible to form any social group with independent goals.

INEQUALITY AND CORRUPTION

The thrust of Chinese reforms has been gradually to reallocate the possession of social resources. However, as this author has repeatedly pointed out, the principal form this has taken has been a process of privatization of juridically public assets by the power-holding stratum. Its most striking feature has therefore been a glaring inequality in the distribution of national resources – an inequality that has been the starting point of the restructuring of class relations in China in the past twenty years ...

Though the total size of the elite that now controls a stock of 'all-encompassing capital' is not large, it enjoys commanding power over political, economic, and cultural life. Most of its members made their fortunes not through technological innovation or industrial enterprise, but by reproducing and exploiting monolithic positions of power to accumulate personal wealth ...

In the 1980s and early 1990s, malversation was mainly an individual affair ... But by 1995, corruption had developed from an individual to an organizational stage. Often the leaders of social organizations were those most heavily implicated in cases of corruption ...

By about 1998, corruption in China had developed further, from an organizational to an institutional or systemic stage ... Firstly, corruption has now permeated the bulk of the Party and state apparatus. Secondly, corruption has become an established arrangement within institutions, as official posts are traded as counters in the redistribution of political, economic, and cultural power ...

POLITICAL AND ECONOMIC ELITES

Chinese society today can now be broadly categorized into a small elite layer, a much larger middle layer, and a burgeoning layer of marginalized groups beneath (although the composition of these layers, and the relations between them, remain fluid). Within the elite itself one can distinguish three distinct groupings, possessed of different types of resource: political, economic, and intellectual ...

Together, China's political and economic elite today comprises about seven million people, or one per cent of the employed population. The political elite proper consists of top state officials, high- and middle-ranking local officials, and functionaries of large state-owned, non-industrial institutions. The composition of this elite shows a high degree of continuity, since many of its members previously held positions within the planned-economy system, although others have entered its ranks during the technobureaucratization process of the reform era. Only a small minority of the old elite has lost social status through retirement or defeat in factional struggles. The majority have been able to use their previous administrative roles to ensure a smooth access to market opportunities – and thus to reconstitute themselves and their families as members of the 'second pillar', the economic elite. This group include the managers of state banks and large-scale state enterprises – still preponderant within the Chinese economy ...

The final contingent of the economic elite – the owners of large or medium private companies — can be further divided into three types. One comprises families from an official background, who have been able to acquire wealth most conveniently through a 'one-family, two-system' arrangement (parents in government, children doing business) ... Another group has made its way up from non-official backgrounds, by deft exchange of 'extrasystemic' material assets for 'insider' power resources ... Both of these types are linked to the political elite through personal connections rather than institutional channels ...

By contrast, a third type has achieved success mainly by seizing market opportunities, particularly in the high-tech sector ...

AN INTELLECTUAL ELITE

The intellectual elite is separated from the run of general technical workers by its possession of a commanding social position and credible authority over public opinion. This stratum has experienced drastic splits and fractures during the reform era, taking a rather different path from that of the political and economic elite, with markedly distinct stages to it ...

Although a segment of the intellectual elite has developed into an interest group tied to the ruling politicoeconomic bloc, a far greater number have gained very little from the economic reforms; instead, their relative socioeconomic position has been irreversibly lowered. The attitude of intellectuals towards the reforms is therefore no longer one of unconditional support, but is now guided by the dictates of self-interest ...

A MARGINALIZED WORKING CLASS

Traditionally defined, China's working class consisted principally of employees of state enterprises. Today, however, the Chinese working class comprises two broad sectors. One continues to be those who labour in state-owned collectively owned firms; the other is made up of employees working in foreign, joint-venture, or Hong Kong and Taiwanese firms, or in township and village enterprises (TVEs). The two sectors are differentiated by distinct types of relationship between the workforce and the state (or managerial agency representing it) on the one hand, and the workforce and capital owners (along with their agents) on the other. At present, with the exception of white-collar employees in Euro-American firms, every part of the Chinese working class is in turmoil ...

COLLECTIVE CONTRACTS

The 'collective contract' predominates in state or collectively owned enterprises, which account for about 70 per cent of the industrial labour force, or some 120 million people ...

Under ever-increasing market pressures in the 1990s, state-owned enterprises – generally outdated in their equipment and short of financial reserves – have fallen into a vicious circle, as markets for their products have contracted, funds have been corruptly diverted to private firms or into the pocket of small managerial cliques, and the central government has tightened its fiscal squeeze on them. In consequence, the number of unemployed or 'off-post' workers has steadily increased. By 1999, the shadow of unemployment had fallen over most state-owned firms. Officially published figures put the jobless at 12 million, but the actual number must be far higher than this ...

[The author then notes that the small minority of workers in firms financed by Western investment tend to enjoy relatively good wages and conditions, and worker discontent is directed against incompetent or corrupt Chinese managers, not foreign capital.]

ASIAN FIRMS – BACK TO THE PAST

Elsewhere, regression in capital–labour relations is a stark phenomenon in China today. What we are witnessing is a return to conditions common during the Industrial Revolution of the nineteenth century, of which Marx wrote the classic critique in his monumental work *Capital*. In the PRC today, workers employed in firms financed by Asian capital are typically forced to toil continuously for ten or twelve hours every day, with a three or four minute trip to the toilet at specified times, and no weekend off. Workers in such firms earn very low wages, in poor and dangerous conditions. Accidents occur frequently. Fires due to the absence of safety measures regularly cause dozens of casualties …

This pattern of regression puts the Chinese government in a very awkward position. In name, China is still a 'socialist state where the working class is its own master', and all toilers enjoy basic human rights. In reality, local governments competing to attract overseas capital typically bend to investors' demands …

PEASANTS UNDER PRESSURE

The Chinese peasantry was the beneficiary of the first phase of the reforms. The initial family contract system did for once give peasants the sense of being liberated. However, as the focus of the reform moved to urban areas, rural regions have experienced increasingly grave problems, which many experts and scholars specializing in village and agricultural research have pointed out in recent years …

According to the authorities, the fundamental problems facing Chinese peasants are threefold. Firstly, they labour under excessive economic burdens imposed by the state. A series of governmental apparatuses, known as 'the seven institutes and four offices', has been newly created for the administration of rural localities. These heavily expanded bureaucratic settings host an increasing number of functionaries outside the realm of production, on the backs of a decreasing labour force …

Secondly, incomes from farming remain very low, since the huge size of China's rural population makes it impossible to modernize its agriculture by economies of scale, while current backward farming methods have virtually reached the limit of their output capacity. The combination of massive rural overpopulation and limited arable land is likely to make it for a long time all but impossible to increase the income of the peasants, who still make up 70 per cent of China's 1.2 billion people. In these conditions, increasingly serious conflicts are breaking out between peasants and local administrations in rural areas …

Together, the working class, rural–urban migrants, and the peasantry comprise some 480 million people, about 69 per cent of the total workforce. Whatever the difficulties of their life, compared with the truly marginalized groups in Chinese society, they are at least employed …

A VAST MARGINAL POPULATION

It is estimated that the total 'off-post' unemployed and pauperized rural population together make up some 100 million people, about 14 per cent of the total available workforce. In other words, about 80 per cent of the Chinese people live either at the bottom or on the margins of society. Such a distribution is bound to lead to social instability …

FLOATING CRIMINALS

The large number of wandering peasants in Chinese cities and at the margins of Chinese villages are also a well-spring of various forms of criminal activity in the PRC today. The majority – over 75 per cent – of criminals in big cities such as Beijing, Guangzhou, and Shenzhen, are non-resident 'three-have-nots' … A noticeable new feature of this peasant criminality is its use of specialized skills or facilities for breaking the law. Thus, bus drivers familiar with neighbourhoods along their routes will help to organize repeated hold-ups of their passengers; repair mechanics will steal or alter key parts of other people's motorcycles; locksmiths will open houses for ransacking. …

CONCLUSION

China today had developed a social structure quite different from that which existed before the Reform Era. But this has emerged gradually, without a sharp break with the past, as the power-holders of old have been transformed into a new type of elite. The most crucial missing element in this society is any social movements. The only movements in today's China are demographic – migrations. A country that possesses social movements has a mechanism for self-reflection and self-adjustment. For what these represent is always a collective endeavour to find the shapes and norms of a new life. Judged by this criterion, during the two decades of reform in China, it was only in the mid- and late 1980s that there were traces of an embryonic social movement. To solve China's problems today, what we need is an entirely new social movement – one capable of aiming at a complete reform of both ideas and institutions.

Source: He Qinglian, 'China's Listing Social Structure',
House of Books, **Changsha, March 2000,**
from New Left Review, No. 5, September/October 2000, pp. 69–99 (extracts)

Index